ORDNANCE INSTRUCTIONS

FOR THE

UNITED STATES NAVY.

1866.

ORDNANCE INSTRUCTIONS

FOR THE

UNITED STATES NAVY.

PART I.

RELATING TO THE

PREPARATION OF VESSELS OF WAR FOR BATTLE,

AND TO THE

DUTIES OF OFFICERS AND OTHERS WHEN AT QUARTERS.

PART II.

THE EQUIPMENT AND MANŒUVRE OF BOATS

AND

EXERCISE OF BOAT HOWITZERS.

PART III.

ORDNANCE AND ORDNANCE STORES.

FOURTH EDITION.—PUBLISHED BY ORDER OF THE NAVY DEPARTMENT.

WASHINGTON:
GOVERNMENT PRINTING OFFICE.
1866.

OFFICERS are requested to communicate to the Bureau of Ordnance any suggestions relative to future additions or corrections, with the reasons for any proposed changes, quoting part, page, and paragraph by its number.

CONTENTS.

[A full index will be found at the end of the book.]

APPENDIX.

PART I.

RELATING TO THE

PREPARATION OF VESSELS OF WAR FOR BATTLE.

BUREAU OF ORDNANCE,
NAVY DEPARTMENT, *January 1st*, 1866.

SIR:—

The Ordnance Instructions for the Navy having been again carefully revised, and such additions and corrections made as the new armaments of vessels of the Navy rendered necessary, they are approved by the Bureau, and I have the honor to submit them for the adoption of the Navy Department.

I am, Sir, with high respect,
Your obedient servant,
H. A. WISE, U. S. N.,
Chief of Bureau.

NAVY DEPARTMENT,
WASHINGTON, *January 1st*, 1866.

SIR:—

The revised Ordnance Instructions for the Navy, submitted with your letter of this date, are hereby approved and adopted by the Department, and all officers of the Navy will strictly observe and enforce them.

Very respectfully,
GIDEON WELLES,
Secretary of the Navy.

Commander H. A. WISE, U. S. N.,
Chief of Bureau of Ordnance.

CHAPTER I.

GENERAL DUTIES OF OFFICERS

IN RELATION TO ORDNANCE AND GUNNERY, AND TO MILITARY EQUIPMENTS AND EXERCISES.

CAPTAIN.

1. THE CAPTAIN OR COMMANDING OFFICER will be careful to require that all the Ordnance Instructions are strictly enforced on board the vessel under his command; and although particular duties are assigned, and various instructions given to the other officers of the vessel, yet he is to see that the duties are performed, and the instructions obeyed, by the officers to whom they are respectively addressed.

2. As soon as the crew is received on board the vessel, he shall cause a fire-bill to be prepared, the crew shown their stations, and see that they are duly stationed at quarters for battle (*See* Articles 78 to 103), and exercised at general quarters, and by divisions, particularly the powder division (*See* Articles 180 to 201), until each officer and man is thoroughly instructed in his duties; after which the exercises are to be frequent during the cruise. Exercises which are short and spirited are preferable to those which are long and fatiguing. Distinctions and indulgences to those who excel are recommended.

When the men have become well acquainted with their duties at the guns, and in passing powder, or when the general duties of the ship are unusually fatiguing, the divisional exercises may be confined to those belonging to one watch. It is directed that, unless bad weather prevent, Monday of each week be set apart for general quarters.

3. He will, at least once in two months for the first year of the cruise, and once in three months for the remainder thereof, assemble the crew at quarters in the night, without any previous intimation of his intention to do so, and have a general exercise. He will inspect the ship throughout, and cause an entry to be made in the log-book of the length of time required between the beginning of the call to quarters and the complete preparation for commencing action; also, when every gun is ready for a second fire.

4. In order to ascertain whether the equipments are complete and their uses understood, as soon after the ship has been commissioned as circumstances will permit, he will cause at least one round to be fired, with shot or shell, according to the nature of the gun; and, when practicable, at targets at known distances and with the appropriate service charges. (*See* TABLES OF RANGES, Appendix.)

5. He will immediately endeavor to discover whether defects or deficiencies in the armament or equipment exist, and, if any be found, will remedy them as far as in his power consistently with instructions, representing them to the Commandant of the yard of outfit, if near it; and, if important, to the Chief of the Bureau of Ordnance.

6. On the representation of the Gunner that the Ordnance Stores are injured or liable to injury, he will order the survey called for by Article 49.

7. He will, in each quarter of the first year of the cruise, expend in target-practice six rounds, and in each succeeding quarter-year six broadsides, making the report required by Art. 14.

He will not, however, either for this purpose or for saluting, reduce his supply of ammunition below 100 broadsides.

8. In order to accustom the men to the use of loaded shells, they are frequently to be used in preference to shot. For this purpose, however, empty shells, or those that are "bouched" only, will be carefully fitted, filled, and fused on board, in season, according to the directions (Chap. I. Part III.), and first expended.

They should be fitted only as required to replace those expended; a principal object in supplying a certain number of shells to be fitted on board ships, is to disseminate information on this subject.

9. The relative proportions of "distant," "ordinary," and "near-firing" charges are to be preserved (*See* TABLE OF CHARGES, Part III.) as nearly as practicable, and after action or exercise, deficiencies caused by the expenditure of any particular kind of charge will be made up, without unnecessary delay, from the others on hand.

10. The allowances for target-practice are not to be expended in one or two exercises, but are to be divided in such proportions as to allow target-practice once a fortnight, or at least once a month, when practicable; and at least three-fourths of the charges allowed shall be expended in practice at sea, when it can be conveniently done, opportunities being chosen for that purpose under all the circumstances of wind and weather in which vessels of war are liable to engage in battle.

11. When in port, and circumstances will admit, such places are to be selected for practice as are favorable for the recovery of the projectiles; when the effect of the bursting charge is not important, a blowing charge may be used in shells, to test the efficiency of the fuze without destroying the shell.

In practice the service charges for which the sights are marked are alone to be employed.

Distances within half a mile are preferable for solid shot, as best showing the result. Targets of ten feet high by twenty long will afford the means of general comparison, especially with the practice at the experimental battery at Washington. For shells, the distances should suit the ranges of their fuzes, or time of burning, that the degree of certainty of explosion in direct or ricochet fire may be seen and noted.

12. The whole crew is to be exercised in the use of the musket, carbine, pistol, and sword, and in firing at a target with small arms, by suitable persons, each division under the superintendence of its respective commanding officer. The company and the battalion drill is recommended as often as convenient opportunities of exercise present themselves.

13. He will cause the boats' crews to be exercised in all the preparations for attacking an enemy, either by land or water, and in the use of "boat and field howitzers," and small arms, under all the various circumstances likely to arise in such service, and particularly in embarking and disembarking the "boat and field" guns and ammunition. (*See* Part II.)

14. At the expiration of each quarter he will cause to be prepared, and forward, by the earliest favorable opportunity, to the Bureau of Ordnance, a report of all firing, with or without projectiles, according to the detail given in form C. Appendix; also the Quarterly return of receipts and expenditures in the Ordnance Department.

15. He will, once in every quarter, cause a thorough examination to be made into the condition of the armament, shot and shells; and will see that care is taken to keep the shot and shell lockers dry; that the shot and shells stowed therein are clean and free from rust, and, also, that the diameter of shot kept on deck is not increased above the high gauge by injudicious lacquering or painting, and report to the Bureau of Ordnance that this has been done.

16. He is to take care that especial attention is paid to the fuzes, whether spare or in the shells; and if there be reason to suspect injury from dampness or any other cause, he will have one or more fuzes burned for trial.

17. He will not permit shells to be filled, or their fuzes to be shifted or shortened, without his order; and whenever these operations are to be performed, he will see that a suitable and properly secured place, not in the shell-room, and as far from the magazine as convenient, is selected for the purpose. On such occasions the fires and lights are to be extinguished, and also the further precautions are to be observed, as to the manner of performing the work, contained in the directions for filling and emptying shells. (*See* Chap. I., Part III.)

18. He is not to dismount, strike below, or otherwise render unfit for immediate use, any of the guns on board the ship he commands, except imperative necessity should require it for the safety of the vessel. The particular circumstances of such necessity are to be immediately entered at large in the log, and information is to be given to the Commander of the squadron, and to the Secretary of the Navy.

When guns are to be struck below, or when shipped for transportation, he shall cause all the precautions to be taken to guard them from injury, prescribed in Article 46 of these instructions, and such others as circumstances require.

19. He is prohibited from giving away the arms of any description belonging to the vessel under his command.

20. He will keep the keys of the magazines and shell-rooms, and of the receptacles for percussion caps and primers, and of the cocks for flooding magazines and shell-rooms, in the cabin, where they may be obtained by the Executive Officer in case they should be wanted when the Captain is absent from the vessel; and they are only to be delivered to the Executive Officer, or the Officer of the Powder Division.

21. Before entering any friendly port, he will cause every gun to be drawn and reloaded with cartridge, if necessary to salute.

22. He will not permit friction-matches to be on board under any circumstances, and before sailing will notify all persons of this regulation, and institute a search to see that it has been complied with.

EXECUTIVE OFFICER.

23. The Executive Officer will, under the orders and direction of the Captain, ascertain that all the ordnance stores and equipments ordered or allowed for the vessel are received on board in good order; that they are properly distributed and stowed; that they are only used or expended according to directions from proper authority, and that they are duly accounted for, according to the directions and forms which are or may be prescribed by the Bureau of Ordnance. In small vessels which have no Gunner, he shall receipt for and be accountable for all ordnance stores, making all the returns which the Gunner is herein directed to prepare.

24. He will be particularly attentive to the state of the batteries, small arms, magazines, shell-rooms, and shot-lockers; to the passages leading to and scuttles connected with them; and take care that they are kept clear and ready for action.

25. He will cause convenient places to be assigned for the stowage of spare articles which may be required in action, and see that shot for at least twenty broadsides for shot-guns, and one shell for each shell-gun, are always in readiness upon the respective decks.

26. When salutes are to be fired he is personally to examine, or to direct one of the Officers Commanding a Division to examine, ascertain and report that the necessary preparations are made and precautions taken to avoid accidents. The guns, if loaded, are to be drawn, wormed, sponged and reloaded. They are, nevertheless, to be so laid as to prevent the possibility of mischief, even in the contingency of a shot or wad being left in any of them. Hard wads are not to be used in firing salutes, nor are port-fires. The guns are to be fired either with percussion or friction primers, as the Captain may prefer. These, when in good order, are not apt to fail if the lock-string be properly pulled; as, however, a slight deterioration may interfere with the regularity of salutes, the precaution of dropping a few grains of gunpowder into the vent will be found effectual.

Guns of the lowest calibre and class, when sufficient in number, are to be used for saluting; and no heavier than their "near-firing" charge is to be used. (*See* Table of Charges, Part III.) Two boats' howitzers will be found sufficient for saluting. "Saluting powder" to be used in all guns for this purpose, in preference to "Service powder."

27. In large vessels he will cause a cot with a spare sacking-bottom, or such other apparatus as may be approved by the Surgeon, to be prepared and kept for the purpose of lowering the wounded to the orlop or berth deck.

28. Before the powder is received on board, he, with the Gunner, will carefully inspect the magazines and shell-rooms, their passages and light-rooms, and have them thoroughly cleaned, dried and aired, and will see that the pipes and stop-cocks, and every thing connected with flooding the magazines, are in order, and acquaint himself with their position and mode of operation; the lighting apparatus cleaned and dried; and particularly that the glasses for transmitting light into the magazines and shell-rooms are clear and without fracture; that the light burns clearly, and the box is well ventilated; and shall report to the Ordnance Officer when the magazines are ready to receive the ammunition. (*See* Chap. II., Part III.)

OFFICERS IN CHARGE OF DIVISIONS.

29. Officers in charge of divisions of guns are required to make themselves thoroughly conversant with every particular relating to the equipment, exercise, and management of the guns, as set forth in these instructions, and especially to familiarize themselves with the charges prescribed and the ranges given in the Tables; the principles and practice of pointing guns under all circumstances, and also with every precaution connected with the use of shells, and of percussion and time fuzes.

30. They are carefully to inspect their divisions when called to quarters for inspection or exercise, and see that every thing is, at all times, in place and in order for service; and in case of discovering any defect or deficiency, will report it to the Executive Officer.

31. They will be careful, when instructing the men at quarters, to require a strict adherence to the prescribed mode of performing their duties, and to all the details of execution, in order that general uniformity and the efficiency dependent on it may be secured. When the individuals of the guns' crews have become expert in the performance of their particular duties, then each man shall be instructed by the officer of his division, until he shall have become acquainted with the special duties of every station at the gun.

32. They are at least once a week to examine the guns and all the iron work of the carriages, and see that they are kept free from rust, and especially the eccentric axles, elevating screws, and pivot-bolts, which must be protected by a mixture of tallow and white-lead, or other similar coating. The cap-squares must be frequently removed, the guns lifted and the trunnions cleaned; the elevating screws oiled, but never cleaned with brick or emery paper.

Once a quarter at least, all the connecting bolts, such as cap-square, bracket, breast, and transom bolts, are to be examined and tightened if they require it. To do this it is necessary, after lifting the gun, to turn the carriage bottom up. The threads of the screws of the bolts above named must be coated with the lacquer for small arms.

33. The Officer of the Powder Division will, in like manner, carefully instruct and drill his men, and test the efficiency of the arrangements for passing powder, shot, and shell, in order to insure a sufficient supply of each to all parts of the batteries, without the danger of misdirection or of accumulations in any part thereof. To this end blocks of proper shapes and colors may be provided in the appropriate tanks of the magazines, and passed up instead of powder, when that is not used. These are to be counted and reported by the Officers of the Gun Divisions, and will enable the Executive Officer, and the Officer of the Powder Division, to detect and remedy defects or deficiencies in the system or its details, and to be sure that the men are properly stationed and instructed.

MASTER.

34. The MASTER will see that the number of fighting-stoppers, whips for preventer-stays, preventer-braces, slings for yards and gaffs, relieving-tackles, and other articles in his division which are directed, are all fitted and ready for use in action. At general quarters his division must be regularly drilled in fishing masts and spars, stoppering and knotting rigging, and trimming sails.

CHIEF ENGINEER.

35. The CHIEF ENGINEER will ascertain that all the tools and implements necessary for the prompt and effectual repair of injuries which the engine and its dependencies may receive in action, are received on board and placed at hand.

GUNNER.

36. He shall attend personally at the ordnance store where his stores shall be delivered to him, the Ordnance Officer furnishing him with means of transportation and men for stowing them in their appointed places on board ship, when the crew is not available for this purpose. He is to be especially careful that the equipments and stores belonging to the magazine are arranged therein in conformity to Ordnance Instructions. (*See* Chap. I., Part III. for further directions relative to his duties and responsibilities.)

37. The powder-tanks containing charges for each class of guns are to be stowed on their sides, with the lids next the alleys and hinges down, near the magazine scuttles through which these charges are to be delivered; the charges for "ordinary firing" nearest the scuttle. When tanks are emptied they are to be stowed on the upper shelves in order that the powder may be kept, as much as possible, below the water line.

38. In time of war, passing-boxes are to have charges for "ordinary firing" kept in them ready for passing up at once.

39. In future white will be used for all cylinders, the calibre and weight distinctly stencilled on each bag. In case of a deficiency of white cartridge cloth, the different charges for all classes of guns may be distinguished by the color of the cartridge-bags; white being used for distant firing, blue for "ordinary" firing, and red for "near" firing.

The lid ends of the powder-tanks for service charges are to be painted of the same colors as the cartridge-bags which they contain, and must be distinctly marked with the calibre and weight of the gun for which the cartridges are intended. Tanks for musket-powder must be marked MUSKET-POWDER; and this powder may be put up in either of the kind of charges allowed which will make the best stowage, the bags properly stencilled.

Tanks containing saluting powder are to be marked "SALUTING." It is to be kept in bags, stencilled "saluting."

40. No loose powder is ever to be taken or carried on board ship, and all, whether public or private belonging to officers, must be safely stowed in the magazines.

41. All metallic cartridges for small arms, percussion caps, and percussion or friction primers, or other articles containing fulminating matter, must be kept in boxes prepared for the purpose, and the boxes must be stowed separately from other articles, in a dry, secure, and safe place, under lock and key, and are on no account to be put in the magazine. It is recommended that they be distributed in two or three places, a portion conveniently at hand.

42. The fireworks, after carefully removing all fulminating matter, such as caps or primers, if any such be used to ignite them, are to be stowed in their proper packing-boxes in other light boxes of suitable length, made water-tight, with lock and key, and to fit between the beams and carlines of the gun decks of frigates and berth decks of single-decked vessels. Those for instant use must be placed near the after hatch, and the remainder abaft that position, if possible, so as to be constantly under the care of the sentinel at the cabin doors. In no case, however, are they to be placed over any standing light or lantern on any deck.

43. All ammunition packing-boxes, shell-bags, and metal cases are to be preserved, and returned into store at the end of the cruise.

44. No coopering is ever to be done in the magazines of ships. Should powder be received on board in barrels, the hoops and heads must be started on the orlop or berth deck before entering the magazine.

45. In stowing shell-rooms, filled shells are to be stowed together in boxes or bags; those having fuzes of different times of burning, and each kind of fuze, will be placed in tiers or ranges distinctly separate. (*See* Article ON FUZES, C. IV.) Empty shells are to be stowed by themselves, unsabotted, in bulk, in a dry place.

46. Whenever guns are to be struck below, or prepared for transportation, the gunner will see that the bores are washed with fresh water, carefully sponged, thoroughly dried, and coated with melted tallow, and a wad dipped in the same material inserted, and connected with a tompion by a lanyard. He is to see that the tompion is put in securely, and the vent and all screw-holes stopped by a plug of soft wood, and puttied over.

47. He is to examine and report daily, before 10 A. M. and 8 P. M., whether the guns and all their equipments; the whips for supplying shot and shells;

the arm-chests, armory, and small arms; the supply and reserve division boxes, and other articles furnished as ordnance and ordnance stores, are in good order and in place, and make immediate report to the Commanding or Executive Officer of any defects or deficiencies which he may discover at any other time.

48. The guns and their equipments are to be kept as dry as possible, and no salt water used in cleaning them.

49. If he shall discover any articles to be injured, or liable to injury from any cause, he will ask, in writing, for a survey to be held, to determine the amount, cause, or liability of any of the stores or equipments to damage or deterioration; a copy of this request and report of survey to be furnished to him as a voucher, by the officer ordering the survey.

50. Whenever the magazines or shell-rooms are opened, he is to take every precaution to guard against accident by fire; to examine particularly that all the men stationed in any way in or about the magazine, embracing all stationed within the magazine screen, put on the magazine dress and shoes, and on no account have any thing metallic about them, and that no improper articles are introduced. He will also see that all the articles required for sweeping and removing loose powder are at hand, and that those operations are performed before the magazine is closed.

51. The tanks are never to be opened unless by special order, or when powder is actually required for service; and then no more of the lids are to be unscrewed than is necessary for immediate supply. The strictest attention to this regulation is required of the Gunner, as experience has proved that the preservation of the powder in good condition depends upon the entire exclusion of damp air.

52. When the guns are ordered to be drawn before entering a friendly port, the Gunner is to be particularly attentive to assure himself that no shot or wad is left in any gun.

53. In saluting, he is to guard against accident in loading, pointing, and firing, and to be particularly careful in reloading, where that operation is unavoidable.

54. In the absence or illness of the Gunner, his general duties will devolve on a Gunner's Mate, under the supervision of the Executive Officer.

55. The Gunner shall keep a minute-book of all expenditures in the Ordnance Department, and on Monday of each week shall submit it to the Executive Officer for examination and approval. Within ten days after the expiration of the quarter, he shall make out his quarterly return in the required form, which shall be signed by him, certified correct by the Executive Officer, approved by the Commander, and forwarded to the Bureau by the first opportunity. At the same time the ledger shall be posted.

56. When a vessel returns from a cruise to be refitted or repaired, or placed in ordinary, the Gunner, or person performing the duty of Gunner, is not to leave the ship, unless specially authorized by the Secretary of the Navy, until all the guns, powder, small arms, ammunition, and other articles under his charge, shall have been examined and surveyed, and turned over to his successor, or other person appointed to receive them, or to the Inspector of Ordnance, the receipt for which he shall show to the officer to whom he applies for leave.

CARPENTER.

57. The Carpenter shall ascertain and report to the Executive Officer that there are a sufficient number of tarpaulins to cover all the hatches leading to the fore and after orlops; that the pump-gear of every description is ready and in order for rigging the pumps, and that every preparation can be promptly made before going into action to free the ship, in case of receiving injuries below the water-line.

58. He is also to examine and keep in order the force and channel pumps, the fire-engine, the division-tubs, and, in short, all the apparatus necessary to give a good and speedy supply of water in case of fire in action.

59. He is specially charged with the care and distribution of articles for stopping shot-holes or repairing other injuries to the hull, which may be received in action, viz.: shot-plugs and mauls; pieces of pine board from eighteen inches to three feet long, and from twelve to fifteen inches wide, covered with felt or fearnaught, previously coated with tar or white lead; patches of sheet-lead, all with nail-holes punched; and trouser-slings for lowering men outside the vessel, to be provided with a pouch or pocket, to contain a hammer and nails. Tarred canvas or oakum should be prepared to shove into the shot-holes before the patches of board or lead are nailed on. Although shot-plugs are still to be allowed, the means just described are most to be relied on.

60. In case it shall not have already been done, the Carpenter, under the direction of the Commander or Executive Officer of the ship, will draw a black line, two inches broad, on the ceiling of the ship, to correspond with the ordinary height of the water-line. On this is to be marked, by corresponding intervals and numbers, the position of the ports on the lowest of the gun-decks. By this arrangement the position of the shot-hole can be easily ascertained and communicated, through the Officer Commanding the Powder Division, and a remedy promptly applied. To this end he is to pay habitual attention to keeping the wings clear to four feet below the water-line, and report any obstructions to the Executive Officer.

YEOMAN.

61. The YEOMAN is to charge himself with, and is to be accountable for, all articles of ordnance stores which may be placed in the storeroom under his charge, and is not to issue or expend any article, except by order of, or authority from, the Captain or Executive Officer.

62. On the return of a ship, to be laid up at a yard, or to be refitted or repaired, the Yeoman will be retained to deliver the ordnance stores in his charge into the hands of the Ordnance Officer. If any deficiency in the stores under his charge be discovered, or they are in bad order, the Ordnance Officer will report the same to the Commandant of the yard, who will order a survey, to ascertain the nature and extent of the deficiency, or injury, and whether either were caused by the Yeoman's negligence or fault. If the surveying officers shall find just cause for suspecting fraud or negligence, the Commandant shall suspend the payment and discharge of the Yeoman, until he shall report the case to the Bureau and receive the orders of the Department.

63. No person is to be knowingly appointed Yeoman who has already served in that capacity in any vessel of war of the United States, who cannot produce a satisfactory certificate of his former good conduct as Yeoman.

CHAPTER II.

GENERAL DISTRIBUTION OF OFFICERS AND MEN AT QUARTERS.

64. The following directions for the general distribution of a ship's company at quarters, or for action, are intended to secure, upon the most important points, a degree of uniformity which will promote efficiency, and at the same time leave to the Captains the selection and arrangement of many individuals under their command, according to their own views of the particular qualifications of each.

65. The Captain's station, in action, is upon the quarter-deck.

66. The Executive Officer, the Midshipmen acting as Aides to the Captain, and the Signal Officer, are also to be stationed on the quarter-deck.

67. The stations of the other Officers are to be regulated by divisions, as follows:

The guns upon each deck are to be numbered from forward, beginning with No. 1, and continuing aft, in succession, each gun and its opposite being designated by the same number, excepting pivot and shifting guns, each of which is to have a separate number. The guns on each deck are then to be divided as equally as possible into three or two divisions, according to the number of Lieutenants or other Watch Officers on board, so that each division of guns, and the persons belonging to it, may be commanded by a Lieutenant or other Watch Officer. These divisions are to be numbered consecutively, designating the forward division on the lowest gun-deck as the first division, and passing from the after division of one deck to the forward division of the next deck above it.

68. The command of these divisions of guns is to be assigned, in the order of their numbers, to the Lieutenants or other Watch Officers, according to their rank, assigning the first division to the officer next in rank to the Executive Officer. In case of a deficiency of Watch Officers, the quarter-deck division may be assigned to an Ensign or Midshipman, who will act under the general supervision of the Executive Officer. When the number of officers on board of vessels having pivot-guns will permit, each pivot-gun will be placed under the special charge of a suitable officer of the division of which it forms a part.

MASTER'S DIVISION.

69. This division will comprise all those stationed in the tops, and those appointed to attend to the rigging, sails, steerage, and signals. The Master is to be stationed on the quarter-deck, and to be assisted by the Boatswain, whose station will be on the forecastle. The Boatswain will be charged with all his divisional duties in the event of his death or absence. (For ARMS, *see* Table in Article 101.)

POWDER DIVISION.

70. This division will be under the direction either of a Lieutenant, Master, Ensign, or competent Midshipman. It will consist of all those stationed below the gun-decks, except persons belonging to the Surgeon's Division and the Paymaster and his Clerk.

The Gunner is to be stationed in the main magazine, and a Gunner's Mate or Quarter Gunner in the other magazine when there are two; and those persons of this division who may be stationed in the magazines and passages are to be under the immediate direction of the Gunner and his Mate, respectively. Those of the Carpenter's crew stationed in the hold or wings are to be under the immediate direction of the Carpenter's Mate, who will be stationed with them. All reports, however, are to be made through the Commanding Officer of the division.

DIVISION OF MARINES.

71. All the Marines who may not be distributed to other divisions for action are to compose a Division of Marines, to be under the immediate command of the Senior Officer of Marines on board. He will form his division on such part or parts of the spar or upper deck as the Captain may direct.

SURGEON'S DIVISION.

72. The SURGEON or senior Medical Officer will have the direction of this division, which shall comprise all the Medical Officers and such other persons as may be designated by the Captain to assist in the care of the wounded in action. This division will occupy the cockpit, or such other convenient place as the Captain of the vessel may direct.

THE CHAPLAIN.

73. The CHAPLAIN will be in attendance to perform the duties of his sacred office, and to render such other service as may be in his power.

PAYMASTER.

74. The PAYMASTER's station will be in the ward-room and on the berth-deck, in charge of the money, books and stores belonging to his Department.

ENGINEER DIVISION.

75. The Engineer Division shall be under the direction of the Chief Engineer, and shall comprise the Assistant Engineers and such of the Firemen and Coalheavers as may be detailed for the purpose. An Assistant will be appointed to take charge of the fire party detailed from this Division.

MISCELLANEOUS OFFICERS.

76. Ensigns, Midshipmen, Mates, Captain's and other Clerks, the Sailmaker, and other officers not enumerated, are to be assigned to the different divisions at the discretion of the Captain.

77. In distributing the Petty Officers, Seamen, and others to the guns and other stations in the several divisions, it is desirable, as a general rule, that those stationed at the same gun or near each other at quarters, should be drawn from different stations for working ship; so that a great loss at any one gun may not fall too heavily on any watch station.

Exceptions to this general rule may be advantageously made where the duties of men require their habitual attendance on particular decks. In such cases it will generally be advisable to station them at quarters near to the places of their ordinary duties.

DISTRIBUTION OF THE CREW.

78. Table showing the number of men for the service of each kind and class of gun in use in the Navy, assuming the vessel to have the established complement.

PIVOT-GUNS.						BROADSIDE-GUNS.						
XI-inch of 16,000 lbs., X-inch of 16,000 lbs.,	X-inch of 12,000 lbs., 64-pdr. of 106 cwt.	IX-inch of 9,000 lbs., 100-pdr. rifle.	60-pdr. rifle.	30-pdr. rifle.	20-pdr. rifle.	IX-inch of 9,000 lbs., 100-pdr. rifle.	8-inch of 63 cwt.	8-inch of 6,500 lbs. 8-inch of 56 cwt.	32-pdr. of 57 cwt.	32-pdr. of 4,500 lbs., 32-pdr. of 42 cwt., 60-pdr. rifle.	32-pdr. of 33 cwt., 30-pdr. rifle.	32-pdr. of 27 cwt., 20-pdr. rifle.
24	20	16	10	8	6	16	14	12	12	10	8	6

To the XI, X, and IX-inch 100-pounder rifle, and 64-pounder pivot guns, a Powderman, and to all other guns a Powder-boy is to be added.

The number of men to form crews of guns mounted on carriages of special character, is to be regulated as may be found most advantageous by the Commanding Officer.

79. In designating the Petty Officers and others for particular stations, it is assumed that the intelligence, skill, and force of the men have been equally divided between the two watches, and that the men in the starboard watch have all odd numbers, as 1, 3, 5, and those of the port watch even numbers, as 2, 4, 6.

To preserve this equality, and to secure the ability of those who may be upon deck to prepare the ship for action at night, whilst the watch below are bringing up and stowing the hammocks, all the odd-numbered guns will be entirely manned by men belonging to the starboard watch, and all the even-numbered guns by those belonging to the port watch, as far as practicable. The crews of pivot-guns to be taken half from each watch.

80. Where ports on opposite sides of the same deck are numbered the same, and are both provided with a gun, guns' crews are only to be furnished for the guns on one side. Pivot and shifting guns are each to have full guns' crews.

81. When the complements allowed to vessels of the Navy will permit, it is recommended as a general arrangement that the guns' crews be formed of about one-third Petty Officers and Seamen, one-third Ordinary Seamen, amd one-third Landsmen and Boys, and that this system be observed as nearly as practicable.

82. At least one Quarter Gunner should be stationed at each division of guns; and a Gunner's Mate or Quarter Gunner in the smaller magazine, and in each shell-room.

If there be more shell-rooms than there are disposable Quarter Gunners to attend them, other careful and suitable persons are to be selected to supply the deficiency.

83. Before permanently assigning the individuals which form a gun's crew, to the performance of particular duties connected with its service in action, it is important to ascertain their respective qualifications, as far as may be practicable, by questioning them or by exercising them at the guns.

84. The Captains, especially, should be selected from those in whose skill, coolness, and judgment the greatest reliance can be placed, without regard to their ratings, though at the same time care should be taken to avoid stationing men of a higher rating than the Captains of the guns, to perform subordinate duties at the same guns. They should be examined by the Surgeon with reference to eyesight.

Spongers and Loaders rank next in importance, and, with activity and coolness, should possess the necessary physical strength and stature. For Handspikemen, weight is important, in addition to strength and coolness.

85. Very careful men should be selected for attending the Powder-scuttles on the different decks, as well to prevent noise and contention among the Powder-boys as to guard against accidents, and speedily to repair such as may occur. The boys should be trained to fall into line, to insure an equal distribution of powder.

86. Unless some special reason should require a different arrangement with regard to Boarders, Pikemen, Firemen, Sail-trimmers, and Pumpmen, the following will be observed:

BOARDERS.

87. Half the men composing a gun's crew, excluding the Powderman or Boy, are to be Boarders. When this rule gives an odd number of men, the odd one is to be a Second Boarder.

88. The Boarders are to constitute two divisions, called First and Second Boarders.

89. First Boarders are, generally, to be taken from the second part of a gun's crew; and Second Boarders from the first part.

90. All Petty Officers on the spar-deck, except the Quartermaster at the conn and the Quartermaster at the wheel, are to be First Boarders.—(For ARMS OF BOARDERS, *see* Table, Article 101.)

The Executive Officer leads the Boarders. All the Division Officers on the spar-deck shall be First Boarders, except the officer commanding the quarter-deck division, who shall lead the Pikemen. On gun-decks the officer commanding the second division shall be a First Boarder; the commanding officers of the other divisions shall be Second Boarders. If there are two officers in any division, the second shall lead those Boarders who do not go with his principal. A Lieutenant or other responsible officer should be detailed to command the gun-deck in the absence of the boarders and pikemen.

PIKEMEN.

91. One-fourth of the number of men composing a gun's crew, rejecting fractions, and excepting the Powderman or Boy, and all the men of the Master's division on the spar-deck, except those designated as Boarders and those at the wheel and conn, are to be Pikemen, and compose but one division.

92. For each Pikeman at a gun there is to be a musket or carbine provided, which in action, when not in use, is to be kept with the bayonet unfixed, hooked securely against a carline or beam near the gun; or on a spar-deck placed conveniently at hand. When they are called away they will repair on deck with these arms, when, if ordered, they will place them in a secure place, to be designated by the Executive Officer, and arm themselves with pikes. Pikemen will wear a cartridge-box whenever at general quarters or in action.

Pikemen of the spar-deck divisions will, on being called away, arm themselves as directed.

Should it become necessary, in an emergency, to call "all hands" from below to repel an enemy, the Pikemen will, if not already so armed, arm themselves with muskets or carbines, leaving their pikes to be used by those whose arms are not designated—that is, by the remainder of the gun's crew and Powder Division.

93. One boarding-pike for each gun on covered decks is always to be kept triced up conveniently near it, and this is to be used by the Powderman, or any other person left at the gun to guard the port.

94. Pikemen are to be covered by the Marines with their bayonets fixed.

FIREMEN.

95. With broadside guns, one Fireman is to be taken from each gun's crew, and from pivot-guns two. Each Fireman is to have a fire-bucket at hand near his gun, and to wear his battle-axe in a belt around his waist.

SAIL-TRIMMERS.

96. In all vessels there shall be two divisions of Sail-trimmers, composed of all the men at the spar-deck guns, except 1st Captains, 1st Spongers, 1st Loaders, and Powder-boys. The 1st Sail-trimmers are to be taken from the guns on the forward half, and the 2d Sail-trimmers from those on the after half of the spar-deck.

97. In vessels carrying guns on more than one deck there are to be three divisions of Sail-trimmers, called 1st, 2d, and 3d Sail-trimmers, and the third division is to be made up of one man from each gun's crew on the other deck or decks, as designated in the tables.—(Article 101.)

This third division of Sail-trimmers is to be regarded as a reserved force, and is not to repair on deck at the general call for Sail-trimmers, nor except when specially ordered. Besides serving to re-enforce the other two divisions when absolutely necessary, it is also to re-enforce either the Firemen or the Pumpmen in cases of need.

98. The third division of Sail-trimmers, and all the Pikemen of the guns' crews, and others armed with muskets (*See* Tables, Article 101), may be made to assemble together as a body of Musketeers, either for landing or otherwise. No one gun more than another will be weakened by so doing; and this suggests the propriety of preferring these men ordinarily for the crews of boats.

PUMPMEN.

99. Each gun's crew composed of as many as 14 men is to furnish two, but, when of less than 14 men, one Pumpman only.

100. When Pumpmen are sufficiently numerous to admit of working the pumps with one-half their force, they should compose two divisions, to be called 1st and 2d Pumpmen.

DISTRIBUTION AND ARMS OF MEN AT THE GUNS.

101. The annexed Tables show the stations of guns' crews at pivot-guns, and at broadside-guns, when composed, respectively, of the following numbers of men: 24, 16, 14, 12, 10, 8, or 6; how each man of a gun's crew is to be armed, and the number of small arms of all kinds required for each gun's crew.

N. B.—To these Tables is annexed another, showing the small arms of the Master's Division.

PIVOT-GUN'S CREW, *composed of* 24 MEN *and a* POWDERMAN.

TITLES OF GUN'S CREW ON LEFT SIDE OF GUN.	GUN NOS.		TITLES OF GUN'S CREW ON RIGHT SIDE OF GUN.	ARMS.					
				SWORDS.	REVOLVERS.	PISTOLS.	PIKES.	MUSKETS.	BATTLE-AXES.
1st Loader, 2 B.........	3	...	....	1	1	–	–	–	–
		4	1st Sponger, 2 B........	1	1	–	–	–	–
2d Loader, 1 B..........	5	...	....	1	–	1	–	–	–
		6	2d Sponger., 1 B........	1	–	1	–	–	–
1st Shellman and Pump..	7	...	....	–	–	–	–	–	1
		8	2d Shellman and Pump..	–	–	–	–	–	1
1st Front Lever., 2 B....	9	...	....	1	1	–	–	–	–
		10	2d Front Lever, 1 B.....	1	–	1	–	–	–
1st Compressor. and Pike.	13	...	....	–	–	–	1	1	–
		14	2d Compressor. and Pike.	–	–	–	1	1	–
1st Rear Lever. and Pike.	11	...	....	–	–	–	1	1	–
		12	2d Rear Lever. and Pike.	–	–	–	1	1	–
Tr.-tkl., Deck-block, 2 B..	17	...	....	1	1	–	–	–	–
		18	Tr.-tkl., Deck-block, 1 B..	1	1	–	–	–	–
Tr.-tkl., Slide-block, 2 B..	19	...	....	1	–	1	–	–	–
		20	Tr.-tkl., Slide-block, 1 B..	1	–	1	–	–	–
Shifting-tkl., Deck-block, and Pikeman.........	21	...	....	–	–	–	1	1	–
		22	Shifting-tkl., Deck-block, and Pikeman.........	–	–	–	1	1	–
Shifting-tkl., Slide-block..	23	...	....	–	–	–	–	1	1
		24	Shifting-tkl., Slide-block.	–	–	–	–	1	1
1st Tr. Lev. and Fireman.	15	...	....	–	–	–	–	–	1
		16	2d Tr. Lev. and Fireman.	–	–	–	–	–	1
1st Captain, 2 B.........	1	...	....	1	1	–	–	–	–
		2	2d Captain, 1 B.........	1	1	–	–	–	–
Powderman............	25	...	....	–	–	–	–	–	–
Total number of Arms.........................				12	7	5	6	8	6

Gun's Crew *composed of* 16 Men *and a* Powderman.

Titles of Gun's Crew on Left Side of Gun.	Gun Nos.		Titles of Gun's Crew on Right Side of Gun.	Arms.					
				Swords.	Revolvers.	Pistols.	Pikes.	Muskets.	Battle-axes.
		4	1st Sponger, 2 B........	1	1	–	–	–	–
1st Loader, 2 B.........	3	...	....	1	1	–	–	–	–
		6	2d Sponger, 1 B........	1	–	1	–	–	–
2d Loader, 1 B.........	5	...	....	1	–	1	–	–	–
		8	2d Shell. and 1st Pump..	–	–	–	–	–	1
1st Shellman, 2d Pump..	7	...	....	–	–	–	–	–	1
		10	2d Handspike., 1 B......	1	–	1	–	–	–
1st Handspikeman, 2 B..	9	...	....	1	–	1	–	–	–
		14	2d Side-tackle. and Pike.	–	–	–	1	1	–
1st Side-tackle. and Pike.	13	...	....	–	–	–	1	1	–
		16	2d Port-tackle. and Pike.	–	–	–	1	1	–
1st Port-tackle. and Pike.	15	...	....	–	–	–	1	1	–
		12	2d Tr.-tack. and Sail-trim.	–	–	–	–	1	1
1st Train-tackle. and Fire.	11	...	....	–	–	–	–	–	1
		2	2d Captain, 1 B.........	1	1	–	–	–	–
1st Captain, 2 B........	1	...	....	1	1	–	–	–	–
Powderman............	...	...	....	–	–	–	–	–	–
Total number of Arms......................				8	4	4	4	5	4

N. B.—On other than lower decks, for Port-tacklemen substitute 3d and 4th Side-tacklemen.

Gun's Crew *composed of* 14 Men *and a* Powder-boy.

Titles of Gun's Crew on Left Side of Gun.	Gun Nos.		Titles of Gun's Crew on Right Side of Gun.	Arms.					
				Swords.	Revolvers.	Pistols.	Pikes.	Muskets.	Battle-axes.
		4	1st Sponger, 2 B........	1	1	–	–	–	–
1st Loader, 2 B.........	3	...	....	1	1	–	–	–	–
		6	2d Sponger, 1 B........	1	–	1	–	–	–
2d Loader, 1 B.........	5	...	....	1	–	1	–	–	–
		8	2d Shell. and 1st Pump..	–	–	–	–	–	1
1st Shell. and 2d Pump..	7	...	....	–	–	–	–	–	1
		10	2d Handspike. and Pike..	–	–	–	1	1	–
1st Handspike., 2 B......	9	...	....	1	–	1	–	–	–
		14	2d Side-tackle. and Pike.	–	–	–	1	1	–
1st Side-tackle. and Pike.	13	...	....	–	–	–	1	1	–
		12	2d Tr.-tack. and Sail-trim.	–	–	–	–	1	1
1st Train-tackle. and Fire.	11	...	....	–	–	–	–	–	1
		2	2d Captain, 1 B.........	1	1	–	–	–	–
1st Captain, 2 B........	1	...	....	1	1	–	–	–	–
Powder-boy............	...	...	....	–	–	–	–	–	–
Total number of Arms......................				7	4	3	3	4	4

GUN'S CREW *composed of* 12 MEN *and a* POWDER-BOY.

TITLES OF GUN'S CREW ON LEFT SIDE OF GUN.	GUN NOS.		TITLES OF GUN'S CREW ON RIGHT SIDE OF GUN.	ARMS.					
				SWORDS.	REVOLVERS.	PISTOLS.	PIKES.	MUSKETS.	BATTLE-AXES.
		4	1st Sponger, 2 B........	1	–	1	–	–	–
1st Loader, 2 B.........	3	...	....	1	1	–	–	–	–
		6	2d Sponger, 1 B........	1	–	1	–	–	–
2d Loader, 1 B	5	...	....	1	–	1	–	–	–
		8	2d Shellman and Pump..	–	–	–	–	–	1
1st Shellman and Pike...	7	...	....	–	–	–	1	1	–
		10	2d Handspike. and Pike..	–	–	–	1	1	–
1st Handspike. and Pike.	9	...	....	–	–	–	1	1	–
		12	2d Tr.-tkl. and Sail-trim..	–	–	–	–	1	1
1st Train-tackle. and Fire.	11	...	....	–	–	–	–	–	1
		2	2d Captain, 1 B.........	1	1	–	–	–	–
1st Captain, 2 B........	1	...	....	1	1	–	–	–	–
Powder-boy...........	...	...	....	–	–	–	–	–	–
Total number of Arms........................				6	3	3	3	4	3

GUN'S CREW *composed of* 10 MEN *and a* POWDER-BOY.

TITLES OF GUN'S CREW ON LEFT SIDE OF GUN.	GUN NOS.		TITLES OF GUN'S CREW ON RIGHT SIDE OF GUN.	ARMS.					
				SWORDS.	REVOLVERS.	PISTOLS.	PIKES.	MUSKETS.	BATTLE-AXES.
		4	1st Sponger, 2 B........	1	–	1	–	–	–
1st Loader, 2 B.........	3	...	....	1	1	–	–	–	–
		6	2d Sponger, 1 B........	1	–	1	–	–	–
2d Loader and Pike.....	5	...	....	–	–	–	1	1	–
		8	2d Shellman and Pump..	–	–	–	–	–	1
1st Shellman and Fire...	7	...	....	–	–	–	–	–	1
		10	Train-tackle............	–	–	–	–	1	1
1st Handspike. and Pike.	9	...	....	–	–	–	1	1	–
		2	2d Captain, 1 B.........	1	1	–	–	–	–
1st Captain, 2 B........	1	...	....	1	1	–	–	–	–
Powder-boy...........	...	...	....	–	–	–	–	–	–
Total number of Arms........................				5	3	2	2	3	3

Gun's Crew *composed of* 8 Men *and a* Powder-boy.

Titles of Gun's Crew on Left Side of Gun.	Gun Nos.		Titles of Gun's Crew on Right Side of Gun.	Arms. Swords.	Revolvers.	Pistols.	Pikes.	Muskets.	Battle-axes.
		4	1st Sponger, 2 B........	1	–	1	–	–	–
1st Loader, 2 B.........	3	...	....	1	–	1	–	–	–
		6	2d Sponger and Pike....	–	–	–	1	1	–
2d Loader and Pikeman..	5	...	....	–	–	–	1	1	–
		8	Tr.-tkl., Fireman........	–	–	–	–	1	1
Shotman and Pumpman..	7	...	....	–	–	–	–	–	1
		2	2d Capt. and Handsp., 1 B.	1	1	–	–	–	–
1st Captain, 2 B........	1	...	....	1	1	–	–	–	–
Powder-boy............	...	...	....	–	–	–	–	–	–
Total number of Arms........................				4	2	2	2	3	2

Gun's Crew *composed of* 6 Men *and a* Powder-boy.

Titles of Gun's Crew on Left Side of Gun.	Gun Nos.		Titles of Gun's Crew on Right Side of Gun.	Arms. Swords.	Revolvers.	Pistols.	Pikes.	Muskets.	Battle-axes.
		4	1st Sponger and Pikeman.	–	–	–	1	1	–
1st Loader, 2 B.........	3	...	....	1	–	1	–	–	–
		6	2d Sponger, Fireman....	–	–	–	–	1	1
2d Ldr., Shot., and Pump.	5		....	–	–	–	–	–	1
		2	2d Captain, Handspike., Train-tackle., 1 B.....	1	1	–	–	–	–
1st Captain, 2 B........	1	...	....	1	1	–	–	–	–
Powder-boy............	...	...	....	–	–	–	–	–	–
Total number of Arms........................				3	2	1	1	2	2

SMALL ARMS OF MASTER'S DIVISION.

STATIONS.	RATINGS.	ARMS.
Conn	Quartermaster	Pistol and Sword.
Wheel	Quartermaster and Seamen.	do. do.
Signals	Quartermaster	do. do.
do.	Boys	Pikes.
Relieving Tackles	Quartermaster and O. S.	Swords.
Main Braces	C. A. G.	Pistol and Sword.
Mastmen	B. M.	Pistol, sword, and Battle-axe.
do.	Seamen and O. S.	Pikes and Battle-axes.
Topmen	do. do.	Muskets.
Forecastle	C. F.	Pistol and Sword.
Bell	S. C.	do. do.

102. The Captain will designate the different hatchways which shall be used by the Boarders and others from each gun when they are called upon deck at quarters. Cutlasses should not be drawn nor bayonets fixed until ordered, and, in moving from one part of the deck to another, should be sheathed, to avoid accidents.

103. The use of fire-arms in the tops being dangerous, and only admissible under very peculiar circumstances, they are never to be used there without the express direction of the Captain.

NOTE.—It is proposed to abandon the pike and all muzzle-loading small arms for a breech-loading carbine and pistol, with one uniform metallic cartridge for both.

The revolver pistol does not realize in service with seamen the advantages claimed for that description of arm.

CHAPTER III.

DUTIES AT QUARTERS, IN BATTLE OR EXERCISE.

CAPTAIN.

104. The Captain, when at general quarters, either for exercise or in action, is to superintend and take the general direction of every thing connected with the management of the ship and the service of her armament.

105. He will from time to time carefully inspect the ship, in order, before commencing a general exercise, to ascertain that all the required and proper preparations have been made for battle. When time and other circumstances will permit, he will always make this inspection before going into action, and when prevented from making it personally, he will direct it to be made by the Executive Officer.

106. When engaged with an enemy at so great a distance as to require the guns to be elevated, he will, if practicable, cause the distance to be ascertained by observation, and, when that cannot be done, will estimate the distance, and from time to time send directions to the Officers of gun divisions for what distances the sights of their guns should be set, and the nature of the projectile, and, if a shell be used, the time of the fuze (*See* Article 326), and also the cartridges to be used, whether for "distant," "ordinary," or "near" firing.

107. He will determine and direct when two shot may be fired; when "quick-firing" may be permitted; when small arms shall be distributed and loaded; when Boarders shall be called up, and when they shall assail an enemy. He will receive, through the Executive Officer, the reports from all Officers commanding divisions.

EXECUTIVE OFFICER.

108. The Executive Officer, under the direction of the Captain, and with the aid of the Master, will work the ship when in action or at general quarters. He will receive the reports of the officers of the different divisions and others, and communicate them to the Captain of the ship.

SIGNAL OFFICER.

109. The Signal Officer is to see that every thing is prepared for making and answering signals promptly, and will make all such as the Captain may direct. He will provide himself with a watch, pencil, and signal note-book properly ruled.

110. He will note and report to the Captain all signals that are made to or by other vessels of the squadron, or other vessels in sight, and also note the time at which each signal was made. He will observe and report any material change which may take place in the positions of the vessels of the squadron, or of other vessels, and every event of moment that may occur.

MASTER'S DIVISION.

111. The Master will cause the persons in his division to sling the yards and gaffs, to stopper the topsail sheets, to lead out the preventer and other braces, and will see that they are clear, and toggled, to prevent them from unreeving.

112. He will have the fighting stoppers at hand in the chains and tops for stoppering the rigging; hatchets and axes ready for clearing away any casual encumbrances from the guns; axes and hatchets for this purpose must be sharpened, covered with painted canvas, and labelled "not for general use;" and will cause proper arrangements to be made for applying and securing grapnels, if they should be required.

113. He will see that the hammocks are compactly stowed, covered, and stopped down, and will cause the boat and boom covers to be hauled over and securely stopped down; the relieving tackles to be hooked and ready for use; a compass to be placed to steer by; and see the spare tiller at hand, the chronometer and other instruments put out of the reach of shot, and relieved as much as possible from the jar of the guns.

114. In case the Captain should give orders for sending small arms and ammunition into the tops, he will attend to having them sent there, and will be watchful that they are not so used as to expose the sails and rigging to danger from taking fire; and in order to furnish a sufficient supply of water, in case of accident, he will have four fire-buckets fitted for each top, with lanyards long enough to reach the water from the yard-arms, and these should be filled with water in preparing for action.

115. On the probability of an engagement, when the ship is on soundings, the Master will have the ground-tackling ready and clear; boats ready for getting out, and every preparation made for towing, warping, anchoring, and getting springs upon the cables; and have leads and lines in the chains. If at anchor, he will have the boats dropped astern, the oars secured to the thwarts, and, if directed, have the plugs ready to be taken out that the boats may fill, and also cause the spare spars to be put overboard.

116. Whenever the cables are bent, they shall be kept stoppered until wanted for use.

117. In action, besides aiding the Executive Officer in working ship, the Master is to pay special attention to the steerage of the vessel, and to the rigging, sails, and spars, and will see that the stoppers are properly applied, and damages repaired as speedily as possible.

In vessels where there is no Signal Officer, the Master, in action or general exercise, may be directed to perform the duties of Signal Officer.

118. The Boatswain being the assistant of the Master, is to see that the rigging, especially forward, is kept clear, and that all damages are promptly reported and repaired. In the absence of the Master, all the above preparations will be at once made by the Boatswain, and reported to the Executive Officer by him.

ENGINEER'S DIVISION.

119. The Chief Engineer will see all proper preparations made for repairing damages to the engine and its dependencies, and will have the apparatus for extinguishing fire ready for immediate use. As soon as these preparations are fully made, and his men mustered, he will report his division ready to the Executive Officer. He will also report such damages as may be received in action, and what assistance is required to repair them, and he will have charge of the preparations made for extinguishing fires below.

POWDER DIVISION.

120. The Officer commanding this division, when called to quarters for general exercise or action, will receive from the Captain the keys of the magazines and shell-rooms, and of their respective water-cocks, and will deliver them to the persons in charge, who are not to open them without his special order.

121. He will have the fire-screens let down, and the light-rooms and the deck under his charge lighted.

122. He will see that the shot and shell whips are in place and in working order, and that shot-troughs are placed for conveying shot where required; that the Gunner and his Mates at the magazine hatches and scuttles, and the persons stationed at the shell-room scuttles, are ready to open them when the order is given.

123. That all the precautions mentioned in the duties of Gunner and Carpenter have been taken against fire, namely: that the division-tubs are filled with water, and that wet swabs are placed by them, and under all the lower scuttles through which passing-boxes are returned; that a fire-tub is placed at the bottom of each chute for the return of empty boxes; that it is nearly filled with water, and has its wire grating shipped; that a proper supply of fresh water is provided for the use of the men; that the hatchways of the decks next above that on which the Powder Division is stationed are properly covered; that the air-ports are closed and secured; and that the hose is screwed to the force-pumps and ready for use.

124. He is to see that the means which are provided for lowering the wounded are ready and properly fitted, and that the wounded, when lowered down, are conveyed to the part of the vessel set apart for the Surgeon's Division, by the persons detailed for that purpose.

125. He will also see that all obstructions to the safe and rapid passage of powder, shot, and shells are removed; and when every preparation for action has been made in his division, will report it ready to the Executive Officer.

126. When the order is given from the Captain to open the magazines, shell-rooms, and scuttles, he will direct the Gunner and Gunner's Mate to repair to their respective scuttles, put on their magazine dresses and shoes, divest themselves of every article of metal, and see that the men stationed with them do the same; they are also to see that wet swabs and cans of fresh water are provided.

127. The magazines being opened, the lids of the tanks are not to be unscrewed until orders are given to that effect. Then the Gunner and his Mate, and their assistants in their respective magazines, will open as many, and no more, tanks than are necessary to supply charges of the kind ordered, which they will pass up to the men stationed on the deck above to receive them. These men will be particularly careful to observe the orders transmitted from time to time, designating the kind of charges required at the guns.

128. While at general quarters he will see that the men preserve their proper stations in silence, order, and coolness; and he will give particular attention to the sufficient and correct supply of powder and projectiles to the various divisions, and take care that in time of action, or of exercise with powder, the passing-boxes, after being once taken out of the magazine, are not passed into it again, or even inside of the screen, during the whole of such action or exercise. These duties are of the highest importance.

129. In exercise where no powder is used, he will see that such substitutes for the various charges as the Captain may direct are passed up in their proper boxes, so that the number of rounds and the kind of charge, whether "distant," "ordinary," or "near," may be ascertained, and compared with those ordered. Should any defect or deficiency in the arrangement for giving a full supply to the guns be discovered, it is to be reported immediately to the Captain, in order that a remedy may be applied as speedily as possible, by additional men or other proper means.

130. The Carpenter will see that the hatches on the deck next above the berth-deck or orlop are properly covered with gratings and tarpaulins, and that the air-ports are closed and secured.

131. He will then cause all the pumps to be rigged, namely, the main pumps, for freeing the ship in case of leaks, and the force and channel pumps. He will have the engine also rigged and filled to supply water for extinguishing fire.

132. He will attend particularly to the preparations for stopping shot-holes, and see that all the articles enumerated in his general duties (Article 59) are distributed among his mates and crew.

133. He will, when directed, cause the cabin and other bulkheads to be taken down, and every other obstruction removed which comes within his department, that may interfere with the working of the guns or the passage of ammunition; and having performed this service, will report to that effect to the Officers of the Divisions in which such obstructions existed.

134. When these preparations are completed, he will see that the men under his direction are in their proper stations, and, when all their preparatory duties have been performed, will so report to the Executive Officer, and to the Officer commanding the Powder Division what relates to that division.

135. During an action the Carpenter will attend the pumps, sound the well frequently, and, should he discover indications of serious injury below the water-line, will immediately make them known personally, either to the Captain or to the Executive Officer, and to them only.

136. During an action, such of the Carpenter's crew as are stationed in the wings, or on the orlop, in line-of-battle ships, or on the berth-deck in other vessels, will be constantly on the look-out for shot-holes.

When a shot enters they are to make its position known by reference to the numbers of the ports under or near which the hole is found, and its distance below or above the water-line, as shown by the interior line corresponding to it, already described in the general duties of the Carpenter (Article 60); and are also to apply promptly such remedy themselves as may be in their power.

137. The MASTER-AT-ARMS, assisted by the Ship's Corporals, will see the galley fire and all unauthorized lights put out; that the lamps are in their places, properly trimmed and lighted; and that the lenses and reflectors are cleaned and polished.

After the magazines have been swept, closed, and secured, and the retreat has been beaten, the Master-at-arms will see that the lights in the light-rooms are extinguished, and apply to the Executive Officer for permission to renew the usual lights and fires.

SURGEON'S DIVISION.

138. The SURGEON or senior Medical Officer will see that all necessary preparations are made for the reception and treatment of the wounded, in the part of the ship which may have been set apart by the Captain for that purpose, and report to the Executive Officer when such preparations are completed.

139. He will cause a sufficient number of tourniquets, or temporary substitutes for them, to be distributed to such men of the different divisions, and in each top, as may be appointed to receive them; and he will take care that the persons in his division, and such others as the Captain may direct, are instructed in the use of tourniquets, to prevent, as far as possible, any dangerous loss of blood before the Surgeon or his Assistants can attend to wounded men.

OFFICERS COMMANDING DIVISIONS OF GUNS.

140. Each Officer Commanding a Division of Guns is to see that all persons belonging to it are present; that all the prescribed arrangements are duly and promptly made; that every article designated for use in the division is in order and in place; that the decks are wet and well sanded; that the hand-swabs at the guns are wet; and that any small arms that may be distributed among the men of his division are properly loaded at the time directed by the Captain.

141. In action he will cause the wounded of his division to be promptly and properly conveyed to the Surgeon, but will see that no man leaves his quarters on pretence of assisting the wounded. Four men, "aids to wounded," should be attached to each Division of Guns, so as not to take men from guns for that purpose.

142. On the lower deck of line-of-battle ships, or the main deck of frigates and spar-deck of single-deck vessels, he will see the hatchways in the range of his division properly covered by the Carpenter's crew, assisted by the handspikemen or compressor-men of the nearest guns, and the scuttles and whips duly prepared for passing powder, shot, and shells.

143. He will be particularly careful to prevent the men from loading the guns improperly, or otherwise than may be specially ordered, and will prevent any unnecessary noise.

144. He will see that the guns are very carefully pointed and properly aimed; that there is no firing until correct sight can be obtained, as random firing is not only a waste of ammunition, but it encourages an enemy, when he sees shot and shell falling harmlessly about and beyond him.

He will carefully impress upon the Captains of guns that there is no excuse for several successive bad shots, as observation of the first or second will surely indicate an erroneous estimate of distance, and afford means of correcting it. Accuracy of fire is to be encouraged rather than rapidity.

It is essential to rapidity and accuracy of fire, particularly on covered decks, that the Division Officers shall keep the Gun Captains constantly advised of the position and distance of the object.

145. He will also take care to prevent confusion at the powder-scuttles in the range of his division, and that all orders which require to be repeated are duly passed. In case of accident to the Powder-passers, he will promptly supply their places by such men as can be best spared from his division.

146. He will take care that each gun in his division is provided with all the "Equipments and Implements" prescribed for its use; and that the "spare" articles which may be required in his division in action are in place.—(Article 148.)

147. He will report to the Executive Officer when all preparations have been made for action; and also after action and exercise, when the guns have been properly secured, and the stores and implements belonging to his division have been returned to their places.

EQUIPMENTS AND IMPLEMENTS.

148. Those for broadside-guns, whether mounted on two or four truck carriages, or on slides, are to be as follows, viz.:

ARTICLES FOR EACH GUN.	WHERE THEY ARE TO BE PUT WHEN THE GUN IS SECURED.
Carriage complete, with bed and quoin, or elevating screw	At its port.
Breeching with shackle-bolts and pins	At the gun.
Compressors and levers, pivot-bolt and housing-chock, for Friction Carriages	Do.
Two side-tackles	Hooked to the securing-bolts on each side of the port and to the carriage.
One train-tackle	Hooked to the securing-bolts in the side, with the parts of the fall round the breech of the gun.
Two handspikes[1]	Resting on the bed-bolt, in-board ends secured by beckets.
One tompion with lanyard and wad	In the muzzle of the gun.
One sponge and cap[2]	On the beam or carling over the right side of the gun (on movable brackets).
One rammer[2]	On the beam or carling over the left side of the gun (on movable brackets).
One lock with string and vent-plug complete, with cover and strap	In place on the gun.
One breech-sight with cover	Do.
One reinforce-sight with cover	Do.
One priming-wire and one boring-bit, with beckets for the wrist.	Inside of the brackets of the carriage, near the breech.
One fire-bucket with lanyard	On gun-decks, close to the side, near the beam over the gun; on spar-decks, round the capstan and the boats forward.
One bucket of prepared grease or oil for rifle cannon	On the breast-piece.
One battle-lantern, with candle or lamp trimmed and primed, but provided for gun-decks only; none for spar-decks.	In the fire-buckets. The candle in supply box.
Battle-axes (as prescribed according to the number of men at gun).—*See* Art. 101.	Inside of the brackets.
One hand-swab	On the breast-piece of the carriage.
One deck-bucket and large swab	To be kept in the hold until wanted.
Two chocking-quoins for truck-carriages.	When not in use, between the brackets and the bed.
Two lanyards for each half port	In place.
Lanyards, chain pendents, runners and tackles for tricing up, and bars and keys for securing lower deck ports	In place.
Ten shot for shot-guns	In racks round hatches nearest the gun.
For shell-guns, one shell in its box	Between the trucks on the left side of the gun.
Ten selvagee wads for shot and shell guns.	On the breast-piece of the carriage, strung on a pin.
Two housing-chocks for lower deck guns.	Placed before the *front trucks* when the gun is run in for housing.

[1] *Marsilly* carriages require a roller handspike each.
[2] The rammers and sponges belonging to the broadside-guns of spar-deck divisions of all ships having topgallant forecastles, or other light decks, may be kept under the forecastle or light deck when not in use. In ships not provided with these decks they are to be kept at the guns inside the brackets; or, if that cannot be done, triced up overhead on the next deck below.

149. He will also assure himself that the following articles, which may be required, are in readiness in his division, and prepared for use, namely: One rattle for calling Boarders; one division-tub for fresh water; one spare bed and quoin for carriages requiring them; two spare gun-trucks; four spare handspikes; one worm; one scraper; one bristle sponge for cleaning guns; two spare breechings; four swabs, and, if any of the guns be on slides, a spare pivot-bolt. Of these articles the worm, scraper, sponge, and spare breechings[1] are to be becketed up between the beams and carlings on the gun-decks as far as practicable, and those which cannot be so placed will be kept at hand in the storeroom or other convenient place. A ladle is supplied for each calibre on board, and will be kept ready in such place as may be designated by the Executive Officer.

The above allowance of articles designated as "spare," including worm, scraper, sponge, and swabs, is upon the supposition that each division is composed of five guns and their opposites. In case the number of guns should be either more or less, the articles will be increased or diminished proportionally to the nearest whole number.

150. He will take care that the Quarter Gunners of his division keep the two division-boxes marked "supply" and "reserve" constantly provided with the following articles, all in good order, viz.:

The "Supply" box with a waist-belt for each Boarder, Pikeman, Fireman, Sail-trimmer, and Pumpman; a primed candle for each battle-lantern; a thumbstall and vent-guard for the 1st and 2d Captains of each gun. The belts of Boarders to be furnished with a frog for a pistol, with its cartridges and percussion-caps; those of 1st and 2d Captains of guns with a box containing fifty primers fitted to slip on the waist-belt. Those for Firemen, Sail-trimmers, and Pumpmen to have each a frog for the battle-axe.

The "Reserve" box with one drill-brace; three vent-drills; one vent-punch; two gun-locks and strings complete; a flask of priming-powder; two boring-bits; three priming-wires; eight thumbstalls; four boxes of percussion-primers; one box of friction-primers; one spare lock-string for each gun, and one fuze-wrench; a shackle-punch and pin, and some rags for wiping. These boxes are to be placed by the Quarter Gunners in their respective divisions, near the mast, and on the opposite side to that engaged.

In vessels of the class of Frigates and upward, these boxes are to be, on covered decks, kept in their several divisions and secured overhead.

On spar-decks they are to be kept under the break of the poop and the topgallant forecastle, and, in vessels having neither poop nor topgallant forecastle, between the beams on the berth-deck. They will be kept under lock and key.

---

[1] The spare breechings should never be stowed near the galley nor Engine-room, lest they be damaged by heat and moisture.

151. He will see that such men of the divisions, and others who are appointed for the purpose, obtain the requisite number of tourniquets, and distribute them to the men selected to use them. (*See* Article 139.)

BROADSIDE GUNS.

STATIONS AND GUN-NUMBERS.

152. The following are to be the gun-numbers and stations for a gun's crew composed of sixteen Men and a Powderman, when working broadside-guns on lower decks; on other decks 15 and 16 are 3d and 4th Side-Tacklemen.

Left Side.	Gun-Nos.		Right Side.
First Loader	3	4	First Sponger.
Second Loader	5	6	Second Sponger.
First Shellman	7	8	Second Shellman.
First Handspikeman	9	10	Second Handspikeman.
First Side-Tackleman	13	14	Second Side-Tackleman.
First Port-Tackleman	15	16	Second Port-Tackleman.
First Train-Tackleman	11	12	Second Train-Tackleman.
First Captain	1	2	Second Captain.

Powderman near the midships, and on the left of the gun.

For a gun's crew of fourteen men and a Powder-boy, or of twelve men, the higher numbers are those to be omitted, and the stations and duties of all the others remain unchanged.

With a gun's crew of ten men, all the numbers continue with the same stations and duties excepting No. 10, who becomes Train-Tackleman, and the 2d Captain handles the handspike.

With a gun's crew of eight men, numbers from 1 to 7 inclusive retain the same stations and duties; No. 2 will, in addition to his duties as 2d Captain, also attend to the handspike, and No. 8 becomes Train-Tackleman.

With a gun's crew of six men, all the numbers retain the same stations and duties, excepting that No. 5 also acts as Shotman, and No. 2 attends to the handspike and train-tackle in addition to the duties of 2d Captain.

153. This arrangement exhibits the gun's crew placed as the men should stand when first assembled at quarters, either for inspection or any ordinary exercise. It is intended that the men are then to stand parallel with the gun, and facing in-board.

CALLS FOR ASSEMBLING AT QUARTERS.

154.

BEATS OF DRUM.

1st. THE ORDINARY BEAT will be the call for INSPECTION at general quarters.

2d. The ORDINARY BEAT, preceded by ONE ROLL—EXERCISE at general quarters, without powder.

3d. The BEAT QUICK—ACTION; or EXERCISE at general quarters with powder, as though engaged in BATTLE.

4th. WHEN AT QUARTERS, a roll of the drum will be a signal for "SILENCE AND ATTENTION!" All firing or other noise will immediately cease, and the next order be awaited in perfect silence. It is of the utmost importance to impress this upon the officers and crew.

5th. When the Captain is satisfied that his order has been delivered and understood, he will order TWO TAPS to be beaten, as a signal for the "EXECUTION OF THE ORDER." The roll and the taps to be given sharply and distinctly.

155. On assembling at quarters for inspection or general exercise, unless directed otherwise, in port, the men are first to go to the starboard guns on the spar-deck, the port guns on the main deck, the starboard guns on the next deck below, and so on. At sea they are first to go to the weather guns, or, if the ship be dead before the wind, to the same sides as in port.

156. When assembled for inspection, besides seeing that all the guns and articles belonging to them are in order and in place, it is directed that the men, without arms or implements, or casting loose the guns, shall be frequently called away and mustered in their stations as Boarders, Pikemen, Sail-trimmers, and Firemen; and also practised in shifting from one side to the other, and in taking their places for fighting both sides at once.

157. On assembling for exercise at general quarters without powder, after the men have been mustered and the divisional reports made, the order will be given: "CAST LOOSE AND PROVIDE!"

Then the starboard watch will provide and cast loose the odd-numbered guns, and the port watch will provide and cast loose the even-numbered guns.

The 1st parts of guns' crews on the starboard side providing and casting loose the starboard, and the 2d parts the port guns. The 1st parts of guns' crews on the port side the port, and the 2d parts the starboard guns. In securing guns the same order of distributing the men is to be observed.

When both these services of providing and casting loose have been performed, and the luffs choked or hitched and trucks chocked, the men are all to return to the guns at which they were mustered, and, taking their places, await in silence further orders, if not already given.

158. When assembled for exercise as though actually engaged in battle, besides what is prescribed for an exercise at general quarters without powder, the further preparations indicated hereafter will be made. The guns' crews will proceed at once to provide and cast loose both sides without waiting to be mustered, or for any further orders.

159. The call for BOARDERS to repair to the spar-deck will be by the rattle and verbal order, repeated by the Officer of each division of guns. They should be trained to form promptly on the opposite side to that engaged, near the hatch by which they ascend.

On the first call or order, the first division only will repair to the spar-deck, led by their officers. If the call or order should be repeated before the first division shall have returned to their guns, the second division will immediately repair to the spar-deck.

160. The call for PIKEMEN to "repel boarders" will be by sounding the Gong. At this signal all the Pikemen will assemble on the spar-deck with their muskets.

161. ALL HANDS will be summoned to repel boarders (*See* Article 92) by springing the rattles and sounding the gong together, and by verbal orders.

162. SAIL-TRIMMERS. The particular division that may be wanted at a time will be called by passing the word for it.

163. The call for FIREMEN to repair to the spar-deck will be given verbally and by striking the ship's bell rapidly. The rapid ringing of the bell will be the FIRE-ALARM at all times, when the crew will immediately assemble at quarters.

164. Boarders, Pikemen, and Sail-trimmers of the spar-deck guns, or any portion of them, and of the Master's division, as well as the Marines, may be ordered from their quarters to perform a particular service, without any call, whenever the Captain may deem proper.

165. Men called for any of the foregoing duties will, on reaching the spar-deck, form on the gangway, upon the side not engaged with the enemy, unless otherwise directed at the time.

166. When called to quarters, every person is to repair to his station promptly and without unnecessary noise; and on the order, "to your quarters," all will return to their stations in the same manner.

PREPARATIONS FOR EXERCISE AT GENERAL QUARTERS, WITHOUT POWDER.

167. Sling the topsail yards and gaffs, and put the preventer braces in place; distribute fighting stoppers and jiggers; stopper the clews of the topsails; get whips on each side of the lower masts for tricing up the pendant tackles, and also the mast-bands and fishes required for securing a crippled mast. Make arrangements for using grapnels; get hauling-lines ready for sending small arms and ammunition into the tops; if not on soundings, haul over boat and boom covers and stop them down; bring up and stow, if down, such hammocks as interfere with the guns, or are in the way of the powder division;[1] haul over and secure the hammock-cloths; hook and mouse the relieving-tackles; place the spare tiller and compass at hand; put the chronometers, and other instruments of navigation, out of the reach of shot; distribute the small arms together with their accoutrements and a supply of filled cartridges, to the men appointed to use them; place axes and hatchets at hand on the spar-deck for clearing away incumbrances at guns; grapnels in mizzen channels with whips to after-davits and spanker-boom end, to hook up any gear likely to foul the screw. In steam vessels, topgallant masts and rigging ready to be sent down and all unnecessary gear unrove.

If underway and on soundings, get the boats ready for hoisting out; the ground-tackle ready for use and keep it clear, and make every preparation for towing, warping, and anchoring with springs on cables; stopper the chains; get lights in the light-rooms, including those of the shell-rooms; light powder division; also gun-decks, if at night, and it be ordered by the Captain; drop magazine screens; get shot and shell whips, and buckets or nets, in place; rig canvas chutes for returning empty passing-boxes; remove every obstruction to the free passage of powder; clear away and open shot-lockers; see the hatchways of the next deck above the powder division properly covered; division and fire-tubs in place, with wet swabs by them, and at the landing of each line of scuttles through which the passing-boxes pass; rig main, force, and channel pumps and fire-engine, which fill with water; get light Jacob-ladders and slings ready for lowering the Carpenters outside, and materials for stopping shot-holes; take down cabin and other bulkheads, when directed, and pass them below; sand the decks; place a bucket of water and a wet swab in rear of each gun, and for all rifle-guns a bucket of oil or prepared grease; have spare breechings at hand; rope ladders for hatchways in place; a bag, to be supplied from one reserve-box, containing a flask of priming-powder and the following spare articles: two

[1] The Executive Officer of the ship should appoint a sufficient number of men in each watch for the purpose of stowing the hammocks of the watch below in case of being called to quarters in the night, so as to prevent confusion and insure the greatest possible dispatch in clearing for action.

locks, four lock-strings, eight thumbstalls, two boring-bits, two priming-wires, a shackle-punch and pins and some old rags, to be slung round the neck of the Quarter Gunner of each division of guns; rammers and sponges placed, and the latter uncapped; one worm in place, on each side of the deck, for each division, and a ladle at hand for each calibre on board; pistols, in frogs furnished with cartridges and caps, and cutlasses and battle-axes, belted round the respective persons designated to wear them; marines accoutred and under arms, and distributed as the Captain may direct; tourniquets to be distributed as may be judged necessary. (*See* Articles 139 and 151.)

PREPARATIONS FOR EXERCISE AT GENERAL QUARTERS,

WITH POWDER, AS THOUGH ENGAGED IN BATTLE.

168. Crew cast loose the guns; shell-rooms and magazine are opened; powder and shells passed up, and every thing ready for firing, the order for which is awâited. If the beat is followed by orders from the qnarter-deck to fire, then this is performed as soon as each gun is ready. In this case, besides what has just been prescribed for a General Exercise without powder, the following further preparations will be made: Put out galley fire and all unauthorized lights; light match and place it in manger; open magazines and powder-tanks, and also shell-rooms, when ordered; close and secure air-ports; fill division and fire tubs with fresh water; place cans of fresh water and wet swabs in magazines and shell-rooms; light up the cockpit, or other place, for the wounded; place mattresses, and if there be room, sling spare cots; get ready the amputating-table, instruments bandages, lint, medicines; have a plentiful supply of fresh water and swabs, and sprinkle the decks. Make a particular examination of all the arrangements for extinguishing fire; see that force-pumps and hose are in good order, and the men stationed at them in their places.

Speed being one of the principal elements of military force, steamers will, on going into action, have all the furnaces clean, and the fires in condition to make steam rapidly.

The beat to quarters for action is therefore a signal to start fires in any furnaces not in use.

PROVIDING BROADSIDE-GUNS.

169. When the exercise of broadside-guns is to be confined to one side only, each gun's crew is to provide its own gun, on the side at which it is ordered to assemble, as follows: but when the guns on both sides are to be exercised at once, each part of a gun's crew is to provide its own gun; each Captain, Loader, Sponger, &c., doing separately what is done by both himself and his second when the exercise is confined to one side only.

170. Captains of guns to provide themselves with percussion-primers, thumbstalls, and priming-wire, and to see that the men of their respective parts of the gun's crew discharge their several duties promptly and carefully.

171. Spongers provide sponges and rammers.

172. Loaders provide a bucket of water and a wet swab; and, for rifle cannon, a pot of oil or prepared grease.

173. Shell or shotmen provide a sufficient supply of selvagee and six junk-wads, and supply the racks around the hatchways with shot from the lockers as required.

174. Handspikemen see the handspikes in place, and then assist in getting up shot for the guns; and, if necessary, in covering hatchways in the division.

175. The Powderman or Boy is to provide an empty passing-box, if no powder is to be used; otherwise he is to present himself at the appointed place to receive a full one.

176. The Fireman is to take down the fire-bucket, and place it and the battle-lantern in their appointed places. On gun-decks the lantern should be hung up at the ship's side, or in rear of and between the guns, as may be directed, and lighted when ordered by the Captain, and the fire-bucket directly in rear of the gun. On spar-decks the bucket may be laid on the deck, or hung up in any convenient place in rear of and near the gun.

177. Side-tacklemen provide sand and water, and sprinkle and sand the decks, if directed; and get bucket and swab from the hold, fill the bucket with water, wet the sponge and the swab, and lay it on deck under the sponge.

178. Quarter Gunners of divisions, besides equipping themselves, as already directed (Article 167), with a bag of spare implements, will attend to the "Supply" and "Reserve" boxes of their divisions (*See* Article 150), and distribute the belts, primer-boxes, and other articles which they contain, to the guns' crews, as soon as practicable, and then keep themselves ready to furnish any reserved or spare articles which may be required, such as spare breechings, ladles, and worms, and will see the battle-lanterns provided with candles with primed wicks, ready for lighting when ordered by the Captain.

179. The swords and pistols should be always available for the Boarders, at the shortest notice; but their particular disposition at quarters, and at what time the pistols shall be loaded, will be determined by the Captain, as in his judgment circumstances at the time may require. Pistols should be loaded, on the probability of action, without further orders.

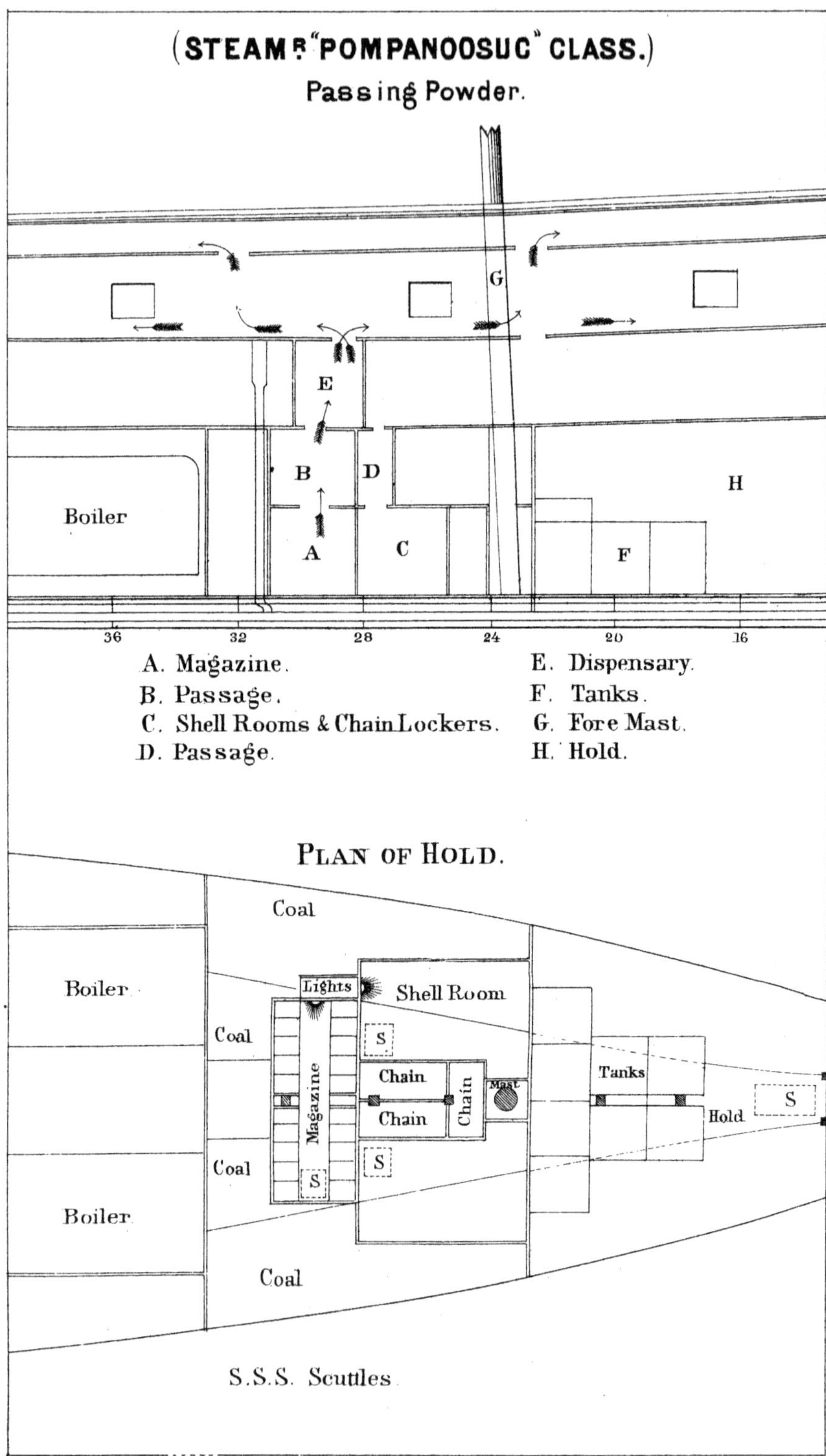
(STEAM^R "POMPANOOSUC" CLASS.)
Passing Powder.
G
E
B
D
H
Boiler
A
C
F
36
32
28
24
20
16
A. Magazine.
B. Passage.
C. Shell Rooms & Chain Lockers.
D. Passage.
E. Dispensary.
F. Tanks.
G. Fore Mast.
H. Hold.
PLAN OF HOLD.
Coal
Boiler
Lights
Shell Room
Coal
S
Magazine
Chain
Chain
Chain
Mast
Tanks
Hold
S
Coal
S
S
Boiler
Coal
S.S.S. Scuttles.
Lith. by J.F. Gedney, Wash'r.
C.K. Stellwagen, del.

ARRANGEMENTS FOR DELIVERING AND DISTRIBUTING POWDER.

180. In making arrangements to deliver and distribute powder from the magazines, for action, the following general considerations and rules should govern:

181. Cartridges, as experience proves, can be passed up each independent chain of scuttles leading from the magazine to the point at which the Powder-boys are to receive the full boxes, at the rate of one every six or seven seconds.

182. Experience also proves that, under the most favorable circumstances, the broadside-guns of a man-of-war cannot be advantageously fired oftener than once in every seventy-five seconds.

Hence it may be received as a rule, that a single chain of passing-scuttles is abundantly sufficient to supply powder for a division of guns as large even as eight of a side; and that it is also sufficient when both sides of such a division are to be used at once, for then the firing of each piece is unavoidably retarded by the division of the guns' crews.

183. No one chain of scuttles should be required to supply cartridges for more than a single description of guns,[1] unless their cartridges be the same in diameter, weight, and form, and their passing-boxes alike, as in the case of the 8-inch shell-gun of 63 cwt. and the 32-pounder of 57 cwt. If, therefore, there be on a deck of guns but one differing from the rest in calibre, class, or assimilation of cartridges, that one should have a separate chain of scuttles for its supply, in order to guard effectually against confusion, or, at least, delay. In a word, each additional calibre or class of guns, unless the cartridges be assimilated and the passing-boxes alike, involves an additional chain of passing-scuttles for its supply; and it should be borne in mind that errors with respect to cartridges of guns of the same calibre, but differing in class, are more to be apprehended than with guns differing only in calibre.

184. If the guns on a deck be all of the same calibre and class, or of like cartridges and passing-boxes, then one chain of scuttles to supply the forward half of those guns, and another to supply the after half, will be all-sufficient.

185. For each chain of passing-scuttles there will probably have to be—

One man in the magazine to deliver charges from the tanks.

One man in the passage to receive and pass those charges through the scuttle in the orlop or berth deck.

One man at the passage-scuttle on the orlop or berth deck, to receive the charges and pass them to the screen.

One man just outside of the screen, to receive the charges through a flapped hole therein, and put them in the empty passing-boxes.

[1] See Table of Charges for Great Guns.

One, two, or three Runner-boys (according to the distance) to run, on the orlop or berth deck, with full passing-boxes, from the screen to the scuttles through the deck, and back again with the empty boxes to the screen.

One man, a very careful one, at the bottom of the canvas chute, to receive the empty passing-boxes, strike them, in an inverted position, over the fire-tub, and inspect them carefully before allowing them to be taken away to be replenished.

One man, on the orlop or berth deck, at the passing-scuttle through the deck above, to pass up full boxes.

One man at the passing-scuttle on the next deck above the orlop or berth deck, to receive and pass up full boxes, or, in the case of a single-deck vessel, or of distribution on the main deck of a frigate, or on the lower deck of a ship-of-the-line, to receive and deliver them to Powder-boys.

One man at the passing-scuttle on the second deck above the orlop or berth deck, to receive and pass up full boxes; or, in the case of a frigate, or distribution on the main deck of a ship-of-the-line of two decks, to receive and deliver them to Powder-boys.

And one man at the passing-scuttle on the third deck above the orlop, to receive and deliver full boxes to Powder-boys on the spar-deck of a ship-of-the-line of two decks.

Thus each chain of scuttles will require—

Seven men to supply its guns on the first deck above; as, for example, the lower deck of a ship-of-the-line, the main deck of a frigate, or the spar-deck of a sloop-of-war, or other single-deck vessel.

Eight men for the spar-deck of a frigate, for the main deck of a ship-of-the-line of two decks, or for the middle gun-deck of a ship-of-the-line of three decks.

Nine men for the spar-deck of a ship-of-the-line of two decks, or for the main deck of a ship-of-the line of three decks.

And ten men for the spar-deck of a ship-of-the-line of three decks.

Besides, each of these numbers—7, 8, 9, and 10—is to be increased by two or three Runner-boys, for the purposes above described.

186. In vessels of and above the class of frigates, or having two magazines—one forward and the other aft—the forward half of the guns on each deck is to be supplied from the forward magazine, and the after half from the after magazine. Thus, for each deck of guns, one scuttle at each of the two magazines, together with its corresponding chain of scuttles, will be sufficient, if all the guns be of the same calibre and class, or have like charges. But the introduction on board of any vessel of guns differing in either of these respects will involve the necessity above stated of a separate scuttle of delivery at the magazine, and also of a distinct chain of scuttles connected with it, for the exclusive supply of each variety of charges that may be introduced.

In this case, the exceptional guns should be supplied, whenever practicable, from the larger magazine, when there are two differing in size.

187. In single-deck vessels carrying more than sixteen guns, all of the same calibre and class, and having but one magazine, two scuttles at that magazine will be sufficient—one to supply the forward half of guns, and the other the after half.

188. In single-deck vessels carrying only sixteen guns, or less, all of the same calibre and class, or having like charges, one scuttle at the magazine will suffice.

189. Should any single-deck vessel be of such great length, or so remarkable in her armament of guns, although all of the same calibre and class, as to render additional scuttles advisable, they are to be cut.

PASSING-SCUTTLES.

190. All the powder is to be passed up from the orlop or berth deck through circular scuttles, cut in the deck or decks at places, as nearly as circumstances will permit, immediately abreast of the middle of the particular set of guns to the supply of which each chain of scuttles is specially appropriated. Besides these scuttles for passing the powder up, there are to be corresponding ones for each set, provided with a canvas chute for returning the empty boxes below. The drawing shows the manner of supplying an upper deck and returning the empty boxes from it. Each deck is to be supplied in like manner, by a distinct and separate arrangement, through as many independent sets of scuttles as may be required by the preceding "Arrangements for delivering and distributing powder."

191. Each scuttle is to have a tompion or other means of closing it, so as to be water-tight when not in use, and to be so placed or regulated in height as not to interfere with the transportation of guns.

192. Should any serious difficulty arise in finding places for cutting any of the different sets of scuttles through the decks, or in the cases of small or very wet vessels, recourse may be had to the gratings of the hatchways. Still, they are always to be cut through the decks whenever it can be done with propriety.

193. For each scuttle at the magazine for the delivery of powder there must be a corresponding flap-hole in the magazine screen, and this is to be regarded as a part of the chain of supply equally with the scuttle itself.

194. When on board ship there are any guns of the same calibre and class, or of assimilated charges, carried on two consecutive decks, all of them may be supplied by the same chain of scuttles, provided the whole number of guns thus made to depend upon this chain does not exceed eight of a side. For instance, under the circumstances stated, the chase, or a few shell or other guns on a spar-deck, may be supplied by a chain of scuttles intended principally for the main-deck guns; or, the shell-guns on a main deck being few, may be supplied by a chain intended principally for the deck below.

195. In delivering cartridges from the magazines for serving guns, they are to be passed up from the magazine to the orlop or berth deck before they are put into the passing-boxes, which, in time of action, or when exercising with powder, after being once taken out of the magazine, are not, on any account, to be allowed to go into it again, or even inside of the screen, during the whole time of such action or exercise. They are to be replenished at the screen, but outside of it.

196. All passing-boxes shall be painted black, with the calibre and charge painted in white letters, two and one-half inches ($2\frac{1}{2}$) long on the side, and one and a half ($1\frac{1}{2}$) on the top.

197. If, however, there are any guns of the same calibre on spar-decks requiring lighter charges, the lower half of the box shall be painted white. For gun-decks in similar case the lower half shall be painted red.

198. Empty passing-boxes returned by the chutes are always to be landed upon wet swabs, and then to be turned upside down, and so struck over a fire-tub, as before directed, to free them from any loose powder.

199. One fire-tub, nearly filled with water, is to be placed on the deck, alongside the bottom of each chute for returning empty boxes. The top of this tub is to be provided with a stout hoop to ship and unship, with a grating of stout copper wire, the meshes of which are to be made small enough to prevent the passing-box from falling into the water, in case of slipping from the man's hand while being struck over the tub.

SHOT AND SHELL.

200. Shot and shell are to be passed up by hand, or whipped up, by the most convenient hatchways. The hands stationed below at the lockers are to work the whips, each of which, being fitted with a toggle, will indicate when the projectiles are hoisted high enough. In case a shot-locker should be somewhat removed from the hatchway, up which the shot are to be passed or whipped, the shot may be speedily conveyed over the distance by means of a wooden trough fitted for the purpose.

HATCHWAY FOR THE WOUNDED.

201. One hatchway, or portion of a hatchway, and that as nearly amidships as possible, is to be reserved for lowering the wounded below, and to be properly provided with a cot or cots, having a whip to each.

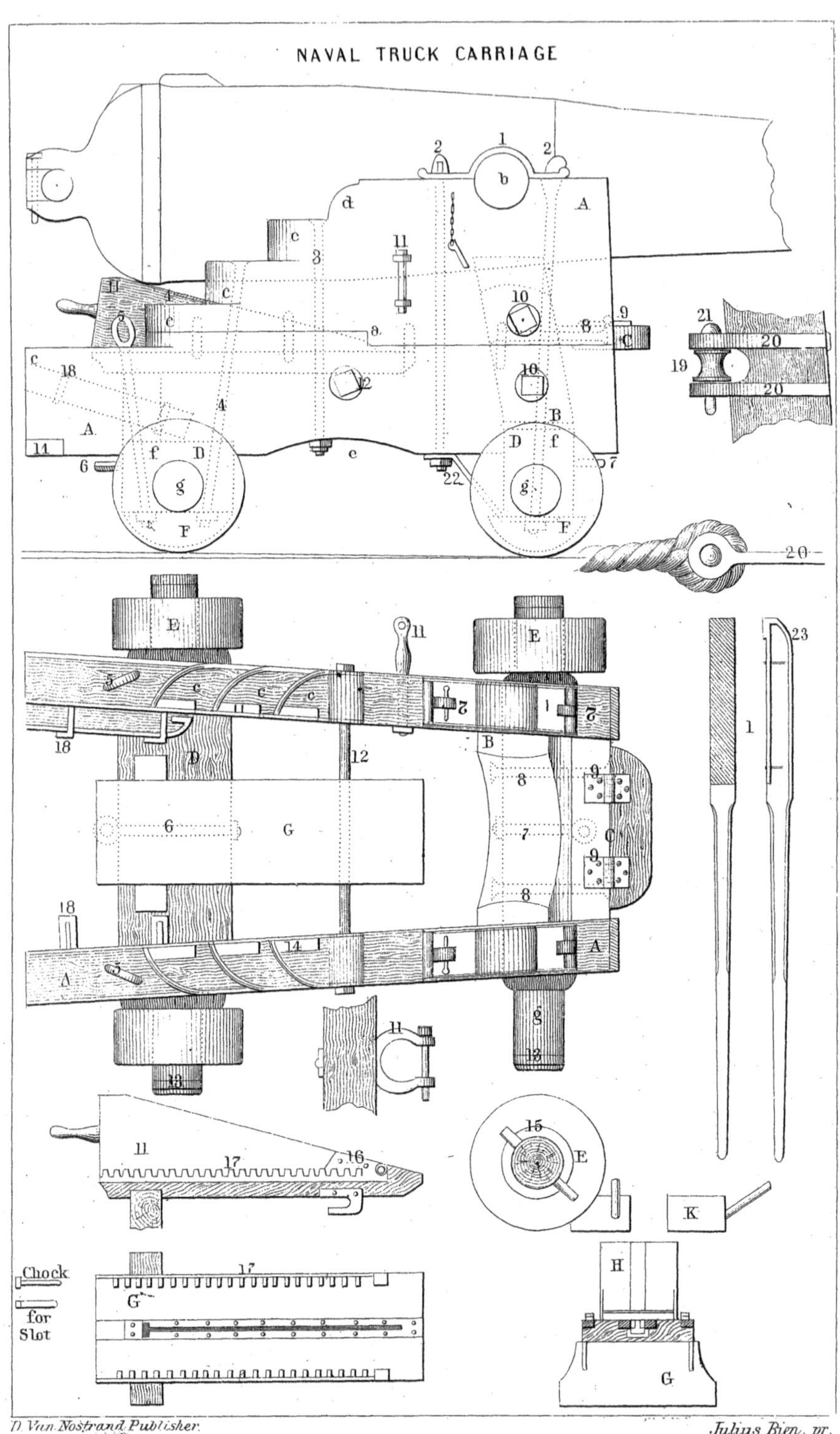

D. Van Nostrand Publisher. Julius Bien, pr.

NAVAL GUN-CARRIAGES.

202. All gun-carriages and their equipments are to be made in conformity with directions from the Bureau of Ordnance.

NOMENCLATURE

OF ORDINARY NAVAL TRUCK-CARRIAGE.

WOODEN PARTS.

Carriage.

A. Brackets of large truck-carriages are made each of two pieces, joined by a jog *a*, and dowelled. The remaining parts of the brackets are the trunnion-holes *b*, steps *c*, quarter-rounds *d*, and arch *e*.
B. Transom, let into brackets.
C. Breast-piece, in two parts—the inner part fixed, by two bolts, into transom; the outer part movable, connected by hinges.
D. Front and rear axletrees, consisting each of square body *f*, and arms *g*, jogged into brackets.
E. Front and rear trucks.
F. Dumb trucks.
G. Bed and stool.
H. Quoin.

Implements.

I. Handspikes.
K. Chocking-quoin.

METAL PARTS.

Carriage.

1. Two cap-squares.
2. Four cap-square bolts and two keys and chains.
3. Two bracket-bolts.
4. Two rear axletree-bolts.
5. Two side-tackle eye-bolts.
6. One train-tackle eye-bolt.
7. One transporting eye-bolt.
8. Two breast-bolts.
9. Two hinges of breast-pieces.
10. Two transom-bolts (upper and lower).
11. Two breeching side-shackles and pins.
12. Bed-bolt.
13. Four axletree bands.
14. Chafing-plates of steps and brackets.
15. Four linchpins and washers.
16. Quoin-plate and stop.
17. Ratchet for quoin-stop.
18. Four training loops.
19. Breeching-thimble (cast iron).
20. Side-shackle bolts for breechings.
21. Shackle-pin, plates, and keys.
22. Two axle-stays.
23. Handspike-shoe.

OF PARTS PECULIAR TO MARSILLY CARRIAGE.

A. The lowest piece of the bracket, in place of the rear truck of ordinary carriages.
B. Rear transom, in place of rear axle.
C. Breast-piece (fixed).
D. E. Sweep-pieces.
D. Fixed below the port-sill.
E. Movable, with brass catches (*f f*) and hooks and eyes (*g g*).
H. Elevating screw and lever, with saucer (I) in place of bed and quoin.
K. Roller handspike.
L. Loop for handspike.

CHAPTER IV.

MANUAL EXERCISE.

EXERCISE OF BROADSIDE-GUNS,

ON ONE SIDE ONLY.

IX-INCH SHELL-GUN (*as an example*).

203. WORDS OF COMMAND.

I. "SILENCE! MAN THE STARBOARD (OR PORT) GUNS!"
II. "CAST LOOSE AND PROVIDE!"
III. "RUN IN!" (preparatory).
IV. "SERVE VENT AND SPONGE!"
V. "LOAD!"
VI. "RUN OUT!"
VII. "PRIME!"
VIII. "POINT!"
IX. "READY—FIRE!"
X. "SECURE!"

It is customary to keep the guns of the Battery loaded at sea; it has been found that the fire of a ship could be commenced in three minutes from the beat of drum, the guns being secured for sea, and no notice of what was contemplated announced to men or officers save by the signal for quarters.

This form of exercise therefore proceeds on the assumption that the cannon are not loaded, but the order of the commands may be varied to suit the circumstances of the case.

204. Guns should never remain loaded longer than necessary, as the cartridge speedily deteriorates by the effects of moisture. If a shell has been loaded twenty-four hours it should be drawn and refuzed.

NOTE.—In order not to incumber the text with details, they are transferred to the "Notes on the Manual Exercise" (Art. 288 to 357), which are to be carefully studied. Also the notes to Pivot-Gun Exercise.

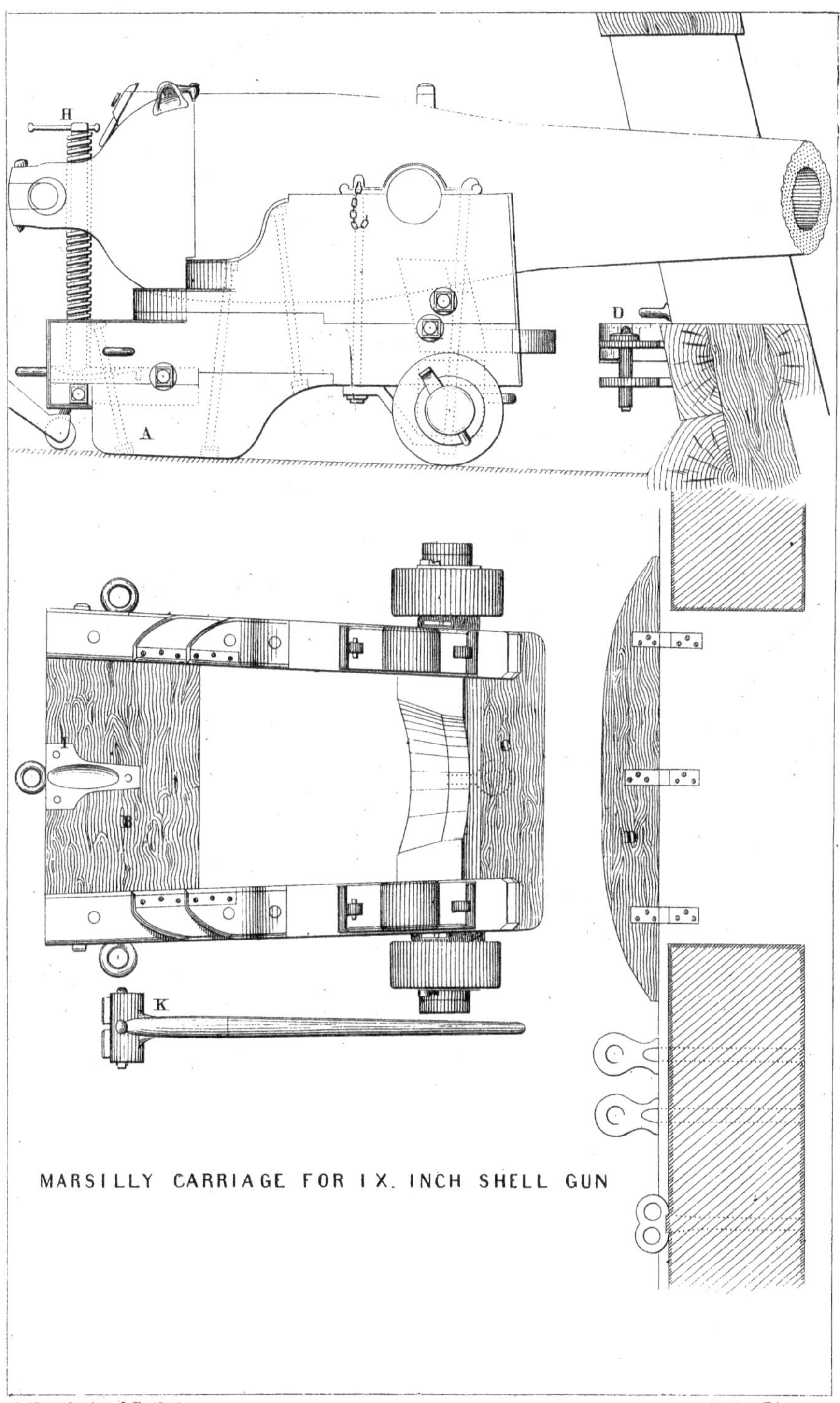

MARSILLY CARRIAGE FOR IX. INCH SHELL GUN

D. Van Nostrand, Publisher.

Julius Bien, pr.

I. "SILENCE! MAN THE STARBOARD (OR PORT) GUNS!"

205. At this preparatory order the strictest silence is to be observed. The Captain faces the port, the men, on the right and left, stand facing the gun; all fix their eyes on the Captain and attentively wait for orders.

II. "CAST LOOSE AND PROVIDE!"

206. The GUN CAPTAIN commands, sees his gun cleared and cast loose, portlid unbarred ready for tricing up, or half ports taken out; side and train tackles hooked, the side-tackle to the side training-bolt, and the train-tackle to the eye-bolt in the deck in the rear of the gun; casts loose and middles breeching and places selvagee straps and toggles amidships; takes off lock-cover, and hands it to the train-tackleman, who places it amidships; buckles on his waist-belt (furnished as directed in Article 150); provides himself with a priming-wire; puts on and secures his thumbstall; and sees that the gear and implements for the service of the gun are all in place and ready for use, and that the men are properly equipped.

When the gun is ready for action he sees that the men take their proper positions, and reports to the Officer of the subdivision to which he belongs.

It is important that the battery shall be completely provided at every exercise, otherwise something is sure to be omitted in preparing for action.

207. 2D CAPTAIN assists in casting loose and middling breeching; takes off and places amidships sight-covers, selvagee straps, and toggles; handles quoin; provides thumbstalls, priming-wires, and boring-bit, and equips himself with the first two; clears lock-string and lays it in a loose coil round the lock, convenient for use, and buckles on his waist-belt furnished as 1st Captain's. If the gun is furnished with an elevating screw, elevates the gun, that the lower half port may be let down.

208. 1ST LOADER, aided by 1st Sponger, casts loose port-lanyards, removes upper half port, and passes it to the men on the left side of the gun, who lay it amidships; lets down the lower half port. On lower deck casts off port-lanyards and muzzle-lashing; removes port-bar and passes it to the men at the left side of the gun, who lay it amidships; bears out port. On all decks places hand-swab and chocking-quoin near the ship's side on the left side of the gun; aids 1st Sponger in taking out tompion.

209. 2D LOADER assists in casting loose; sees the wads in place, and for rifle cannon a pot of grease at hand; hooks outer block of side-tackle to side training-bolt, on the left side of the gun.

210. 1ST SPONGER casts loose port-lanyards and aids 1st Loader in removing upper half ports and letting down lower ones, and on lower decks in removing the port-bar, bearing out the port and taking off the muzzle-lashings; takes out tompion, and passes it to 2d Sponger, who hangs it amidships; places chocking-quoin on the right side of the gun, near the ship's side.

211. 2D SPONGER assists in casting loose; hooks outer block of side-tackle to the side training-bolt, on the right side of the gun.

The Spongers take down the sponges and rammers; take off the sponge-cap and hang it up out of the way; place sponges and rammers together. on the right side of the gun, heads toward the breech, in the brackets overhead on covered decks, otherwise on deck.

The SIDE-TACKLEMEN assist in casting loose; on lower decks, aid Port-tacklemen; moisten the sponge, being certain that the end of the sponge which touches the bottom of the bore is thoroughly wet.

212. SHELLMEN assist in casting loose, provide shot and wads, and proceed to hatchway, ready to pass loaded shell, if ordered.

213. TRAIN-TACKLEMEN lead out and hook train-tackle.

214. HANDSPIKEMEN take out the handspikes on their respective sides, and with carriages using a quoin, each standing between his handspike and the side of the ship, place the heels of their handspikes on the steps of the carriage and under the breech of the gun, and raise it so that the quoin may be eased and the lower half port let down, or, when housed, the bed and quoin adjusted. Then each Handspikeman will lay his handspike on deck, on his own side of the gun, parallel with its axis, clear of the trucks and butt to the rear.

215. POWDER-BOY repairs to his proper scuttle for his passing-box, which having received he returns and stands a little to the left and in rear of the gun, keeping the passing-box under his left arm and the cover closely pressed down with his right hand.

216. When there are fourteen or more men at a gun, the PORT-TACKLEMEN and SIDE-TACKLEMEN, on lower decks, lead out port-tackle falls and assist in tricing up the port, and, when high enough, belay the fall.

217. In the temporary absence of the first Captains, Loaders, or Spongers, when at quarters on one side, their Seconds will take their places and perform their respective duties.

When exercising by divisions, or single gun's crews, every station should be filled; if necessary, taking men from the Master's or Powder division to fill vacancies. The guns will be sufficiently exercised in working with reduced crews at general quarters.

218. With a gun's crew of ten or more men, No. 7 will take the place of No. 5, and No. 8 of No. 6, when Nos. 5 or 6 are absent temporarily.

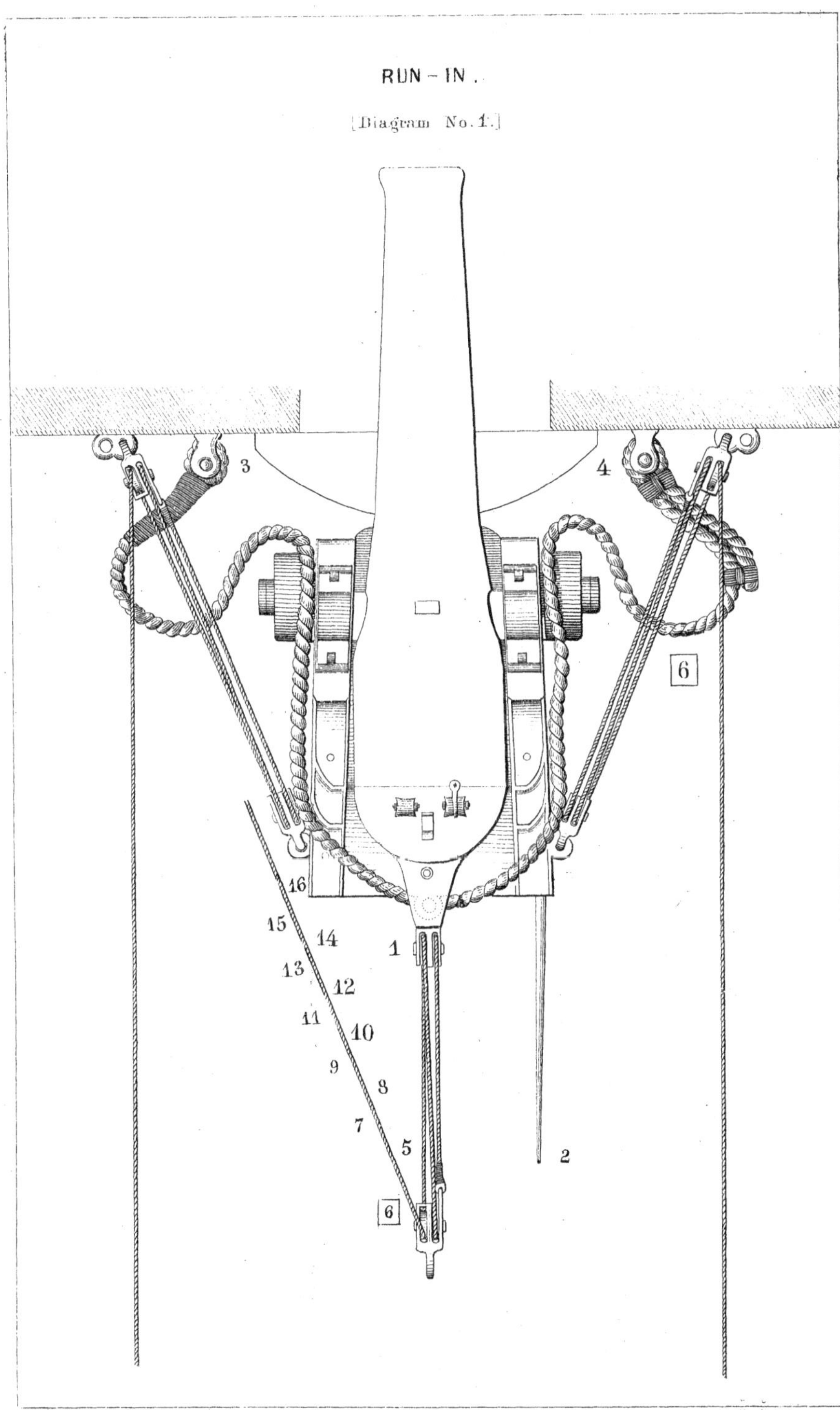

RUN-IN.

[Diagram No. 1.]

D. Van Nostrand, Publisher.

Julius Bien, pr.

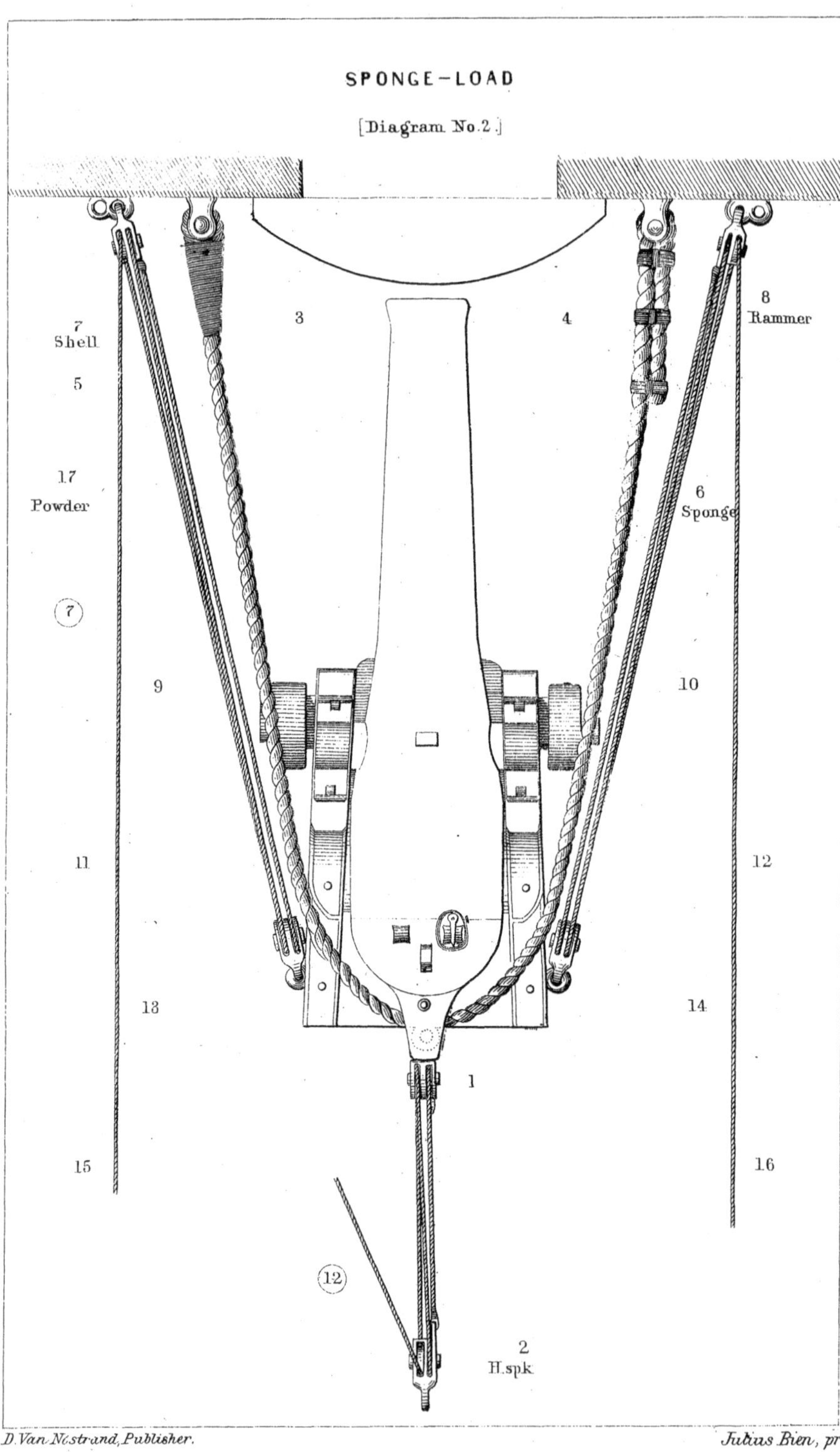

D. Van Nostrand, Publisher. Julius Bien, pr.

III. "RUN IN!" (*preparatory*).

(Diagram No. 1.)

219. Nos. 7, 8, 9, 10, 11, 12, 13, 14, 15, 16 (and, if necessary, 5, 6), man the Train-tackle.

2d Captain ships and works Roller Handspike. Nos. 3, 4, overhaul or tend the Side-tackles.

The gun having been run in, No. 12 chokes luff of Train-tackle, assisted, if there is much motion, by No. 11.

Nos. 3, 4 place Truck-quoins in front of Trucks.

No. 6, with back square to gun, and facing over left shoulder to Sponger, takes up the Sponge, head in-board, and stands ready to hand it to 4.

No. 8, facing to the gun, and outside of 6, does the same with the Rammer.

The rest of the men go to their stations.

IV. "SERVE VENT AND SPONGE!"[1]

(Diagram No. 2.)

220. Gun Captain serves and then stops the Vent. No. 4 receives the moist Sponge from 6, right hand over, left under, sends it home, and, assisted by 3, presses it to bottom of bore; then, turning it round two or three times, from left to right, in the direction which is needed to have the worm take, withdraws it, and, when out, strikes the staff several smart taps under the muzzle, then hands it back to 6, who lays it on the deck or lodges it overhead on the hooks, if they are provided. No. 10 examines and clears sponge-head and worm.

After the Sponge is withdrawn, Gun Captain serves the vent with his priming-wire and again closes it.

No. 8 hands Rammer to 4 as soon as the Sponge is taken from him by 6. Should 4 observe that the Gun Captain neglected to serve the vent, he is to call his attention to it.

No. 3 stands ready with Charge he has taken from Powderman.

No. 5, assisted by Shellman, opens Shell-box, disengages the Shell, and has it in readiness to pass to No. 3.

V. "LOAD!"

(Diagram No. 2.)

221. No. 3 places Charge in muzzle, seam from the Vent, small end in, and pushes it well into the Bore.

No. 4 stands ready with the Rammer, enters it into the muzzle, and pushes the Charge steadily to the bottom of the Bore, which will be shown

[1] See notes on this command and the succeeding one, "LOAD," for further important details.

by the mark on the rammer handle; 3 assists with one hand, and the charge is on no account to be struck.

While 4 withdraws the Rammer, 3 is to receive the Shell from 5, lift and enter it, sabot first, into muzzle, fuze out, as soon as the rammer is clear thereof.

As the shell lies just fair with muzzle, 3 removes cap from Fuze, which is to be passed along to the Gun Captain, and pushes the Shell into the Bore.

No. 4 enters Rammer, and, assisted by 3, pushes in the Shell until the mark on handle shows it to be in place. It is most strictly forbidden to strike the Shell with the Rammer.

No. 6 takes Rammer from 4 and lays it down.

Whilst this has been doing, the preparation for the next order has been proceeding, thus:

2d Captain ships Roller Handspike. Nos. 7, 9, 11, 13, 15,—8, 10, 12, 14, 16 take hold of Side-tackles; Gun Captain feels if Vent is clear, and Charge home.

Action.

(This is equivalent to the order "Together.")

Nos. 5, 6 assist at Side-tackles.

Nos. 3, 4 attend Truck-quoins and keep the Breeching clear of Front-trucks.

No. 12, assisted in heavy rolling of lee guns by 11, prepares to tend Train-tackle. If necessary with a round turn round all parts of the fall.

VI. "RUN OUT!"

(Diagram No. 3.)

222. The execution of this order is to be controlled by the gun being to windward or to leeward, and also by the nature of the Roll.

To *leeward*, and with much motion, the cannon will rush out violently unless prevented; therefore 11 assists 12 at the Train-tackle; 7, 9, 11, 13, 15, and 8, 10, 12, 14, 16 start the gun cautiously.

2d Captain heaves up on Roller Handspike, but is careful to let down the Carriage if it begins to start out rapidly; it may even be advisable not to use the Roller Handspike at all.

Nos. 3, 4 remove Truck-quoins and tend breeching.

Action.

If to *windward*, 2d Captain heaves up Carriage fully on Roller Handspike.

Nos. 5 and 6 assist at Side-tackles.

No. 12 only tends Train-tackle if the Roll should need it; otherwise he overhauls it and assists at Side-tackles.

Nos. 3, 4 remove Truck-quoins, and keep Breeching from fouling the

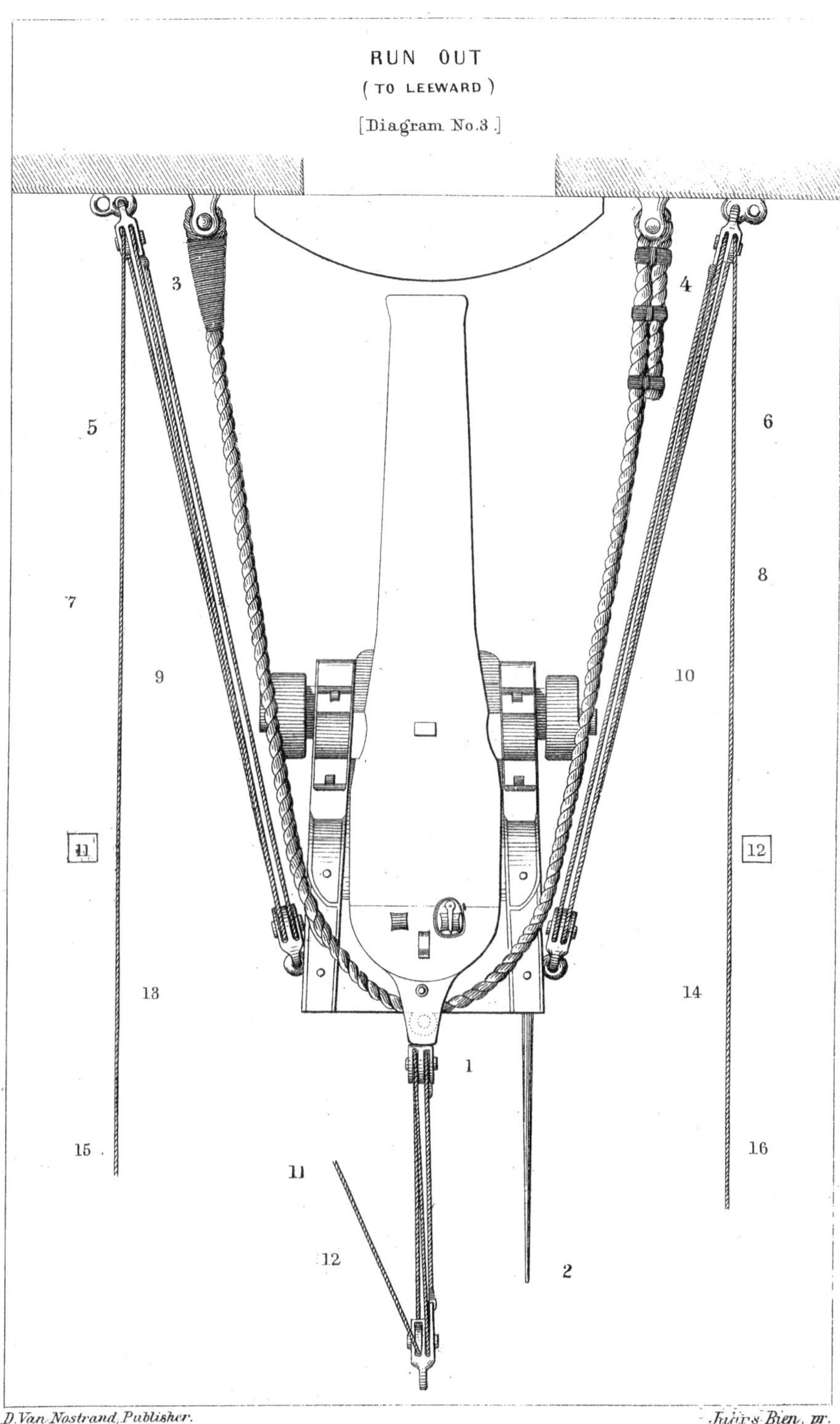

D. Van Nostrand, Publisher.

Julius Bien, pr.

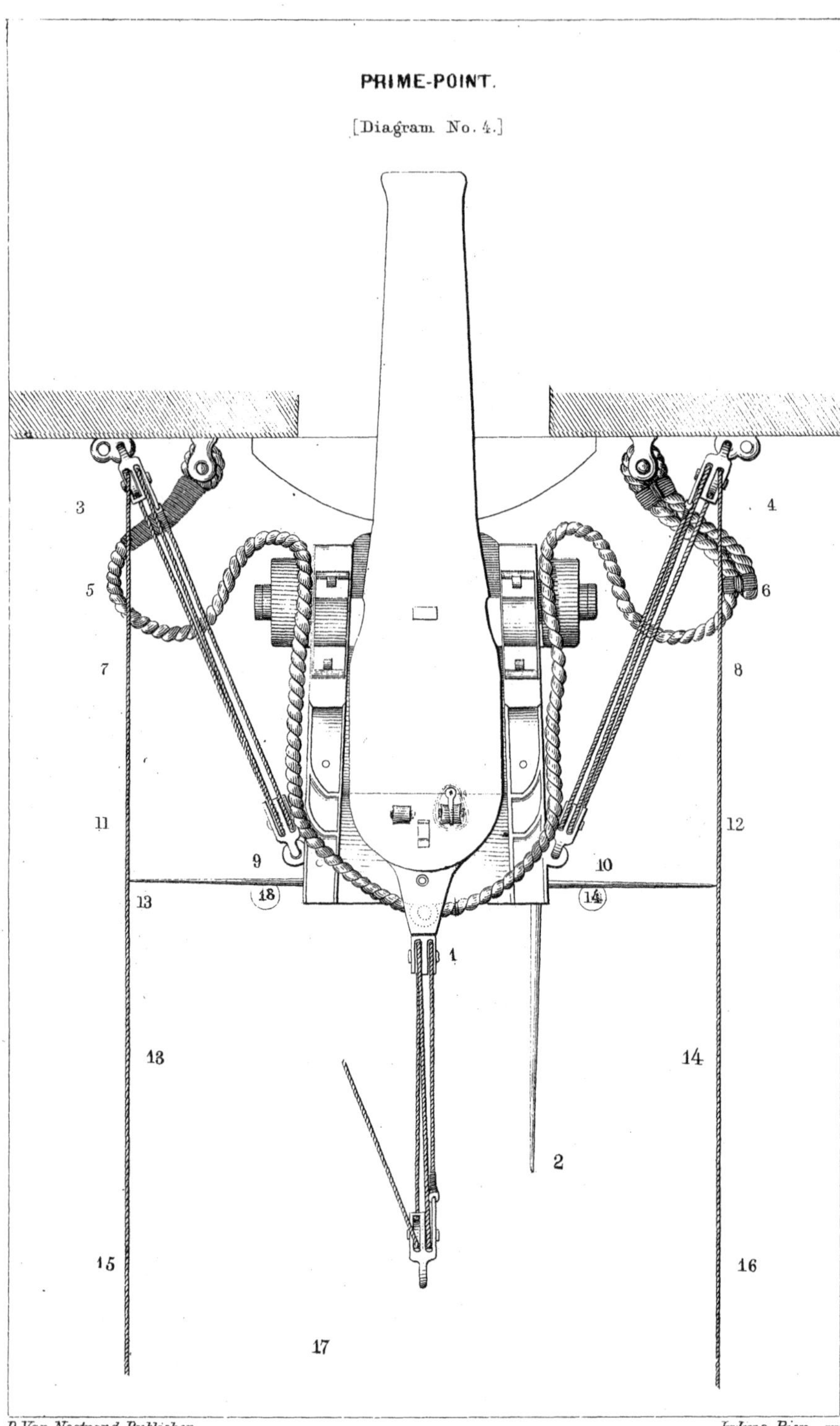

D. Van Nostrand, Publisher. Julius Bien, pr.

Front-trucks; 7, 9, 11, 13, 15, and 8, 10, 12, 14, 16 set taut the Side-tackles.

When the gun is out the 2d Captain swivels the Roller Handspike for training, or removes it altogether if the Handspike alone be preferred for this operation.

Nos. 5, 6 choke and retain hold of luffs of Side-tackles, while 3, 4 place Truck-quoins in rear of trucks, if the movement of the ship requires it. Crew close up; rear man coils end of fall, clear for running.

If the training is to be sharp, the proper Side-tackle will be hooked to the further eye-bolt inside; 12 unhooks the Train-tackle, and hooks it also to the proper eye-bolt in deck.

VII. "PRIME!"

(Diagram No. 4.)

223. Gun Captain again makes sure that the Vent is clear, and, in so doing, lets down his wire quickly into the charge.

He inserts a Primer, and turns down the Hammer upon it.

Meanwhile 9, 10 take up handspikes, and place themselves at rear of bracket conveniently to heave forward or aft.

In sharp training Nos. 13, 14 assist them.

Nos. 3, 5, 7, 11, 13, 15, and 4, 6, 8, 12, 14, 16 man Side-tackles.

VIII. "POINT!"

(Diagram No. 4.)

224. Gun Captain adjusts or verifies Sliding-Bar of Rear Sight to proper distance given by the Officer of Division, and falls back so as to be clear of the recoil, lanyard in hand, face to the Port, standing *directly in the rear of the gun*, with his eye ranging over the sights, and keeping in view the water-line of the opposing ship, trains the gun by voice or sign.

No. 6 throws back the Hammer, and takes hold of lever of Elevating Screw. (If Roller Handspike is not used in training, 2d Captain performs this.)

At word "Right" or "Left," 3, 5, 7, 11, 13, 15, or 4, 6, 8, 12, 14, 16 haul on the proper Side-tackle, and 9, 10 heave correspondingly on handspikes. Nos. 3 and 4 keep their eyes on handspikemen opposite to them, to give the time to the other Nos. for hauling on the fall.

No. 6 (or 2d Captain) Elevates or Depresses as directed.

Action.

2d Captain unships the Roller Handspike if it has been used in training. Nos. 9, 10 withdraw handspikes, and step back clear of recoil.

Nos. 3, 4 overhaul Side-tackles to mark, unless the motion does not admit of it.

No. 12 overhauls or holds up Train-tackle.
Nos. 7, 8 remove quoins from Trucks.
Men to their stations.

IX. "READY—FIRE!"

(Diagram No. 5.)

225. The Gun Captain, standing as already placed, waits patiently, but sharply, for the coincidence of the sights upon the object, which, if a ship, is always the water-line. When a correction of elevation or of direction is required, he repeats such of the previous orders as may be necessary; and these are to be re-executed accordingly.

If the gun is to leeward, the men stand ready to take hold of the Train-tackle and jerk the cannon into a taut breeching.

When sure of his aim the Gun Captain, who has held the lock-lanyard just taut, draws it promptly and firmly, bearing in mind that in no case is he to attempt moving from his post.

The 2d Captain stands ready with a primer, and, in the case of failure, throws back the hammer and inserts another. If necessary, serves the Vent. If a second failure occurs, it is a certain indication that the charge is not home.

Action.

Instantly with the explosion, 11, 12 jerk away the parts of the train-tackle, or hook it if it has been unhooked.

Nos. 3, 4 place quoins in front of trucks. 9, 10 lay down handspikes.

When the gun is not in to a taut breeching, the 2d Captain ships the Roller Handspike.

Nos. 7, 8, 9, 10, 11, 12, 13, 14, 15, 16, take hold quickly of Train-tackle, and run in to a taut breeching.

When in, 3, 4 move up the Truck-quoins, 12 chokes luff of Train-tackle.

Gun Captain puts back the hammer and coils up lanyard.

No. 6 takes up Sponge, and the exercise proceeds as already directed.

If necessary, No. 2 levels the gun for loading, and lays it fair for running out.

226. If the exercise is to be continued, it is resumed at the fourth command:

"SERVE VENT AND SPONGE!"

"CEASE FIRING!"

227. Whenever this order is given, either by the roll of the drum, or by passing the word, if the gun is primed, the Gun Captain immediately removes the primer, and with the crew stands at "Attention."

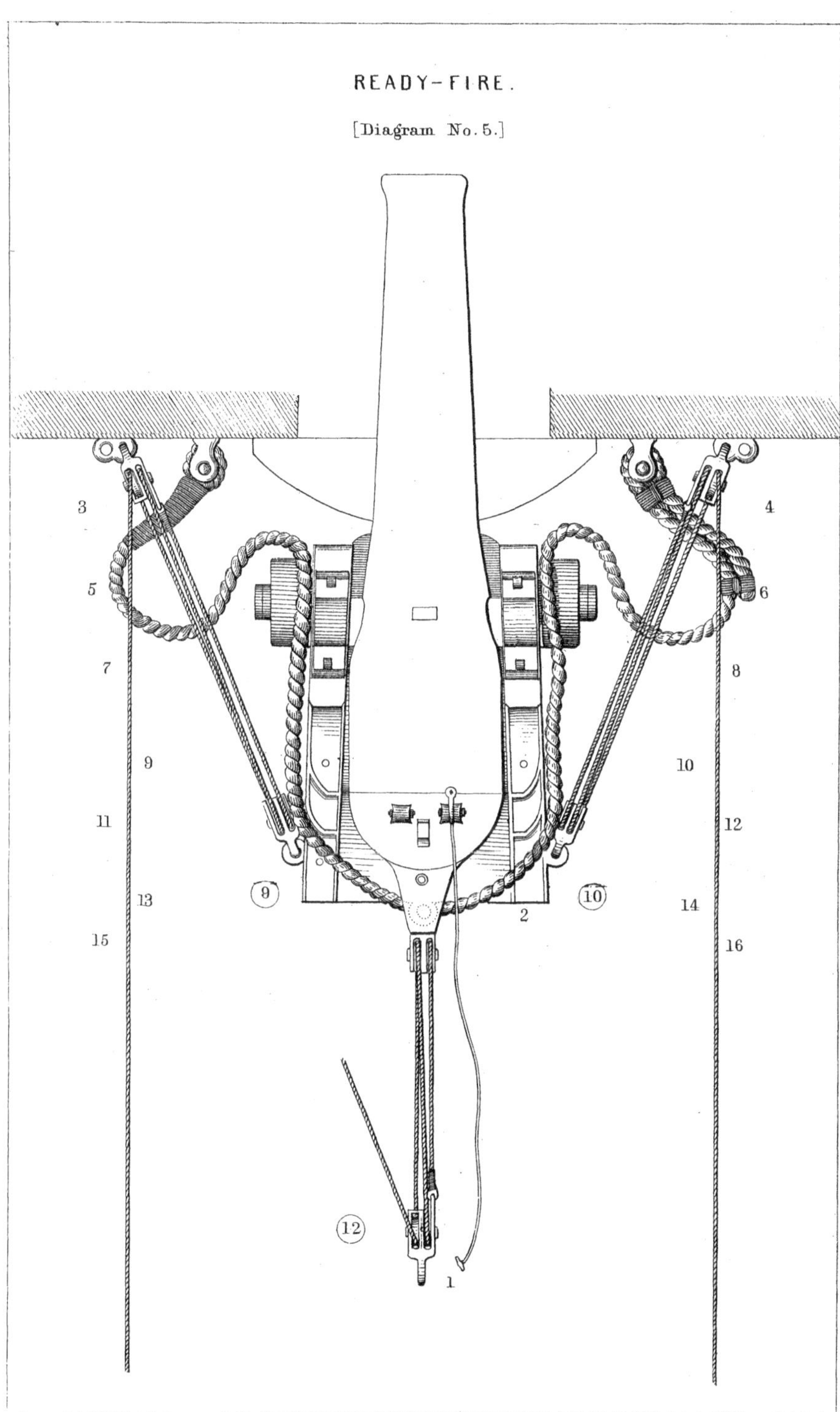

D. Van Nostrand, Publisher.
Julius Bien, pr.

228. NOTE.—The breechings of IX-in. guns are to be so fitted that the face of muzzle when in shall be 18 inches from inner face of side, for two reasons:

To prevent the gun from returning to the port, and to give room for the handling of such large shells.

Seventeen men are a proper number for working a IX-in. gun under any circumstances.

Rammer handles are to be marked for place of charge and of shell.

Side and train tackles are also to be marked to the proper overhaul, so as to avoid slack rope.

Breast-sweeps are useful at lower sill of port, for training more than a point.

X. "SECURE!"

229. The Powder-boy returns the spare powder and the passing-boxes to the magazine. The Shellmen return the shells and empty shell-boxes, if any remain on deck, to the shell-room.

The Gun Captain directs the gun to be laid square in the middle of the port.

When the guns are to be secured without being housed the Loader and Sponger place the chocking-quoins square up against the rear part of the front trucks and put in the tompion. The Handspikemen, if there is a quoin, free the quoin and lower the breech, the 2d Captain handling the quoin. When the gun is fitted with an elevating screw this operation is performed by the 2d Captain alone, who handles the screw.

The Gun Captain, assisted by the 2d Captain, hauls the breeching through the jaws of the cascabel to the left side of the gun, forming with the bight a turn over the breech and cylinder, taking care to keep the breeching well clear of the elevating screw to prevent chafe, and securing the parts on each side with selvagees and heavers; or, if this should interfere with the breech-sight, by crossing the breeching at the side and securing it with selvagee straps and toggles. In this case the breeching should be secured after alternate exercises right and left.

The Loader and Sponger haul up and secure the lower half-ports, put in tompion, and secure muzzle-bag. The Gun Captain puts in the vent-plug, lays the hammer of the lock in its place, and the lock-string in a coil around it. The 2d Captain takes the lock-cover from the Train-tackleman and secures it over the lock, and in like manner covers the breech and reinforce sights.

The men at the side-tackles unhook the outer blocks from the training-bolts and hand them to the Loader and Sponger, who hook them to the securing-bolts at the sides of the port. The men on both sides haul them taut and stop the parts of the tackles together, with knittles provided by the Quarter Gunner, and then expend the remainder of the falls by passing them around the breech of the gun, through the jaws of the cascabel, and stopping the bights alternately to the eye-bolts on each side of the port until expended: or, at four-truck carriages, take two half hitches over the tail of the brackets, and expend the ends of the falls.

The Train-tacklemen hook the train-tackle to the side-tackle bolts on each side of the port, the double block on the left side, haul the tackle taut, expend the end round the breech, and stop the parts in with the side-tackles.[1]

The Gun Captain then directs the Handspikemen, or if the screw is used, the 2d Captain, to raise the breech so as to level the gun and bring all parts of the tackles and breeching taut.

The Loader and Sponger put in and secure the upper half-ports, if directed, and the Loader swabs the deck to collect any loose powder which may have been scattered on it.

The several persons who provided the arms and implements used in the exercise, return them to their proper places, or to the persons appointed to take charge of them, care being taken that the small arms are unloaded and reported so before they are sent below, unless otherwise directed by the Captain.

HOUSING LOWER-DECK GUNS.

230. If the lower-deck guns are to be housed, the Gun Captain directs the gun to be laid square in the middle of the port and run in to a taut breeching, and if loaded, the load to be drawn. The Loader and Sponger place the housing-chocks before the front trucks.

The gun is then run close up against the housing-chocks, and the chocking-quoins are placed square up behind the rear trucks.

The Handspikemen raise the breech to free the quoin; the 2d Captain withdraws it and the bed; the Handspikemen lower the breech upon the axletree, so that in case the gun should break adrift, the muzzle will take the upper port-sill; and the Port-tacklemen lower the port-lid.

The 2d Loader and 1st Shellman bring the port-bar to the Loader and Sponger, who put it in place across the port, hook the port-hooks in the ring-bolts in the port-lids, and drive in the keys until the port is perfectly closed.

The men on both sides shift the side-tackles from the training-bolts to the securing-bolts, haul them taut, and expend the ends between the blocks. The Loader and Sponger pass the frapping lashing round both parts of the breeching, in front of the brackets, and with the assistance of the men nearest them bowse it well taut; and secure the muzzle by placing the grommet over it and the housing hook-bolt, and by frapping the two parts

[1] With the nib-blocks the train-tackle cannot be used to assist in securing the gun, unless a special eye-bolt is placed for this purpose.

together with the lashing. When the housing-bolt is an eye-bolt, a toggle will be necessary to keep the grommet in its place.

In moderate weather the train-tackle is unhooked from the deck, and made up and stopped along the side-tackle, on the forward side of the gun. In bad weather it is kept hooked, bowsed taut, and the end expended through the ring-bolt and round the arms of the rear axle.

The manner of housing guns, mounted on truck-carriages, on other decks, in bad weather, does not vary materially from that just described, excepting that the upper half-ports and the port-bucklers are put in and secured.

When there are no housing-chocks the ordinary chocking-quoins may be used as such. It will be an additional security to take off the rear trucks, and to tighten the muzzle-lashing by raising the breech.

GENERAL REMARKS ON THE MANUAL EXERCISE.

231. The exercise of the great guns has a double object: 1st, To teach the crew all the details necessary to Load, Point, and Fire the gun; 2d, To develop their activity, intelligence, and muscular force.

The principal object, the base of all this instruction, is loading and pointing; too much care and attention cannot be devoted to obtain exactitude in all the movements. There is a tendency to devote too much time to such exercises as shifting carriages from side to side. There is always sufficient time for these manœuvres. The most important are the management of the rammer and sponge in loading and the handspikes in pointing.

232. At the time of reception on board, the crew may be considered as made up of three classes: 1st, The Captains, Loaders, and Spongers of guns, who may be considered as competently instructed in the manual; 2d, another part, who have had some instruction and are competent to fill the secondary duties; 3d, The remainder, who are entirely ignorant.

The directions in the manual are more particularly devoted to the instruction of a crew completely formed, omitting all the minor details of position and exactness in the performance of the motions under the different commands, which are to be supplied by the Instructor. These details would break the connection of the several commands, and increase the bulk of the work. The precepts of the manual are not for self-instruction of the ignorant, but to produce a uniform system of commands in the Instructors. The important point, is to instruct the last two classes by gun's crews, and then by divisions. This is accomplished by drilling the guns' crews separately, until each man has acquired some facility in his particular duties, and then selecting the most deficient for special instruction, combining them as a gun's crew, in order not to uselessly fatigue those who are already expert or readily acquire the drill. Whenever a new order is to be executed, it should be first thoroughly and minutely explained; and as soon as all have heard and appear to understand, execute it. If not correctly performed, repeat the explanation.

233. When the individuals of each gun's crew have become well acquainted with, and expert in the performance of their several special duties, they are to be successively transferred, temporarily, to the performance of the duties of some other station, until each man shall have become acquainted with the special duties of every station at the gun.

In exercising each man of a gun's crew in the duties of all the other men of that crew besides his own, it is to be done thus:

The system supposes that, beginning with the 2d Captain to take the place of the 1st Captain, the men are to be called to perform the duties of the latter in a regular succession agreeably to the way they are placed at the gun; *i. e.*, after the 2d Captain, the 2d Train-tackleman is to do the duties of Gun Captain; and so on all round the gun. Each man is to fleet his position one remove or place, in a direction "with the sun," so that instead of the interchange of duties being confined to two individuals only, it is to extend to the whole gun's crew. Thus, for instance, when the 2d Captain is called upon to do the duties of 1st Captain, the latter, by moving one place "with the sun," becomes the 1st Train-tackleman, the 1st Train-tackleman the 1st Port-tackleman, and so on all around the gun throughout the whole crew, the person at the muzzle of the gun on its left side crossing over and taking the place of the one at the muzzle on the right side. Next in order, the 2d Train-tackle. is required to take the place of the 1st Captain, then the 2d Captain becomes 1st Train-tackle., the 1st Captain the 1st Port-tackleman, the 2d Port-tackleman the 2d Captain, and so on throughout.

If it should be desired to take, at first, a man from the middle of the crew of the gun, or even still further towards the muzzle, to do the duties of 1st Captain, then it must be done under the supposition that all the men preceding him in the order above mentioned have already been exercised in those duties, and the men are then to take their stands accordingly.

After the guns' crews have been well trained by giving the words of command, it will be expedient to exercise them without giving the several detailed commands, by directing them to "load and fire!" At this command the different individuals should, each in proper order of time, silently perform his prescribed duties of sponging, loading, running out, training, and pointing, the Captain of the gun regulating the elevation and depression, by raising or lowering his hand, and by holding it horizontally and steady when the gun is "well;" and in pointing, by moving his hand to "right" or "left" as the gun requires to be trained, and by bringing it down to his side when it is "well." Before firing, he is to throw his hand well up as a signal for the men to "drop tackles," and is to give the word "fire" when he pulls the lock-string.

When casualties occur at the guns, the Captain of the gun will order "close up," and then equalize the crew on each side. If the Powderman is disabled the highest number takes his place.

234. Whenever the crew of a gun becomes so greatly reduced in action that men enough are not left to work the piece, it may be fired while partially run in. In such case, however, the breeching should be frapped forward of the carriage, the ends crossed under the muzzle or otherwise arranged so as to keep the muzzle outside of the port; the side-tackles left loose; the chocking-quoins placed square up against the outer part of the front trucks; the train-tackle hauled taut, the end of the fall passed through the train-bolt and well secured, and wet swabs placed up against the forward part of the rear trucks and sprinkled with sand or ashes. After three or four rounds the train-tackle should be re-secured; the chocking-quoins will require re-placing after each fire. The greatest possible care should be taken to guard against accident from fire, and minimum charges of powder used.

Experiment proves that a gun may be fired in this manner without injury to the ship's side or the breeching, and by three or four men.

It must be apparent to every officer that both the rapidity and the accuracy of fire to be obtained from guns in vessels at sea, must depend, in a great degree, upon the care which may be taken to explain to the men the best mode of performing their respective parts of the exercise, and the particular object for which each part is intended, and especially on such frequency of exercise and target-firing as will make the men perfectly familiar with their prescribed duties. The importance of this instruction, which may decide whether an action shall result in victory or defeat, will, it is hoped, insure due attention to it from all officers, and especially from the officers of divisions at quarters.

THE GUNS ON ONE SIDE BEING MANNED,

TO CHANGE SIDES,

OR BOTH SIDES BEING MANNED,

TO MAN ONE SIDE ONLY;

COMMAND.

"MAN THE STARBOARD (OR PORT) GUNS!"

235. Whenever this or any other order is given which requires all the men suddenly to leave the gun which they are working, they are not to do so until it is properly loaded, and well secured by hauling taut the side and train tackles, and hitching their falls around the straps of the inner blocks; nor on lower decks of ships-of-the-line till the ports are down and secured by their lanyards. A strict compliance with this injunction is indispensable to guard against excessive or imperfect loading and other accidents.

When these precautions have been duly taken, the men will shift over in obedience to the command.

EXERCISE OF BROADSIDE-GUNS,

ON BOTH SIDES AT ONCE, BY MANNING ALTERNATE GUNS WITH FULL CREWS.

236. In the event of being required to fight both sides, it is generally conceded that a more effective fire is maintained by handling alternate guns with full crews.

In this case the preparatory order will be given:

"SILENCE! MAN BOTH SIDES, EVERY OTHER GUN WITH FULL CREWS."

Upon which the guns' crews of the guns of the starboard watch will man the odd-numbered guns on the starboard side, and the guns' crews of the port watch will man the even-numbered guns on the port side, and the exercise will be the same as prescribed for "broadside guns on one side only."

MANNING ALL THE GUNS.

GENERAL REMARKS.

237. Arrangements have been made to enable each gun's crew to work together and fire alternately a pair of guns on the same side of the deck. Experience, however, shows that this can only be continued with effect for three or four rounds, and is in general results inferior to those obtained by manning alternate guns with full crews.

QUICK FIRING.

238. The service of the guns consists, essentially, of two distinct parts, pointing and loading. The first of these, pointing, cannot be performed too carefully and methodically, and requires extreme coolness and attention on the part of the Captain of the gun; loading, on the contrary, cannot be executed with too much rapidity, provided neither the safety of the gun nor of its crew be compromised.

It is clear that if two hostile vessels meet equally matched in all the ordinary points of equipment and preparation, and manned by crews equally skilled in gunnery, the advantage will be in favor of the ship that loads quickest; and should it happen that nicety of aim becomes a matter of secondary importance, in consequence of the closeness of the action, then, evidently, rapidity of fire will determine the affair.

These considerations appear decisive, and every care should be taken in the instruction of guns' crews, that pointing be executed with deliberation, care, and method, and loading with all possible dispatch. In order, therefore, to insure the great advantage of rapid firing, officers are enjoined frequently to exercise the crews in setting the cartridge, shot, and wad home together, in one motion, of such guns as may be loaded in this manner, without inconvenience. This is the case with all the guns, chambered as well as unchambered, excepting the 8-inch shell-gun of 63 cwt. of patterns earlier than 1851; it is not recommended, however, to practise simultaneous loading with guns of higher calibre, such as IX-inch and upwards, as nothing will be gained by it in point of time.

To prevent the shot from rolling on the tie of the cartridge and jamming it, the end of the cartridge-bag, outside of the tie, should be shortened as much as security will permit, unless it has been specially prepared for this use, by stitching back the end in the form of a cockade.

With the view of affording the Loader a certain and independent means of knowing when the whole load is really home, the handle of the rammer should have a mark upon it, easily distinguishable either by day or night, and this should be suited to the "ordinary firing" charge of powder, due allowance being made for the others.

COMMAND.

"LOAD IN ONE MOTION!"

239. The Loader receives the cartridge and puts it in the gun, as already described; he also receives the shell or shot and wad and introduces them accordingly.

As soon as the whole charge has been introduced, the Sponger and Loader together thrust it down smartly with the rammer, as in ordinary loading. When home, the men run the gun out as quickly as possible; the Captain of the gun clears the vent, primes in running out, points and fires in the usual manner, but as rapidly as is consistent with a good aim, taking care that the muzzle is clear of the port-sill, and on lower decks that the port is triced up clear of the explosion.

SHIFTING BREECHINGS IN ACTION.

COMMAND.

"SPONGE, LOAD, AND SHIFT BREECHING!"

240. Supposing the gun's crew to be reduced to six men and the Powder-boy, that being the least number required to perform the evolution, and the gun to be discharged and run in. The Captain hauls taut the train-tackle and chokes the luff, and the Loader and Sponger place the chocking-quoins forward of the front trucks, and proceed to sponge and load the gun in the usual manner. The 2d Sponger and 2d Loader haul taut side-tackles and choke luffs, or, if rolling deep, hitch the falls round the straps of the blocks, and then unshackle the old breeching and shackle the new, which is to be brought to the gun by the 2d Captain.

The Captain removes the old breeching from, and places and secures the bight of the new one in the jaws of the cascabel, after the gun is sponged. The 2d Captain passes the old breeching amidships, and the men resume their usual duties at the gun.

When there are more than six men at the gun, the 2d Sponger and 2d Loader, after securing the side-tackle falls, will assist to load the gun, and the additional men will assist in unshackling the old and shackling the new breeching, but one of these will do all the duties just assigned to the 1st Captain, so as not to interfere with his ordinary duties in loading.

SHIFTING TRUCKS.

241. The operation of shifting a truck can only be required when the gun is "run in" after firing. At the order to shift any one of the trucks that may be designated:

With the MARSILLY CARRIAGE.—Heave up with the roller handspike under the end of the bracket on the side on which the truck is to be removed; handspikemen pass inside the breeching and place their handspikes under the axletree as near the truck as possible, and, assisted by 5 and 6, lift the gun while the shellman removes the old truck and side-tackleman puts on new one.

With the ORDINARY CARRIAGE.—To shift a rear truck, handspikemen lift under the rear axletree. To shift a front truck the rear truck on the opposite side should first be taken off, then handspikemen lift under the fore axletree.

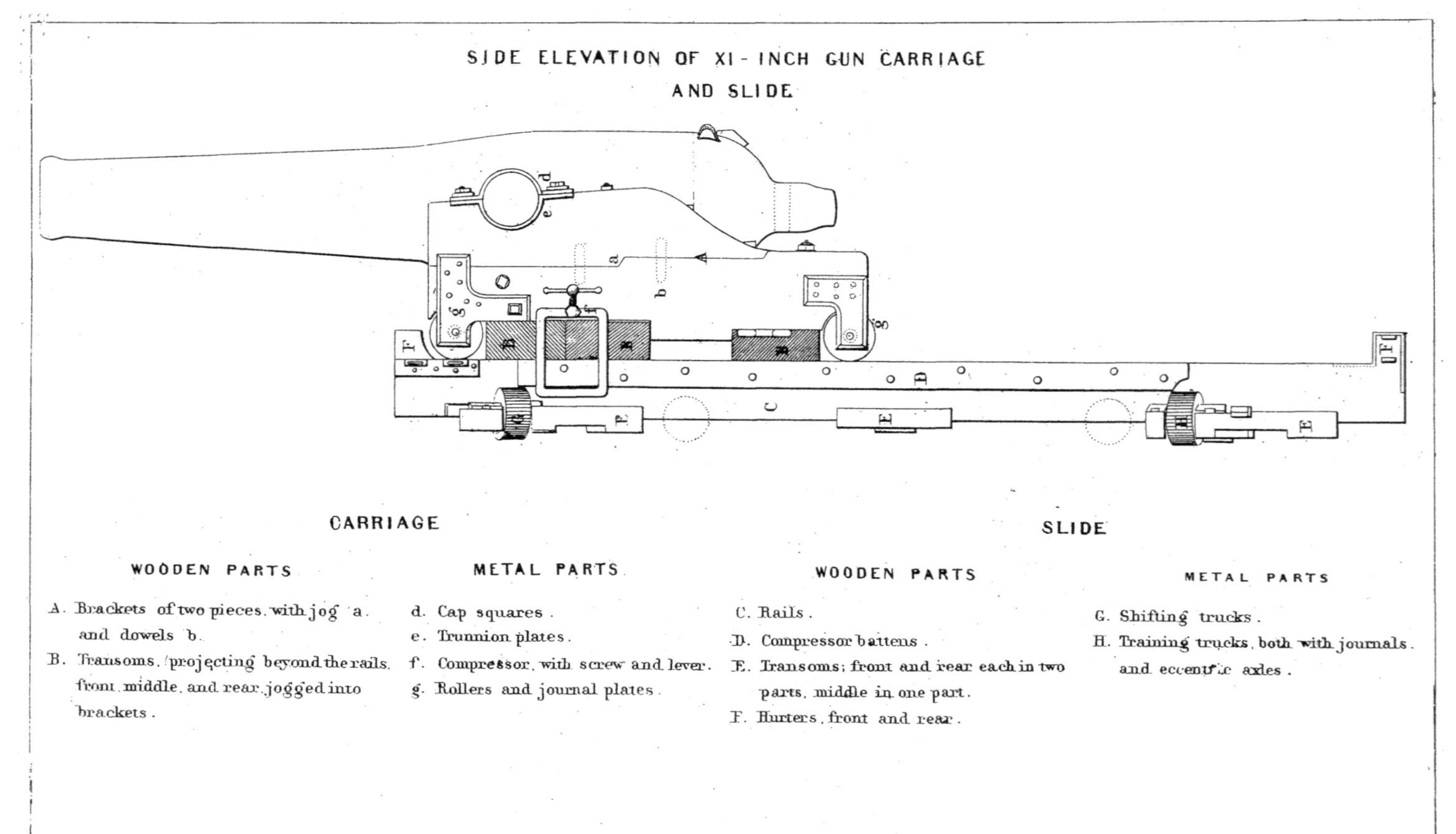
SIDE ELEVATION OF XI-INCH GUN CARRIAGE
AND SLIDE
a
b
d
e
f
g
g
A
B
B
B
C
D
E
E
E
F
F
G
H
CARRIAGE
WOODEN PARTS
A. Brackets of two pieces, with jog a. and dowels b.
B. Transoms, projecting beyond the rails, front, middle, and rear, jogged into brackets.
METAL PARTS
d. Cap squares.
e. Trunnion plates.
f. Compressor, with screw and lever.
g. Rollers and journal plates.
SLIDE
WOODEN PARTS
C. Rails.
D. Compressor battens.
E. Transoms; front and rear each in two parts, middle in one part.
F. Hurters, front and rear.
METAL PARTS
G. Shifting trucks.
H. Training trucks, both with journals and eccentric axles.
D. Van Nostrand, Publisher.
Julius Bien. pr.

SECTIONAL VIEW OF XI INCH GUN CARRIAGE AND SLIDE

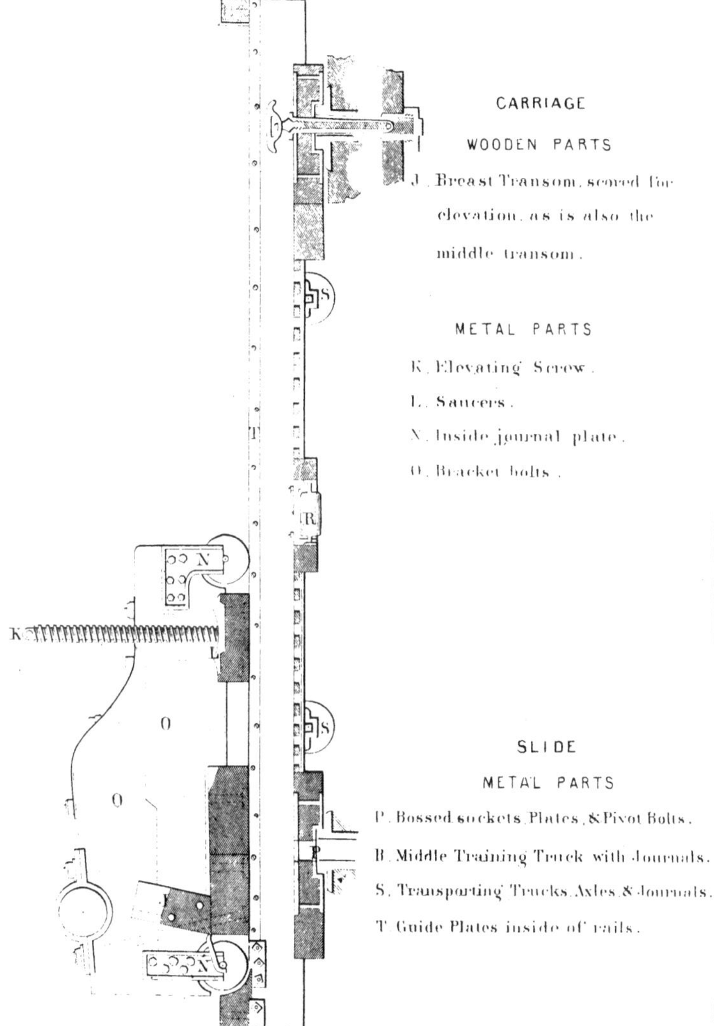

D. Van Nostrand, Publisher.

Julius Bien. pr.

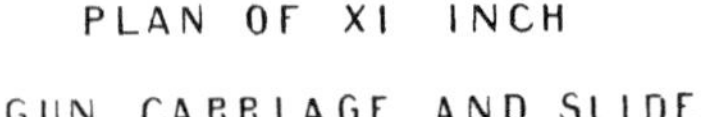

WOODEN PARTS

X. Battens and Slats.

Y. Preventer Breechings.

METAL PARTS

Z. Upper Pivot-plate.

1. Middle Roller-plate.

2. Eyes for Tackles.

3. Hurter Straps.

4. Rail Plates.

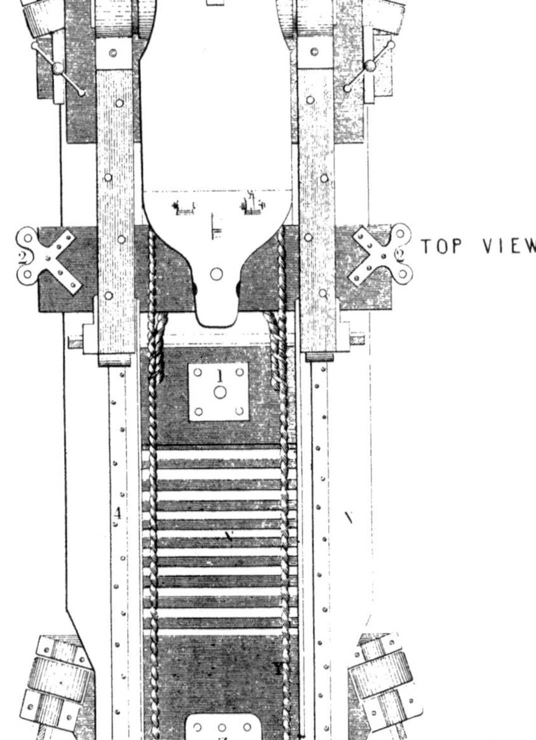

D. Van Nostrand, Publisher. *Julius Bien, pr.*

PLAN OF SLIDE FOR XI-INCH GUN CARRIAGE

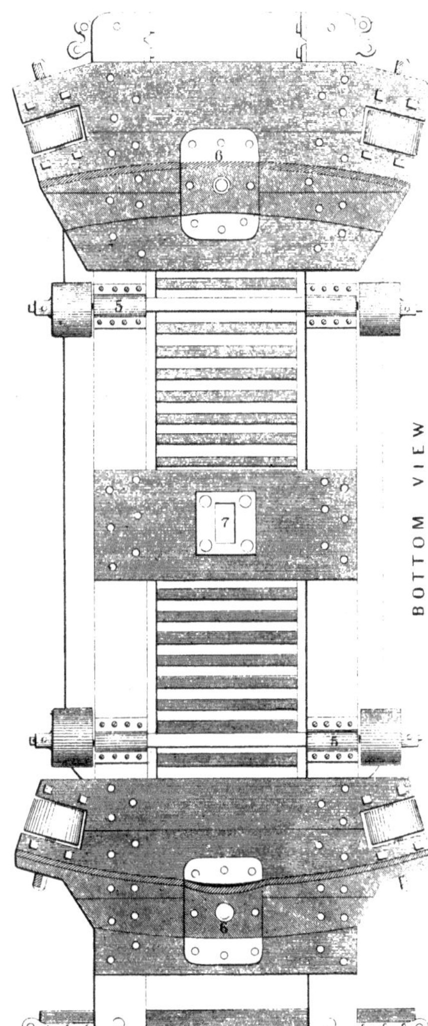

METAL PARTS

5. Transporting journals

6. Pivot plates & guide-flanges

7. Middle roller

Note All metal parts are composition except the axles, levers, elevating screw & bracket-bolts.

D. Van Nostrand, Publisher. *Julius Bien, pr.*

EXERCISE OF PIVOT-GUNS.

XI-INCH SHELL-GUN

(As an example.)

242. Arranged to traverse on circles fitted with Bossed Sockets for pivoting, and with clevis-bolts and sockets for housing.

Equipments and Implements.

Articles for each Gun.	Where they are to be put when the Gun is Secured.
Carriage and slide complete, with elevating screw and pivot-bolts.........	In place.
Two front roller levers.................	Becketed to brackets.
Two rear do.	
Two levers for training and shifting trucks.	
Two in-tackles.......................	Hooked in place.
Two out-tackles.......................	Do. do.
Two shifting-tackles..................	Made up on slide.
Two training-tackles..................	Do. do.
Breeching..........................	In place.
Preventer..........................	Do.
Lashings for securing gun.............	Do.
Tompion, with wad and lanyard........	Do.
Sponge and cap.......................	Becketed to beams between decks, or inside the brackets.
Rammer.............................	
A pot of oil or prepared grease for rifle cannon.............................	Breast of carriage.
Lock, with string....................	In place.
Vent-plug...........................	
Lock-cover and strap.................	In place on gun.
Breech-sight and cover...............	Do. do.
Reinforce-sight and cover.............	Do. do.
Trunnion-sight.......................	In box between decks.
Priming-wires........................	Inside brackets.
Boring-bits..........................	
Water-buckets and large swab..........	Hold, until wanted.
Hand-swabs..........................	Breast of carriage.
Selvagee-wads........................	Do. do.
Battle-axes, as allowed (Art. 101).......	On breast-transom.
Two transporting axles and trucks......	In storeroom, at hand.
One shell in box.....................	On slide.
Shell-bearer.........................	Do.
Rail transom-chocks[1].................	Under rails.

[1] These should always be kept under the centre transom when the carriage is not in use; also in firing at high angles of elevation to relieve the rails of the shock.

STATIONS AND GUN-NUMBERS.

243. The following are to be the gun-numbers and stations for a gun's crew of twenty-five, including the Powderman, the XI-inch shell-gun being taken as an example:

Left Side.	Gun-Nos.		Right Side.
First Loader..................	3	4	First Sponger.
Second Loader.................	5	6	Second Sponger.
First Shellman.................	7	8	Second Shellman.
First Front-Leverman...........	9	10	Second Front-Leverman.
First Compressman.............	13	14	Second Compressman.
First Rear-Leverman...........	11	12	Second Rear-Leverman.
Tacklemen....................	17	18	Tacklemen.
	19	20	
	21	22	
	23	24	
First Train-Leverman...........	15	16	Second Train-Leverman.
First Captain..................	1	2	Second Captain.
Powderman....................	25		

To reduce from 24 men and Powderman to 20, omit four highest numbers.

To reduce from 20 men and Powderman to 16 men and Powderman, omit four next highest numbers.

To reduce from 16 men and Powderman to 12 men and Powder-boy, omit four highest numbers; 7, 9, and 10 become Pikemen, 11 and 12 Compressmen and Train-Levermen, in addition to other duties.

To reduce from 12 men and boy to 10 men and boy, omit two highest numbers; 5 becomes Pikeman, 7 becomes Fireman, 9 and 10 Compressor and Train-Levermen, in addition to other duties.

EXERCISE FOR HEAVY GUNS

MOUNTED ON PIVOT-CARRIAGES.

XI-INCH SHELL-GUN. (*As an example.*)

244. The gun is supposed to be secured amidships, fore and aft, over the housing pivot, and not loaded.

The exercise will proceed in conformity to the following words of command, viz:

I. "SILENCE! CAST LOOSE AND PROVIDE!"
II. "RUN IN!"
III. "SHIFT PIVOT!" (TO THE RIGHT OR LEFT!)
IV. "SERVE VENT AND SPONGE!"
V. "LOAD!"
VI. "RUN OUT!"
VII. "PRIME!"
VIII. "POINT!"
IX. "READY—FIRE!"
X. "SHIFT TO HOUSING-PIVOT, AND SECURE!"

N. B.—It is always to be understood that when any of their respective duties under one command are executed, the men will at once proceed to prepare for those which follow next in order. The exercise must be considered as a whole, though the details are necessarily divided under the several words of command.

EXERCISE OF PIVOT XI-IN. CANNON.

GUN SECURED FOR SEA AMIDSHIPS.

I. "SILENCE! CAST LOOSE AND PROVIDE!"

245. No. 1, Commands; sees his gun cleared and cast loose; circles cleared and swept; tackles hooked; levers shipped; lock and sights in place; elevating apparatus, pivot-bolts, and compressors in working order; takes off lock-cover and hands it to 23, who lays it clear of circle: provides himself with waist-belt and primers, priming-wire, boring-bit, and thumb-stall; and sees that all the gear and implements are ready for use, and the men at their respective stations.

No. 2, Takes off sight-covers and hands them to 22, who lays them clear of circle; removes rail-chocks and assists in casting loose. He provides waist-belt and primers, and sees that the men on his side of the gun execute promptly their several duties.

CAST LOOSE.

(Diagram No. 1.)

Clear away the Bulwarks	15.16.17.18.23.24.	
Lashings of Gun—Adrift	3.4.11.12.	
In-Tackles—Cast loose	15.16.	
Out-Tackles—Cast loose	13.14.	
Training-Tackles—Cast loose	19.20.21.22.23.24.	
IMPLEMENTS	QR. GUNNER.	
Powder	25.	
Shells, Shell-Ladle, &c	7.8.	
Sponge, Rammer — Take down	5.6.	
Front Carriage-Levers, Ship[1]	9.10.	
Rear Carriage-Levers—Ship		11.12.
Slide-Levers—Ship forward		15.16.
Sight-Covers—Take off. 2d Capt. and hands to 22.		
Buckets of Water[2]—Fill; Wet Swabs—Bring.		5.6.
Outer Tackles hook as Shifting-Tackles — to Deck		21.22.
Outer Tackles hook as Shifting-Tackles — to Slide		23.24.
Inner Tackle[3] hook — to Deck		17.18.
Inner Tackle[3] hook — to Slide		19.20.
Attend Compressors		13.14.
Man In-Tackle	11.15.17.19.21.23. 12.16.18.20.22.24.	
Man Carriage-Levers	Front. 9.10. Rear. 11.12.	

[1] When the trucks are to be brought into play, the levers should be shipped on their axle-squares so as to heave upwards, past the centre, and rest against the wood of the Carriage or Slide; otherwise they must be kept in place by hand or by a pin, neither of which entirely secures the Levers from flying back and doing mischief. If hove down, they are apt to interfere with the Tackles.

In order to ship the Levers expeditiously on the proper square, both are to be marked with a cold chisel.

The Fore Carriage-Levers require the efforts of two men at each, as the weight of the gun has most bearing there; each of the other levers is readily worked by one man.

[2] Principally to moisten the Sponge, which ought never to be omitted, as there is nothing so effectual in extinguishing any fragments that might remain burning in the Bore, and cause accidental explosion in loading, particularly in blank firing. It is a mistake to suppose that this practice increases the foulness of the Bore; on the contrary, it prevents it from hardening and accumulating, as long experience has shown. Sometimes it is convenient for the Spongers to dip the Sponge alongside, and they soon acquire the habit. Superfluous moisture is easily gotten rid of by twirling the Sponge at the handle.

[3] Were it practicable to hook a tackle so that it would move the gun, even from amid-

STATIONS BEFORE CASTING LOOSE

(Diagram No. 1.)

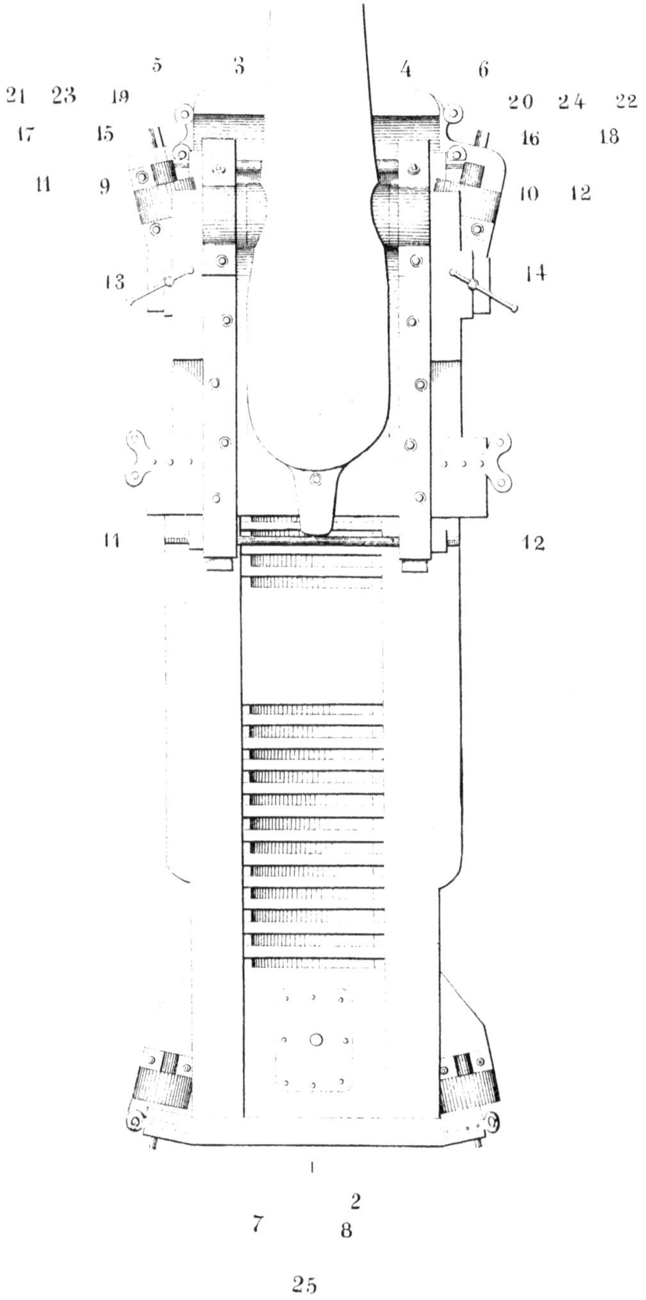

5 3 4 6

21 23 19 20 24 22

17 15 16 18

11 9 10 12

13 14

11 12

1

2

7 8

25

D. Van Nostrand, Publisher. Julius Bien, pr.

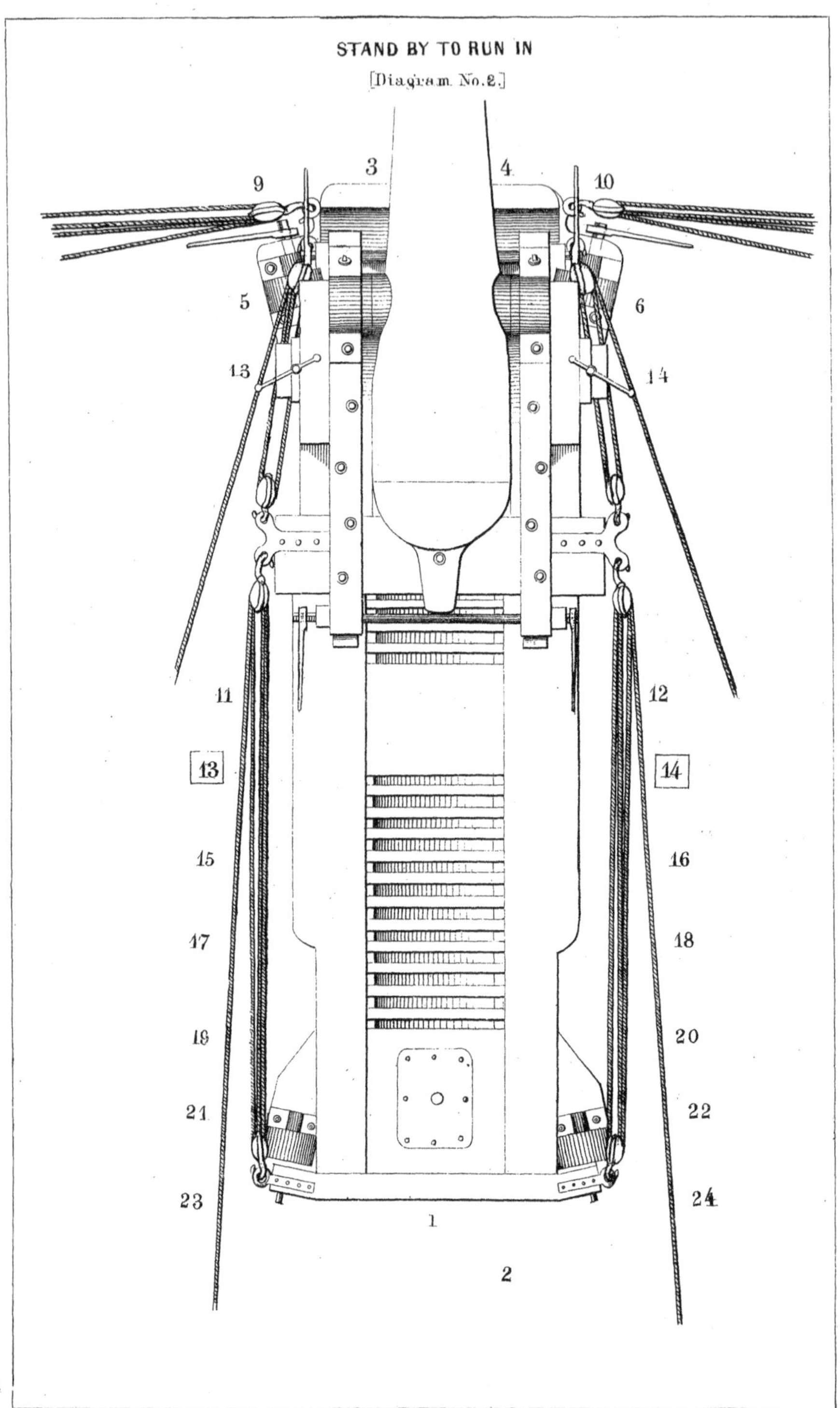

STAND BY TO RUN IN

[Diagram No. 2.]

D. Van Nostrand Publisher

Julius Bien, pr.

246. STAND BY TO RUN IN.

(Diagram No. 2.)

Ease Compressors[4] and go to In-Tackles...........	13.14.
Up Carriage-Levers[5].........................	Front. 3.9. and 4.10. Rear. 11.12.
Tend Out-Tackles...........................	5.6.

II. "RUN IN!"[6]

Haul on In-Tackles...........................	11.13.15.17.19.21.23. 12.14.16.18.20.22.24.
Out-Tackle block—Unhook from Slide, to leave room for hooking Inner Shifting-Tackle.............	5.6.
Down Carriage-Levers.........................	Front. 3.9. and 4.10. Rear. 11.12.
Tauten Compressors..................................	13.14.

247. STAND BY TO PIVOT.

(Diagram No. 3.)

Draw Fore Pivot-Bolt....................................	3.4.
Up Shifting Slide-Levers..................................	15.16.
Man Outer Shifting-Tackle...............	3.11.5.9.13.15.17.19.21.23. or or or or 4.12.6.10.14.16.18.20.22.24.
Attend opposite Outer Shifting-Tackle...............	19.3. or 20.4.
Stand by to hook Inner Tackle, when the Outer Shifting-Tackle is a-block........	17 or 18.

ships to the port, without being shifted, or were it prudent to leave the gun free while shifting the tackle, there would be no need of a second tackle. But it is not possible, in pivoting, to exert direct action for more than the eighth of a circle by one position of a tackle, and it is absolutely dangerous at sea to leave the Slide unconfined for an instant. When, therefore, the Outer-Tackle is a-block, the second tackle must be hooked and set taut.

[4, 5, 6] These orders are to be executed in quick succession, so as to be nearly simultaneous; that is, the compression is first relieved by backing its lever, upon which the Front-Levermen instantly bring the carriage on its trucks, and the gun is run back by the In-Tackles, the Out-Tackles being eased gradually, so as to check any violent movement; for the trucks, being fitted with friction rollers, allow the heavy piece to move suddenly and rapidly.

III. "PIVOT TO RIGHT OR LEFT!"

(Diagram No. 3.)

Haul on—Outer Shifting-Tackle[7]........ { 3.11.5.9.13.15.17.19.21.23.* | or | 4.12.6.10.14.16.18.20.22.24. (3 or 4, 11 or 12, 5 or 6, 9 or 10, 13 or 14, 15 or 16, 17 or 18, 19 or 20, 21 or 22, 23 or 24)

Ease away opposite Shifting-Tackle............19.3 or 20.4.

Hook to Slide, Inner Tackle and Haul Taut......17. or 18.

Unhook Outer Shifting-Tackles................21.22.23.24.

In Fore Pivot-Bolt......................... 3. or 4.

Shift Inner Tackles as Train-Tackles { To rear of Slide..... 19.20.
To Deck........... 17.18. }

Down Shifting Slide-Levers, unship them and ship them on Rear Slide Training-Trucks[8]....... 15.16.

Hook Out-Tackle Block to Slide............... 5.6.

Take stations for next order—which, if the gun is loaded, will be "Run Out;" if not loaded, will be "Sponge."[9]

When the Gun is Run Out—

Shackle Breeching[10]..................... 3.13.—4.14.

Draw the Rear Pivot-Bolt............... 2.

---

* Other numbers may be called to assist, if needed.

[7] The pivoting of so heavy a Gun is the most complicated of all the operations with it, and demands special drill. When done to windward, the hearty effort of the whole Gun's crew is required, particularly if there be much crown to the deck and no deck circles; to leeward there is no difficulty, and the time at sea to pivot from side to side may vary from four to seven minutes. The advantage of the Pivot-Boss will now appear, as it secures the coincidence of the hole in Slide with that of the Socket, and permits the Bolt to be removed out or in easily. Hitherto the difficulty of doing so without a Boss has caused delay, and contributed more than any thing else to the objections entertained against such heavy Ordnance, which have been in nowise obviated by either the Pivot Shifting-Screws of our own Navy, or the Pivot-Flap of the English Navy.

[8] Some difference of opinion may arise in regard to the shipping of these levers before the gun is run out, and they are required for pointing. To ship them now amounts to having them on the whole time—to which the only objection is, that if on, before wanted in pointing they may be in the way of the men; and, on the other hand, if not on, more attention may be demanded from 15, 16.

The question will not be material when the men are well drilled.

[9] The gun being now pivoted to the Port, the Breechings should be shackled and the rear Pivot-Bolt drawn, in regular order. But neither of these can be done without running out the gun a few feet. For in order to pivot with the greatest ease, the carriage had been previously run back on the Slide to the rear Hurter, so as to bring the weight of the gun as near as possible to the Rear pivot, the very best position being with the Trunnions of the Gun just forward of the Rear pivot. The shackling of the

STAND BY TO PIVOT

STARBOARD

[Diagram No. 3.]

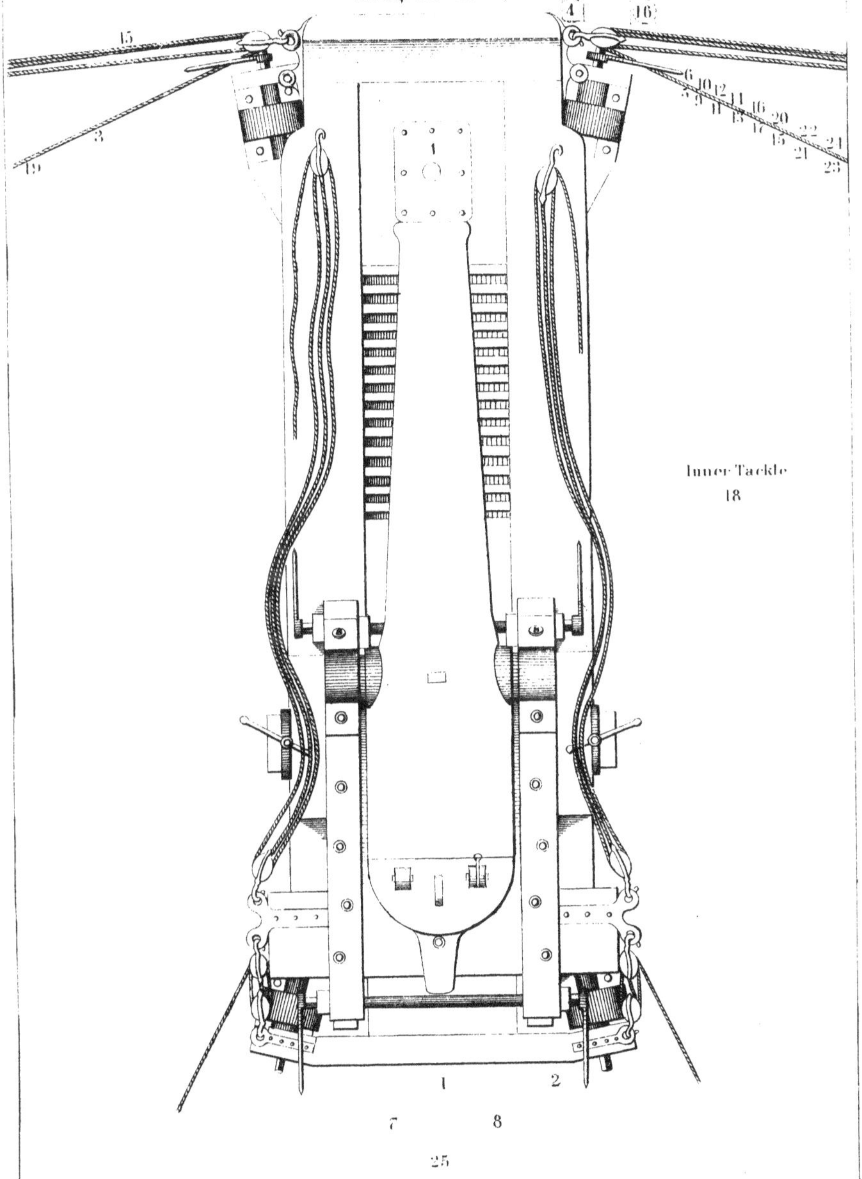

15

3

19

4

16

6 10 12 14 16 20 22 24

9 9 11 13 17 15 21 23

1

Inner Tackle
18

1 2

7 8

25

D. Van Nostrand, Publisher

Julius Bien, pr.

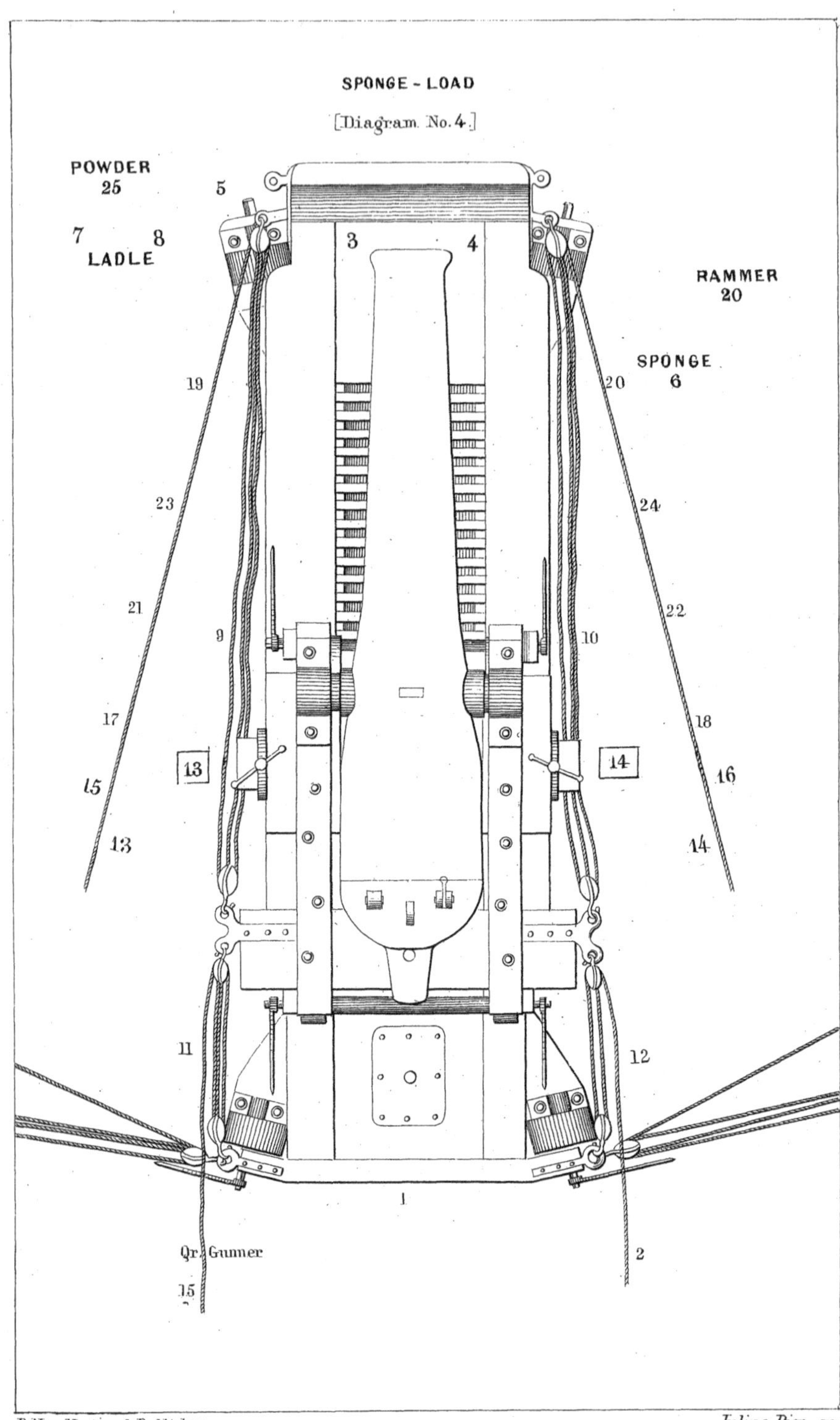

D. Van Nostrand, Publisher. Julius Bien, pr.

IV. "SERVE VENT AND SPONGE!"

(Diagram No. 4.)

248. No. 4 is to receive the moist sponge from No. 6, right hand over, left under, to send it home, and, assisted by No. 3, to press it to the bottom of the Bore, then to turn it around two or three times from left to right, in the direction that the worm may take,[11] withdraw it, strike the staff several smart taps under the muzzle, then return it to No. 6, who will receive it and lay it down;[12] the Gun Captain serves, then stops the Vent,[13] and as soon as the sponge has been withdrawn, serves the Vent with his priming-wire and again stops it.

This being done—

No. 20 hands the Rammer to No. 4 as soon as the latter has been relieved of the Sponge by No. 6. Should No. 4 observe that the Gun Captain has neglected to serve the Vent, he is to call his attention to it.

No. 3 stands ready with the Powder which he has taken from No. 5, to whom it was passed by No. 25.

Nos. 7, 8, open the Shell-Box, disengage[14] the Shell, and place it in the Ladle, in readiness to pass to Nos. 3 and 5. (Special drill.)

Breeching and the removal of the Bolt are, therefore, deferred until the Gun has been run out in the subsequent proceedings.

The Breeching is always to be shackled to the Ship's side—not to the Slide, which needlessly strains the pivoting, and also causes the shackle with its appliances to interfere with the working parts at the forward end of the Slide.

[10] It is generally expected that the Compressors are to supersede the necessity for a Breeching. But experience shows that in firing it is better to rely habitually on the Breeching, and use the Compressors to assist. Thus, in firing to windward at Sea, the Compressors are always to be set, but only so hard as may be required to ease the shock on the Breeching. In firing to leeward, the Compressors are not wanted, except to secure the gun in its place when in. When the Ship is not steady, but rolling, the discretion is to be exercised.

The Preventer, or Inner Breeching, will be found indispensable to avoid accident when running out to leeward in a sea-way. For with a trained crew, and all precaution in handling the levers and In-Tackles, there is a liability to the gun getting away, in which case it moves out with great violence, and may do serious damage. On one such occasion an XI-in. gun cracked the stout iron straps of the Compressors, and seemed but just prevented from freeing itself entirely and going overboard over the Port-sill. Not being able to replace the Straps, the Compressors were useless till late in the cruise. Preventer Breechings were then fitted, and answered so well that the practice was continued at sea as usual. They now form part of the equipment of all XI-in. guns, and should be just taut when the gun is out, and the Trucks of the Carriage reach but do not ascend the curve of the forward Hurter.

[11] This is to detach from the bottom of the Chamber the fragments of burnt Flannel that are apt to adhere and solidify.

[12] This practice encumbers the deck, and interferes materially at times with the management of the gun. Trial was therefore made on board the *Plymouth*, where the gun was on a covered deck, of hooks attached to the beams above, near each piece, in which the Sponges and Rammers were placed after having been used. The only objec-

V. "LOAD!"

(Diagram No. 4.)

249. No. 3 places the charge in the muzzle, seam from the Vent,[15] small end in, and pushes it well into the Bore.

No. 4, who stands ready with the Rammer, enters it into the muzzle, and pushes the charge home steadily, until the mark on the Rammer handle shows the charge to be in place.[16] No. 3 assists with one hand, and the charge is on no account to be struck.[17]

Whilst No. 4 withdraws the Rammer, Nos. 7, 8 each take a handle of the Ladle, lift up the Shell,[18] and, assisted by No. 5, pass it on to Nos. 3 and 4, who enter the shell into the muzzle, sabot first and Fuze out, as soon as the Rammer is clear of the muzzle.

As the Shell lies just fair with the muzzle, No. 3 removes the cap from Fuze,[19] which is passed along to the Gun Captain, and pushes the Shell into the Bore.

No. 4 enters the Rammer, and, assisted by No. 3, pushes in the shell until the mark on the handle shows it to be in place. It is most strictly forbidden to strike the shell with the Rammer.[20]

No. 6 takes the Rammer from No. 4 and lays it down, or lodges it overhead on the hooks. Whilst this has been doing, the preparation for the next order is to go on.[21] Nos. 13, 14 ease compressors, if no motion. If there is, they stand ready to ease at next order. The Out-Tackles are manned by Nos. 19, 21, 23, 17, 15, 11, 13, and 20, 22, 24, 18, 16, 12, 14. The Inner Tackles tended by No. 2 and Qr. Gunner. The Front Carriage-Levers grasped by 3, 9, and 4, 10. The Rear by 11, 12.

---

tion was, that too much time might be lost in so doing; but after continued trials this was found not to be the case, when the men had been properly trained.

[13] Stopping the Vent is omitted by many practised artillerists, as unnecessary in extinguishing fragments of the cartridges. But as so much importance has been and still is attached to its performance, and it costs so little trouble, it seems better to continue the practice, particularly when so many accidents occur from premature explosion, not only to untaught and careless people, in saluting on holidays, but also on shipboard, where they ought not to happen.

[14] Sometimes the box has been fitted too tightly to the Shell, or has contracted on it, and delay is caused in loading. This should be attended to in season.

[15] Otherwise the stout stuff and seams found necessary with heavy charges might resist the primer, and cause a failure to explode the powder.

[16] It was the habit at the Experimental Battery, and in the experimental cruise of the *Plymouth*, to mark the handle of the Rammer, so that there should be no doubt as to the charge being home. This is always useful, but particularly so in case of the gun bursting, as it makes sure of an important fact.

[17] It is a common practice in loading, to expend much zeal in striking the cartridge one or two blows to insure its being home, which is quite unnecessary when the mark on the handle affords so much better evidence thereof.

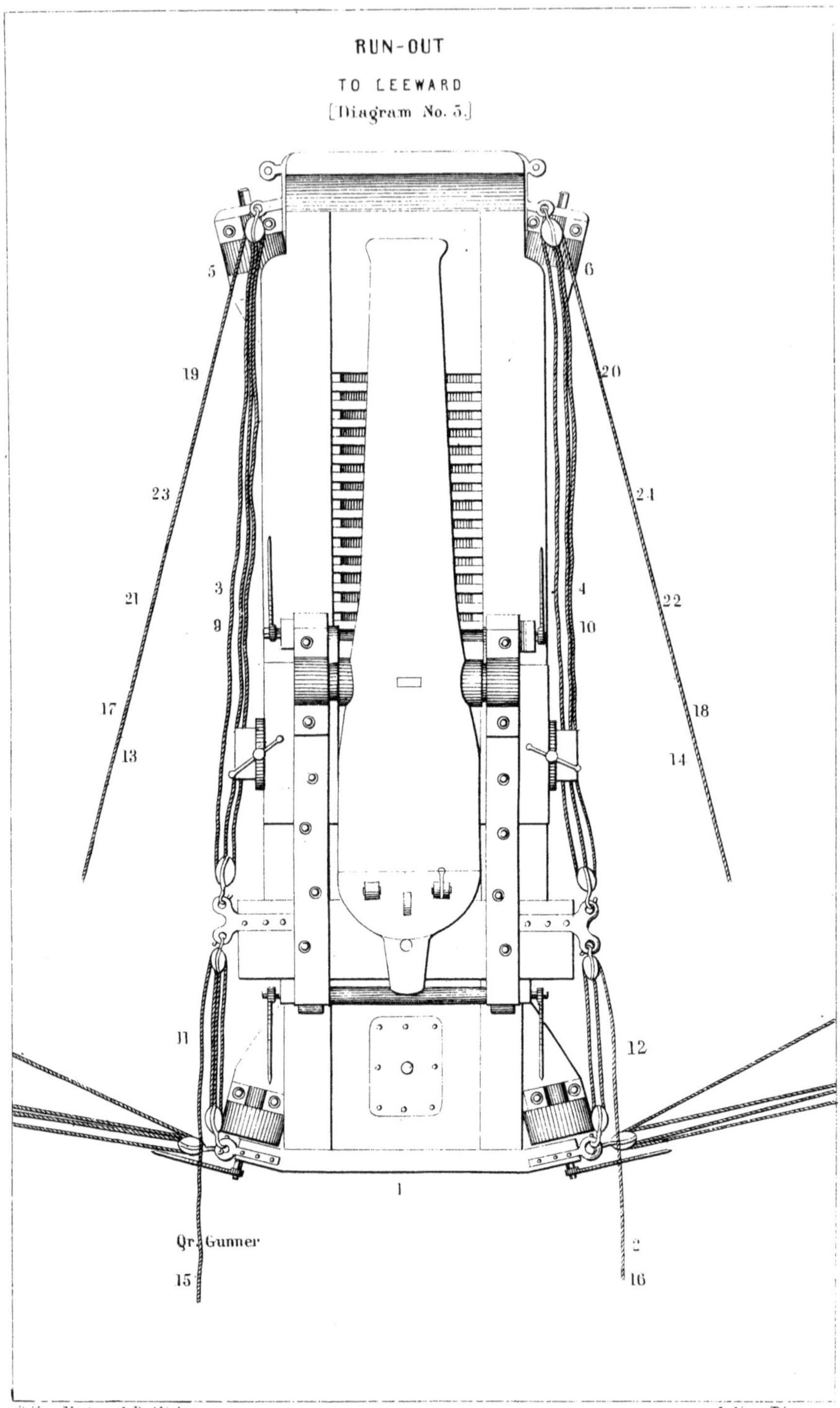

D. Van Nostrand Publisher. Julius Bien pr.

VI. "RUN OUT!"

(Diagram No. 5.)

250. The mode of executing this order will vary with circumstances—by the gun being to windward or to leeward, and by the nature of the rolling motion.

To leeward, and with much motion, the tendency is to go out with dangerous violence.[22]

Therefore, Nos. 5, 19, 21, 23, 17, 15, 13, and 6, 20, 22, 24, 18, 16, 14, haul cautiously on the Out-Tackles, the Qr. Gunner and No. 2, assisted by 15, 16, holding well back on the In-Tackles with a turn caught; 13, 14 ease the compressors; Nos. 3, 9, and 4, 10 heave up the Front Carriage-Levers; Nos. 11, 12 keep down the Rear Carriage-Levers, unless it is seen that they are necessary.

In running out to windward[23] the compressors may be eased at once, the In-Tackles slacked, the Carriage hove up on its trucks, and the gun run out by the Out-Tacklemen, assisted by any of the numbers not employed in other duties. When out, the Carriage-Levers are let down promptly and unshipped. The compressors are set[24] and Rear Slide-Lever shipped.

---

[18] The XI-in. Shell weighs, when loaded, 135 lbs.; the lifting and entering it into the muzzle was one of the objections of those who were opposed to the use of heavy calibres. There was not one of the crew of the *Plymouth's* XI-in. gun who was not found able, on trial, to take up the Shell and unassisted to put it in the Bore, when the ship was still. At sea a very simple implement was used—an iron segment with a bent handle on opposite sides. The Shellmen, 7, 8, turned the shell out of the box into this ladle, placed on the deck near No. 3, the Loader, who, when ready, took the left handle, and No. 5 (the 2d Loader) the right. These two lifted the Shell towards the muzzle, and No. 4 (Sponger), standing on the Slide, received the right hand from No. 5 as soon as within reach. No. 3, stepping on the Slide, and No. 4 continued to raise the Shell to the muzzle, which was not difficult, because of the Bore being conveniently high above the Slide on which they were standing; the Sabot projecting beyond the Ladle was entered into the muzzle, and the Shell pushed in, No. 5 taking the ladle back and laying it on the deck.

[19] As this is very firmly fixed in the recess of the metal stock, it is to be removed by pulling directly on the tail, which, if twisted, will be likely to break, and thus cause a loss of time. The patch is passed to the Gun Captain, who puts it in his belt-box, and is afterwards handed to the Quarter deck by the Lieut. of Division, in order to verify the number of shells fired. When the Fuze has been uncovered, care must be taken not to let it be touched by the moisture of the hand, or by the sea-water.

[20] As the blow might dislodge the priming of the Fuze and prevent its ignition. It is well to dispense with any wad, even a grommet, if possible.

[21] A good exemplification of the principle assumed for this exercise, that when any one of the men has executed an order, he shall not remain in position until the order is given which requires him elsewhere; for he may not have any part in the next order, or even in that second next, as occurs after pivoting, when only a few numbers participate in the following orders: Sponge—Load, the remainder only doing so at the third following, viz.: Run Out.

VII. "PRIME!"

(Diagram No. 6.)

251. The Gun Captain again makes sure that the Vent is clear,[25] and in so doing lets his wire down quickly into the charge.[26] If all is right, he inserts a primer.

If the Slide-Levers have not been shipped, or have been unshipped, they must now be put on the axles of the Rear Slide-Trucks—15, 16.

The Rear Train-Tackles will be manned by

Nos. { 13.15.17.19.21.23.5.
14.16.18.20.22.24.6.

VIII. "POINT!"

252. The Gun Captain adjusts or verifies the Sliding-Bar of the Rear sight to the desired range,[27] and steps off the slide directly to the rear, lock-lanyard in hand. The 2d Captain takes hold of the Elevating screw,[28] 15, 16 heave up the levers of Rear Slide-Trucks, and the Training-Tackles are manned by

Nos. { 13.15.17.19.21.23.5.
14.16.18.20.22.24.6.
(Right or Left.)

---

[22] No operation with this gun requires more care. There is a weight of 20,000 lbs. moving on friction Rollers along a metal plate, down an inclined plane—if once permitted to get loose and to be propelled by the motion of the ship, the momentum is immense, and must disable some of the apparatus, perhaps the Gun-Carriage itself. On such an occasion the preventer breeching is invaluable, and will be the best safeguard, if fitted so that when well stretched it will not permit the fore trucks to ascend on the curve of the Fore-hurter, for it is this which strains the strap of the Compressor.

Permitting the gun to go out with much force also displaces the shell, whether a grommet-wad be used or not.

[23] To windward, with a steady inclination, the precautions used to leeward are unnecessary. On the contrary, the difficulty is to move so great a weight up the inclined plane. Therefore, the carriage is released from all restraint, and all the available force put at the Out-Tackles, taking advantage also of whatever roll there may be to windward.

[24] This must, of course, be regulated by circumstances, as already mentioned in Note 10; as to windward, set the compressors moderately; to leeward, not at all; off the wind, according to the roll. Let the compression be so adjusted as to allow the muzzle just to come in.

[25] It is an old custom for the Gun Captain to keep the Priming-Wire in the vent while the loading is going on, feeling from time to time if the charge is home. It is a bad practice, because there is a liability of being caught by the charge as it comes along the Bore, and having the wire bent, thus spiking the vent, for a while at least. The mark on the Rammer handle is the best evidence that the charge is in place. The object now is only to clear the vent of pieces of cartridge stuff, which not unfrequently get into the vent, and choke it so as to prevent the primer from exploding the powder.

[26] Though the primers seldom fail to penetrate the flannel stuff of the cartridge, it is

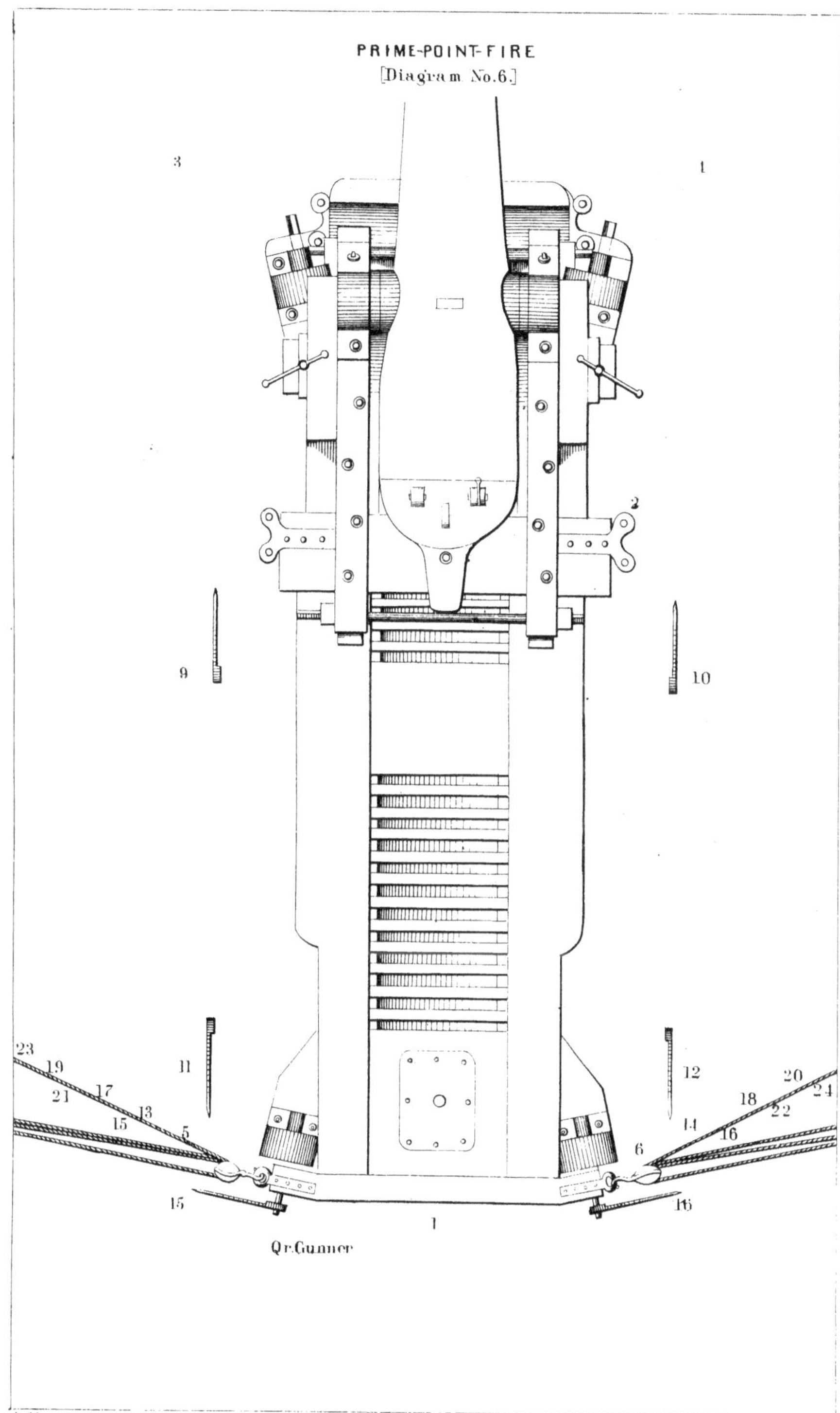

D. Van Nostrand, Publisher.
Julius Bien, pr.

IX. "READY—FIRE!"

253. The Gun Captain, with lock-lanyard just taut and his eye ranging over the sights, but kept well down to the bottom of the notch in head of sliding-bar, and over the point of middle sight, awaits these being brought into coincidence by the roll with the object, which is always the WATER-LINE—the Slide being trained constantly as desired by voice or sign.[29]

When sure of his aim, the Gun Captain draws the lock-lanyard promptly and firmly.

If the primer miss, the 2d Captain removes it, clears the vent, and puts in a fresh primer.

If the gun, when fired, does not come into its place for loading, ship Carriage-Levers, heave up, and run in by the In-Tackles to a taut breeching.

Down all levers and set Compressors.

If the firing or exercise is to continue, the next order is "Sponge."

If not, unshackle the breeching, then—Run in, back to rear hurter for pivoting—"Stand by to Pivot"—"Pivot to right or left;" when amidships—In Pivot-Bolt—"Run out," and secure for sea.

X. "SHIFT TO HOUSING-PIVOT, AND SECURE!"

254. The gun is brought into the housing position amidships and pivoted to the socket farthest from the extremity of the vessel, and run out.

No. 1 puts in the vent-plug, wipes and lays the hammer in place and the lock-string around it, then puts on the lock-cover; sees his gun properly secured, and the implements and spare articles returned to their places.

No. 2 levels the gun and wipes off and re-lacquers rear pivot-bolt and elevating screw; puts on sight-aprons; puts in rail-chocks and assists in securing lashings and breeching.

Loaders put in the tompion and on muzzle-bag, and wipe off and re-lacquer the front pivot-bolt.

Spongers return rammer and sponge to place, and assist in securing lashings and breeching.

---

well to pierce the latter with the wire, so as not to omit any means that may insure the instant discharge of the gun.

[27] The Sight-Bar of the XI-in. Gun is graduated to its own charge only; if reduced charges are ever used, it will only be at short distances, when the gun needs no elevation. The Bar will then be down entirely, its head resting on the Box.

[28] One turn of which is equal to one degree of the quadrant, and may be of service when the Sight-Bars are not.

The carriages of Gun Sloops and other vessels carrying XI-in. guns allow of an elevation of 20°.

[29] When the vessels are moving, it is best to train the gun a little ahead, watching when the object draws in line; then, as the roll brings the piece right in elevation, it is fired.

Levermen wipe off and re-lacquer their respective levers and eccentrics, secure levers in place, and assist in securing the gun.

Compressormen wipe off, re-lacquer, and tighten the compressors, and assist Carpenter in replacing and securing bulwarks.

Shellmen return shells, empty boxes, and shell-bearer to their places, and assist in securing bulwarks.

Powderman returns spare powder and passing-box to the magazine.

Tacklemen tighten and secure "in" and "out tackles," and make up and stow "shifting" and "training tackles" on the slide; ship the clevis-bolts, pass and tighten the gun-lashings, and assist in replacing bulwarks.

The men who provide implements and spare articles return them to their places.

TRANSPORTING PIVOT-GUNS FROM ONE END OF A VESSEL TO THE OTHER.

255. The gun must be pivoted and trained so as to bring its muzzle towards the direction in which it is to be transported, the transporting-trucks shipped and secured to their axles, the chocking-quoins placed, the training-trucks thrown out of action, the compressors brought to bear to confine the gun near the middle of the slide, some of the tackles hooked for dragging, and others, with capstan-bars, for guiding and steadying it. The pivot-bolts are to be removed, and the gun's crew, aided by others if required, transport it to the desired position at the other end of the vessel. The slide is then brought over and pivoted upon a fighting or outer centre, the transporting-trucks removed, and the training-trucks brought into action. When the implements for working and loading the gun are brought to it, it will then be ready for action.

When the forward and after slides are of different lengths, and the traversing circles of different diameters, the longest slide will be fitted with an additional rear pivot-hole and plate, to correspond with the smaller circle, in order that the gun may be worked from the midship pivot-bolt and shifted to the different fighting centres or pivot-bolts of the smaller circle.

Thus, when only one pivot-gun is mounted forward and one aft, and when they can both be brought to bear from only one end of the vessel, the force may be doubled at that extremity by pivoting one gun on each bow or quarter, as the case may be.

For heavy guns this is practicable in smooth water only.

Arrangements are made for shifting the broadside-guns both to the bow and stern, in aid of the pivot-guns, when the distance of the enemy is not too great. When the stern gun is pivoted over the rudder, one of the broadside-guns may be worked on each side of it, in firing right aft. Guns mounted on pivot-carriages may be fought upon the rear pivot, on the common or shifting centre, and fired from any point of the traversing or shifting circle, if the elevation be such as will not endanger the decks. In this case the training must be done with the gun run in over the rear pivot, as after it is run out the training will be difficult, and the helm must be relied on to bring the gun on with the object.

Guns should never be transported about the deck of a ship when loaded.

NOTES UPON THE MANUAL EXERCISE.

FOURTH COMMAND.

"SERVE VENT AND SPONGE!"

"The Gun Captain-serves, then stops the vent!"

256. A difference of opinion being entertained among artillerists with regard to the utility of stopping the vent, the continuance of the practice, as directed in the text, is recommended.

The thumbstall has been made of various materials, but its use is somewhat inconvenient for the Gun Captain, and he cannot feel that the vent is stopped. At the Experimental Battery of the Ordnance Yard the naked thumb is used, and experience shows that the gun is never so hot as to occasion the least inconvenience, except with howitzers.

257. It has been the uniform practice at the Experimental Battery at the Ordnance Yard, Washington, and also on board the Gunnery Ship *Plymouth*, in 1857–'58, to use a moist sponge; and as no accident from premature explosion has taken place in either case, the inference is that the method is a safe one, and might obviate other precautions, especially where reloading is necessary, as in firing salutes, when, there being no shot over the cartridge, it is imperfectly consumed.

258. "Strikes the staff several smart taps under the muzzle!" to shake off any adhering fragments of the cartridge. Should any burning fragments be drawn out, the Loader extinguishes them with the wet swab; the Gun Captain again commands "Sponge."

259. Gun Captain "serves the vent with his priming-wire!" If at any time he should find the vent obstructed, and be unable to clear it with the priming-wire or boring-bit, he will at once report to the officer of division, who will order the vent-punch used; or, if this should fail, have recourse to the vent-drill and brace in charge of the Quarter Gunner. The boring-bit, vent-punch, and drills should be used with caution, as, being of steel, they are liable to be broken off in the vent and thus effectually spike the gun. After clearing the vent the bore should be sponged.

260. Spongers and Loaders are to be careful to keep their bodies as much within the port as practicable, otherwise at close quarters they will be picked off by musketry.

FIFTH COMMAND.

"LOAD!"

"*No.* 3 *removes cap from fuze!*"[1]

261. The cap is never to be removed until the shell has been entered in the gun. With high elevations, or when rolling, care should be taken that the shell does not slip down the bore before this is done.

The cap or patch is removed by taking hold of the lug with the forefinger and thumb, first raising it a little, and without twisting; a pull readily removes it. The patch is passed to the Gun Captain, as an evidence that the priming has been exposed; the patches to be preserved and accounted for at the end of the firing.

262. The Loader must be careful not to touch the fuze composition with his fingers, for fear of injuring it by moisture. Where the firing is not hurried it is advisable to raise the priming of the fuze, to insure its ignition. All of these details should be carefully explained to the crew.

263. No wad is required over a shell, but a selvagee wad may be used in heavy rolling.

264. When loading with shot a selvagee wad is placed over it. A part —half or a third—of a selvagee wad, is equally efficient in holding the shot in place.

265. Shells should be used against Ships at all distances where the penetration would be sufficient to lodge them. They are of no service in breaching solid stone walls, but are very effective against earthworks, ordinary buildings, and for bombarding. For these purposes a good percussion or concussion fuze is desirable, but no reliable fuzes of these kinds have as yet been devised.

266. Solid shot should only be used when great accuracy, at very long range, and penetration are required.

267. If, in loading, a shot or shell jams in the bore, no attempt should be made to force it down, but it should be withdrawn. This may be done with the ladle, by depressing and striking the muzzle against the lower sill of the port, or by running the gun out hard against the side at extreme depression.

268. A gun is not to be loaded with more than a single shot at once, without the express sanction of the Captain, and never with more than a

[1] Many officers are of the opinion that this order should be divided—"Load with Cartridge," and "Load with Shell." But those guns would be very badly served which should wait until this time to give the order for the species of projectile or class of fuze required. *After* "Load," is the proper time to give subsidiary order to Shellmen what projectile and length of fuze to bring for next fire.

single shell. Solid shot are not to be fired from shell-guns without a direct order from the Captain.

269. Experiments show that firing two loaded shells together should never be practised. With quite reduced charges [of from $\frac{1}{8}$th to $\frac{1}{12}$th the weight of the single shell], of 88 loaded shells thus fired, 25 were broken and 43 did not explode, and some of the remainder were exploded too soon by the shock of discharge. Of 50 unloaded 8-inch shells, fired two at the same time, with 6 lbs. of powder, only one was broken by the shock of the discharge. This difference between loaded and empty shells is accounted for by the fact that a small hole is generally broken into the outer shell, through which its charge is ignited. *See* p. 13, Report of Admiral Farragut, dated August 31, 1853, on experiments made at Old Point Comfort.

270. In loading with a shell, the most exact attention is required to all the precautions relating to the position of the fuze and the mode of setting home the shell. The Loader is to be specially instructed that unless the leaden patch is stripped off, to expose the priming, the fuze will not ignite, and consequently the shell cannot explode.

271. Grape-shot have not sufficient penetration to be used with effect, generally, against ships-of-war beyond 150 yards. When the men on the spar-decks of the enemy are exposed, by the heeling of the ship, grape or canister may be used against them, at distances varying from 200 to 300 yards. Against light vessels, a single stand of grape from heavy guns may be used at about 400 yards. The dispersion of the balls is about one-tenth the distance, and is practically independent of the charge.

272. The XI-inch gun, at 10° elevation, gives for the mass of grape or canister a range of about 1,300 yards; the spread about 10°. They may therefore be used with great effect against boats or exposed bodies of men.

273. A stand of grape is not to be used with any other projectile.

274. Canister or case-shot, prepared for immediate use, are supplied for all guns, including boat and field howitzers, and are effective at short distances against boats or exposed bodies of men; they may be used also, under favorable circumstances, against the tops of an enemy.

275. Shrapnel-shell or spherical case-shot is intended to exceed the range of canister, and is to be used only under the same circumstances, but at an increased distance. Canister is more effective at from 250 yards with the 12-pdr. howitzer, to 400 yards with the XI-inch; but beyond those distances shrapnel should be used up to 900 yards for the 12-pdr., and 1,500 with the XI-inch. A well-delivered shrapnel-shell from a heavy gun must sweep away the crew of a pivot or other gun, on a spar-deck not protected by bulwarks. The 'distant firing' charge is always to be used with shrapnel.

SEVENTH COMMAND.

"PRIME!"

"*He inserts a primer and turns the hammer down upon it.*"

276. To prevent the primer from being blown out of the vent by the blast of the next gun, as occasionally happens on light-covered decks.

With guns of the old pattern this cannot be done, because, if turned down, it would interfere with the aim.

277. It is essential that the head of the primer shall be placed flat and pressed close upon the vent, that the hammer may strike it fairly. The tip of shellac, by which the lower end of the tube is sealed, occasionally obstructs the jet of flame so as to split the tube. In this case the flame is dispersed laterally, and fails to ignite the charge; it is therefore a good precaution to pinch the end of the tube before putting it into the vent.[1]

278. The tubes of all the primers are carefully gauged before issuing them for service; but such as, from any cause, become so much enlarged as not to go easily into the vent, should be rejected without attempting to force them down.

It will occasionally happen, either from carelessness or inattention to the instructions given for the proper manner of pulling the lock-string, that the head of the primer will be crushed without exploding it. Frequently a second and stronger pull will have the desired effect, if the fulminate has not been dispersed; in case, however, this attempt should prove unsuccessful, the tube of the primer should be drawn out, if possible, before using the priming-wire to clear the vent.

279. In case either lock or primer should entirely fail, recourse will be had to the friction-primers or to the spur-tubes. In using the first, the Captain of the gun, after taking the primer from the box, will raise up the twisted wire-loop until it is on a line with the spur; place the tube in the vent with the spur towards the muzzle of the gun, and so that this spur will rest on the lock-piece; then hook the lanyard into the raised loop, and pull it, when otherwise ready to fire the gun, as though it were a lock-string, using, however, a less degree of force. The lanyard may be hooked to the loop before the tube is put into the vent. When the spur-tubes are used, the Gun Captain exposes the priming and the 2d Captain applies the match.

280. The men should be practised at unloaded guns, in placing the primers, both percussion and friction, properly, and in pulling the lock-string so as to insure their explosion, until this very essential knowledge and skill have been perfectly attained.

---

[1] "In 10,000 fires, when testing guns of different calibres, with the regulation locks, less than fifty primers failed from all causes."

EIGHTH COMMAND.

"POINT!"

"*His eye ranging over the sights!*"

281. The Gun Captain gives the necessary order, "Right" or "Left," "Raise" or "Lower," by voice or sign. He alone should speak, giving his orders in a sharp, clear tone, but not louder than necessary for his own crew to hear him.

282. He should make use of the following signs to assist in making himself understood, which, when the crew become well drilled, are sufficient without the verbal orders.

IN POINTING.—He should move the left hand, held vertically, to the right or left, according as he wishes the right or left tackle hauled upon.

IN ELEVATING.—He should move the hand, held horizontally, up or down, according as he wishes the breech raised or lowered.

283. Officers of divisions, while instructing the men in aiming, should be particular in impressing upon their minds the necessity of bringing the eye to an exact level with the bottom of the sight-notch, as otherwise they will fire too high.

284. In lateral training, when the direction of the gun is frequently changed by the coming up or falling off of the ship, or when the position of the object to be fired at is rapidly changing by passing in opposite directions, or from other causes, it is better to train a little beyond, and then watch the proper moment for firing, instead of endeavoring to train at once directly on the object.

285. The lateral training, or pointing, when considerable, should always precede the elevation; because, the jarring of the gun is apt to alter the elevation.

286. "If roller handspike is not used in training." A great difference of opinion exists on this point. The use of the roller handspike somewhat facilitates extreme train, but the gun cannot be fired until it is unshipped, which alters the elevation and consumes time. It is perhaps preferable to use one handspike under the bracket, manned by two men, and the other to lift and slue the gun, manned by one man, under the transom.

287. "Elevate or Depress as directed!" If the carriage is fitted with a quoin, handspikemen standing between the handspikes and the side of the ship, place their handspikes on the steps of the carriage and raise the breech. As soon as the quoin is free, the 2d Captain takes hold of it with both hands and withdraws the quoin to the full extent; handspikemen "raise" or "lower" the gun slowly and steadily. When the proper elevation is given, the Gun Captain gives the word "Well!" and the 2d Captain forces the quoin tight under the breech, giving the word "Down!"

288. To facilitate the operation of pointing guns according to the distance of the object aimed at, sights are prepared and fitted to each gun; and breast-sweeps for all truck-carriages of heavy guns.

The ordinary sights consist of two pieces of bronze gun-metal, one of which, called the reinforce-sight, is a fixed point, firmly secured to the sight-mass, upon the upper surface of the gun between the trunnions. The heads of the sights should not be bright, otherwise it interferes with the aim when they are exposed to a bright sun.

289. The other, or breech-sight, is a square bar or stem, with a head, in the top of which is a sight-notch. It is set diagonally, so as to expose two faces to the rear; the rear angle chamfered, to afford a bearing for the clamp-screw. This bar or stem is made to slide in a vertical plane, in the sight-box fixed to the breech sight-mass, and is held at the various elevations for which it is graduated by means of a thumb-screw. Its length is sufficient for all the elevation which can be given—about 5°—before the muzzle appears above the front sight, after which a long wooden sight must be used, graduated for the whole length of the gun, using the notch in the muzzle.

The bar or stem of the sight has lines across its faces denoting for all the old guns degrees of elevation, each of which is marked with the number of yards at which a shot or shell will strike the point aimed at, when that line is brought to a level with the top of the sight-box, and the gun is loaded with a specified charge of powder; for the guns of the new system, the ranges are marked in even hundreds of yards.

The uppermost line on the stem marked level is the zero of the other graduations, and when adjusted to the level of the top of the sight-box, the bottom of the notch in the head of the breech-sight and the apex of the reinforce-sight show the dispart of the gun. When the line of sight coincides with these points, it is parallel to the bore, and when continued to a distant horizon, the gun is laid level or horizontal.

Sights should invariably be made so that the level line on the stem will correspond with the bottom of the head when it rests on the sight-box, and thus secure a dispart-sight in case of accident to the screw in the sight-box.

A white line, one-fourth (.25) of an inch wide, drawn on top of the gun from the breech-sight to the notch on the swell of the muzzle, has been found to greatly facilitate the aim. For night-firing a broad wooden block, painted dead-white, to ship over the reinforce-sight, leaving $\frac{1}{4}$ of an inch of the sight exposed, will assist in preventing the aim from being too high.

290. For shot-guns the ranges in yards for one shot with the distant-firing charge of powder are marked for each degree of elevation on the right in-board face of the sight-bar; for the ordinary firing, on the left face.

291. The gun being placed a certain height above the water, depending on the class of vessel and the deck on which it is mounted, it is evident that, when the axis of the bore is horizontal, the shot will have a range proportionate to this height. This range or distance is commonly called point-blank, or point-blank range, and is the number noted in the column marked P. B., or 0°, or level in range tables.

This point-blank, therefore, depends on the class of gun, the charge, and the height above the water.

292. A preferable definition of this distance is "range at level."

293. The aim is always supposed to be directed at the water-line. But, with the sight-bar at level, if a gun is aimed by it at the water-line of a vessel at point-blank range, the shot would strike short of the point aimed at by about one-quarter of the distance; or, if aimed, under similar conditions, at the upper part of the hull, the shot would fall a distance below the point aimed at equal to the height of the gun.

294. In firing at small objects, particularly boats, within point-blank range, it is therefore important to attend to this source of error. It is desirable that all sights should be marked, from 100 yards to the greatest range, and thus avoid all consideration of point-blank.

In fitting new guns, or those upon which the sights require replacing, the sight-bar will be fitted as described in Article 289, and graduated from 100 yards downwards.

For shell-guns the ranges are marked for shells on the sight-bars, in the same manner as those for the shot of shot-guns.

295. These sights being each adjusted to a particular gun, and marked with its class and number, do not, in strictness, admit of being transferred to other guns, even of the same class.

296. When used, the stem of the breech-sight must be raised or lowered, to correspond with the ascertained or estimated distance, in yards, of the object aimed at, and firmly secured there by the thumb-screw. Then, if the ship be steady, elevate or depress the gun until the line of sight from the bottom of the notch of the breech-sight, the top of the reinforce-sight, and the point to be struck, will coincide; but if the ship have a rolling motion the gun must be so laid, after the sight is set for the distance, that this coincidence may be obtained, if possible, at the most favorable part of every roll which the ship makes.

297. The inclination of the line of metal to the axis of the bore varies in guns of the same class, as well as in those of different classes. Aiming, therefore, by the line of metal cannot be relied on for definite ranges; besides that, within those ranges, it is apt to mislead by giving too much elevation to the piece. Therefore, when the established sights are not furnished, or have become unserviceable, wooden dispart-sights lashed on the reinforce should be immediately substituted. A narrow groove in the upper surface of the wooden sight, made to coincide with the plane of the line of sight marked on the gun, will assist the Gun Captain in getting the true direction quickly.

Half the difference between the diameters of the gun at the base-ring and swell of the muzzle, or at any intermediate point on the line of metal, will give the proper height of the dispart-sight at the point where the least diameter was taken, to which must be added the height of the lock-piece above the base-ring, in order to get a line of sight over it, parallel to the axis of the bore.

The guns of the Dahlgren pattern are cylindrical for a certain distance forward of the base-line, always giving a line of sight parallel to the axis of the bore.

298. All the new guns are marked on the top of the lock-piece, base-ring, the reinforce sight-mass, and the swell of the muzzle, by notches which indicate a vertical plane passing through the axis of the bore, at right angles to the axis of the trunnions.

299. Pivot-guns have been supplied with trunnion-sights, designed to be used when the ordinary sights do not give the required elevation. This instrument, however, gives but a rude approximation in either elevation or direction.

300. The rifled cannon in service have the breech-sight on the side of the breech and the front sight on the rimbase, which permits the gun to be accurately aimed and the object kept in view at all elevations. It is intended in future to apply this arrangement to all cannon mounted on pivot-carriages.

301. Various modes have been practised to ascertain at sea the distance from the object aimed at, so as to regulate the elevation of guns, but none can be depended upon for giving it with minute accuracy, and even when obtained it is continually varying; therefore, when the projectile is seen to exceed or fall short of the object considerably, the sight-bar must be readjusted accordingly. It thus becomes, under ordinary circumstances, the best instrument for approximating distances. In correcting the elevation, however, the variation of range to the first graze, attributable to eccentricity, differences of windage, and other causes, must be taken into consideration, as, under the most favorable circumstances, at the Experimental Battery of the Ordnance Yard, this variation is found to equal fifty yards, more or less.

302. In addition to the errors arising from these sources, we have also those due to the direction and force of the wind, the movement of the ship across the line of fire, and to sheering round a pivot when performing evolutions.

303. They can be obviated or diminished by the following means:

1st. Allow the Gun Captain to estimate the distance to windward or to leeward, right or left, to be allowed for the deflection; or,

2d. Indicate the number of yards right or left of the object; which, after all, depends on his estimation of distance.

3d. Furnish a sight which, in addition to the elevation, allows for the deviation, and permits the Gun Captain in all cases to aim directly at the target.

Such a sight is furnished to the Parrott rifles, and is desirable for all guns.

304. In case the ordinary sights should be lost or rendered useless, tangent firing may be resorted to against ships, by pointing with the wooden dispart-sight at such part of the ship as the Tables indicate for the distance, and according to the class of gun in use at the time.

A Table of this kind is appended, which has been calculated for the 8-inch and some of the heavier of the 32-pounder guns when loaded with single shot and distant-firing charges.

The different classes of sailing ships-of-war, whether of the same or of different nations, are not of the same length, nor are their masts of the same height from the deck, or from the water. They, however, correspond so nearly, for the same class of ships of the same nation, that calculations made from the angles subtended by the average height of their masts, will generally give their distance with sufficient accuracy for general firing.

Tables are inserted at the end of the book, in which the distances corresponding to different angles made by the masts of English and French ships-of-war are shown—from which the intermediate distances due to other angles may be estimated, and the sights regulated accordingly, if circumstances should render it desirable. Also an abridged Table, in which the height of our own mast is used as the base.

305. Officers of divisions and Captains of guns should be occasionally practised in measuring the distances of objects by the eye, at times when opportunities offer of verifying the accuracy of their estimate by comparing it with the distance obtained by the foregoing methods, or any other which will afford the best means of comparison.

306. Within point-blank range, if the hull of an enemy's vessel is obscured by smoke or darkness, the aim may be directed by the flashes of his guns.

307. Most naval guns are now fitted with elevating screws, passing through a hole in the cascabel of the Dahlgren system, and for those of the old system attached to the carriage: but the ordinary beds and quoins are also still in use; they are arranged to allow the extreme elevation and depression of the guns which the ports will admit with safety. When the inner or thick end of the quoin is fair with the end of the bed in place, the gun is level in the carriage; or horizontal, when the ship is upright. The degrees of elevation above this level, which may be given to the gun by drawing out the quoin when laid on its base, are marked on the side or edge, and those of depression on the flat part of the quoin, so that when the quoin is turned on its side for depressing, the marks may be seen. The level mark on the quoin is to correspond with the end of the bed. When the quoin is entirely removed, and the breech of the gun rests on the bed, the gun has its greatest safe elevation; and when the quoin is pushed home on its side, the gun has the greatest safe depression that the port will admit.

Care must be taken that the stop on the quoin is always properly lodged, to prevent the quoin from flying out or changing its position, and that the bed is secured to the bed-bolt.

Porter's bed and quoin has been adopted for all carriages requiring quoins. This quoin, being graduated to whole degrees, requires a small additional quoin for slight differences of elevation in smooth water.

When the elevating screw is used, a quoin should be at hand to place under the breech of the gun, when at extreme elevation, to relieve the screw from the shock of the discharge, and prevent a change of the elevation, as well as to take the place of the screw if it should be disabled. When the fire is continuous at the same distance, the lever of the elevating screw should be secured by a lanyard, to prevent the screw from turning and altering the elevation.

308. If a greater elevation for broadside-guns should be desired for any special purpose, it may be obtained by placing inclined planes behind the rear trucks, for them to recoil over and produce a corresponding depression of the muzzle of the gun as it comes within the port. But it will be observed that, beyond the elevation which the ports will admit of, the sights can no longer be taken by the tangent or any other top sight, as the upper sill of the port interferes. The gun must therefore be laid by the quoin and pendulum.

Additional depression may also be obtained by placing inclined planes for the front trucks to recoil upon, or by raising the breech by means of a wooden toggle placed vertically under it. One end of a tripping-line is fastened to the middle of the toggle, and the other to the breeching-bolt in the side of the ship; by this arrangement the toggle is tripped from its place at the commencement of the recoil, and the muzzle is raised so as to clear the port-sill by the preponderance of the breech.

NINTH COMMAND.

"READY—FIRE!"

"Waits patiently for the coincidence of the sights upon the object."

309. The exact moment for firing, at sea, necessarily varies with circumstances; but when these are favorable the following general principles should govern:

310. When the ship is steady, the gun should be fired when the line of sight is brought upon the object; but when the ship has much rolling motion, the moment for firing should be chosen a little before, so that the shot will probably leave the gun when the roll brings the line of sight upon the object aimed at.

When practicable, and too much time will not be lost, it will be best to fire when the vessel is on the top of a wave and just begins to roll towards the object. If the loss of time should be found objectionable, the gun may be fired at any other instant, when properly pointed, giving a preference, however, to the moment when rolling towards rather than when rolling from the object, and making due allowance for the probable change of elevation by the roll of the ship before the shot leaves the gun.

311. If, from any cause, the firing should be delayed after the gun has been pointed, it should be carefully pointed again before the order to fire is given.

312. The great object is to fire low enough to strike the hull if the shot preserve the intended direction, and as a general rule to strike it near the water-line.

313. To avoid loss of shot from lateral deviations, it is recommended to direct all the guns to be pointed to strike somewhere between the fore and mizzen masts of an enemy; when quite near, the guns of the forward divisions should be pointed in preference to that part of the hull about the foremast, and one or two of the after guns at the rudder, if it should be fairly exposed.

REMARKS ON THE DIFFERENT KINDS OF FIRING.

314. Firing at Will.—By this is meant firing the guns independently of each other, each Captain of a gun seizing the most favorable opportunity. This firing should always be used in action—unless ordered to the contrary—whenever the object is visible, the smoke from one gun not greatly impeding the firing of another.

315. Firing in Succession.—By this is meant firing one gun after another in regular order, commencing from the foremost or after gun, according as the wind is blowing from aft or forward. This firing may be used with advantage in the commencement of an action, or whenever a continuous, steady fire is desired, as the smoke from one gun will not impede the firing of the next.

316. Quick Firing.—By this is meant rapid firing at will, the tangent-sight not being raised. This firing should be used only when close alongside an enemy, as then but little pointing would be required.

317. When the guns are laid for the projectile to strike the object aimed at without grazing between the gun and the object, the firing is said to be direct. This mode of firing is to be preferred when the object fired at is so near that the chances of hitting it are very great, and also when the intervening surface between the gun and object is so rough or irregular that a projectile striking it would have its velocity much diminished or destroyed, and its direction injuriously affected.

Direct Firing requires a good knowledge of distance, and precision both of elevation and lateral direction, in order to strike an object which is comparatively a point. It is always to be preferred when the distance is accurately known.

318. When the guns are so laid that the projectile makes numerous grazes between the gun and the object, and continues its flight, the firing is denominated ricochet.

That properly so called is performed at level, or at most at three degrees of elevation; shot will often ricochet at much greater angles, but it is not what is meant by ricochet firing.

Ricochet Firing, upon a smooth surface within certain distances, has some important advantages over direct firing. When the guns have very little or no elevation, and are near the water, as they are in a ship's battery, the projectile strikes the water at a very small angle; its flight is not greatly retarded by the graze, and it rises but little above the surface in its course. The distant charge should always be used, but the penetration is not to be depended on beyond 1,500 yards against ships-of-war.

Ricochet firing at low elevations requires only correct lateral direction, since the projectile would rarely pass over and would probably strike a vessel if within its effective range, whether the actual distance had been correctly ascertained or not.

The deviation of projectiles is, however, generally increased by ricochet, and in proportion to the roughness of the surface of the water. Even a slight ripple will make a perceptible difference not only in direction, but in range and penetration, and the height to which the projectile will rise in its bounds.

Although these facts demand attention, yet when the estimated distance does not require an elevation of more than three degrees, projectiles from guns pointed rather too low for direct firing will probably ricochet and strike the object with effect, even when the water is considerably rough. This may be called "accidental ricochet."

When the water is not smooth, the most favorable circumstances for ricochet firing are when the flight of the shot is with the roll of the sea, and that roll is long and regular.

Ricochet will be effective against small objects up to 2,000 yards, but should not commence at less than 600 yards; at less distances it is preferable to fire direct. Ricochet is of no value from rifled guns firing elongated projectiles, as they lose all certainty of direction on the rebound.

Upon smooth water, a shot fired horizontally from the 32-pdr. of 33 cwt., with 4½ lbs. powder, ricocheted and rolled about 3,000 yards; the greatest range obtained from an elevation of 5°, with the same gun and charge, was less than 1,800 yards. *See* Dahlgren's Report on 32-pdr. of 32 cwt., p. 90.

Shot rarely ricochet at all with elevations above 5°, and the bounds are always higher, with equal charges from the same gun, as the elevation of the gun is increased.

319. Concentration of fire may be desirable under certain circumstances; and arrangements have been sometimes made to secure it by the simultaneous discharge of a number of guns upon some part of an object whose distance is known.

The advantages of these arrangements are not very obvious, excepting in cases where the position of the enemy may be visible from one part of a ship and not from all the guns in the batteries.

The object sought to be obtained is therefore to aim from in-board at an invisible target, the distance and direction of which are indicated by the Captain. It is consequently necessary that he shall be so placed as to obtain a distinct view of the enemy, or have suitable observers to inform him of his exact position.

320. In general, this sort of fire has been of little efficacy; but by the aid of a simple implement, readily made on board ship, it is believed that good results may be obtained, and particularly at night, when firing from guns on covered decks is now absolutely ineffective.

It consists of a simple metal or wooden batten, sliding in two beckets attached to the outer or inner sides of each of the brackets of the carriage, retained in any position by a thumb-screw. This batten is graduated by experiment or calculation for either the parallel or converging fire, for such points on the bow, beam, or quarter, as may be deemed advisable.

A small knob is screwed into the inner end of each batten, and a cod-line provided, with a loop in each end, somewhat longer than the width across the transom. If, then, one of the battens be drawn out to the graduation representing the degree of train required, the line stretched taut from the two knobs and hitched, and guns trained until this line is parallel to a mark on the deck, or one of the seams of the deck-plank—if they are parallel to the keel—the guns will all make the required angle, and may bo fired simultaneously or in succession, as ordered.

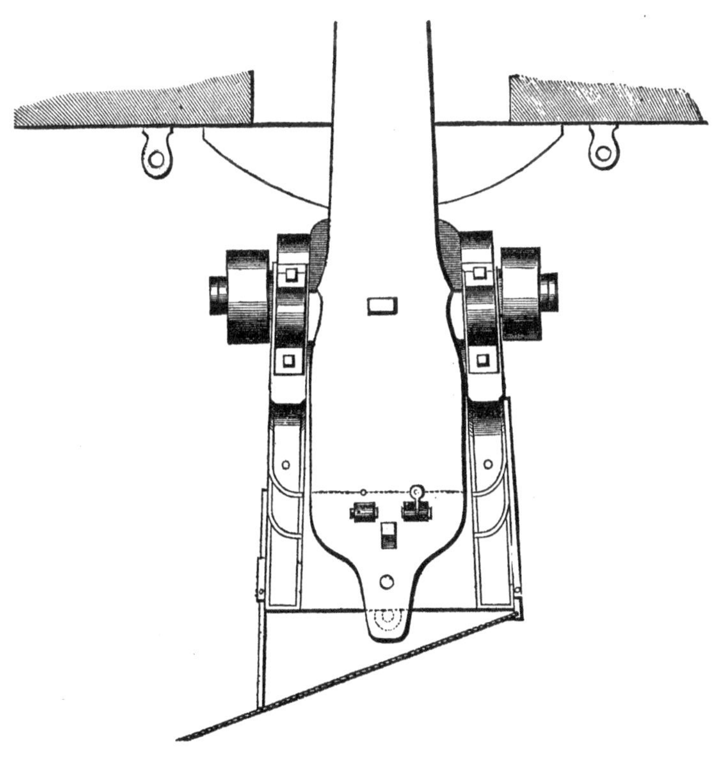

321. The principal object in view, therefore, is so to prepare the training by anticipation, that when the smoke rises, or on sheering the vessel, the enemy shall be visible to all the Gun Captains at the same time; giving them the choice to fire at will, or on a given signal, if simultaneous fire be desired.

It diminishes the great disadvantages of guns on covered decks, where the Gun Captains can only with difficulty ascertain the direction of the enemy; and places the whole battery more completely under the control of the Commander.

322. The principal care of the Commander must be to keep his guns always bearing on the enemy, and never pass the limits of extreme train for all his guns, unless absolutely necessary in manœuvring.

This he must regulate, either by one of the guns in his vicinity, or, better, by the aid of a bearing-plate, a species of plane-table which gives the angular bearing of the object.

323. Concentration of fire upon a particular part of an enemy's vessel may also be obtained by a general order for the guns to be aimed to strike that part when visible, leaving the Captains of guns to determine the proper time for firing, according to circumstances at the moment. This obviates the objections due to simultaneous firing, and would generally be equally effective at distances beyond point-blank. In this, as in all other cases of firing at sea, success depends mainly upon the skill, judgment, and coolness of the Captains of the guns.

THE USE OF FUZES.

324. All spherical shells, except those for the 24 and 12 pdr. howitzer, and all shrapnell, are fitted with the Navy time-fuze.

This fuze is composed of a composition driven in a paper case, and then inserted in a metal stock which screws into a bouching fitted to the shell.

The composition is covered with a safety-cap, which protects it from moisture and accidental ignition; also with a water-cap of peculiar construction, intended to protect the flame from being extinguished on ricochet.

A safety-plug at the lower extremity prevents the communication of fire to the powder in the shell, in the event of the accidental ignition of the fuze after being uncapped.

325. It is strictly forbidden to show or explain to foreigners or others the construction of any fuzes, except so far as may be necessary for the service of the guns.

326. These fuzes are of 3½, 5, 7, 10, 15, and 20 seconds time of burning; which are supposed to offer a sufficient variety for most of the exigencies of service. There are also supplied paper-case fuzes of greater length, which, when used, are always to be inserted in metal stocks.

All the Navy time-fuzes—paper case as well as metal stock—being intended for use under a water-cap, burn a longer time in the open air.

All shells, unless otherwise ordered, are fitted and issued from the shell-houses with the 5-seconds fuze, which is to be regarded as the general working fuze.

For greater or less distances this fuze may be drawn, and any of the others substituted.

The Navy time-fuze is rarely extinguished by several ricochets on water; and near the end of its flight, when fired direct, frequently acts by concussion.

The fuze used should not be of longer time of burning than requisite to reach the object; the shorter times are of quicker composition, therefore more certain; also in firing on ricochet the shell may sink short of the distance necessary for its explosion, and consequently be supposed to fail.

327. For special firing, as for example, at shore-batteries or masses of uncovered troops, any of these fuzes may be shortened. To do this, unscrew the water-cap and back the paper case out from the lower end with a drift and mallet; cut off from the lower end with a fine saw, or sharp knife struck with a mallet, the proportional part required, and insert the upper part in the stock, forcing it down with a few gentle blows with the drift; screw on the water-cap. It is preferable, however, when circumstances will admit, to take up such distance as will correspond with the time of flight of one of the regulation lengths. When firing against ships or earthworks, the fuze should be a little longer than necessary, in order to reach the object before bursting; but a little shorter when firing against boats or masses of troops, in order to insure its bursting in front of them.

328. The Bormann fuze is fitted to the 24-pdr. and 12-pdr. howitzer ammunition, and all shrapnell. It has also been fitted to certain shells used for special firing. The length of fuze is the limit of the distance within which this fire is effective.

This fuze is opened at the required number of seconds, by cutting close to the right of the mark on the index-plate. The cut should be made down to the plane of the table, in order to expose the composition; and is best made at two or three efforts, instead of trying to effect the cut at once. This fuze should be carefully explained to the men, as shells have been taken from guns with the cut made into the priming-magazine, which would explode them at the muzzle.

329. There are also on trial for the rifled cannon the percussion and time fuzes of Schenkl, Hotchkiss, Parrott, and others.

No reliable percussion or concussion-fuze has as yet been arranged for spherical shells.

330. These fuzes will be exhibited and explained by the Ordnance Officer on the application of Commanders of vessels, who, with the Executive Officer and Gunner, are enjoined to make themselves thoroughly acquainted with this most important part of the equipment.

331. Commanders of vessels will carefully note and report the efficiency of all fuzes fired in action or exercise; giving the elevation of the gun, the estimated or measured range, the number fired, the name of the inventor, whether percussion or time, the number of failures to explode the shell, premature explosions, and satisfactory action. Great waste of ammunition is frequently occasioned by an under-estimate of the distance.

332. The times of flight and length of fuze for all projectiles, so far as ascertained at the Experimental Battery at Washington, are given in the Table of Ranges, Appendix B.

333. The best effect of a percussion-fuze is obtained by firing into a mass of timber. They frequently fail if fired into a bank of soft earth, sand, or other material which does not offer a sufficiently sudden resistance; also, if fired at high angles of elevation, owing to the fact that the rifle-shells do not generally strike point foremost.

334. Time-fuzes are also very unreliable in rifle-guns; expanding projectiles cut off the flame from the fuze.

With the Parrott shell, however, the Navy time-fuze is the most certain of ignition and regular in its time of burning. The safety-plug should be removed when the Navy time-fuse is used in rifled cannon, as recent experiments show that it is a probable cause of premature explosions of shells.

In testing the Navy time-fuse by the watch, or michronometer, the safety-plug must be removed: otherwise the fuze will burn longer than the time for which it is marked.

BOARDERS.

335. It is not supposed that any directions can be framed which will entirely provide for all the various circumstances which may require attention when about to board an enemy, or to repel a similar assault made by an enemy upon our vessels.

The following general suggestions are, however, presented for the consideration of Captains, in order that some degree of uniformity may be preserved when other more important considerations do not prevent it.

336. Upon the signal for Boarders, the divisions called should form on the gangway of the side which is not engaged, properly armed, and remain there until ordered elsewhere, provided there be time to make this disposition of them. In all movements from one part of the ship to another, cutlasses should be sheathed and pistols in the frogs. The men of each division should be united as much as possible under their own officer. Bayonets not fixed until ordered.

"PREPARE TO BOARD!"

(FROM ANY SPECIFIED PART OF THE SHIP.)

337. The Boarders should repair to the place directed, taking care to keep themselves down so as not to be seen by the enemy, and form close to the bulwarks, until the order is given to—

"BOARD THE ENEMY!"

338. The Boarders should then gain the enemy's deck as quickly as possible, keeping near enough to each other for mutual support, and to act in concert against the opposing force, using every possible exertion to clear the enemy's decks by disabling or driving the men below.

In case the intention of boarding should be discovered by the enemy, and he collects his men to repel the attack, the marines and small-arm men should take positions where they can best fire upon the men thus collected; and, if possible, the spar-deck guns loaded with grape, and howitzers loaded with canister, should be used for the same purpose before the Boarders are ordered to make the attack.

So long as the contest is continued after boarding, the fire should be kept up against the enemy from all the guns with as much vigor as the number of men remaining at them will allow.

The guns should then be much depressed, in order that there may be little or no danger to our own men. Much positive injury may be inflicted on the enemy in this way, besides the advantages of dividing his attention at such an important moment.

If it should be necessary to repel Boarders from the enemy, the Boarders and Pikemen must be called, and at the order—

"PREPARE TO REPEL BOARDERS!"

(AT ANY SPECIFIED PART OF THE SHIP.)

339. The Pikemen should arrange themselves in rear of those armed with swords, and in situations which will allow them to rest the points of their pikes on the hammocks or rail, and cover that part of the ship and the parts where the assault is expected. The marines, with their muskets loaded and bayonets fixed, may be formed behind the Pikemen, or at any other place from which their fire on an assailing enemy may be most effective and least dangerous to our own men.

340. The moment an enemy commences his assault, the order—

"REPEL BOARDERS!"

Should be given, and every effort made to prevent his gaining or retaining any foothold in the ship.

It will, of course, be important to bring grape and musketry to bear at once upon the enemy's men when they are assembled for boarding, if they should be discovered in time.

The men left at the guns must be watchful that the enemy does not gain an entrance through ports or quarter-galleries.

341. In case the enemy should effect a landing on the decks, the pikes may, from their length and the press of the contending parties, become less efficient than the swords. Whenever this occurs, the sword must be brought into full use, as the most efficient weapon for attack or defence at such close quarters.

342. The howitzers, mounted on the field-carriage and charged with canister, should be ready for use in case of the enemy's getting a footing on the spar-deck.

343. Unless induced by circumstances to attempt to board the enemy first, the most favorable opportunity for attack will present itself when his men have been driven back; and to guard against the contingency of being repulsed, in all cases where the Boarders are called to attack the enemy they are to be covered by the marines and all the available small-arm men on deck.

344. The men, and especially the Boarders and Pikemen, must be exercised and encouraged to practise with the single stick and sword, as far as circumstances will allow.

GENERAL PRECAUTIONS

TO BE OBSERVED IN TIME OF WAR.

345. In time of war, unless otherwise ordered by the Admiral commanding, every cruiser should at nightfall carefully extinguish all lights not absolutely necessary, and shade all those that are indispensable, that they may not be visible from out-board.

346. The watch on deck shall be mustered at their quarters, and the guns so far cast loose as the state of the weather will permit.

347. The officer of the watch shall, on taking the deck, ascertain that the means of making and answering signals and a competent signal-man are always at hand. It is his duty to make himself fully acquainted with all the day and night signals.

348. Before making night-signals, every light should be extinguished or covered.

349. Particular care is required, when it is expedient to conceal the lights of the ship, to look well to the cabin and wardroom lights. Ports and air-scuttles there, are more apt to be imperfectly masked or thrown open heedlessly by servants.

350. If in company with other vessels, two guns in each broadside must always be ready for making signals of immediate or urgent necessity.

351. No vessel cruising shall allow a strange or suspected vessel to come within gunshot, without the watch being at quarters and ready to open fire.

352. It is the duty of the officer of the watch to immediately inform the Commander of all suspicious movements which he may observe, or which may be reported to him, and of all unknown vessels or boats that may appear in sight.

353. Speed being one of the principal elements of military force, Steamers will, on going into action, have all the fires lighted and in condition to make steam.

The beat to quarters for action is therefore a signal to start fires in all the furnaces not in operation.

354. If at anchor singly or in squadron in our own waters, in those of an ally, or elsewhere within our right to exercise control, and where liable to an attack by an enemy in any form, no strange or suspicious vessel must be permitted to be underway between evening gun-fire and daylight. The nearest vessel must require her to anchor, and send an armed boat to ascertain her character.

355. If the Senior Officer opens fire on any vessel, the nearest vessel in a position to do so will also be prepared to fire to bring her to, if signalled. All boats to be hailed and ordered alongside to give the countersign, or to lay off on their oars to be visited by the guard-boat.

356. If at anchor in or about an enemy's waters, steam shall be kept up at night at all times, sufficient to move the vessel at half speed at least, and the engines moved certainly every hour, or oftener if necessary, to keep them in a condition for immediate service. In vessels with single engine, liable to be caught on the centres, means for turning it off to be kept at hand, and suitable persons stationed to attend to it.

357. The cable must be kept ready in every respect for slipping, with a stopper forward of the bits, and even unshackled, if the weather will permit, with a steady man stationed to slip or cut as may be requisite.

358. Some of the guns, and those such as may be brought most conveniently to bear upon the probable quarter of attack, must be loaded with grape and some with canister, and ample supplies for reloading be kept on deck. Appliances for extreme depression should be at hand for broadside-guns; a gun here and there depressed extremely. The Howitzers, on field-carriages, in place, and loaded with canister. Pikes distributed about the decks ready for use.

359. Small vessels lying in rivers or sounds, and liable to be attacked and carried by boarding, will have their boarding-nettings of wire rope secured at evening quarters; the guns cast loose; the watch completely armed and on the alert, and every preparation made for instantly slipping and getting under way and repelling boarders.

360. At the hail by the look-out of "Boat ahoy," without further orders or the striking of the bell, the engine should be started *immediately*, the slip-rope cut, and all boats are to be received while under way and the crew at quarters.

361. It is important that the arms of the watch below should be as accessible as possible, that no confusion may take place in case of being summoned suddenly. The engineer and watch in the fire and engine room must always be armed.

362. On dark, foggy, or hazy nights, no lights should be shown, nor the bell struck or watch piped to indicate the position of the vessel.

The look-outs, increased and cautioned to greater vigilance, relieved at least hourly, and visited by either the Commander or Executive Officer half hourly.

363. The safety of small vessels at night requires that they shall be always either underway, or else in readiness to be got so at the shortest warning.

364. If circumstances prevent this, the greater the necessity for increased precaution and vigilance, and therefore a picket or advice boat should be kept out in the direction from which attack may be expected; and, indeed, the resort of picket-boats should be observed whenever practicable and at all likely to be of service.

365. In case of sending away a boat that is to return before sunrise—which is always to be avoided, if possible—a concerted signal, such as a certain number of flashes of a light, preceded or followed by the firing of a certain number of muskets, must be made at the distance from the vessel of about one-half mile, the number to be agreed upon for each night as the boat leaves the vessel. A countersign is also to be given; but if not understood by the look-out, he is to call out "Enemy," at the same time warning the boat to keep off, at which the vessel will be got underway at once.

366. The boat must be furnished with suitable and reliable fireworks or other means for announcing instantly the approach of an enemy, and no excuse can be taken for a failure on the part of the picket to give the alarm. The capture of the picket-boat is a minor consideration.

367. When confident of being able to repel any force, the boat should return to give timely notice for preparation; and in this case it may be expedient to be prepared to light up the adjacent waters, to enable an effective fire to be opened on the enemy from guns and howitzers.

368. Commanding Officers of vessels situated as described in Art. 359, are required to practise their crews, by going on deck and hailing, "Boat ahoy," at least once a week.

The time taken for the execution of this order to be noted on the log.

369. In times of anticipated attack from rams or mail-clad vessels upon a fleet or single ship, it is recommended to load the guns with maximum charges and solid shot; but where there is doubt of the character of the assailant, the guns should only be loaded with the service powder charge, having ready at hand shot, shell, shrapnell, grape, or canister, as the case may demand.

DIRECTIONS IN CASE OF FIRE.

370. In the following directions, no other object is proposed than to notice some of the more prominent and common preparations which may be generally made, and the measures to be adopted in vessels on the alarm of fire. The variety of circumstances under which that danger may be presented can only be successfully met by properly stationed, well-trained and disciplined men, judiciously directed by the Captain, and superintended by officers whose coolness and presence of mind are proof against every form and degree of danger, which alone will enable them to adopt and execute the best plans the emergency may require.

To this end the Captain will, as soon as the crew is organized, cause a Fire-bill to be prepared, adapted to the particular arrangements of his ship, and in accordance with these Directions, by which the crew is to be drilled once a week till expert, and after that occasionally. This fire-bill should, as far as possible, conform to the arrangement for extinguishing fire during exercise at General Quarters. Much confusion has been known to arise from requiring different duties from the same person at Fire Quarters, and in case of fire when at General Quarters.

371. Should the alarm of fire be given when the men are not at Quarters, that alarm of itself is to be considered as a call to Quarters, and the men must repair to their stations at once. This must be impressed upon the men by the Division Officers. But the ordinary call for inspection is to be given as soon as practicable, by way of enforcing the order.

The alarm will be given by the sentinel near the bell, by ringing quickly and loudly successive peals for ten or fifteen seconds, with short intervals between.

The bell is to cease, however, as soon as the drum begins to sound the call to Quarters.

Should it be deemed necessary to water and provision the boats, preparatory to lowering them, the drum will beat the usual call for provisions, when the men stationed for these purposes will promptly proceed with their duties. In this case the shot shall be drawn or discharged from the guns, to guard against accidents in leaving the vessel, should it be impossible to save her.

372. The Captain will direct the Executive Officer, and such others as he may deem proper, to visit the place of the fire, and to transmit reports to him, by officers, of its character and extent, and to suggest the measures which will most speedily and certainly subdue it, or prevent its extension.

373. He will, if at sea, cause the ship to be hove-to, or steered in such direction as will be least likely to increase the activity of the fire, or will best enable the men to use the means in their power for controlling and extinguishing it.

374. If fire should take place in a ship at anchor in port or harbor, his attention must be given to prevent the communication of the fire to other vessels or combustible objects, and to have the cables ready for slipping, boats ready, and, if advisable, springs prepared to change the position of the ship, in order to prevent danger to other vessels.

375. He will decide whether the magazines and shell-rooms shall be flooded, and give orders accordingly; whether the hammocks shall be brought up and stowed; where sentinels shall be placed, and what disposition shall be made of the sick and prisoners.

If hammocks are to be brought up, each man not a Fireman, Pump-man, Hoseman, Axeman, or Smotherer, or belonging to the Carpenter's gang, or detailed as a Sentinel over boats' falls or spirit-room, will lash and carry up two hammocks and stow them in the nettings on his way to Quarters. Blankets, or other woollen materials, when wet, afford an excellent means of smothering fire, and should be left out by the party lashing up the hammocks and collected by the Smothering party, in charge of an officer, whose duty it will be to see them properly used.

376. The Officers of the respective divisions will enforce the strictest observance of orders from those under their command, and allow no one to leave his station, unless by express orders or permission. At the same time they will direct the most trustworthy of their men to perform any particular duty within their divisions which may tend to check the spreading of the fire, or furnish the means of extinguishing it.

377. Officers of gun-deck divisions will be prompt to detach, under proper officers, men who may be directed for any particular service, or who may be called from the guns by the calls for Firemen, Sail-Trimmers, or Boarders. Should the call for Boarders be made in case of fire, the men will answer it without any other arms than their swords or battle-axes. Divisional Officers near the main or other pumps, will cause the men of their divisions to aid in rigging and working them. The ship's buckets are to be passed up to the pumps, as soon as possible, by the persons who may be stationed near them, and these and the fire-buckets and division-tubs filled. The swabs are also to be got up and thoroughly wetted.

Division-boxes, and all powder or explosive materials not in the magazines, must be taken in charge by the Quarter-Gunners and placed in the safest positions, ready to be thrown overboard if ordered.

378. The Officer commanding the Powder division will himself deliver the keys of the magazines, shell-rooms, and water-cocks to the Gunner, his Mate, and the men stationed at the water-cocks, and see that they are prepared to flood the magazines, if orders should be given to that effect; but he must take especial care that the magazines, passages, and shell-rooms are kept closed until orders to open them are received from the Captain.

379. He will also take care that the air-ports are immediately closed, and all other means adopted for diminishing currents of air, especially if there should be a hope of confining the fire to the lower parts of the vessel.

He will at once have the hose led from the bilge-cock, the cock turned, and, if the forcing-pump or engine is worked below the gun-deck, will see it manned and worked by some of the men of his division.

380. The Master will cause windsails to be taken down; and, if set, courses, spanker, and all lower sails hauled close up; head, channel, and all other pumps which work on upper deck, and fire-engine, if on deck, to be rigged and worked by the men of his division stationed nearest to each of them. If practicable, sails, rigging, boats, spars, and the sides of ship must be kept wet, and every exertion made to furnish a full supply of water for extinguishing the fire. Rigging-axes and battle-axes must be ready for use, in case they should be wanted for any purpose.

381. The Chief Engineer will detail such Assistant Engineers and men as may be needed to take charge of steam-pumps, to lead out hose, and to use such other means of extinguishing the fire as may be ordered or deemed advisable. If under steam, the main engine will be slowed on the first alarm of fire, unless otherwise expressly ordered, and the steam-pumps started.

382. The Surgeon and his assistants will be in readiness to destroy, if required, all inflammable fluids, or other medical stores which would increase the fire; and to superintend the removal, if necessary, of patients who may be lame or confined to hammocks or cots.

383. Exercises, by order of the Captain, following false alarms of fire, known only to him and the Executive Officer to be false at the time of giving the alarm, may, it is believed, be resorted to with advantage, especially at night.

Such alarms furnish the best means of ascertaining practically whether the necessary preparations for extinguishing fire have been duly attended to; and what degree of silence, calmness, and promptitude may be expected from officers and men in repairing to their stations, as well as in the performance of their duties in a real case of fire.

False alarms, frequently repeated, may perhaps lead some of the men to move slowly, under the impression that every alarm given is false, and merely intended for exercise; and this impression may be entertained even when a fire has actually taken place. This evil would, however, be comparatively small, since it will be readily admitted by any one who has witnessed the effect of a fire upon a crew at sea, that the great difficulty in such cases is to obtain that necessary quiet and orderly attendance at Quarters which is essential to the success of all subsequent measures.

CHAPTER V.

RIFLED CANNON.

384. THE rifled cannon at present in service are—

PARROTT.

DENOMINATION.	WEIGHT.	CHARGE.	WEIGHT OF SHELL.	WEIGHT OF SHOT
	lbs.			
6.4-inch, or 100-pounder..	9,700	8 lbs. rifle.	80 lbs.	70 lbs.
5.3-inch, or 60-pounder ..	5,400	6 lbs. rifle.	50 lbs.	60 lbs.
4.2-inch, or 30-pounder ..	3,550	3¼ lbs. cannon.	29 lbs.	30 lbs.
3.67-inch, or 20-pounder..	1,750	2 lbs. cannon.	18 lbs.	20 lbs.

DAHLGREN.

DENOMINATION.	WEIGHT.	CHARGE.	WEIGHT OF SHELL.	CHARGE.
	lbs.			
4-inch, or 20-pounder, bronze howitzer..	1,340	2 lbs. cannon.	18 lbs.	0.86 lb.
3.4-inch, or 12-pounder, bronze howitzer.	880	1 lb. cannon.	11 lbs.	0.50 lb.

385. CHARGES FOR PARROTT'S SHELL.

		8-INCH.	100-PDR.	60-PDR.	30-PDR.	20-PDR.
		lbs. oz.	lbs. oz.	lbs. oz.	lbs. oz.	lb. oz.
Long..................	....	–	–	3.4	1.8	1.
Short	....	–	3.11	2.2	–	–

386. SHELL AND SHOT GAUGES.

		100-PDR.	60-PDR.	30-PDR.	20-PDR.
Greatest	....	6.36	5.27	4.17	3.64
True diameter	....	6.35	5.26	4.15	3.63
Least	....	6.33	5.24	4.14	3.61

387. In the rifle-guns of Mr. Parrott, provisionally adopted, it is intended to retain the full charge of powder which a smooth-bore gun of the same calibre would have with a round shot. The projectile for the rifled gun is to be usually ten times the weight of this charge.[1]

388. To obtain greater initial velocity, projectiles of less than the full weight have been provided—solid shot of 70 pounds for the 100-pounder, with the front end "chilled." Such projectiles, though not suited for long ranges, will be effective at 1,000 yards or less, and are well calculated to act against oblique surfaces of iron.

389. The powder for the 100-pounder and 60-pounder should be of Rifle (or, as formerly called, No. 7):—for the smaller calibres, 30-pounder and 20-pounder, of Navy cannon powder. The cartridge-bags are the same as those prescribed for similar calibres of smooth-bore guns.

390. The Parrott guns have been arranged for the use of a certain kind of projectile, supplied by the inventor. These have reference not only to the calibre and mode of rifling, but to the design of the gun itself. For these reasons, the inventor objects to the use of any other than his own form of projectile in the guns of his invention. This request has been acceded to in the heavier calibres. The shells of Schenkl and Hotchkiss have also been used, however, in the smaller calibres.

It is not considered expedient to describe these projectiles, and it is therefore directed that the Commander, Executive Officer, and Gunner shall make themselves thoroughly acquainted with their construction, and the percussion and time fuzes issued with them, before sailing. The Ordnance Officer will furnish them with any information on these subjects in his possession.

391. The projectiles consist of shells, shrapnel, and solid shot. All rifled projectiles used in the Navy are of the expanding class; that is, forced into the grooves by the action of the charge of powder, and require no other precautions in loading than common spherical shells.

392. It is, however, essential—

1st. That the base of every rifle-projectile, especially the Parrott, shall be thickly greased before entering it into the gun.[2] For this purpose common pork slush, prepared by several washings in hot fresh water, may be used.

2d. That the bores of all guns shall be frequently washed, the grooves

---

1 Owing to the recent accidents which have taken place with these guns, the 150-pounder has been withdrawn from service, and the charge of the 100-pounder provisionally reduced to eight (8) lbs. of Rifle powder, and the short shell of eighty (80) lbs. only is to be used.

2 The Schenkl, Hotchkiss, and some other projectiles, have a small quantity of grease attached.

of rifled guns cleaned of all residuum and dirt, and a moist sponge invariably used. After firing, the bore should be oiled with a sponge.

The attention of Commanding Officers is especially called to this requirement; and the Bureau desires that the action of Parrott's and other rifle-projectiles fired under the above conditions, may be carefully observed and reported; for it is believed that nearly all the failures of projectiles in actual service result from the grooves being filled, after a few rounds, with a hardened residuum of powder.

393. It is also necessary that the shell shall be close home on the powder, otherwise the necessary expansion will not take place, and the shell will tumble immediately after leaving the gun, utterly destroying its range and accuracy.

394. In order to be certain that the projectile is properly home, the rammer-handle must be marked to indicate it.

395. It is very important that dirt, sand, or other foreign substances should not be carried into the gun on the sponge or the projectile, or by the wind in batteries on shore.

In using guns on shore, a canvas muzzle-bag, a soft wad, or a light stopper of wood, suggest themselves as means of security during the interval between loading and firing the gun. The cover or stopper might be removed, or left to be blown away at each discharge.

The longer the interval above alluded to, and the higher the elevation at which the gun is kept, the more important and necessary are these precautions.

396. Much care is taken to give the projectiles uniformity of size; and if the powder is of suitable quality, those now supplied will almost invariably take the grooves. Should difficulty in this respect, however, be experienced, it may be remedied by separating the brass ring from the iron at three or four points of the circumference. This should be done with a cold chisel, very slightly, and so as not to interfere with the loading. It is only necessary to sever the contact of the two metals.

397. As the projectile slides in the gun with very little friction, particularly when greased, the gun should therefore be elevated and eased out when firing to leeward, that the shot may not be started from its seat. An experiment to test this, showed that running a 100-pounder out with the force of its crew against the forward hurter, the gun being level, started the shot forward nearly two feet.

Placing a grommet or other wad over elongated projectiles is positively prohibited.

398. The 100-pounder and 60-pounder guns being, respectively, of the calibres of the 32-pounder and 18-pounder spherical shot, and fired with the same charges, these shot may be fired from them with excellent effect, particularly on ricochet. The round shot should be sewed up in canvas or felt, strapped to a sabot, or snaked between two grommet-wads.

399. Both percussion and time fuzes are supplied for these rifle-guns. When the object to be fired at presents a sufficient resistance, such as masses of timber or earth, ships, or solidly-built houses, the percussion-fuzes alone should be used from rifled cannon. They will, however, frequently fail to explode the shell at long ranges, owing to the shell not striking on its apex; or, if fired into loose earth, which checks its momentum too slowly to make the plunger strike with sufficient force.

400. It has been observed that time-fuzes burn with greater rapidity in shell thrown from rifled cannon. Being in front, they are subjected to greater pressure from the air. A similar effect is produced when the fuze is confined under a water-cap, as in the naval time-fuze.

401. The fuze-holes of the heavy shells are cast larger than the diameter of the regular fuze-stocks of the navy, which can, however, be used with the aid of a bouching or an adapting ring, always sent with the shells.

This bouching has heretofore been made of cast zinc. Others with a flange and washer and the thread cut are now supplied, and the use of the old rings is prohibited.

402. If it be desired to explode the shell in front of or in the midst of a body of troops, or after having penetrated some resisting obstacle, the time-fuze should be used. This is the only fuze to be used with shrapnel.

403. The Vent is made in a bouching of pure copper screwed into the gun. In the largest calibres the interior orifice is lined with platinum.

The upper portion of the copper in naval guns is replaced by steel, to obtain a harder surface for receiving the blow of the hammer. The steel is three-fourths ($\frac{3}{4}$) of an inch thick.

A new vent can be readily put in, after getting out the old one, without injury to the screw-thread. This can be done by boring out the bouching with a drill, which leaves a thin shell containing the thread. Into the hole thus made insert a square mandrel about four inches, driving it lightly; by wrenching it, a portion of the shell of the bouching can be detached and removed by unscrewing. This may be repeated, and the whole of the old copper removed. The screw-thread is then to be cleaned out, and the new vent-plug screwed in.

404. Sights.—These consist of a fixed sight upon the right rimbase, and a brass movable sight placed in a socket which is screwed into the rear of the reinforce at the breech of the gun. The movable sight is furnished with a sliding eye-piece, and is graduated up to 10°. The eye-piece is also capable of lateral adjustment to allow for the drift as far as 10°, and for the effect of the wind. It is desirable that the sights should be placed on both sides of the breech; otherwise, in firing from a port at extreme train, there is a considerable loss of lateral aim. Furthermore, with the sight on the right rimbase, it is not convenient for the 2d Captain to attend the screw without interfering with the aim.

405. These guns are all rifled to the right, by which it is understood that the upper surface of the projectile is made to turn from left to right, the observer looking from the breech towards the muzzle of the gun.

406. Drift.—This is a deviation caused by the direction of the rifling, is always to the right when uninfluenced by the wind, and is to be allowed for.

407. The drift is in practice confounded with the deviation produced by the direction and force of the wind, which may either annul or increase it, according to whether it blows from right or left across the line of fire. At long range it is also necessary to consider the motion of the vessel across the line of fire. Suppose this to be at the rate of six knots, and the gun is elevated 15°, the time of flight would be by the Tables, 18 sec., while the deviation arising from this cause would be upwards of 60 yards. It is therefore of great importance that the Captain of the gun shall be carefully instructed in making this adjustment of the eye-piece.

408. Elevating Screw.—To obtain readily the changes of elevation necessary in the use of rifled cannon, the heavier calibres are made with very small preponderance, and are supplied with an elevating screw which is attached to the carriage at the lower end, while the nut is connected with the cascabel of the gun. Both screw and nut admit of movements by which the screw can take any position required in the various degrees of elevation. The parts should be allowed a certain amount of play; if binding is prevented, it is believed that the evident advantages of the screw may always be obtained.

409. Ranges and Time of Flight.—So far as ascertained, are contained in Table VII., Appendix B.

410. Precautions to be Observed.—In the use of these rifled cannon, it is of the utmost importance that all the directions relative to the lubrication of the shell, its being close home, charge and kind of powder used, and lining of the shells, shall be carefully observed.

Many premature explosions of shells having taken place in these guns, which are attributed to various causes, such as,—defects of metal, porosity, faulty fuzes, concussion and friction of the powder within the shell,—it is ordered that, on the occurrence of a premature explosion or rupture of a shell within the gun, it shall be immediately washed out and a careful examination made of the interior of the bore, by the mirror and by taking impressions in wax (*see* Mode of Taking Impressions, p. 16, Part III.), and all the circumstances of the case reported to the Bureau, specifying the kind and calibre of the shells, kind of fuzes, the charge and kind of powder, with its manufacturer's name: and,

Were the shells filled completely, and with what kind of powder?

Were the shells coated inside with any kind of composition?

Are any cracks or marks of scoring visible in the bores?

In rifled cannon, cracks or injuries produced by firing, or the rupture of shells, are to be sought for—thus,

1. Around and in rear of the vent-bouching.
2. On the top of the bore, between the trunnions and reinforce-band.
3. On the lower side of the bore, near the seat of the shot, at the junction of the lands and grooves.
4. Near the inside of the muzzle, caused by explosion of shells.

Although shells have been frequently ruptured in the guns without leaving any visible traces of injury, yet they may be developed after a certain number of rounds. Thus, in proving a gun at West Point, a shell exploded in the gun at the second fire: on examination, no traces of injury could be perceived; but, on a re-examination of the gun after the tenth fire, a fine transverse crack was discovered in the rear of the vent, extending two-thirds round the bore. It is therefore important that frequent examinations shall be made, even if no apparent injuries exist, as it is the opinion of the inventor of the guns that the principal, if not the only cause of failure of these guns in service, is due to the rupture of shells within the bore.

Experiments have been made, and are still in progress, which appear to show that these premature explosions may be to a great extent obviated, if not altogether prevented, by lining or coating the rough surface of the interior of the shell with a smooth and elastic coating.

All rifle-shells, except those for howitzers, before being issued for service, shall therefore be lined or coated on the interior with a mixture composed of—

16 ounces of soap—common yellow, not salt-water soap.

7 ounces of tallow.

7 ounces of rosin.

The tallow should be melted first, then melt and add the rosin, and lastly, the soap, bringing the mass to a heat that will make it *very* fluid.

The shells having been first thoroughly cleaned, fill them about one-third full of the composition, roll them slowly so as to spread the mixture over the whole interior surface, and then pour off the residue. This coating should be about five-hundredths (0.05) of an inch in thickness, and is expected, from a series of experiments made for the purpose, to prevent the premature explosion of shells in the bores of rifled guns.

The Bureau further directs that hereafter the charge of the 100-pounder, or 6.4 inch, Parrott rifle, shall be reduced to eight (8) pounds of rifle, or No. 7 powder, and that only the short shell or solid shot, not exceeding eighty (80) pounds weight, and spherical projectiles, prepared as directed in the Circulars of February 24th and July 6th, 1864, be used in this gun.

411. Exterior Dimensions of Boxes containing Parrott's Projectiles.

	Long.	Wide.	High.
	Inches.	Inches.	Inches.
100-pounder, short................ 1..	18¾	8¾	8¾
60-pounder, ...	....	....	....
30-pounder, containing ....10..	25¼	11	15¾
20-pounder, containing ....10..	25¼	10½	13

412. Hotchkiss's Projectile for 20-Pounder and 12-Pounder Howitzer.

	Long.	Wide.	High.
20-pounder, containing........... 5..	24	12	6½
12-pounder, containing...........10..	20	9	9

413. Schenkl's Projectile for 20-Pounder and 12-Pounder Howitzer.

	Long.	Wide.	High.
20-pounder, containing........... 5..	24	14	7
12-pounder, containing ....10..	22¼	9½	11½

414. J. A. D. Projectile for 20-Pounder and 12-Pounder Howitzer.

	Long.	Wide.	High.
20-pounder, containing........... 3..	15	12¼	7
12-pounder, containing...... .... 5..	19	10¼	6

CHAPTER VI.

MONITORS.

The diagram represents the interior arrangement of the turret of the Monitors for the long and short XV-inch guns.

415. NOMENCLATURE.

A. Ammunition-scuttle.
B. Starting-bar for revolving turret and training gun.
C. Shaft on which turret revolves.
D. Travelling-bar on which moves the shell-whip.
E. Position of Engineer stationed at bar to revolve turret and train guns.
F. Compressor-wheel to check recoil, hove taut before firing.
G. Crank for running gun in and out.
H. Smoke-box of XV-inch (*Passaic* class).
O. Officer at sight-hole.
P. Port-hole.
R. Port-stopper.
S. Sight-hole.

416. In the *Passaic* class the ports for the XV-in. gun are only of sufficient dimensions to allow the passage of the shot at such elevations and depressions as were judged necessary: the gun being fired entirely within the turret. In order to protect the crew of the gun from the blast of the explosion, the smoke-box was devised, which to a certain extent accomplished the desired object, but at the expense of rapidity of loading.

417. In designing the *Tecumseh* class it was decided to enlarge the port, so as to allow the face of the muzzle to run out flush with the exterior of the turret. The gun was therefore lengthened sixteen (16) inches, and the muzzle turned down to the minimum size.

418. The contracted space within the turret rendered it necessary to introduce additional mechanical aids in lieu of manual labor in running out, loading, and checking the recoil.

MONITOR TURRET.

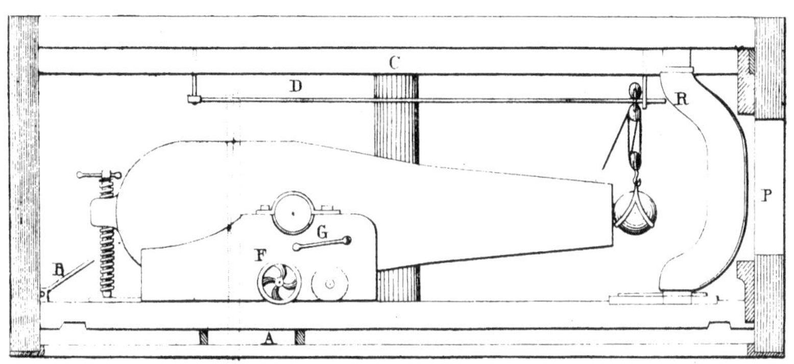

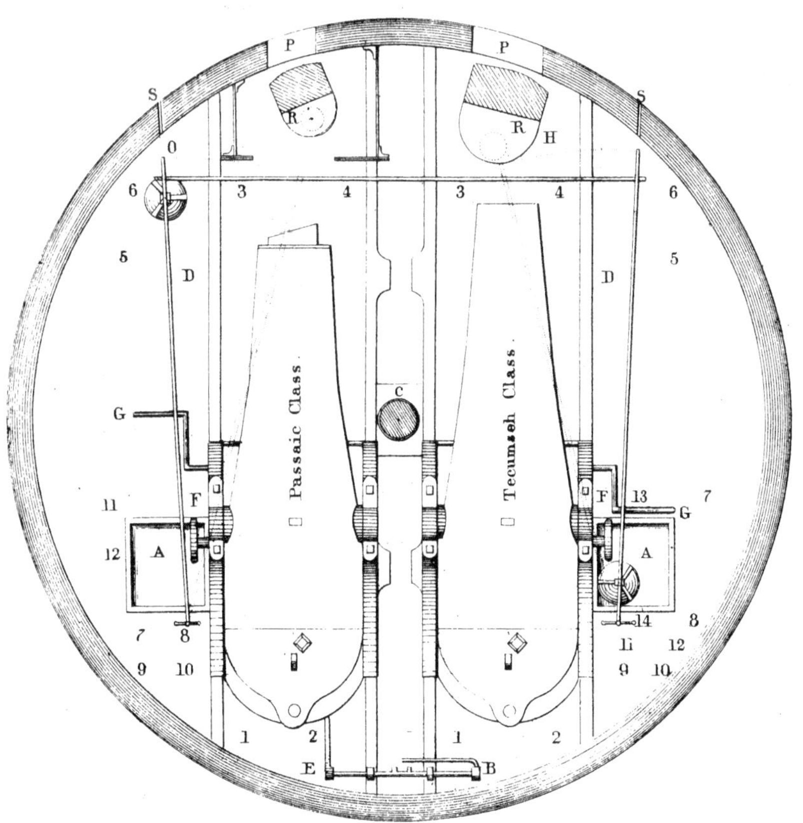

419. The exercise therefore conforms to the established exercise for great guns only as far as circumstances will admit.

The gun is supposed to be run in, and not loaded.

420. WORDS OF COMMAND.

I. "PROVIDE THE GUNS!"
II. "SERVE VENT AND SPONGE!"
III. "LOAD!"
IV. "PRIME!"
V. "ELEVATE!" (OR DEPRESS).
VI. "RUN OUT!"
VII. "TRAIN!"
VIII. "READY—FIRE!"
IX. "RUN IN!"
X. "SECURE!"

MANUAL EXERCISE.

(RIGHT GUN.)

II. "SERVE VENT AND SPONGE!"

421. Gun Captain serves, then stops the Vent. No. 3 passes to left of muzzle. No. 4 receives the moist Sponge-head from 6, and, assisted by 3, enters it in the Bore and forces it down as far as the first section. No. 6 passes the successive sections of the staff to 4 as needed, and receives them from him as the sponge is withdrawn.

After the sponge is withdrawn, Captain serves the Vent with his priming-wire, and again closes it.

III. "LOAD!"

422. No. 4 receives Cartridge from 5, to whom the box has been passed by 13, assisted by 3, enters it in the Bore; receives Rammer-head and successive sections from 6, and, assisted by 3, rams home. Nos. 3 and 4 fall back from the muzzle. Gun Captain serves the Vent to feel if the Charge is home.

Nos. 3 and 4 return the rammer.

Nos. 7 and 8, 11 and 12 whip up Shot (or shell), as has been previously ordered. Nos. 11 and 12 choke luff of whip. Nos. 7 and 8 run shot (or shell) to the muzzle. No. 5, assisted, if necessary, by No. 6, bears over, when 3 and 4 enter and ram home by sections.

No. 4 removes Patches and passes them to 7, who hands them to Gun Captain.

IV. "PRIME!"

423. Gun Captain again makes sure that the Vent is clear. No. 2 primes with priming-powder from a flask or a blank musket-cartridge.

V. "ELEVATE!" (OR DEPRESS).

(Always done before running out.)

424. No. 2 handles lever of Elevating screw under the direction of the Officer of the piece, who sets the trunnion-sight at the proper degree of elevation and clamps it there. When the bubble of the trunnion-level is in the centre,—"Well."

Nos. 3 and 4 lift the muzzle by a section of the rammer-handle; the preponderance not being sufficient to overcome the friction of the trunnions in the cap-squares. No. 3 passes to the right of the muzzle.

VI. "RUN OUT!"

425. Nos. 7, 8, 11, and 12 man Truck-crank to run out. Nos. 9 and 10 ease compressor. Nos. 3, 4, 5, and 6 man port-tackle: as muzzle approaches port-stopper, "Open Port!"

As soon as the gun is out, Nos. 11 and 12 unship truck-crank and place it clear of gun-slide. No. 9 to Compressor-wheel, which he heaves hand taut. No 10 ships ratchet-levers and heaves well taut.[1] Gun Captain inserts percussion-primer.

VII. "TRAIN RIGHT!" (OR LEFT).

426. The officer of the gun sights through sight-hole, and orders "Right!" or "Left!" as the muzzle is to go. The Engineer at the starting-bar revolves the turret.

No. 1 to lock-string; when the object comes in view, Officer of piece gives order.

VIII. "READY—FIRE!"

427. Gun Captain pulls lock-string. No. 3 lets go port-tackle. No. 5 closes port. Engineer revolves the turret so as to point the gun abeam. (This gets the scuttle clear for passing up ammunition.)

If necessary,

Nos. 11 and 12 ship crank, and, with 7 and 8, run the gun in; Nos. 9

[1] The compressor-shaft should be marked as a guide to No. 1 to know when compressed sufficiently.

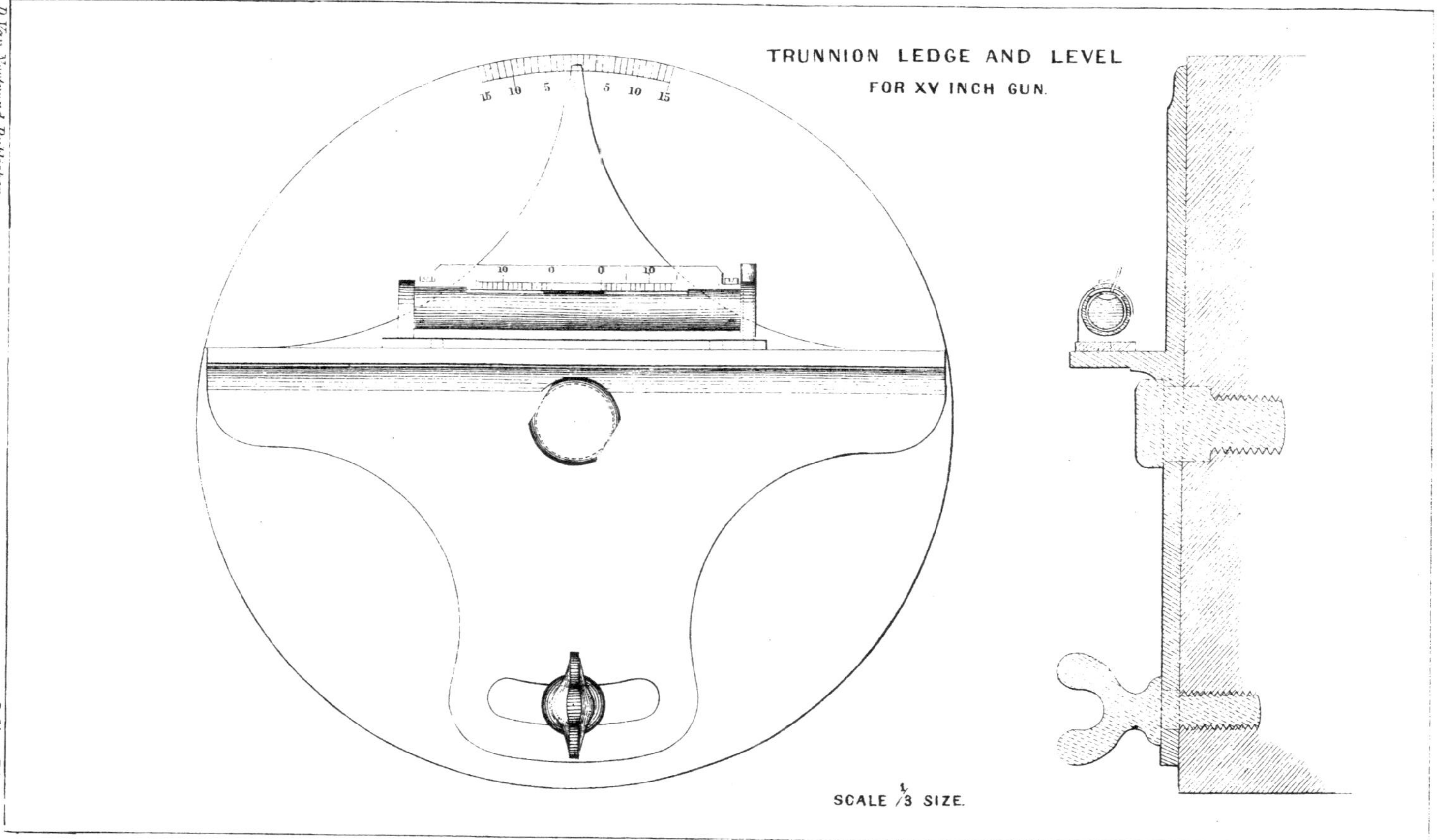

D Van Nostrand, Publisher.

Julius Bien, pr.

and 10 easing compressor. No. 10 ships ratchet-lever to ease compressor, No. 9 easing it further by hand. The gun is now ready for loading, and the exercise proceeds as before.

428. The exercise of the left gun is in all respects the same, except that Nos. 3 and 4 exchange duties.

429. The crew of the XV-in. gun consists ordinarily of 14 men, but the gun may be readily worked by 8 men; indeed, some officers prefer the smaller number as being equally efficient, giving more room in the turret, and affording the very great advantage of relief crews during a protracted engagement. The same remarks apply to the XI-in. gun.

Working XV-in. by Half-Crew.

"SERVE VENT AND SPONGE!"

430. No. 1 stops vent. 3 passes to left of muzzle. 5 passes sponge-head and sections as required to 3, and assists in sponging.

"LOAD!"

431. No. 13 receives passing-box at scuttle and holds it to 5. 5 receives cartridge from 13, enters it in muzzle, passes rammer-head and sections, and, assisted by 3, rams home. Gun Captain serves the vent, 3 and 5 falling back.

Nos. 9, 11, 13, and 15 whip up shell and attend it to muzzle.

Nos. 5 and 3 steady shell and enter it in muzzle.

No. 5 removes patch, passes it to 7, who hands it to 1.

Nos. 5 and 3 ram home by sections as before.

"ELEVATE!"

432. Nos. 3 and 5 raise muzzle by section of rammer.

No. 1 tends elevating screw.

"PRIME!"

433. No. 1 serves vent and primes with powder.

"RUN OUT!"

434. Nos. 7, 11, and 15 man crank.

No. 9 eases compressor.

Nos. 3, 5, and 13 open port.

When out,

No. 1, Gun Captain, inserts percussion-primer.

No. 11 unships crank.

No. 9 heaves compressor hand taut.

No. 15 ships lever and heaves well taut.

The gun is trained as before.

"FIRE!"

435. Nos. 3 and 5 close port.

Nos. 7, 11, and 15 man crank, and 9 eases compressor. The above is given for the 1st part of gun's crew; for 2d part substitute next high numbers in each station.

SHELL AND POWDER DIVISION.

436. To the Shell and Powder Division is assigned the most laborious and difficult of all the duties—that of keeping up a supply of projectiles.

437. It is therefore necessary to have it strongly manned, and a system of frequent reliefs for all the important stations, particularly in the magazine and shell-locker.

438. There are required three gangs of four each for the passage of projectiles: one to whip them out of the hold, or shell-room; a second to pass them to the door of the turret-chamber; and a third to pass them to the scuttle and adjust them in the bearer. When working with half-crews, the third gang assists at the shell-whip, the fall being dropped down to them.

439. The XV-in. passing-box requires two men to carry it to the turret-chamber.

440. The allowance of projectiles can only be determined by the character of the service expected, and the stowage capacity of the vessel, which is limited to about 150 rounds per gun for sea-service.

441. By reason of the contracted space in these vessels, all shell should be filled, and all powder must be made up into cartridges.

442. All XV-in. shell shall be fitted with three fuze-holes, and issued for service fuzed with 3½, 5, and 7 seconds fuzes.

443. When the distance of the object is known to be less than the range of the shortest fuze, and time will admit of doing so, uncap all the fuzes. At other times uncap the fuze suited to the distance, and the one of longest time of burning.

NOMENCLATURE OF 13 INCH MORTAR, CARRIAGE AND CIRCLE.

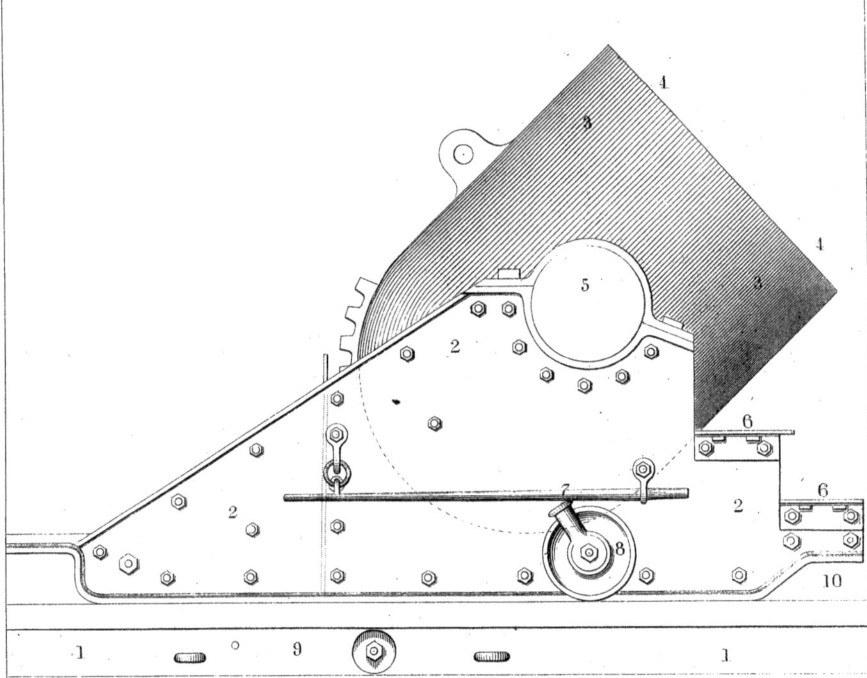

1, 1.	Circle	6.6.	Steps of Carriage
2.2.2.	Bracket	7.	Carriage excentric Socket
3.3.	Mortar	8.	Wheel
4.4.	Face	9.	Circle excentric Bar
5.	Trunnion	10.	Hurter

D. Van Nostrand, Publisher. *Julius Bien, pr*

CHAPTER VII.

MORTARS.

444. TITLES OF MORTAR CREW.

(See Diagram 1.)

No. 1. First Captain.
" 2. Second Captain.
" 3. First Loader and Trainer.
" 4. " Sponger and Trainer.
" 5. Second Loader, Front Eccentric Trainer.
" 6. " Sponger, " " "
" 7. Left Circle Eccentric Trainer and Shell-carrier.
" 8. Right " " " "
" 9. Left Circle Eccentric Trainer and Shell-hoister.
" 10. Right " " " "
" 11. Rear Circle Eccentric Trainer and Shell-hoister.
" 12. " " " "
" 13. Powder-man.

During exercise or action, Nos. 9, 10, 11, and 12, in addition to their other duties, will hoist up shell from below.

445. IMPLEMENTS AND EQUIPMENTS.

Articles.	Where they are placed.
Handspikes	Two on each side of the bed against the cheeks, leaning upon the manœuvring-bolts, the ends towards the vessel's sides, and those of the front handspikes even with the front of the cheeks.
Haversack	Containing fuzes, and a pair of sleeves, attached to the tompion.
Tube-pouch	Containing the priming-wire, friction-tubes, and lanyard, attached to the tompion, and lying on the mortar.
Gunner's Pouch	Containing gunner's level, gimlet, vent-punch and chalk, attached to tompion.
Quadrant Plummet Scraper Wiper Shell-hooks	In a basket between the cheeks of the mortar-bed.
Tompion	In the muzzle.
Quoin	Under the mortar upon the bolster, with handle to the left.
Maul Wrench Pincers Broom	With the basket.

Directly over each mortar must be rigged a gun-tackle purchase-whip, with seven-inch block, to whip up and lower the bomb into the mortar.

One empty bomb and one empty cartridge-bag must be ready for drill.

SILENCE

(Diagram 1.)

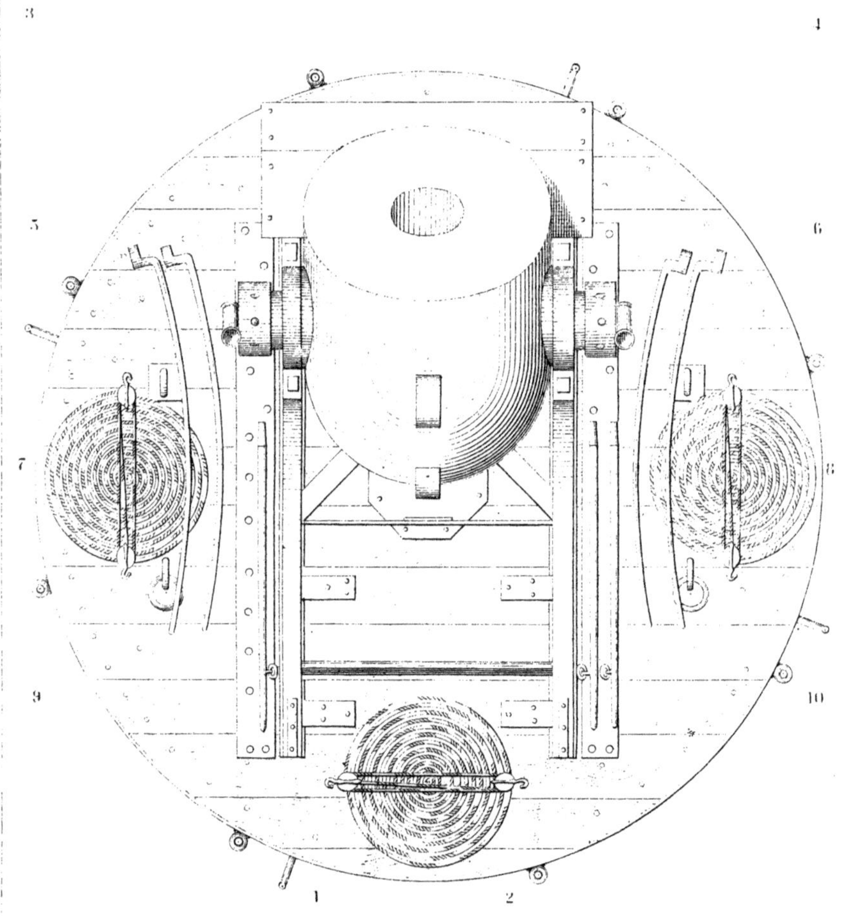

D. Van Nostrand, Publisher

Julius Bien, ph

MANUAL EXERCISE.

XIII-IN. MORTAR.

446. **WORDS OF COMMAND.**

I. "SILENCE!"
II. "CAST LOOSE AND PROVIDE!"
III. "TRAIN!" (RIGHT OR LEFT).
IV. "SERVE VENT AND SPONGE!"
V. "LOAD!"
VI. "ELEVATE!"
VII. "PRIME!"
VIII. "READY—FIRE!"
IX. "MORTAR FRONT!"
X. "SECURE!"

The exercise commences with the supposition that the **Mortar** is secured fore and aft, but not loaded.

I. "SILENCE!"

(Diagram 1.)

447. At this preparatory order the strictest silence is to be observed.

The Captain faces the breech, the men on the right and left stand facing the mortar; all fix their eyes on the Captain, and attentively wait for orders.

II. "CAST LOOSE AND PROVIDE!"

(Diagram 2.)

448. 1st Captain commands; sees his mortar cleared and cast loose; canvas covers taken off; Eccentric Bars in their place; Train-Tackles over-hauled and placed fore and aft on deck; Shell-whip hooked into mast-head span; small shell-hooks moused on lower block of shell-whip; Shell-tongs ready for use; Grommet for resting shell on deck at hand; basket of implements on deck to the rear of mortar; Tompion taken out and placed to the rear; sees that there is a Gunner's Quadrant and plumb-line in the basket; a boring-bit between beckets; a breeching and tackle, if it should be wanted; buckles on his waist-belt, furnished with a primer-box; equips himself with a priming-wire and lanyard; places elevating lever on the right side of mortar ready for use.

2d Captain gets basket of implements and spirit-level from the Gunner; places basket on deck to the rear of the mortar; screws spirit-level to trunnion, and adjusts it to an angle of 45° with the axis of the bore.

No. 3, First Loader, removes mortar-cover; takes out tompion and places it to the rear of mortar-circle, out of the way; provides grommet for resting shell on deck; gets scrapers and spatulas out of basket.

No. 4, First Sponger, assists in removing mortar-cover; gets his sleeves out of basket and puts them on; provides an empty cartridge-bag for wiping shell.

Nos. 5 and 6, Second Loader and Second Sponger, hook shell-whip into mast-head span, and bring it perpendicular over the bore; mouse small shell-hooks on to lower block; get breechings and tackles ready for hooking; ship front eccentric bars.

Nos. 7 and 8, Shell-carriers, get shell-tongs for carrying shell; assist in shipping eccentric bars on their respective sides of circle.

Nos. 9 and 11 overhaul left train-tackle to its full length, and place it on deck fore and aft, near the ship's side; ship left circle eccentric bar, and place lever for carriage-eccentric on the circle, butt to the front, and close to the side of carriage.

Nos. 10 and 12 execute the same duties on the right side of the mortar.

Nos. 11 and 12 also ship rear eccentrics.

Nos. 9, 10, 11, 12, hook tackles for hoisting shell from below.

No. 13, Powder-man, repairs to the proper scuttle for his passing-box, returns, and stands a little to the left and in rear of the circle.

III. "TRAIN!" (RIGHT OR LEFT).

(Diagram 3.)

449. Nos. 5, 6, 7, 8, 9, 10, 11, and 12, throw circle eccentric into gear, and pin eccentric bars down. Nos. 5 and 6 then hook double blocks of train-tackles into circle on their respective sides. All the crew, except Nos. 1 and 2, will bowse on train-tackles, until the mortar is in the desired direction, when the order "Well!" will be given by No. 2, who attends spirit-level and trunnion-sight.

At the command "Well!" Nos. 5 and 6, 11 and 12 will unhook their respective blocks and lay the train-tackle fore and aft on deck, near the ship's side; Nos. 5 and 6, 7 and 9, 8 and 10, 11 and 12, throw the circle eccentrics out of gear.

IV. "SERVE VENT AND SPONGE!"

450. 1st Captain inserts his priming-wire and clears the vent. No. 3 scrapes the chamber and bore, removes scrapings with the spoon. No. 4 takes the empty cartridge-bag and wipes out the mortar, then uses the sponge to thoroughly cleanse the chamber and bore; as soon as this operation is

TRAIN.

[Diagram. 2.]

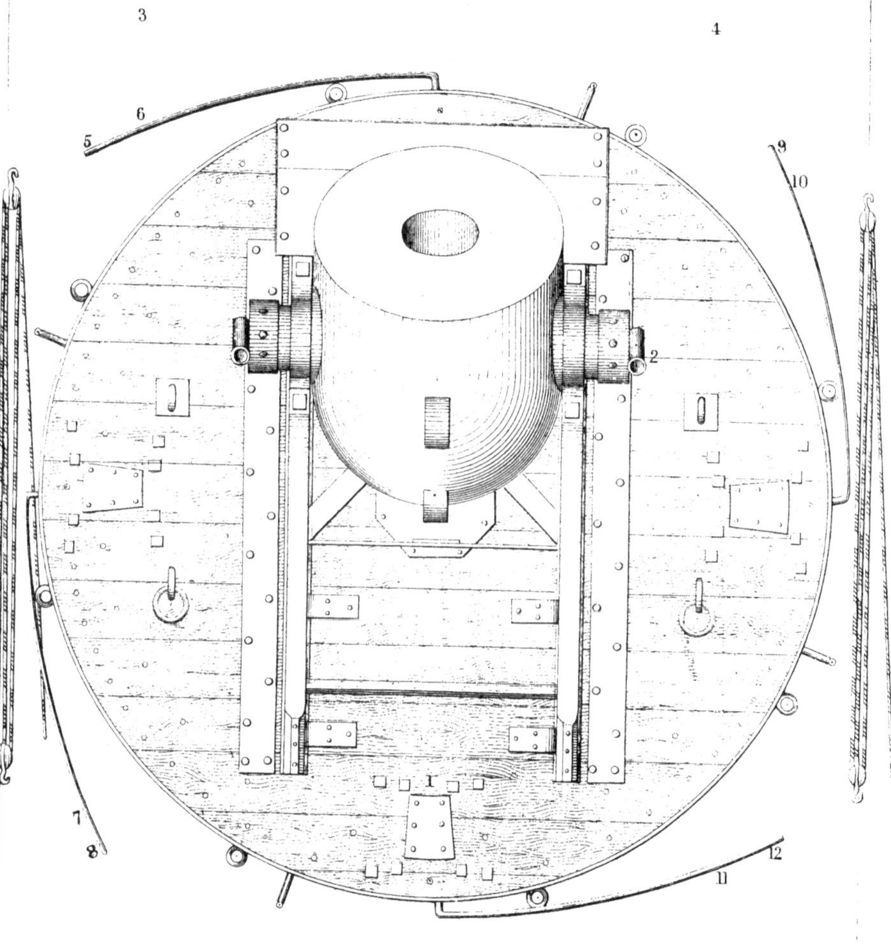

D. Van Nostrand, Publisher.

Julius Bien, p.

RIGHT OR LEFT

[Diagram. 3.]

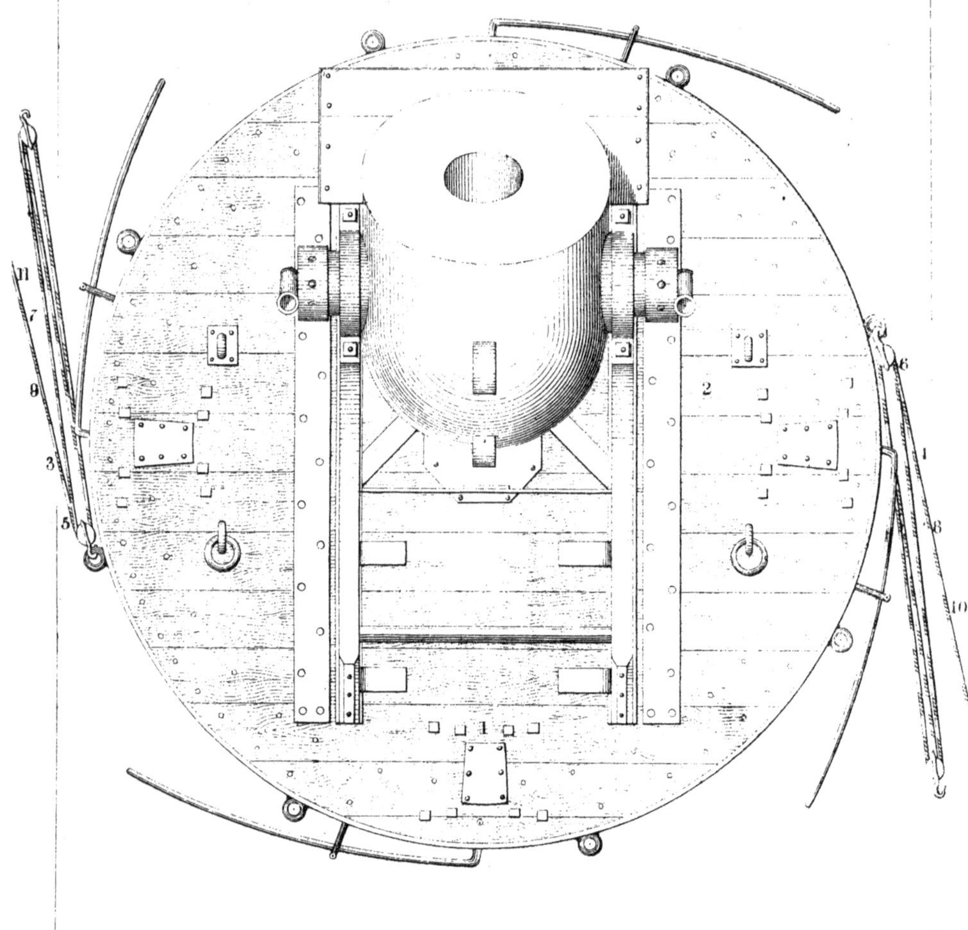

D. Van Nostrand, Publisher.

Julius Bien. pr

performed, the Captain again serves the vent. Should there be any fire or dirt pushed down, the sponging will be repeated.

V. "LOAD!"

451. The Powder-man, No. 13, goes to the scuttle for a cartridge, and brings it to No. 3 (always passing on the side not engaged), who empties it carefully into the chamber, keeping the cartridge-bag in his hand, to be used in wiping the shell before it is lowered into the bore. No. 4 takes spatulas, levels off the powder, and calls out "Shell!" which is brought to the front of the mortar by Nos. 7 and 8, Shell-carriers, and landed in the grommet, which has been put in its proper place by No. 5. Nos. 5 and 6 hook shell on and whip it up; when high enough, No. 3 calls out, "High!" wipes it clean with empty cartridge-bag, and, assisted by No. 4, steadies it over the bore; it is then lowered carefully upon the charge, keeping the fuze exactly in the axis of the bore. No. 4 then removes the paper covering and exposes the priming of the fuze, handing the covering to No. 2, as an evidence that it has been removed. After an exercise or an action, these paper coverings will be compared with the account kept by the Officer having charge of the Powder Division. Nos. 3 and 4 now step down on deck, ready to assist in training, should any be required.

VI. "ELEVATE!"

452. The 2d Captain, having adjusted the trunnion-sight[1] to a given angle with the axis of the bore (usually 45°), orders "Raise" or "Lower;" and at the same time the 1st Captain inserts the elevating lever through elevating loop, on to ratchet, and raises or lowers according to direction from 2d Captain, who will give the word "Well!" when the mortar has its proper elevation.

VII. "PRIME!"

453. 1st Captain inserts his priming-wire to ascertain that the vent is clear; takes a friction-primer, raises the loop nearly in line with the spur, hooks it on his lanyard and inserts the primer into the vent, being careful that the lanyard has been led through the loop at the rear of mortar-carriage for that purpose; then retires to the rear of mortar to the full length of the lanyard, and gives the word.

Officer in charge takes station to watch the effect of the bomb, which shall be recorded in a suitably ruled note-book.

[1] If the Spirit-Level should be damaged, he will apply the Gunner's Quadrant to the face of the mortar.

VIII. "READY—FIRE!"

454. At the word 'Fire!" the Captain pulls the lanyard with a quick draw: there should be a pause of about two seconds between the words "Ready" and "Fire," in order to allow every one time to retire to the rear.[1]

IX. "MORTAR—FRONT!"

455. Nos. 1 and 5, on the left side, Nos. 2 and 6, on the right side, step on the circle; take carriage eccentric levers and throw eccentrics into gear; withdraw the lever from the sockets, and insert them into holes in the wheel, and heave the mortar-carriage up against the front hurter; throw eccentric out of gear; place levers on the circle close to Brackets, butts forward, and retire to their stations.

X. "SECURE!"

(Diagram 1.)

456. Train fore and aft, face of mortar forward, throw circle out of gear; 1st Captain stops vent; 2d Captain unscrews spirit-level. Nos. 3 and 4 put in tompion, put on mortar-cover, put scrapers, spoons, sleeves, and empty cartridge-bags into basket. Nos. 5 and 6 unhook shell-whip and coil it up on the lower step of carriage; put small shell-hooks into basket; put grommet between brackets of carriage; coil up breeching-tackle, and put it on the lower step of carriage; secure the mast-head span to the rigging; unship front circle eccentric. Nos. 7 and 9 coil left train-tackle on the circle, left side of carriage, unship left circle eccentric bar. Nos. 8 and 10 coil right train-tackle on the circle, right side of carriage, unship right circle eccentric bar. Nos. 11 and 12 coil shell-tackle on the circle in rear of carriage; unship rear circle eccentric bar. Eccentric bars to be placed on the circle in the following manner: left and front bars, on left side of brackets; right and rear bars on the right side of brackets. Nos. 7 and 8 put shell-tongs on circle to the rear of carriage. 1st Captain puts his lanyard and priming-wire into the basket, which, together with the spirit-level, is carried to the Gunner by 2d Captain; the crew then resume their stations as at "SILENCE."

[1] To lessen the shock of the discharge and the concussion on the ear, the crew should be instructed to stand on their toes at the moment of firing, keeping at the same time their mouths and ears open.

MAGAZINE AND SHELL-ROOM.

457. Vessels specially constructed for mortar purposes have regularly-built shell-rooms, while others, fitted for temporary service, have merely spaces set apart, which should be protected by screens fitting tightly to the beams and deck, with tubs of water always at hand during practice, and likewise wet swabs laid to cut off trains of powder.

458. Before the vessels leave port, every thing must be arranged in the magazines for the rapid and safe transmission of ammunition to the mortars, and any deficiencies should be promptly reported to the Officer commanding the division, and by him to the Officer in charge of ordnance.

459. The Officer in command of each vessel is to be present at the embarkation of the ordnance, to stow and check the lists.

460. All the implements accompanying the mortars are to be kept in lockers used solely for that purpose, and under the charge of the Gunner or his mate.

461. The full service-charges for the mortars will be sent on board ready filled in white cotton bags, and their transmission from the magazines will be in leather passing-boxes.

462. The powder is to be emptied into the mortar, the bag well shaken and beaten over the lee-side to remove dust and fine grains of powder, and the bag placed in the rear to wipe out the mortar-chamber after every round.

None of these bags should be returned to the magazine during the action, as the loose powder would be likely to form trains.

463. Large tubs of water are to be kept near the magazines, with buckets at hand to drown the cartridges, or to extinguish fire; and every precaution taken to cut off trains of powder with wet swabs.

464. The forward part of the vessel above decks will be used as the most convenient place for cutting or preparing fuzes, and a heavy screen, spread tent-fashion, should be rigged to protect the fuzes from fire from the mortars, or rain.

In filling shells, the Gunner and two assistants will be detailed for this purpose, besides the men stationed to pass powder from the magazines.

All fire and lights must be put out when the magazine is opened for action.

465. In firing against the wind, the flame is thrown back in-board; therefore care should be taken beforehand to wet the sides, decks, and rigging of the vessel; the sails covered with tarpaulins; and men stationed with buckets to put out fire.

466. One hundred bombs are at all times to be kept ready filled in the shell-room.

A vessel properly organized ought to throw at least 20 bombs an hour.; but should circumstances prevent, the mortar may be properly served if even one bomb can be filled before the previous one is fired.

467. A beech plug must be temporarily put in the fuze-hole of the bomb when filled; and the men who fill cartridges and charge the bombs are to wear flannel sleeves and magazine-shoes.

468. When ranges are desired to be obtained by reduced charges, the measuring and filling of the cartridges must always be done in the magazine, no matter how inconvenient it may be; and the utmost exactness is to be observed in filling the powder-measures and levelling off the top, as an ounce of powder makes an important variation in the range of the bomb.

469. Extra cotton bags are to be provided to receive the reduced charges, which are to be stowed in half barrels.

470. Every precaution that suggests itself to the officers in command to prevent accidents, should immediately be put in force, and a memorandum of the matter transmitted to the Ordnance Officer of the squadron.

GENERAL RULES AND OBSERVATIONS.

471. To estimate the distance by the bursting of a bomb, where the flash can be seen, multiply the number of seconds which elapse between it and the sound of the report by 1,100, and the product will be nearly the distance in feet.

472. The officer in charge of a mortar must always note the time of flight and distance, by the above rule, for every bomb that is fired, and likewise note when the report is not heard from the bursting charge.

473. When going into action for a bombardment, the fore-rigging must be come up on the side where the mortar is to be used, the fore-topmast sent down, foresail unbent, boom and gaff laid on deck, rigging lashed in close to the mast, head-sails to be thoroughly wetted, spring on the cable, boats lowered from the side davits, and all the hatches covered with tarpaulins.

474. The broadside-guns must be kept ready for action, and muskets loaded and at hand, in case the squadron should be attacked by the enemy's gunboats.

475. Besides bombs, various other projectiles are fired from mortars, such as carcasses, which are shells having three holes of similar dimensions to the fuze-hole, pierced at equal distances apart in the upper hemisphere, with their exterior openings touching the great circle which is perpendicular to the axis of the bore.

476. These carcasses are placed in the mortar in the same manner as the bomb, and are filled with inflammable mixtures, and should be transported in a vessel by themselves, as they are dangerous companions. Thirteen-inch carcasses weigh 194 pounds each.

477. Bombs are sometimes fired with a port fire stuck into the fuze-hole, which is an almost certain mode of igniting many kinds of buildings.

478. Mortars can also be fired with a bag of one-pound balls, or ordinary grape-shot, with very reduced charges, and a wad between the powder and the balls. One pound of powder will project a 200-lb. bomb 302 yards; the same weight of grape-shot thrown in among boats would prove destructive; and especially a lot of canister fired in this manner would cause great havoc.

479. It is not expected, however, that much execution could be done after the first discharge in a fleet of boats moving rapidly; but combined with the batteries of the Squadron, it is presumed that an enemy would be deterred from an attempt to capture a vessel by boarding.

TAKING THE DISTANCE.

480. An inexperienced officer will find difficulty in estimating distances by the eye alone, as it requires long practice and studied observation. The sextant, however, offers a surer method of approximately fixing a position by taking the angles between any three points, which are generally found to be accurately laid down on the Coast Survey charts; then plotting the angles with a horn protractor, or working them out by the three-point problem, which is given in all surveying books.

481. If the object to be assaulted is a large one, a practical man can, by the exercise of moderate judgment after two or three fires, throw the bombs near the work; but, at the same time, the sextant is the more certain means for determining the true distance, and the Officer in command should make himself acquainted with the simple manner of measuring horizontal angles.

482. If points are not visible in line, then measure a base on shore, angle on the object to be aimed at, and from the angles of the base-line, you can fix the position of the mortar-vessel.

483. When a vessel once gets her position accurately determined, and it becomes necessary after a bombardment to remove out of the line of battle, a small buoy with the vessel's name or number should be dropped under foot, so that the same position may, if necessary, be resumed.

LOADING MORTARS.

484. After the powder has been emptied through the funnel out of the cotton bag into the chamber, the bomb, loaded and fuzed, is to be carefully lowered into the bore by the hooks, and allowed to rest upon the charge.

485. The friction-tube is not put into the vent until the piece is about to be fired.

FUZES.

486. The wooden fuzes used at present for the 13-inch bombs are in sections, and marked according to the estimated distance in practice, viz.:

Seven inches extreme length; and each section one inch, giving a flight for every section of seven seconds, and a total of forty-nine seconds.

487. The plugs are of the proper size for the fuze-hole; the axis bored cylindrically from the large end down, to within a short distance of the small end, which is left solid; the orifice is filled with composition pressed hard and evenly as possible. At the large end a cup is hollowed out and filled with mealed powder moistened with alcohol.

488. The rate of burning is ascertained by experiment, and marked on a water-proof cap, which is tied over the cup.

489. A fuze-saw must be at hand during practice to cut the fuze the required length.

490. Fuzes for sea-coast mortars are also driven in a conical paper case, which is inserted in a metal or wooden plug previously driven in the fuze-hole and accurately reamed out.

491. The paper-case fuze is marked with the number of seconds it burns per inch, and it may be cut, where no danger from ignition can take place, with a sharp knife.

PROCESS OF FILLING BOMBS.

492. Having been inspected to see that they are clean and dry, place the bombs on a block made for the purpose, or on grommets of rope, or on the ground, with the eyes up. The charge, having been carefully measured, is then poured into the chamber through a funnel, while, at the same time, the fuze is cut to the proper length by resting it on a groove made in the block, and sawing it across. The fuze is then tried in the hole, and should enter $\frac{3}{4}$ths of its length; if it does not, it must be reduced by rasping.

493. The head of the fuze having been covered with tow to prevent breaking the composition, the fuze-setter is placed on it, and the fuze driven with the mallet until the head is about $\frac{2}{10}$ths of an inch above the surface of the bomb.

POINTING MORTARS.

494. First give the elevation by applying the quadrant to the face of the piece, and adjusting the quoin or ratchet until the required number of degrees is obtained.

495. In pointing mortars on shore, it is an easy matter to get the direction, because the mortar is stationary; but on shipboard, owing to the motion, it is attended with difficulty, especially when the vessel is rolling and the line of fire can only be approximate.

496. On shore, the plan of giving the direction is to determine practically two fixed points, which shall be in a line with the piece and the object, and sufficiently near to be readily distinguished by the eye. These points being covered by a plummet, is the vertical plane including the line of metal, which becomes the plane of fire.

497. In mortar-vessels other expedients are resorted to, such as trunnion-sights, or a white line painted on the mortar-bed parallel to the axis of the bore when level; but the first plan is preferable.

498. The circles on which the mortars stand being fitted with eccentrics, are made to revolve so as to point the mortar at the object without the trouble of swinging the vessel or moving the mortar round with hand-spikes.

499. Before firing, care must be taken that the eccentrics are thrown out of gear, and the circle flat upon the platform on which it revolves.

TABLES OF CHARGES, ELEVATIONS, AND RANGES FOR 13-INCH MORTARS.

500. CHARGES FOR 13-INCH MORTAR-BOMBS.

CHARGE.	13-INCH.	
	lbs.	oz.
Of shell filled	11	0
To burst shell	6	0
To blow out fuze	0	6
Ordinary service-charge	7	0
Incendiary, match, or other composition	0	8

501. RANGES WITH SEA-COAST 13-INCH MORTARS, 20° ELEVATION.

CHARGE.	MEAN TIME OF FLIGHT.	LEAST RANGE.	GREATEST RANGE.	MEAN RANGE.
Lbs.	Seconds.	Yards.	Yards.	Yards.
4	8.	840	877	869
6	9.5	1209	1317	1263
8	11.66	1653	1840	1744
10	12.50	2010	2128	2066
12	14.25	2369	2688	2528
14	15.25	2664	2780	2722

502. Ranges with 13-Inch Mortars, at 45° Elevation.

Weight of Shell, 200 lbs.

Charge.		Flight.	Fuze.		Range.
Lbs.	oz.	Seconds.	Inches.	10ths.	Yards.
7		21.4	4	$2\frac{2}{3}$	2190
7	8	22.4	4	4	2346
8		23.2	4	6	2480
8	8	23.8	4	$7\frac{1}{2}$	2600
9		24.4	4	$8\frac{3}{4}$	2734
9	8	24.9	4	$9\frac{3}{4}$	2853
10		25.4	5	1	2958
10	8	25.9	5	$1\frac{3}{4}$	3026
11		26.3	5	$2\frac{1}{2}$	3150
11	8	26.7	5	$3\frac{1}{2}$	3246
12		27.0	5	4	3327
12	8	27.4	5	$4\frac{3}{4}$	3404
13		27.7	5	$5\frac{1}{2}$	3470
13	8	28.0	5	6	3552
14		28.3	5	$6\frac{1}{2}$	3617
14	8	28.5	5	7	3681
15		29.0	5	8	3739
15	8	29.1	5	$8\frac{1}{4}$	3797
16		29.2	5	$8\frac{1}{2}$	3849
16	8	29.4	5	$8\frac{3}{4}$	3901
17		29.6	5	9	3949
17	8	29.8	5	$9\frac{1}{2}$	3997
18		29.8	5	$9\frac{3}{4}$	4040
18	8	30.0	6		4085
19		30.2	6	$0\frac{1}{4}$	4123
19	8	30.3	6	$0\frac{1}{2}$	4160
20		30.5	6	1	4200

503. TABLE OF ALLOWANCES.

Subjoined is a list of articles which are indispensable for the service required, and must be kept in readiness at or near every mortar, in some secure position:

Article	Quantity
Tube-boxes	4
Straps for boxes	4
Quill-tubes	400
Friction-tubes	600
Fuze-composition for priming	12 lbs.
Powder-bags	250
Port-fires	100
Port fire-sticks	4
Rasps, half round	4
Cotton wick	4 lbs.
Hand-hatchets	2
Sheep-skins	6
Diagonal scale	1
Compasses	2
Copper funnel, 13 in	1
Wood mallets	2
Fuze-extractor	1
Iron pincers	2
Augurs	2
Cutting-knives	2
Scissors	2
Thread	1 lb.
Brass quadrants	1
Sponges with staves, 13 in	2
Handspikes	6
Claw-hammers	1
Lead plummets	3
Tallow	20 lbs.
Shell-hooks, 13 in	2
Shell-hooks, with thimbles	2
Cotton quick-match	6
Punches for mortar-vents	2
Corkscrews	2
Blocks for driving fuzes	2
Drifts of iron tapped with copper	4
Copper ladles for fuzes	2

Leather buckets	3
Elm plugs	60
Brass pickers	2

SPARE ARTICLES.

Cap-squares	
Eye-pins	
Keys for pintles, large	2
Keys for pintles, small	2
Washers	2
Bolts, traversing	4
Bolts, dog	4

CHAPTER VIII.

MISCELLANEOUS OPERATIONS.

GETTING IN GUNS ON COVERED DECKS.

504. AFTER bracing the yard over the port through which it is intended to take the guns, secure the lizard round the yard five or six feet outside of the ship, and hook the top burtons just outside of the lizard.

Haul taut, and bring an equal strain on the burtons and lifts. Hook a rolling-tackle on the opposite side of the yard, bowse it well taut, and the trusses also, if they be of rope. Pass the end of the pendant of the gun-purchase through the thimble of the lizard; take the end up and make it fast round the top-mast, just above the lower cap. Have the port lined with pine boards, to keep it from being chafed.

Bore a hole in the deck or decks through which it is intended to pass the garnet, as nearly as possible over the rear end of the gun-carriage, and as near in line with the centre of the port into which the guns are to come as the beams will allow. Pass the upper end of the garnet through the hole, and turn in the thimble, to which hook the pendant-tackle. Place a tackle across the deck ready for bowsing the gun into its carriage through the port.

Bring the gun under the yard and sling it as follows: place one bight of the slings under the neck of the cascabel, and pass the lashing which is attached to the slings round the chase, at such a distance from the trunnions as will allow them to go into the trunnion-holes without bringing too great a pressure of the slings against the upper port-sill. Then toggle or hook the gun-purchase to the outer bight of the slings, and sway away. When the breech of the gun is above the port-sill, hook the garnet and the thwart-ship-tackle to the cascabel, and bowse on both. When the slings bear hard on the upper port-sill, lower the gun-purchase, and bowse on the garnet until the breech is high enough for the trunnions to clear the cap-square bolts in the carriage; then bowse on the thwart-ship-tackle until the trunnions are over the trunnion-holes, lowering the purchase as required to bring the gun into its place.

As each gun is mounted unhook the purchase and garnet, take off the slings, run the carriage to its proper port, and place another for the next gun.

TAKING IN GUNS OVER ALL.

505. Sling the gun slightly breech-heavy, to render it more manageable. If it is to be mounted on the spar-deck, place the carriage in the gangway; if on the main-deck, close to the main hatchway on that deck. In place of the garnet, hook the stay-purchase for lowering the gun into its carriage.

GETTING OUT GUNS THROUGH PORTS.

506. Secure the yard as in getting in guns, and sling the gun in the same manner. Hook the garnet and haul it taut, so as to raise the breech of the gun as much as the port-sill will permit; hook or toggle the gun-purchase, and sway away. As soon as the trunnions are clear of the carriage haul it from under the gun, ease away the garnet, and let the gun go out the port. As soon as the gun is perpendicular to the purchase, unhook the garnet and lower the gun into the lighter, or on the wharf, as the case may be.

If the gun is to be taken out over all, the stay-tackle is to be substituted for the garnet, only it is to be hooked to the same end of the slings as the gun-purchase, and the lashing on the slings is to be passed around the chase of the gun, as near the trunnions as possible, without being in the way of the brackets.

MANNER OF USING THE GRIOLET PURCHASE FOR DISMOUNTING OR MOUNTING GUNS ON COVERED DECKS.

507. In practice, guns are rarely shifted from one carriage to another during action: it is only during a cessation of firing. While the action is going on, the crew of a disabled gun are more usefully employed in replacing the killed and wounded. Furthermore, spare carriages are not so numerous as to permit this operation to be performed frequently. Nevertheless, each gun's crew should be thoroughly exercised, in order to develop their strength and skill.

508. The gun is to be run in, in the direction required to bring the muzzle under the housing-bolt, and the breech under the hole bored in the deck to receive the screw-bolt of the upper block of the breech-purchase. This hole should be bored through the plank in the deck, as nearly abreast the middle of the port as the beams will allow, giving the block room to play clear of the beams and carlings.

With a gun's crew of twelve men the operation may be performed as follows:

At the word "Stand by to dismount!" the Quarter-Gunner of the division on the deck above that in which the gun is to be dismounted removes the screw-tap, and stands ready to place the washer, key and un-key the bolt of the breech-purchase block.

All the numbers, except 1, 2, 3, and 4, man the train-tackle.

No. 1 gives the word "Run in!"

While the gun is coming in, Nos. 1 and 2 remove breeching from jaws of cascabel, and 7 and 8 remove it from side-shackle. Nos. 1 and 2 throw its bight over the reinforce. No. 1 removes sight-bar and screws up the thumb-screw firmly.

When the gun is in position—Nos. 1 and 2 adjust upper and lower block of breech-purchase and secure the latter with the cascabel-pin. Nos. 3 and 4 chock fore-trucks, provide muzzle-purchase, and, assisted if necessary by 5 and 6, adjust its upper block. Nos. 5 and 6 unshackle breeching from ship's side, and shove toggle-block of muzzle-purchase into the bore and back it to the breech-purchase.

Nos. 7 and 8 un-key and throw back cap-squares and choke luffs of side-tackles, or, if rolling deeply, hitch them round the straps of the blocks.

Nos. 9 and 10 provide breech-purchase and assist 1 and 2 in adjusting it.

No. 11 chokes luff of train-tackle, or hitches it, if required; provides and hooks tackle of muzzle-purchase; belays and lowers.

No. 12 provides and hooks tackle of breech-purchase; belays and lowers.

These preparations made, all the numbers man the breech-tackle fall, or divide themselves to bowse upon both falls together, as the position of the gun in the battery may render either mode most convenient.

At the word "Dismount!" the gun is swayed out of the carriage.

Nos. 3 and 4 attend chocking-quoins, and 11 attends train-tackle, if required.

All the numbers, excepting 11 and 12, who attend purchase-falls, move up to their ordinary stations for serving the gun, unhook side-tackles, and remove the old carriage, under the direction of No. 1; and—

At the word "Mount!" the same men bring the new carriage into position for mounting.

At the word "Lower!" Nos. 11 and 12 lower the gun into its place; all the numbers then proceed, respectively, to reverse what they had done in dismounting.

Guns on covered decks may also be dismounted by means of a muzzle-lashing, the runner and the train-tackles, assisted by the handspikes.

The gun is run in and laid square under the housing-bolt, the bed and quoin removed, the muzzle elevated and secured as in the housing position; then, after un-keying and throwing back the cap-squares, the breech is bowsed up clear of the carriage by means of the train-tackle, hooked in the eye of a runner, the block of which hooks in an eye-bolt in the beam over the gun. If preferred, this mode of dismounting may be adopted by substituting the muzzle-lashing for the toggle-block of the griolet, and toggling the runner-block in the hole made in the deck for the breech-purchase of the griolet.

THROWING GUNS OVERBOARD.

509. The gun's crew being assembled at Quarters, remove the pin and chock from the cascabel, into the jaws of which place a selvagee strap; hook the double block of the train-tackle into the housing-bolt over the port, and its single block into the selvagee strap; remove the cap-squares, and place a round block of wood on the sill of the port, high enough to let the chase bear on it when slightly depressed; raise the breech as much as possible, without lifting the gun out of the carriage. When all is ready man the train-tackle well; have the handspikemen also ready to assist in raising the breech; and if the vessel is not rolling, it will be well to have additional handspikes under the rear of the carriage to lift it also, so as to give free egress to the gun. When all is ready, give the order: "All together—launch!" In a gale of wind advantage should be taken of a favorable roll to give the word, that the action of the sea and of the men at the guns may be simultaneous.

If the guns are to be thrown overboard for the purpose of lightening a ship which is aground, they must be buoyed, and care is to be taken that each buoy-rope is of a proper length and strong enough to weigh the gun. The best mode of securing the buoy-rope to the gun is to form a clinch or splice an eye in the end which goes over the cascabel, and take a half-hitch with the bight around the chase of the gun, and stop it with spun-yarn.

The buoy must be sufficient to float the rope when saturated; or, in deep water, a smaller line may be used for the buoy, and attached to the rope intended for weighing the gun, that it may be hauled up when wanted.

PART II.

EQUIPMENT AND MANŒUVRE

OF

BOATS.

EQUIPMENT AND MANŒUVRE

OF

BOATS.

EQUIPMENT OF BOATS.

WHEN DIRECTED TO BE MANNED AND ARMED FOR SERVICE.

1. BOATS must be provided according to the time of absence and nature of the service they are to perform, keeping in view the details prescribed in Table (Article 5).

The number and class of Boat-Howitzers are assigned by the Bureau of Ordnance.

2. When boats manned and armed are ordered, the Officers detailed to command them will see that they are thus furnished, and report when the boats are ready. They will also see that all articles are safely returned, or duly accounted for, when the boats return to the vessel.

If the boats are directed to assemble alongside of any particular vessel, the officers must report as they arrive there. If signalled alongside of the ship of the Commander of the Squadron for exercise or for inspection, they are to be inspected, if he shall so direct, by an Officer appointed by him, whose duty it shall be to report those which may be particularly well prepared, and those which he may find deficient in equipment or arrangement, specifying particulars.

3. Whenever the Howitzers are to be used in boats they must be fitted for the purpose as directed in "EXERCISE AND MANŒUVRE OF BOAT-HOWITZERS;" their crews being armed with swords and revolvers.

4. Boarding-parties are to be supplied with swords, revolvers, and rifles loading at the breech, with filled cartridge-boxes.

5.—TABLE OF BOAT EQUIPMENTS, ARMS, AND STORES FOR EXPEDITIONS.

Departments.	Names of Articles.	Line Ships and 1st Class Screw Frigates.			All other Frigates.			Razeed Frigates and 1st Class Screw Sloops.			All other Sloops and Brigs.		
		Launches.	1st and 2d Cutters.	3d and 4th Cutters.	Launches.	1st and 2d Cutters.	3d and 4th Cutters.	Launch.	1st Cutter.	2d and 3d Cutters.	Launch.	1st and 2d Cutters.	3d Cutter.
Gunner's.	Boat-Carriage, complete	1 ea.	1 ea.	–	1 ea.	1 to 1st	–	1	1	–	1		
	Field-Carriage, complete	–	1 "	–	1 "	–	–	1	–	–	1		
	Ammunition-Chests (various in size & contents)	Either one or all, as the nature of the service may require.											
	Ammunition-Pouches	One for each man of the field-howitzer's crew, except Nos. 1 & 3.											
	Match-Rope (lengths)	1 ea.	1 ea.	1 ea.	1 ea.	1 ea.	1 ea.	1	1	1 ea.	1	1 ea.	1
	Primers (tin-boxes)	2 "	2 "	–	2 "	2 to 1st	–	2	2	–	2		
	Spare Lock, complete	1 "	1 "	–	1 "	1 ea.	–	1	1	–	1		
	Haversack for Captain of Howitzer	One for each field-gun.											
	Swords	One for each man in the boat.											
	Breech-Loading Arms	One for each man of the boat's crew.											
	Minié-Rifles	When extra men in the boat, one for each.											
	Revolvers	One for each man of the boat's crew.											
	Cartridge-Boxes, filled	One for each rifle, breech-loading gun, and revolver.											
	Empty Powder-Tank, as a Magazine	1 ea.	1 ea.	1 ea.	1 ea.	1 ea.	1 ea.	1	1	1 ea.	1	1 ea.	1
	Boat Arm-Chest	1 "	1 "	1 "	1 "	1 "	1 "	1	1	1 "	1	1 "	1
Carpenter's.	Masts and Spars (set)	1 "	1 "	1 "	1 "	1 "	1 "	1	1	1 "	1	1 "	1
	Cranes for Spars and Spare Oars (set)	1 "	–	–	1 "	–	–	1	–	–	1	–	–
	Set of Oars	1 "	1 "	1 "	1 "	1 "	1 "	1	1	1 "	1	1 "	1
	Spare Oars for one Thwart (set)	1 "	1 "	1 "	1 "	1 "	1 "	1	1	1 "	1	1 "	1
	Boat-Hooks	3 "	3 "	3 "	3 "	3 "	3 "	3	3	3 "	3	3 "	3
	Tools and articles for repairing damages (set fixed)	1 "	1 "	1 "	1 "	1 "	1 "	1	1	1 "	1	1 "	1
	Bucket	1 "	1 "	1 "	1 "	1 "	1 "	1	1	1 "	1	1 "	1
	Tarpaulin	1 "	1 "	1 "	1 "	1 "	1 "	1	1	1 "	1	1 "	1

SAIL-MAKER'S.	Sails....................(set)	1 ea.	1 ea.	1 ea.	1 ea.	1 ea.	1 ea.	1	1	1 ea.	1	1 ea.	1
	Awning....................	1 "	1 "	1 "	1 "	1 "	1 "	1	1	1 "	1	1 "	1
	Tent-Awning (see drawing)....................	1 "	1 "	1 "	1 "	1 "	1 "	1	1	1 "	1	1 "	1
BOAT-SWAIN'S.	Thrum-Mats for muffling oars..........(sets)	1 "	1 "	1 "	1 "	1 "	1 "	1	1	1 "	1	1 "	1
	Hand-Grapnels....................	2 "	2 "	1 "	2 "	2 "	1 "	2	1	1 "	1	1 "	1
	Anchors....................	1 "	1 "	1 "	1 "	1 "	1 "	1	1	1 "	1	1 "	1
	Chain or Rope for Anchor..........(15 f'ms long)	1 "	1 "	1 "	1 "	1 "	1 "	1	1	1 "	1	1 "	1
	Marlinspike....................	1 "	1 "	1 "	1 "	1 "	1 "	1	1	1 "	1	1 "	1
	Spun-Yarn..........(balls of)	1 "	1 "	1 "	1 "	1 "	1 "	1	1	1 "	1	1 "	1
	Grease..........(lbs.)	1 "	1 "	1 "	1 "	1 "	1 "	1	1	1 "	1	1 "	1
	Fishing-Lines and Hooks....................	Three lines for the larger boats and two for the smaller, with 1 dozen assorted hooks per boat.											
MAS-TER'S.	Boat-Compasses....................	1 ea.	1 ea.	1 ea.	1 ea.	1 ea.	1 ea.	1	1	1 ea.	1	1 ea.	1
	Lead and Line....................	1 "	1 "	1 "	1 "	1 "	1 "	1	1	1 "	1	1 "	1
	Signals..........(sets)	One for the senior officer of the boats belonging to each ship.											
	Spy-Glasses....................	Do.		do.		do.			do.				
	Ensign....................	1 ea.	1 ea.	1 ea.	1 ea.	1 ea.	1 ea.	1	1	1 ea.	1	1 ea.	1
	Lantern....................	1 "	1 "	1 "	1 "	1 "	1 "	1	1	1 "	1	1 "	1
	Candles..........(lbs.)	1 "	1 "	1 "	1 "	1 "	1 "	1	1	1 "	1	1 "	1
	Tinder-Box, with Flint and Steel....................	1 "	1 "	1 "	1 "	1 "	1 "	1	1	1 "	1	1 "	1
YEO-MAN'S.	Boat-Stove and utensils for cooking..........(set)	1 "	–	–	1 "	–	–	1	–	–	1	–	–
MAS-TER'S.	Fuel..........(quantity)	As may be judged necessary.											
	Breakers of Water..........(number)	To be regulated, like the fuel, according to the nature of the expedition and ballast required.											
PAY-M'STER'S.	Provisions....................	Do.		do.			do.			do.		do.	
SUR-GEON'S.	Articles for treatment of sick and wounded..........	Do.		do.			do.			do.		do.	

DETAILS OF THE FOREGOING TABLE.

FIXTURES IN BOATS FOR BOAT-GUNS.

6. Two eye-bolts on each bow, to receive the hooks of the skid; two cross-pieces, of yellow pine, to bear the carriage, so as to carry the muzzle of the howitzer just above and clear of the gunwale and stem.

One piece of yellow pine scantling, placed lengthwise and amidship, mortised into the rear cross-piece to sustain the carriage in sweeping.

MOVABLE PIECES.

7. Six pivot plates and bolts—one at the stem, one at the stern, one at each bow, and one on each quarter; two light wooden tracks to lay along the thwarts for the wheels of field-carriages and the slide of boat-carriage; one midship wheel-track for the trail of field-carriage; two stout skids, each fitted at one end with two hooks, and connected at the shore end by an iron brace.

The chocks with rollers at the stem and stern posts of launches, are arranged to be removed when the gun is used.

8. *Implements for Shifting the Howitzer from Boat to Field-Carriage.*

One muzzle-block.

One selvagee strap.

One shifting-spar.

One short iron or wooden bolt, to keep the piece on the right sluc.

9. *Implements, complete, for Serving and Working the Howitzer.*

Breeching for boat-gun, if deemed necessary.

Lock with lock-string.

Elevating screw.

Sight.

Priming-wire.

Boring-bit.

Vent-cloth.

Sponge and rammer.

" " spare.

Spring-spike.

Rat-tail file.

Haversack, with strap, for Captain of howitzer, to contain a supply of primers, spare fuzes, spare lock, vent-bit, vent-cloth, and implements for spiking; leather ammunition-pouches for each of the men of the field-gun, except Nos. 1 and 3, to be supplied by the Quarter Gunner, with one round of ammunition each, and two primers, when the order to land is given.

Drag-rope, fitted with hooks and handles.
Trail handspike.
A rope, or chain, to lock the wheels in descending slopes.
Transporting-boxes.

10. AMMUNITION.

A chest containing shrapnel.
" " shell.
" " canister.

These chests are of two sizes; the single, holding nine, and double, eighteen rounds.

A key is becketed to each box for unscrewing the lid

Cutting-tool for opening the Bormann fuze, one in each box of shell and shrapnel.

FOR SMALL ARMS.

11. Cartridge-boxes and belts, furnished with cartridges and percussion-caps, screw-driver, cone-key, and wiper.

An empty powder-tank for magazine, to contain filled cartridge-boxes and spare cartridges.

SMALL ARMS.

12. Breech-loaders, in loops or brackets, under the gunwale of the boat, protected by a water-proof canvas covering, running round the rising of the boat.

Rifles.
Revolvers.
Swords.
Boat arm-chest.
A good tarpaulin to cover ammunition.

13. PROVISIONS.

Pork. To be cooked if there be time.
Bread, in water-proof bag.
Cheese, or canned meats.
Fresh water, in breakers; always to be used for ballast when ballast is required.
Fuel and kindling.

14. UTENSILS AND ARRANGEMENTS FOR COOKING.

Launch-stove and utensils.
Mess-kettle.

Tin pots and spoons.
Funnel.
Bucket.

15. TOOLS AND ARTICLES FOR REPAIRING DAMAGES.

Axe,	One for each boat.
Hatchet,	" "
Hammer,	" "
Hand-saw,	" "

Nails, 2 pds. for each launch; 1½ pds. for each large cutter; and 1 pd. or each of the rest.

Sheet-lead, 3 square feet for each launch; and 2 square feet for each cutter.

Tacks (number), 100 for each launch; 75 for each large cutter; and 50 for each of the rest.

Marlinspike.
Spun-yarn.
Grease.

16. MISCELLANEOUS ARTICLES.

Boat ensign.
Set of signals for boat of Senior Officer.
Boat-compass.
Spy-glass.
Lead and line.
Lantern.
Candles.
Tinder-box, with flint and steel.
Fishing-lines and hooks.

17. FOR TREATMENT OF SICK AND WOUNDED.

Tourniquets.
Bandages.
Lint.
Medicines.
Surgical instruments.

18. BOAT-GEAR.

Masts.
Spars.
Rigging.

A set of oars, fitted with trailing-lines long enough to allow them to trail alongside in the water.

Three boat-hooks.

Spare oars, with trailing-lines, for one thwart.

Cranes on the gunwale to hold spars and spare oars, raised sufficiently high above the gunwale (9 inches) to allow the oars to be got out or trailed. The spars thus arranged form a considerable protection against musketry.

Small thrum-mats for muffling oars when required.

Anchor.

Chain, or rope.

Hand-grapnels, fitted with a fathom of light chain, and five fathoms of line.

Sails.

Awning and stanchions.

Tent awning. (*See* Drawing.)

N. B.—In order to avoid delay and confusion when boats are called away for service, it is recommended that the articles required by the foregoing lists should be kept separately in the store-rooms, in convenient packages for stowage in the boats and protection against the weather. The contents of each package must be marked on it, together with the name of the boat for which it is intended. Particular attention should be paid by the Executive Officer of the vessel to the best and most compact stowage of all articles required for boat expeditions, which will, necessarily, vary according to the size of the boat and the nature of the service she is to perform. The occasions will be very rare when all of these articles are required at the same time.

FORM OF EXERCISE AND MANŒUVRE

FOR THE BOAT-HOWITZERS OF THE UNITED STATES NAVY.

NOMENCLATURE.

19. The Cascabel is the part of the gun in the rear of the base-ring; and is composed of—

The breech-plate.
The knob.
The neck.
Base-ring.
Cylinder.
Chase.
Loop, with hole for bolt.
Lock-lugs.
Mass-sight.
Mass for breech-sight.

The Bore includes all the part bored out, viz.:

Cylinder of bore.
Chamber.

These guns must not be polished bright.

BOAT-CARRIAGE COMPLETE, consists of—

Bed.
Slide.
Compressor-plate.
" bolts.
" handles.
Lugs for loop.

FIELD-CARRIAGE COMPLETE, consists of—

Axle.
Trail.
Braces.
Supports for transporting boxes.
Lugs for loop.
Trail-wheel or runner.
Bolt for do.
Socket for handspike.

HOWITZER AND BOAT CARRIAGE

D. Van Nostrand, Publisher. Julius Bien, pr.

HOWITZER ON FIELD CARRIAGE

D. Van Nostrand, Publisher.

Julius Bien. pr.

Elevator.
Disk of elevator.
Box for elevator.

EXERCISE OF THE BOAT-HOWITZER.

20. While preparations are in progress for clearing out the boats, the Officer of each boat will see that the howitzer, and its various equipments, are also in readiness. The Junior Officer or Officer of the piece will attend to the gun itself and its carriages.

The Quarter Gunner will get up the ammunition from below; also the lock, sights, sponges, spare fuzes, ammunition-pouches, and primers. Spare article box.

This will be the proper time for examining the shrapnel and shells, which must receive the particular attention of the Officer who is to command the boat.

The Captain of the gun will look after the traverses, tracks, and pivot-plates.

The Coxswain will have ready the thwarts, oars, masts and sails.

When the boat has been cleared for hoisting out, lay the thwarts and traverses, and bolt the pivot-plates on the bows and quarters; if the stem and stern pivot-plates interfere with the purchases, they can be secured after the boat is in the water. If the field-carriage is to accompany the gun, lay the wheel and trail tracks.

In a sea-way, it may be better to place the howitzer in the launch, laying it athwartships, and bolting the two ends of the slide into the bow pivot-plates, which will hold it perfectly firm.

As a general rule, the howitzer is not to be handled separately from one of its carriages. It may be hoisted into the launch on either field or boat carriage, as circumstances may dictate.

When the boat-carriage is preferred, sling it with a stout strap passed through the loop-lugs and brought up round the gun, into which hook the purchase; previously shove the bed a little towards the rear end of the slide, so that the carriage will hang square, and set the compressors tight.

When the boat has been hoisted out, the howitzer, its ammunition, and equipments, should be stowed in it conformably to the requirements of the occasion.

Ordinarily, the howitzer may be placed in the bow on its boat-carriage, bolted to the stem-pivot; the field-carriage aft, with its wheels resting on the floor of the stern-sheets and bearing against the after thwart; the trail laid over the quarter-rail, so as not to interfere with the steering; and the ammunition stowed in the stern-sheets, or elsewhere, as may be most convenient for trim of boat. or for its own preservation.

These arrangements can be subsequently changed as circumstances may require.

The Captain of the howitzer slings his haversack and deposits in it a supply of primers, a vent-bit, and vent-cloth, which are handed to him by the Quarter Gunner.

The equipment of the boat will be much facilitated by assigning to each man special duties of preparation and providing articles.

As the bow-oars cannot well be pulled when the howitzer is mounted in the bow, Nos. 1 and 2 do not ordinarily assist at the oars.

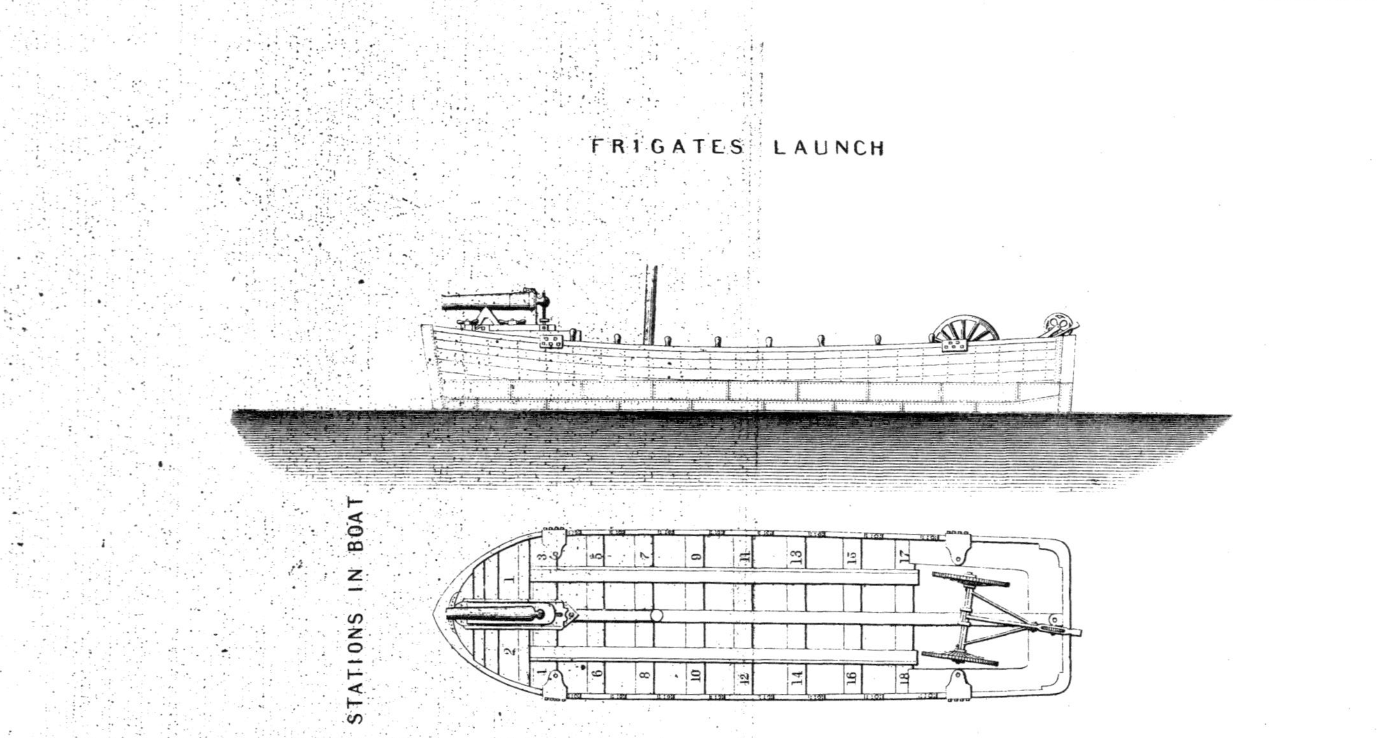

FRIGATES LAUNCH

D. Van Nostrand Publisher
Julius Bien, pr.

STATIONS.

21. For 20 men the stations in the boat and at the howitzer will be as follows; if fewer are employed, the higher numbers are to be omitted:

BOAT. *Stations.*		HOWITZER. *Duty.*
Quarter Master,	Stern-Sheets.	Signals and assists with ammunition.
Quarter Gunner,	Ammunition.	Ammunition.
Cockswain,	Helm.	
Chief of Piece,	Bow.	Superintends the firing.
Port.	*Starboard.*	
1. ———	Bow-oar.	Captain of howitzer, points and fires the gun, superintends orders, and gives orders in absence of an Officer.
If the lock and sight are on left side Captain will take station on port side.		
2. Bow-oar.	———	2d Captain, tends vent and primes.
3. ———	2d oar.	Sponger, sponges and pushes home charge.
4. 2d oar.	———	Loader, receives and enters ammunition.
5. ———	3d oar.	Tends forward compressor.
6. 3d oar.	———	Tends after compressor.
7. ———	4th oar.	Train rope.
8. 4th oar.	———	
9. ———	5th oar.	
10. 5th oar.	———	
11. ———	6th oar.	
12. 6th oar.	———	
13. ———	7th oar.	
14. 7th oar.	———	
15. ———	8th oar.	
16. 8th oar.	———	
17. ———	9th oar.	Runs field-carriage forward when landing.
18. 9th oar.	———	Runs field-carriage forward when landing.

Officer of boat directs the whole of the operations, or may take especial charge of the howitzer.

Officer of the gun is in command of the piece, unless otherwise ordered by the Officer of the boat.

(Preliminary Order)—"MAN THE HOWITZER!"

22. The Captain of the gun sees that the elevator, sight and lock are in order for firing.

Nos. 1, 2, 3, 4, 5, 6, 7. Trail oars.

No. 3 goes to starboard side of muzzle, having the sponge and rammer ready.

No. 4 goes to port side of muzzle, takes out tompion.

No. 5 to starboard side, near forward compressor.

No. 6 port side, near after compressor.

No. 7 after-end of slide, and hooks training-rope.

No. 2 tends the vent and puts in primer.

If the gun is unloaded, it must be run in.

I. "SPONGE!"

23. No. 2 closes vent. (*a*)

No. 3 enters the sponge, and, pressing it firmly to the bottom of bore, turns it round and withdraws it. (*b*)

Quarter Gunner takes a round from the ammunition-box, and, if shell or shrapnel be used, holds it for the Officer in command of gun to adjust the fuze.

II. "LOAD!"

24. Quarter Gunner passes forward with the fixed charge, protecting it under his jacket. (*c*)

No. 4 receives the charge from Quarter Gunner and enters it.

No. 3 pushes home to the mark on rammer-handle. (*d*)

No. 2 puts in primer and covers it with his hand until Nos. 3 and 4 are clear of the gun. (*e*)

III. "POINT!"

25. Nos. 5 and 6 ease compressors. (*f*)

All six men and Captain of gun run out the howitzer. (*g*)

Nos. 5 and 6 then tighten compressors.

Officer of gun puts up the sight as directed by Officer of boat. (*h*)

Captain of gun brings the elevation within the limits of the boat's motion, and causes No. 7, with the assistance of some others, to train nearly to object if the boat is under way.

IV. "FIRE!"

26. If the boat has motion, or is under way, a discretionary execution of this order is necessarily implied.

The assumed elevation having been given by the elevator, a slight motion of the helm is made to sweep the piece laterally, so as to cross the object.

The Captain of the gun closely watches this movement, with his eye down on the sights, and holding the lock-lanyard firmly, draws it as soon as the sights coincide with the object.

Immediately after firing he coils up the lanyard and pulls from the vent any pieces of the quill that may remain, and also enters the bit to clear it entirely through. (*i*)

NOTES TO THE FORM OF BOAT EXERCISE.

27. (*a*) The necessity for closing the vent is a mooted question; but as the operation itself is a slight one, having no appreciable effect in complicating or delaying the manœuvre of the gun, it is not deemed advisable to omit it in this "Form." An equally sure method, is merely to lay a piece of untwilled woollen cloth over the vent, and press it down with the hand; or else turn the lock on it, and hold that down.

(*b*) Too much care cannot be used in sponging, as a premature explosion endangers life and limb. A moist sponge is to be preferred, for contact with it must surely extinguish every trace of fire in the bore.

It may be considered as a safeguard against accident, for during many years' practice, in proving pieces and exercising the men to fire rapidly—ordinarily, seven or eight times in a minute—not a single instance of premature explosion has occurred.

(*c*) The head of the fuze-composition must be guarded against moisture from the fingers, rain, or spray of the sea; otherwise, there will be a failure to ignite.

(*d*) The ammunition is never to be struck with the rammer-head, but pushed home, and with very moderate force; particularly omitting a very common practice of forcing the charge after it reaches the bottom of the bore. In pushing home the charge, No. 2 should always keep his body at the side of the chase, and not before the muzzle.

(*e*) It is not necessary to pierce the cartridge when percussion-primers are used; their fire being always sufficient to pass through it.

(*f*) It is only necessary to give the compressors a turn, or a part of a turn; this will relieve the nip completely, and time is saved subsequently in compressing.

(*g*) Some will take hold of the standard of the carriage-bed that receives the loop of the piece, others of the breech or bed, as may be convenient, to run out the gun.

(*h*) In tightening the thumb-screw that holds the breech-sight in position, do not turn it too hard; the thread may be stripped by continuing to do so. The sight may descend by the shock of the discharge, but this is of no moment.

In point-blank firing, the breech-sight is not required; the eye must then range along the cylinder and muzzle-sight.

(*i*) The charge may not be fired; if this arises from not properly drawing the lock, it will be evident at sight, as the wafer of the primer will not flash; in this case No. 2 throws back the lock.

If the primer explodes without acting on the charge, care must be taken not to approach the piece too soon, as it may only hang fire, and the recoil will injure any one in the way of it. After a seasonable pause, the Captain of the howitzer will remove the residue of the primer, pass the bit down the vent, and insert another primer.

PIVOTING THE HOWITZER.

28. The sweep allowed by the stem-pivot is about one point and a half, starboard or port; if this is not sufficient to train the piece on the object, without diverging too much from the course or position of the boat, then the bow-pivots may be used.

The Officer of the boat gives the order—

"PIVOT ON THE PORT (OR STARBOARD) BOW!"

29. No. 7, with the assistance of the others, trains the rear end of the slide into the bow-pivot which is not to be used. No. 2 bolts it in. No. 3 draws bolt out of stem-pivot, and, with assistance, draws round the forward end of the slide into the pivot to be used; drops in the bolt. No. 2 withdraws the bolt from rear end of slide.

The sweep on the bow-pivots includes an arc of about 120 degrees.

It is not advisable to train the howitzer more than a point abaft the beam if forward, or more than a point forward the beam if aft; as the accidental explosion of a shell near the muzzle, and even of a shrapnel, might be dangerous to those in the boat.

On the bow-pivot, the piece may be pointed nearly from the direction of the keel to a little abaft the beam.

SHIFTING THE HOWITZER.

30. If the howitzer does not bear on the object with such assistance as is admissible from the helm, then the Officer in command may direct it to be shifted to the other end of the boat.

The light 12-pounders, with their boat-carriages, average 660 pounds each; and can be transported by hand from one end of the boat to another.

With their boat-carriages, the 12-pounders of 750 average 1,200 pounds each; the 24-pounders about 2,000 pounds, and will probably be more conveniently managed, especially if the boat has motion, by placing rollers $2\frac{1}{2}$ to $2\frac{3}{4}$ inches in diameter on the tracks laid for the field-carriage. On these the boat-carriage can be shifted from one end of the boat to the other, using light falls to keep it under command.

DISEMBARKATION OF THE HOWITZER.

I. "PREPARE TO LAND!"

31. The Quarter Gunner fills the pouches with one round each, and passes them to the men, each of whom, except Nos. 1 and 3, slings a pouch over the right shoulder, and buckles the strap as short as possible, so as to keep the ammunition clear of the water when leaving the boat.

The Captain of the gun also shortens the strap of his haversack

"TRAIL BOW AND STROKE OARS!"

32. Nos. 1 and 2 adjust the bed of the boat-carriage to its proper place on the slide for shifting; place the muzzle-block, and make the muzzle bear on it by means of the elevator; pass the strap around the neck of the cascabel and put the shifting-spar through the strap; the Quarter Gunner, assisted by the men from the after oars, raises the field-carriage up on the tracks.

II. "TRAIL!"

33. The boat being beached in season, the men trail oars and jump to their stations.

Nos. 3 and 4 over the bow to adjust the skids, which are launched by Nos. 5 and 6.

No. 2 attends the elevator.

No. 3 attends the muzzle.

Nos. 8, 10, 11, and 13, the shifting-spar, assisted by as many of the crew as can take hold.

No. 7 draws the loop-bolt.

The Stroke Oarsmen run the field-carriage forward, the Quarter Gunner guiding it on the track by the trail.

III. "SHIFT THE HOWITZER!"

34. Nos. 1 and 2 clear the elevator; heave up the breech of the gun by the spar; Nos. 5 and 6 back the bed on the slide; run the field-carriage a little forward, so that its lugs come under the loop of the howitzer; lower the piece; put in the loop-bolt and elevator; hook on the drag-rope and ship the trail-handspike in its socket.

IV. "LAND!"

35. Nos. 5, 6, 7, and 8 now jump out of the boat, and, with Nos. 3 and 4, divide to each skid; not standing between them, but keeping outside of them. The Stroke Oarsmen wheel the piece up to the gunwale by the spokes, the Quarter Gunner guiding the trail by the trail-handspike, and the rest of the crew take hold of the drag-rope to ease the gun down from the bow, the Quarter Gunner still guiding it down the skids.

When down off the skids and on the bottom, the drag-rope is hooked around the axle, and the howitzer run up on the beach.

The Captain of the howitzer superintends and assists whenever it may be necessary.

The sponges and rammers are now to be attached in their places on the trail.

The transporting-boxes will also be filled.

EMBARKATION OF THE HOWITZER.

36. When the howitzer is to be embarked, the transporting-boxes should be taken off and put in the boat separately.

The men unsling the ammunition-pouches, and pass them into the boat, which is to be brought to a convenient distance from the beach, and the skids laid and secured.

The field-carriage is then pointed with the trail towards the boat, and drawn down to the skids, with a wheel resting on each.

Nos. 3, 4, 5, 6, 7, and 8 divide at the wheels, and take hold of the spokes, so as to assist the carriage up. No. 14 ships the trail-handspike and tends it with No. 15. The rest of the men get into the boat and take hold of the drag-rope. At the word "HEAVE!" the men at the wheels bear the carriage up on the skids, those in the boat haul on the drag-rope, and the two at the trail bear it up, so that the Quarter Gunner, who stands at the bow, can get hold of the trail-handspike and guide the carriage fairly.

When the howitzer is in the boat, the skids are unhooked and put in the boat by Nos. 3, 4, 5, and 6.

The howitzer may now be shifted to the boat-carriage, by reversing the process already described in orders Nos. 1, 2, and 3, for shifting to the field-carriage.

CREW AT THEIR STATIONS

FOR ACTION

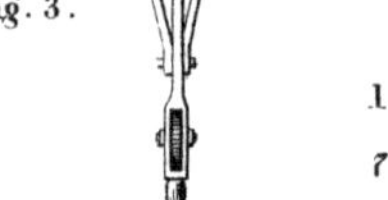

CREW AT THE DRAG ROPE

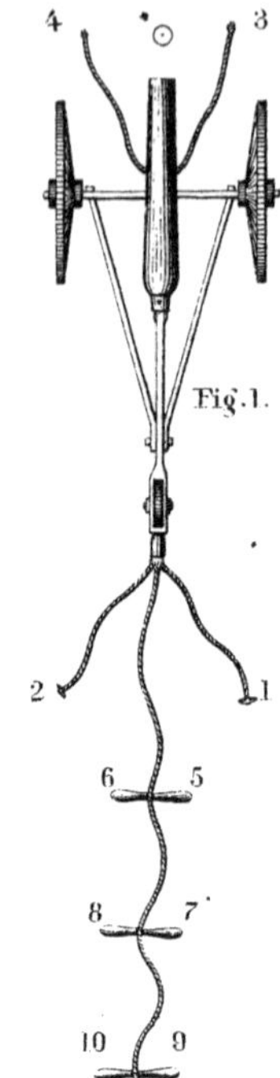

Fig. 2.

Crew to the Rear.

Crew to the 12 10 8 6 4 2 Rear.

1 3 5 7 9 11

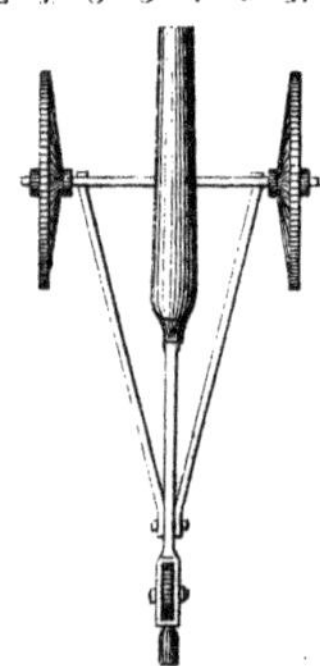

Crew to the 11 9 7 5 3 1 Front.

2 4 6 8 10 12

Crew to the Front.

D. Van Nostrand Publisher Julius Bien, pr.

37. EXERCISE WITH HOWITZER ON FIELD-CARRIAGE.

Gun's Crew.

Stations.	Duty.
Quarter Gunner.	Charge of ammunition and spare equipments.
No. 1. Captain, rear of breech, to the right (or left, depending on the position of lock and sight).	Captain of piece—points and fires the howitzer, superintends orders, and gives orders in absence of an Officer.
2. Rear of breech, to the left.	Closes the vent, puts in primer.
3. Right side of muzzle.	Sponges and rams home.
4. Left side of muzzle.	Receives and enters ammunition.
5. Rear and outside of right wheel.	Assists at right wheel.
6. Rear and outside of left wheel.	Passes ammunition, assists at left wheel.
7. Five yards rear of right wheel.	Assists at right wheel, attends bolt of trail-wheel and trail-handspike.
8. Five yards rear of left wheel.	Passes ammunition, assists at left wheel.
9. With No. 7.	Assists at right wheel.
10. With No. 8.	Assists at left wheel.

(Preparatory Order)—"MAN THE HOWITZER!"

38. The men go to their stations as above designated, the Captain of the howitzer with his haversack, previously supplied, and all the men, except Nos. 1 and 3, with one round in a pouch.

No. 3 takes the sponge and rammer.

No. 6 unbolts trail-wheel, and ships handspike in its socket of trail.

The transporting-boxes, if there be any with the howitzer, are to be deposited about twenty-five yards in its rear, in charge of Quarter Gunner.

The drag-rope is deposited with the ammunition-boxes.

I. "SPONGE!"

39. No. 3 enters the sponge, and, pressing it firmly to the bottom, turns it round and withdraws it. No. 2 serves the vent.

Quarter Gunner takes a round from the ammunition-box, or from the pouch or passing-box of one of the men; and, if shell or shrapnel be used, holds it for the Officer in command of the piece to adjust the fuze.

II. "LOAD!"

40. The charge is to be passed along by the Quarter Gunner to No. 8, and by No. 8 to No. 6, and by No. 6 to No. 4, who enters it into the muzzle.

No. 3 pushes home to the mark on rammer-handle.

No. 2 puts in primer, and covers it with his hand until Nos. 3 and 4 have withdrawn to their stations outside the wheels.

III. "POINT!"

41. Officer of gun puts up the sight, as directed by Officer in command.

The Captain of the gun gives the piece the proper elevation with the screw, and causes No. 7 to train the gun with the trail-handspike to the desired direction. He then withdraws as far as the lock-lanyard permits, standing on the quarter of the breech, and outside of the wheel.

No. 2 stands outside of the left wheel. Nos. 3 and 4 fall back, and the remainder of the gun's crew take the stations first assigned them.

IV. "FIRE!"

42. The Captain of the howitzer instantly draws the lanyard at the word.

No. 2 closes the vent.

Nos. 4, 6, and 8 go to the left wheel; 5, 7, and 9 to the right wheel, taking hold of the spokes, ready to wheel the carriage forward, as may be directed by the Officer in command.

(Concluding Order)—"SECURE THE HOWITZER!"

43. The Quarter Gunner secures the transporting-boxes, and gets ready the lashing.

The Captain of the howitzer coils the lanyard around the lock.

No. 7 bolts the trail-wheel.

No. 3 may carry the sponge in his hand if the fire is merely suspended.

No. 7 may also carry the trail-handspike.

Nos. 8 and 9 hook on the drag-rope, and lead its parts fair for taking hold.

Wheel the piece to the ammunition-boxes, and place them on the axle.

The piece is now ready for any change of position.

REMARKS ON THE USE OF NAVAL LIGHT ARTILLERY.

44. The facility with which the Naval Howitzers are handled is apt to cause a misconception of the purposes for which Naval Light Artillery should ordinarily be used on shore; which are, to be landed from boats in such numbers as may be required, or admitted by circumstances, supported by the seamen and marines of a squadron, and not to be assembled as a battery, to replace, or be substituted for, regular field-artillery.

45. The force landed should be handled as light infantry, for which the individuality of sailor-life so well fits the men; while the character of the gun, and the usually broken nature of the shore-line renders this formation necessary.

46. Open order in approach, in landing, in motion, and in action, is therefore advisable; because a compact formation requires too much attention to position, distances, and alignments in any of them, with more perfect drill than can well be obtained; and which, under fire, exposes too much of a mark to every shot fired.

47. The evolutions in the field should constitute but a small part of the general system of drill, either with a single howitzer or a battery, and should be assimilated to those of light infantry,—that is, the most extended order that the ground admits of,—never massing the guns in close order, but habituating the seamen to open out with them in skirmishing order, keeping on their flanks, never in their rear, using every cover of ground, trees, or, if time will admit, throwing up some earth as a protection against riflemen or the wide-spread fire of shrapnel,—while at the same time the fire is concentrated to prevent attack on the pieces in detail, or is dispersed, as may be required.

48. Such a drill will best develop the scope and efficiency of the gun as a naval arm, and will render most effective the peculiar advantages of its lightness and mobility in rapid movements.

49. Evolutions in action, or preparatory thereto, should always be performed with the ammunition in the pouches; it being a common error in the service to use the ammunition-boxes at such times, when they are only designed for service out of action.

50. If liable to be attacked, all the ground within musket range, especially if it is broken by ravines, should be reconnoitred, particularly on the flanks; and, if possible, all the approaches by which the enemy, and particularly cavalry can approach, should be obstructed; and all obstacles to a retreat or change of position removed.

51. Although commanding positions are to be preferred, the top of a hill should not be chosen where the men and pieces are relieved against the sky, forming a much better mark.

52. Shell and Shrapnel produce a greater moral effect than grape or canister, and in general a greater real injury, as the latter are generally fired at too great distances.

NOTES ON THE USE OF BOAT-HOWITZERS.

53. N. B.—Before equipping boats with howitzers, notice attentively the Hints for General Service, commencing at page 146, Boat Armament of the U. S. Navy, and Suggestions for Landing, of that system, which relate more especially to the condition and management of boat-guns.

54. Too much care cannot be taken to be fully provided, and to have each detail in good condition; for, after the boat has left the ship, it may be impossible to compensate for failure in some seemingly trivial article.

55. The chief purposes of naval light artillery are:

1. To attack small vessels that are lightly armed, and furnish but slight protection to the crews.
2. To contend with other armed boats.
3. To cover the landing of troops.

56. The landing of seamen is rather a remote contingency in the naval service, and should never be resorted to when opposed by good infantry, or when the object to be attained would take the seamen too far from their boats, which should be the base of operations.

57. Boat-Guns.—No tackles are required to run out 12-pdrs.; but 24-pdrs. may possibly require them.

58. The hole in the cascabel for reeving a breeching has been purposely omitted in howitzers, as hitherto the use of a breeching has not been found necessary. Should one be required, a thimble may be fitted to the neck of the knob to serve in place of this hole.

With a breeching, the piece may be fired as if on an ordinary carriage.

59. The recoil is controlled by compressing the slide between the bed and the lower plate. It is necessary, however, that the surfaces of the carriage in contact should be plane. If they are not so, dismount the gun and examine them, and where the wood is worn smooth, remove it in the slightest manner, and correct the surfaces generally. In making the surface plane, it is by no means necessary that it should be rendered smooth. It ought to be as little so as possible for the present purpose.

60. Field-Carriage.—In order to moderate the recoil on smooth ground,

IMPROVED SHRAPNEL

D. Van Nostrand, Publisher

SECTION OF 12 PDR. SHRAPNEL

With Bormann Fuze and Filling of Sulphur.

(full Scale.)

take out the axle or pin of the trail-wheel and turn the wheel up on the trail.

For using the howitzer on shore, two transporting-boxes are supplied, placed on a support and lashed to the axle of the field-carriage. When more than a single piece is landed, it may be found convenient to secure the trail of one field-carriage to the axle of another, and then, by means of pieces of stuff, or boat's spars, secured from axle to axle, to place the ammunition-boxes, provisions, and pouches upon them.

61. Shrapnel may be effectively used where the dispersion of common canister becomes too great and its effects feeble. It takes the place of common shell, to a great extent, when uncovered masses of men are in view, and is designed to burst in front of troops, at just such a distance and height as to disperse the balls among them.

62. Similar terms are used in marking the sight and the fuze. Thus, if the fuze be adjusted to 2 seconds, and the piece elevated by the sight raised to the line on it marked 2 seconds, then the shrapnel will burst about 500 yards from the piece, and spread its balls from that point to a considerable distance further—effectively at least 150 yards.

The adjustment of the fuze to the distance and the altitude of explosion are regulated to the elevation; and, therefore, the three conditions to good effect may be said to depend mainly on a correct knowledge of distance.

63. The 12-pdr. shrapnel contains 80 musket-balls, and if its explosion occurs at one hundred or one hundred and twenty yards in front of and fifteen to twenty yards above the object, one-seventh of the number of balls may be relied on to take effect upon an object 20 by 10 feet in size.

64. Shells may be advantageously substituted for shrapnel when the hostile force is sheltered, especially by such quarters as small craft or merchantmen afford, or when material of any kind is the object of the fire.

65. At two hundred yards canister, only, is required.

In case of a want of canister, the shrapnel or common shell furnishes an excellent substitute by cutting into the magazine of the Bormann fuze, which will cause it to explode at the muzzle.

66. When provided with the Bormann fuze, the shrapnel, or shell, as issued, is complete. The upper surface of this fuze is graduated into seconds and fourths of seconds; and it is only necessary to lay bare the composition contained in the fuze, by the cutting-tool, to prepare the projectile for instant use. In this respect the Bormann fuze has an advantage over the ordinary fuze. The length of the fuzes limits the distance within which the fire of these guns is considered as effective.

67. The introduction of the 12-pounder rifled howitzer has greatly extended the accuracy and effective range of the boat and field artillery.

Solid shot and shell have sufficient penetration to be effective against ordinary wooden vessels at any distance which the elevation allowed by the respective carriages will reach. *See* TABLE OF RANGES.

The shrapnel has sufficient velocity at 2,000 yards to disable men and horses.

Hitherto no certain or efficient time-fuze has been adopted for rifled howitzers.

There are objections to firing grape and canister from rifled guns, as the grooves are injured thereby, and the rotary and irregular motion given to the mass diminishes its effect. If used, the balls should be of lead or zinc.

68. Fixed ammunition is preferable, on the score of greater convenience, and of avoiding difficulties.

For MANŒUVRES OF BOATS ARMED FOR SERVICE, see "Naval Howitzers Afloat;" by Commander Foxhall A. Parker, U. S. N.

LANDING SEAMEN, MARINES, AND HOWITZERS

FOR EXERCISE OR SERVICE ON SHORE.

69. As the efficiency of seamen when landed in any considerable number depends most materially upon a proper system of organization and training previous to their being landed, and without which they are inefficient, the following system is recommended :

70. The small-arm men are to be formed into companies of 80 men, with four petty officers. Each company to be commanded by a Lieutenant, with two other officers. The company to be subdivided into two platoons, and each platoon into two sections, and to be exercised in such movements as are absolutely necessary to manœuvre as a company and in battalion, by the officers who are to command them.

71. Small vessels should furnish a platoon of 40 or section of 20 men, that the companies formed by their aggregation may be of equal strength.

72. The companies when landed are to fall in, and number from the right according to the seniority of the Captains of their respective ships, so that they at once will fall into their places according to their number when landed.

73. Each ship landing two companies is to be prepared to land with the small-arm men six Pioneers—2 with a saw and axe each, 2 with a pickaxe and spade each, 2 with a small crowbar and sledge-hammer, or such intrenching or other tools as the nature of the expedition may require ; the tools to be slung on the men's backs ; smaller detachments a proportionate number.

74. The ship's bugler, if she have one, or drummer, will be sent with the men. He is to be able to sound the "Assembly," "Retreat," "Close," "Extend," "Commence Firing," and "Cease Firing," which sounds the men are to be accustomed to on board ship.

75. If the men are likely to be on shore during the night, they should have a haversack and blanket slung across their shoulders.

76. As muskets are apt to miss fire the first time if not properly clean, the greatest precaution is to be taken to see that the nipple is perfectly clear before loading ; first, by blowing down the barrel and placing the finger before the nipple, to feel that the air passes through it, and afterwards snapping a cap off to dry up any oil or moisture that may be in the barrel. To avoid accidents, it is better not to cap the muskets until after landing.

77. When field-pieces are landed, the guns shall be numbered from the right in the same manner as a company.

78. One or more armorers should be sent with each landing party with cleaning-rods, screw-drivers, and spare nipples.

79. The boats should be formed in divisions, according to the seniority of the Captains of their respective ships—or of the Commanding Officers of the divisions—numbering from the right. The seamen and marines, having been told off in companies previous to leaving their ships, on landing they will form immediately in the same order.

80. The howitzers being mounted as boat's guns and prepared for landing, are brought at once into action, or remain in the boats, according to circumstances.

81. Each division of boats should have a distinguishing flag; and scaling-ladders, intrenching tools, and other implements, should be carried by designated boats.

82. The boats will always land a boat's length apart. Before leaving the ship four boat-keepers should be appointed to each boat carrying a howitzer, and two for the others, with an officer in charge of each division of boats, who are on no account to leave them. Should there be a probability of the landing party being attacked on a re-embarkation, the boats should be hauled off to their anchors, with a long scope of cable, having a stern-line to the beach, and a man in the boat to veer in, that the troops may be readily embarked. The officer left in charge of the boats should be careful to avoid being surprised; and, if circumstances admit, strengthen his position by cutting down trees and throwing up small breastworks a short distance in front.

83. A fast-pulling boat with Medical Officers will attend in rear of the line, designated by a yellow flag.

84. Should the distance from the point of landing be considerable, the boats of each division, in tow of each other, lightest boats leading, will fall in—the leading boat of each division abreast (Art. 72), leaving space for the whole line to form abreast when ordered. On approaching the beach the tow-ropes should be cast off, and the launches with howitzers dress up in line ready to open fire, if necessary, to clear the landing. The officer in command will commence firing from the howitzers when he thinks fit; but no musketry is to be fired without special orders.

85. When the Commanding Officer perceives the beach to be clear, or when he considers it proper, he will order "Cease firing!" and direct the boats with skirmishers and light howitzers to pull in and land as quickly as possible. On landing they will immediately extend, advance, and seize the first cover near the beach, if there be any, but will not open fire till the Officer commanding them sounds "Commence firing." The main body then pull steadily in and land, forming line in rear of the covering party. The howitzers form on the flanks of their divisions, or as ordered. Pioneers and scaling-ladders as ordered. The main body being formed, will advance in line or column, according to circumstances, preceded by the skirmishers firing, if necessary. When firing in close order the front rank should fire kneeling, as, owing to the shortness of muskets, accidents frequently occur. Under certain circumstances, as advancing on an open beach, the boats might be employed on the flanks to cover the advance or retreat.

86. Should the boats be employed for the disembarkation of troops, the same arrangement should be made. It will then be desirable that every boat should carry a flag similar to that of the Commanding Officer of its division; and, when in large numbers, the boats should also be painted according to the colors of the flags, that the troops may readily know their own boats.

87. The re-embarkation should be conducted on similar principles to the disembarkation—the skirmishers and light howitzers extending in rear of the line, which will then pass through the intervals, forming again, if necessary, to support the skirmishers, who will retire firing, and re-form in rear of the line. The main body will then embark, followed by the covering party under cover of the boats' guns.

88. When landing in a heavy surf, the ammunition should be put in one or more small powder-tanks, with the lids well screwed down.

PART III.

ORDNANCE

AND

ORDNANCE STORES.

PART III.

CHAPTER I.

ORDNANCE AND ORDNANCE STORES.

1. All articles of Ordnance and Ordnance Stores, when duly delivered at any Navy Yard, are to be borne on the books of the Inspector of Ordnance, and duly accounted for, according to such regulations as may, from time to time, be established by proper authority.

2. He will make monthly estimates and requisitions for all materials and articles which may be required by the master workmen in the Ordnance Department, and which he may deem necessary; which requisitions are to be forwarded to the Chief of the Bureau for his approval.

No articles are to be purchased without previous requisitions, nor any to be used until duly inspected, approved, and receipted for.

Before reception, every article shall be carefully examined by the master workman in whose department it is required, and such other person as the Inspector shall appoint, and compared with samples, to see that it conforms to the standard, and is, in quantity and quality, as called for by the requisition or order of the Bureau for its delivery.

He will keep on hand standard Patterns and Drawings, approved by the Bureau of Ordnance, to which all articles of manufacture or issue shall strictly conform; notifying the Bureau of any discrepancies therefrom in articles received from other Yards, that unauthorized variations may be checked and the manufactures of each Yard be identical.

3. The Inspectors of Ordnance at all Navy Yards shall have the immediate custody of all articles appertaining to ordnance, and they shall be kept in suitable places, separate from the other articles in the Yard.

And they will promptly inform the Bureau of all orders received from Senior Officers, which may in the least affect the execution of the instructions given by the Bureau in relation to their duties.

4. Inspectors of Ordnance having charge of the articles above mentioned are, under the direction of the Commandant of the Yard, to be responsible for their being carefully attended to, and preserved from injury.

5. Whenever any of them shall require repairs, other than those which can be made in the ordnance workshops, the Inspector will apply to the Commandant of the Yard, or to the Bureau through him, for the necessary means to keep all articles in his charge in order and ready for service.

6. He shall require from master workmen employed on ordnance work reports in the required form (see blank forms) of the expenditure of materials and labor upon each and every object under their immediate superintendence, at which time they will make a return of all unexpended material on hand. They will also be responsible for all waste and improper use of material by those under their general superintendence.

7. The Inspector of Ordnance shall have authority over all master and other workmen employed on ordnance work, and direct all its details.

He will examine and certify to the correctness of all bills rendered for materials, supplies, or labor in the Ordnance Department, and examine and certify to the correctness of the pay-roll of all persons employed on ordnance work.

8. No Inspecting Officer or person employed by the Bureau is to show to, or leave in the way of persons not authorized by the Bureau, any drawing, descriptions, or dimensions of guns under contract, nor to permit the examination by such persons of the guns themselves.

9. The resident and other Inspectors are to inform the contractors of this strict requirement on the part of the Bureau, and to request them to cause it to be rigidly enforced by all persons under their control.

10. It is most positively forbidden to communicate any information whatever in relation to ordnance matters, or to show or describe ordnance work, of any description, to any person not in the employ of the government, unless by superior authority.

Inspectors are also directed not to hold correspondence in writing with manufacturers, contractors, or other parties in relation to ordnance supplies, unless specially directed by the Bureau.

Officers on Ordnance duty will give no official opinion, to Inventors or others, upon the merits of any invention appertaining to Ordnance, which may be submitted to them officially or unofficially for examination, unless by special direction of the Bureau of Ordnance.

All such opinions will be forwarded to the Bureau, to whom parties must be referred for information.

11. The Inspectors of Ordnance at the several Yards and stations are required to enjoin upon all their employés the strictest secrecy in relation to every thing connected with their duties. No information whatever is to be given to any one in relation to the prices of articles, the details of work, or the condition of ordnance or ordnance supplies.

Any breach of this order is to be followed by prompt dismissal from employment.

12. Whenever any ordnance stores shall be furnished to vessels, or for any other purpose, the Ordnance Officer shall take proper receipts for them from the officer to whom they are delivered. These receipts shall be signed at the Ordnance office, and the commander is required to ascertain before sailing if the proper officers have signed all receipts and vouchers.

13. The Ordnance Officer will deliver with them an Invoice of the number and cost of such stores, retaining a receipted duplicate, approved by the commander, to be forwarded to the Bureau of Ordnance.

One Ledger, one Invoice, and twenty blanks for Quarterly Returns to the Bureau of Ordnance, are to be furnished each vessel fitted for sea.

If any articles are purchased abroad, or obtained from other stations after the vessel is regularly fitted for sea, they should be duly entered in the Ledger, and a note made therein stating when, and from what source received; and, if practicable, their number and cost should be inserted in the Invoice of other articles supplied the vessel.

14. A separate list shall be furnished to all commanders of vessels of the ammunition furnished, which list is to be returned to the Ordnance Officer of the Yard to which the vessel shall return, with any additional supplies which she may receive during the cruise entered on it.

15. The allowances which are prescribed for the different classes of vessels in the Table of Allowances are not to be exceeded, except by the express sanction of the Chief of the Bureau of Ordnance.

16. It shall be the duty of any commander of a vessel, before making or approving requisitions, to examine the allowance table and expenditure books, to see that the amount required, together with that on hand, does not exceed the allowance, and that the articles required are allowed. If these articles are not allowed, or are in excess of the allowance, but are, in his opinion, necessary for the use of the ship under his command, he will state on the requisition, opposite the article, "in excess of allowance," or, "not allowed," and the reason why considered necessary, before sending it to the Commandant of the Yard or Squadron for his approval.

In case he shall neglect so to do, the Inspector of Ordnance will only furnish the allowance, and shall return the requisition for correction, calling the attention of the approving officer to this neglect.

17. All Ordnance Stores, except the ammunition, shall be delivered to the Gunner, or other officer appointed to receive them, at the ordnance storehouses, the Inspector of Ordnance furnishing him with the means of transportation, and men for stowing them in their appointed places on board, when the crew are not available for this purpose.

In order to guard against the loss or misdirection of Ordnance Stores, which has frequently been found to occur whilst they were being transferred from the Ordnance Store-houses to vessels going into commission, or in the case of vessels landing their stores on returning from a cruise:

The Bureau directs that whenever Ordnance Stores of any kind are to be received from or delivered on board of a vessel, a responsible officer be present, whose duty it shall be to take an exact account of them and see them safely delivered at their destination, indorsing the Receipts and Invoices with his name.

For any loss that may occur in the performance of this duty, that officer will be held pecuniarily responsible; and whenever any stores are found to be missing, the name of the officer who superintended their removal is immediately to be forwarded to the Bureau.

The Inspector of Ordnance will be vigilant in seeing this order strictly carried out.

18. All stores landed from ships will be received at the Ordnance Store-houses, when all responsibility on the part of the officer delivering them shall cease, and a survey be held, as soon thereafter as practicable, to determine the quantity of stores, and the condition in which they are delivered.—(See form of survey.)

When the vessel returns to a yard to be refitted or to be laid up at the end of the cruise, her Ledger and Invoice are to be handed to the Ordnance Officer of the yard for his examination, and for the use of the officers who may be ordered to hold a survey upon the Ordnance Equipments and Stores; and when the survey is completed, both Ledger and Invoice are to be forwarded to the Bureau of Ordnance with the report of survey.

19. It having been found that in the "Reports of Survey" made at the different Navy Yards on the Ordnance Stores of vessels returning from sea, many articles are put down as "deficient by Returns" without these deficiencies being in any way accounted for, the Bureau directs that the Surveying Officers shall require the Gunner (or other officer having charge of the Ordnance Stores, in case there be no Gunner on board) to show a just cause for said deficiencies; a statement of which, properly signed, is to be forwarded to the Bureau with the Report of Survey. In case of his failure to do so, he will be held responsible for the loss, and the value of the deficient articles checked against his pay.

Where arms or other articles are lost or destroyed in action, the fact must be properly authenticated by the signature of the Commanding or Executive Officer.

20. Ordnance Ledgers of all vessels coming from a cruise shall be signed by the Gunner or Executive Officer and the officer in command before leaving the Yard or station.

Invoices and Receipts must invariably be given and taken of all ordnance, ordnance stores, equipments, and small arms, when transferred from the keeping of one officer to another.

And whenever any article of ordnance is lost or mutilated, the fact shall be reported to the Bureau, with all the circumstances of the case, and the value of the same will be deducted from the pay of the person having it in his possession at the time, unless sufficient reason for a contrary course should appear.

21. It shall be the duty of the Inspector of Ordnance (or of the officers who inspect a ship on her return from a cruise) to report to the Bureau the condition in which the articles under the charge of the Gunner may be transferred, that his care and attention may be properly known and appreciated.

22. Officers upon Ordnance duty at Navy Yards may correspond with the Bureau on subjects connected with Ordnance duties, forwarding their communications open, to the Commandant of the Yard for transmission.

23. The dates of all circulars, orders, telegrams, or letters to which reference is made in corresponding with the Bureau, shall be distinctly quoted.

And the same rule is to be observed in forwarding triplicate Bills, Bills of Lading, and Invoices, the date of the order or orders being written across the face in red ink; and the receipt of all telegrams must be immediately acknowledged.

24. The Commandants will, in forwarding communications, accompany them with such remarks or recommendations as they may deem proper, and at any other time make such suggestions as they may consider will promote the public interest.

25. In shipping or forwarding stores each box or package shall be numbered, and have the nature of its contents stencilled or marked on the outside, and noted on the Invoice. The Invoice should in all cases of shipment accompany the articles.

All stores intended for shipment to squadrons, shall be legibly and conspicuously addressed to the Commander-in-Chief of the squadron, and marked for that squadron.

INSPECTION AND PROOF OF NAVAL GUNS.

26. All cannon for the navy, cast at private foundries, will be fabricated in strict accordance with the terms of the contract made with the Bureau of Ordnance, and subject to the inspection of an officer detailed to supervise the operations. (See "Instructions for the Inspection and Proof of Cannon, 1864," for further details.)

27. New guns are to be closely examined and measured, inside and out, for defects of metal or manufacture, and the results recorded in the prescribed forms by the Inspector resident at the foundry, as soon after being finished as possible, if he has not already done so in the various stages of manufacture, which is preferable, as the detection of errors which pass the limits of toleration may save useless subsequent labor. Internal defects of metal will, for instance, generally be betrayed by a close examination of the core-pieces. As rust tends to conceal defects, this examination of the guns is to take place before exposure to the weather. And previously to the final examination and proof of guns, they are not to be covered with paint, lacquer, oil, or any material which may hide defects of metal.

If it is ascertained that any attempt has been made to conceal defects, the gun or guns so treated are to be rejected without further examination.

As the water-proof, which is of great importance in detecting defects of metal not otherwise developed, necessarily succeeds immediately the powder-proof, and can be effectively applied only in fine weather, and when the temperature is above the freezing-point, final inspections are to be made at such times only.

DESCRIPTIVE LIST OF INSTRUMENTS REQUIRED AND USED IN THE INSPECTION AND PROOF OF GUNS.

28. 1st. A mirror for reflecting the sun's rays into the bores. Two will be required if the sun be in the rear of the Inspector.

2d. A lamp attached to a staff for examining the bores when the sun is obscured, or the guns are under cover.

3d. A standard cylinder gauge. This is a hollow cylinder of iron, turned to the least allowed diameter of the bore, and one calibre in length. It has a cross-head at each end, one of which has a smooth hole through its axis to fit the staff, and the other is tapped to receive the screw in the end of it.

4th. A measuring-staff of steel or iron, in joints of suitable length, connected together by screws. Each joint is provided with a light brass

DAHLGREN SHELL GUN

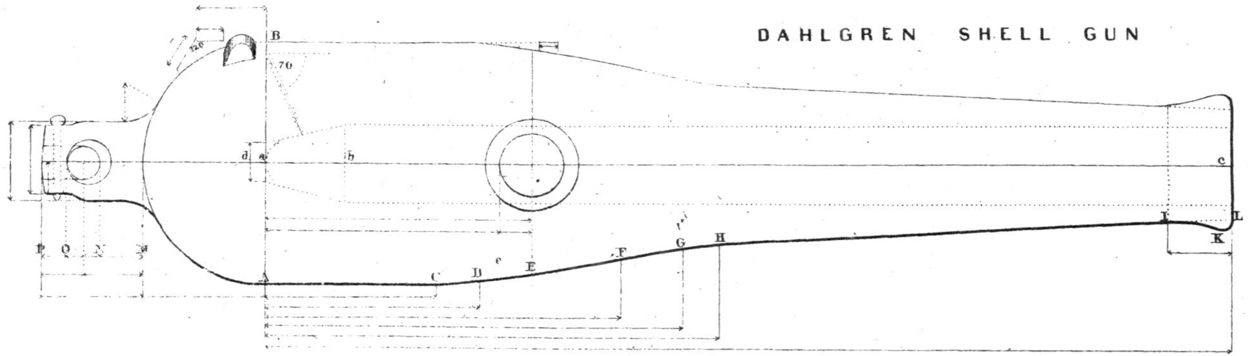

PARROTT RIFLE GUN 1864.

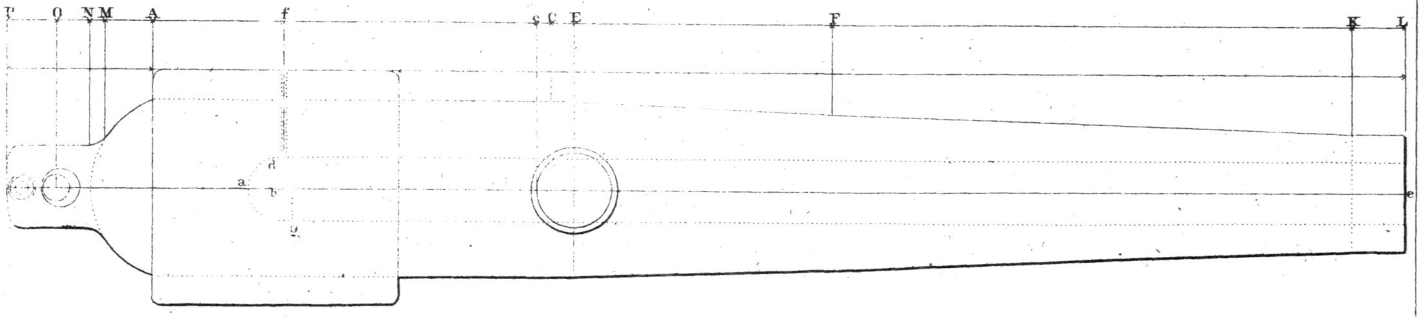

D. Van Nostrand, Publisher. Julius Bien, pr.

disk, the diameter of which is 0.05 inches less than that of the bore. Through the centre of the disk there is a hole which fits upon a shoulder at the joint; the whole is so arranged that when the joints are screwed together the disks between them are held firmly in place, while the length of the staff is not affected by them. A steel point is screwed on to the end. When pushed to the bottom of the bore, the staff coincides very nearly with its axis. The outer joint is graduated to inches and tenths. A slide is made to play upon it with a vernier scale, graduated to hundredths of an inch. On the inner end of the slide a branch projects at a right angle, sufficiently long to reach across the muzzle face, and, when in contact with it, to indicate the precise length obtained from that point to the end of the measuring-point on the other end of the staff. A half disk of wood, made to fit the bore, with a groove for the staff to rest in, placed just inside of the muzzle, is useful in preventing any springing of the staff.

The point being taken off, the staff can be used with the cylinder gauge, to measure the distance to which the latter descends. But as the gradu ation is intended for the points, care must be taken in this case to allow for the difference.

5th. A chamber-gauge for verifying the shape and size of conical chambers.

The head should be made of close-grained, well-seasoned wood, and of the exact dimensions of the chamber. Two planes, crossing each other at a right angle, coinciding with the vertical and horizontal central sections, have been found better than a solid block. The edges should be bevelled. A metal socket in its centre connects it with the measuring-staff. Being pushed to the bottom of the bore, if the length coincides with that obtained by the point, it is obvious that the chamber is large enough, provided the cylindrical part has not been bored too deep, in which case a shoulder would be found at the junction. The edges of the gauge should be chalked before it is inserted. When withdrawn, if the chalk-marks are visible all around the chamber, it is evident the chamber is not too large. With slight modifications, this arrangement may be applied to the slope of cylindrical chambers, and to the curve at the bottom of the bore of any guns. Should the inspection of guns with conical chambers or slopes take place at the foundry, an examination of the chamber reamer will be very satisfactory. If found correct in size and shape, the impossibility of making the chamber too large will be apparent.

6th. A star-gauge, for measuring the diameters of the bores and of cylindrical chambers. This instrument is composed of the staff, the handle, and a set of points for each calibre.

The staff is a brass tube, made in three pieces, for convenience of stowage, and connected together, when required, by screws. Its inner end expands into a head, in which are placed four steel sockets, at equal distances from each other, which receive the points. Two of the sockets opposite to each other are secured permanently. The two others are movable. A tapering plate or wedge, the sides of which are cylindrical, runs through a slit in the head; an aperture in the inner ends of the movable socket embraces the cylinder, so that when the plate is moved forward or backward, the sockets are projected or withdrawn. The tapering of the plate has a certain known proportion to its length, so that if it is moved in either direction a given distance, a proportional movement is imparted to the sockets, and to the points which they contain. It is easy to see how, in this manner, a movement of .10 in. may increase or diminish the distance between the points .01 in. Therefore there would be no difficulty in estimating, to a considerable degree of accuracy, a difference of .001 in. between the points. In general, however, the distance on the plate required to move the points .01 in. is about .06 in. only.

A square sliding rod is connected with the tapering plate, and runs through the whole length of the tube, projecting some inches beyond the outer end. This rod has as many parts as there are joints in the staff, and, like them, connects by screws. Each section of the rod works in its proper joint, through a square socket at each end, and is prevented from falling out by pins. When screwing the joints together, if the ends of the rod are pressed up to each other they become connected by the same motion.

The staff is graduated to inches and quarters, so that the distance of the points from the muzzle of the gun may always be known. A centre line, starting from the centre of the upper socket, is marked upon the staff throughout its length.

The handle in use at present is of brass, made to fit over the outer end of the staff, and to connect with the sliding rod by a screw, having a large milled head at the outer extremity of the handle. It may be used on either joint, as required. A slit through the handle permits a part of the staff near the end to be seen beneath. A scale on one side of the slit is graduated with the distance that the rod moves, to throw the points .01 in. apart.

That part of the handle containing the slit and scale is separated from the other part; it is made to fit closely over it. On each side there is a small tube; a thread is cut in one, through which a fine screw, held by a stud on the permanent part of the handle, works and gives it motion; a guide runs through the other. Seen through the slit is a small plate of silver inserted in the staff, and a fine mark upon it to show the place of zero, when the points are adjusted. The zero-mark on the scale is made to correspond with it by means of the screw just mentioned.

The points are of steel, with a strong shoulder at one end, below which the screw is cut that fits into the socket in the head. A wrench is made to fit the other end, so as to turn the point firmly into its place. They are made of such a length that they will just pass into the adjusting-ring when they are all in place. To this instrument belong the adjusting-rings and the muzzle-rest in the form of T; of the rings there is one for each calibre, reamed out to the exact minimum diameter of the bore. The latter can be used for any class of guns. Its office is to keep the staff of the star-gauge in the axis of the bore. For this purpose it contains a groove, above the perpendicular branch, to receive the lower half of the staff. There is a movable slide on each branch, which can be adjusted to marks for each calibre, so that points projecting from their rear will enter the muzzle and hold the rest in place. In this position the upper edge of the transverse branch coincides with the diameter of the bore.

A hook is pivoted on the inner side of the transverse branch, on one side of the groove, and so fitted that when the star-gauge is in the gun, it embraces one-half of that portion of the staff which is above the groove. Therefore, if the transverse branch be placed so as to coincide with the axis of the trunnions, the hook thrown over the staff, and the latter turned so that the centre line just meets the end of the hook, the perpendicular points will be perpendicular to the axis of the trunnions. If the staff is then drawn out carefully, the measurements will all be taken in the same plane. A notch in the end of the hook, made to coincide with the plane of the muzzle, may be used for marking the distances on the staff.

The upright branch is movable, and is made to fit into the end of the transverse branch, for convenience and security in packing.

In examining the bores after proof, it has been found that the greatest indentation occurs in general near the seat of the projectiles. But, as it is not always found at precisely the same point of the circle of the bore, a convenient mode of searching for it is desirable. This is supplied by a disk for circular measurements, which may also be considered as belonging to the star-gauge. It is made of composition, and is divided into halves, with a hole through the centre to receive the staff of the star-gauge.

It is turned so as to fit into the muzzle of the gun closely, with a projecting lip two or three inches broad to hold it in place, and with cleats overlapping the edges, to keep it from going in too far. The face is a plane surface. The circumference is divided into as many equal parts as may be thought desirable, which are numbered in regular order. The centre hole is reinforced on the inside by a projection which is turned to receive a collar that fits closely around it, and holds the two halves together when they are placed on the staff.

When ready for use, the face is in the plane of the muzzle-face. Its zero-mark is made to coincide with a light punch-mark on the muzzle-face, directly below the line of sight.

On the staff of the star-gauge a brass slide is fitted, having a thumb-screw to hold it in any position; from the inner end a point extends at a right angle to its axis, of sufficient length to meet the points at the circumference of the disk; a centre line extends from the base to the apex. The slide being moved so as to make its inner end coincide with any mark upon the staff, at which a circular measurement is required, and the centre line of the point being made to coincide with that of the staff, it is secured by the thumb-screw. The point of the slide is then in the same plane with the perpendicular measuring-points, and its direction always indicates them; a series of measurements, made before proof, may thus be compared with another made at the same points after proof.

It is obvious that the determinations will not be absolutely accurate, for when the gun is worn, should the stationary points be perpendicular, the movable points, being then horizontal, would fall below the true horizontal diameter, and the measurements would be more in error than it would be with the points in any other direction. Still, if care is taken to preserve the points at the greatest length possible, a very tolerable degree of accuracy may be attained. In the inspection of guns arranged on skids, the gun itself should be turned, which will insure accurate measurements. Care must also be taken not to allow the joints of the staff to become so loose that the coincidence of the centre line is destroyed when they are screwed together. If this should occur, however, a few turns of thread, placed between them at the time of putting the instrument together, would remedy the difficulty.

7th. An instrument for verifying the interior position of vents.

When the vent is drilled in the vertical plane of the axis, as in the guns of old patterns, a simple head, shaped to fit the bottom of the bore, or the chamber, with a staff fitted to it, is sufficient. But for the Dahlgren guns, with two vents, some other plan is better. The following has been found satisfactory:

A head of well-seasoned wood, which is fitted to the chamber, is attached to a wooden disk of the diameter of the main bore. The surface of the head corresponds with a longitudinal central section of the chamber; at the point where the projection of the vent would meet it a piece of hard wood is inserted. A central line drawn through its length, crossed at a right angle by another line at any known point from the smaller end, will afford convenient points to measure from. A stout square wooden staff is attached to the axis of the head; at a distance equal to the length of the bore, the end is jogged into the centre of a half disk of wood, which is fitted to the bore. The whole is so constructed that the straight edge of the half disk (or the chord) is in the same plane as a horizontal section of the head. A few holes are bored through the disk attached to the half head, to allow the instrument to pass freely into the gun and out of it.

A wire of untempered steel, of the size of the vent, with a sharp, well-centred point, and a small spirit-level, are required to use with this instrument.

The gun being levelled, and the instrument being pushed to the bottom of the bore, the upper edge of the half disk near the outer end of the staff is then brought to a level. The surface of the half head then corresponds with the horizontal central section of the chamber. The point of the wire being pushed gently to meet it, will show very accurately the interior position of the vent.

8th. Profile-boards for distances in front and rear of the base line.

Their lower edges are adapted to the shape of the gun, and the upper ones are parallel to the axis of the bore.

The distances from the base-line of the several parts, and of the points at which diameters are to be measured, are laid off accurately on the upper edge, and then marked in lines perpendicular to it on the sides and lower edges of the profile. An iron strip is attached to the upper edge to prevent warping, and the whole is well coated with shellac varnish, to keep it from absorbing moisture.

The following instruments are used in connection with the profile-boards:

A rule for verifying the marks, of such a length that not more than one fleeting may be necessary, to be graduated decimally according to the standard.

A small square of steel, to be used in referring the marks on the board to those on the rule.

A steel straight-edge, long enough to extend across the muzzle-face, and several inches on the board, to ascertain the extreme length from base to muzzle. It is also used for the same purpose at the extreme end of the cascabel.

A steel scratcher, to mark the gun at points not otherwise indicated, where diameters are to be measured.

9th. A trunnion-square of steel or iron for ascertaining the position of the trunnions, with reference to the axis of the bore. This instrument is a square with two branches, one of which is fixed and the other movable. The foot of each branch is in the same plane, and is parallel to the upper edge of the main piece which connects them. The latter is graduated to inches and tenths. The movable branch slides on the main piece, and may be secured to it by two thumb-screws. It is provided with a vernier scale graduated to hundredths of an inch. Between the branches there is a slide, also provided with a vernier graduated as before, with a thumb-screw to secure it firmly; in its centre there is a sliding-point, moving vertically, with a thumb-screw to fasten it. Above the foot of each branch there is a slit to receive the shank of a plate, on the end of which a thread is cut; the lower edge of the plate forms a right angle with the branch, and the plate is fastened to the branch by a nut, at a point from the end equal to the semi-diameter of the trunnion, which is marked on each branch.

When the feet of the branches, or the lower edge of the plates, rest upon the trunnions, the upper edge of the main piece is parallel to their axis, if their alignment is correct. When in the latter position, the edges of the feet will lie close against the sides of the trunnions.

A graduated steel wedge is used to measure the deviation of the trunnions from the feet of the square.

10th. A trunnion-gauge, which is an iron ring of the proper diameter of the trunnions. Its outer edge coincides with the diameter of the rimbases.

11th. A trunnion-rule, to measure the distance of the trunnions from the base ring, or line. This is an iron rod with a head at one end, through which passes one branch of a small square. The centre of the rod is marked on the end, and the square is set so that the inner edge of the branch which is parallel to the rod is at a distance equal to the semi-diameter of the trunnion from the centre. It is secured in this position by screws and clamps.

The upper side of the rod is graduated to inches and tenths. A slide with a slot through it, to show the graduation beneath, traverses upon it, and is kept from turning by a guide on the lower side. There is a vernier upon the slide, graduated to hundredths of an inch; a thumb-screw serves to secure the slide at any point on the rod. That end of the slide from which the graduation of the rod commences has both of its sides drawn out, to form knife-edges; the knife-edges and the end of the slide are in the same plane. When the square at the end is placed on the trunnion, the end of the rod will touch its side at the point of its greatest diameter. The rod being held parallel to the axis of the bore, with the side of the head pressing the rimbase, the knife-edge will be in a proper position to fall into the base line when moved to find it.

12th. A beam-calliper for measuring diameters is a square of steel or iron, with two branches, one of which is fixed and the other sliding. The inner edges of the two branches, when pushed together, lie, of course, in contact with each other throughout their length. The beam is graduated to inches and tenths. A vernier is attached to the sliding branch, graduated to hundredths of an inch. The latter is provided with a thumb-screw, to fasten it at any point.

The length of the beam must be rather greater than the diameter; and that of the branches than the semi-diameter of the guns to be inspected, at their largest points.

13th. A cascabel-block is a wooden cylinder of the proper diameter of the breeching-hole, the size of which it is used to verify.

The opening between the jaws may be ascertained by measuring the iron block which is fitted to go between them, or by a template.

14th. A vent-guide, to be used with vents in guns of Dahlgren's pattern.

This instrument is made of bronze or composition. When placed upon the gun, one of its branches coincides with the curve of the cylinder, and the other, starting from its centre, lies along the cylinder in contact with it longitudinally. The lower edges of the branches are a right line and a curved line, making two right angles with each other. The length of that of the transverse branch is equal to the distance between the centre of the two vents. The rear surface of the transverse branch is curved and quadrilateral. Its sides are inclined, so that their rear edges show the exact direction of the vents. Every point in the upper edge lies in the same horizontal plane. The height is sufficient to permit the edges to give an accurate direction to the drill.

The upper edge of the other branch runs off in a sloping curve to its extremity.

A centre line is drawn through the lower edge of the longitudinal branch, and is continued upwards on the rear surface of the transverse branch to the top.

The guide being placed with its centre upon the centre mark of the gun, and the centre line of the longitudinal branch being made to coincide with the centre line scribed upon the cylinder, the rear lower edge of the transverse branch will then coincide with the base-line, its extremities will indicate the centres of the vents, and the rear edges of the sides will show their true direction.

15th. Vent-gauges of untempered steel wire, with shoulders to prevent them from slipping into the vent. One should be of the proper diameter of the vent, one of the greatest, and one of the least diameter allowed.

16th. A vent-searcher, a steel wire of the length of the vent, bent to a right angle at the lower end and pointed. It is used for detecting imperfections in the sides of the vents.

17th. A semicircular protractor of metal for measuring the inclination of vents, or for ascertaining their deviation from the guide.

18th. A set of templates for verifying the shape of lock-lugs, the angle of the rear sight mass, the curve between the base-line and the front of rear sight mass, that at the end of the cascabel, the bevel of the breeching-hole, the opening of the cascabel, and the shape of the muzzle swell.

If the inspection should take place at the foundry, the templates used in chipping might be verified and used for inspection.

For guns of Dahlgren's pattern, a bronze model, showing the shape of the lugs and rear sight mass, and the position of the vents, is furnished as a guide to the contractors.

19th. A standard foot-rule for verifying measures.

20th. A foot-rule of steel for measuring the masses, the length of the trunnions, and for other purposes. The graduation should be extended to each end.

21st. A set of ring-gauges, large, medium, and small, for inspecting the projectiles used in proof.

22d. A small beam-calliper, with outside edges, for examining the adjusting rings and the ring-gauges.

23d. A platform balance, for weighing the projectiles used in proof, and for bringing the shells up to the standard weight. For use with the above there should be provided a bag of dry sand, a funnel, some wooden plugs for the fuze-holes, and a hammer.

24th. A set of implements for loading and cleaning, viz.:

A rammer, faced with hard wood or metal, with a graduated scale on the staff, near the muzzle, to show the distance of the front of the projectiles from the muzzle.

A bristle sponge with a worm in its end, for ordinary use in firing.

A sheepskin sponge, for drying the bore after cleaning it.

A gun-scraper.

A ladle.

A boring-bit.

A priming-wire.

A lock and lanyard, should navy primers be used in firing; but if friction primers are used, then a lanyard with a hook in its end will be required, only.

A breeching and a couple of tackles, if the guns should be fired on skids.

Six handspikes.

Six buckets and a large tub, for washing out the guns.

If the firing is made into a butt, a couple of wheelbarrows, with two or three pickaxes and half a dozen shovels, will be necessary.

25th. A searcher, with six or more points, to detect injuries or cavities in the bore.

26th. A machine for taking the interior impression of vents.

This consists of a wooden head, one-half of which is cylindrical, and the other half is of the shape of the chamber, both being rather smaller than the parts of the bore that they are intended for. A staff, flat on its upper side, and rounded on its under side to fit the curve of the bore, is mortised into the circumference of the cylindrical part of the head. A mortise is cut through the chamber part of the head, extending several inches in rear and front of the position of the vent. Into this mortise a loose piece is fitted, capable of free motion upwards and downwards, the top of which is pierced with holes to secure the wax or composition which is spread over its surface. This movable piece rests on a wedge attached to a flat rod running through a slot in the head; there is a slot in this rod about four inches long, a pin passing through it into the staff. To use the instrument, withdraw the rod as far as the slot will permit, which will allow the movable piece on which the composition has been spread to drop below the surface of the head, and protect it. Push the head to the bottom of the chamber, and arrange the position of the staff so that the movable piece will cover the vent, then press the end of the rod home. This motion will throw out the composition, and a distinct impression of the vent and of fire-cracks (should there be any) will be left upon its surface; draw the rod back as far as the slot will allow, and withdraw the instrument: the impression, being protected thereby, will come out uninjured.

Impressions of injuries or cavities in the bore may easily be taken by a similar contrivance.

27th. Hydraulic pump and apparatus for the water-proof.

Any of the various patterns of this machine may be applied to the proof of guns. An iron cross-head is secured to a stout wooden block which fits into the muzzle, and which has a flange or shoulder to cover the muzzle-face; rings of caoutchouc or gutta-percha are placed between them; an iron rod with a ring in one end, to fit over the trunnion, and with a thread cut on the other end, is used on each side of the gun, to connect the trunnion with the cross-head. The whole is set up with nuts, and the pressure upon the rings makes a tight joint; a coupling upon the cross-head receives the hose, and the water is forced into the gun through a hole in the wooden block. Care should be taken that the valve is loaded with the proper weight for proof.

28th. Dies for marking guns.—A full set of figures, with such capital letters as may be required for the inspection-marks; these should be one inch in length. Also, small letters of suitable size to mark "lbs.," and a full set of half-inch figures.

USE OF THE INSPECTING INSTRUMENTS.

29. The guns having been freed from rust, and their foundry numbers noted, in the order of their relative positions, on the field-book, the inspecting officer will proceed to verify the instruments to be used in their measurement, if this has not been previously done in a manner entirely satisfactory to him.

He will then examine carefully the guns, inside and out, for defects of metal or of manufacture, and note the results.

The interior of the bore is to be examined by reflecting the rays of the sun into it from a mirror or mirrors; or, if the sun is obscured, and there can be no delay, by means of a spirit-lamp, or of a wax taper, on the end of a rod, taking care not to smoke the surface of the bore.

The cylinder-gauge is then to be introduced, which must pass freely to the bottom of the cylindrical part of the bore. If obstructed, the depth to which it reaches should be noted.

The star-gauge is used to ascertain the exact diameter of the bore, and of the cylindrical part of the chamber. The bore must be measured at intervals of $\frac{1}{4}$ inch from the bottom of the cylindrical part to the seat of the shot; of 1 inch from that point to the trunnions; and of 5 inches from the trunnions to the muzzle. If any marks of the reamer or other defects are seen in the bore, they are to be searched for, and their depths and positions noted. These results are to be tabulated according to the blank forms furnished. The whole length of the bore is ascertained by means of the measuring-staff, with the point screwed on, supported in the axis of the bore by the disks and half-tompion.

In the absence of this instrument, a pine rod, having the proper length of the bore marked on it, and the end rounded to the curve of the bottom of the bore, will answer as well, using a thread or a straight-edge across the face of the muzzle.

The shape and dimensions of the chamber, and the position of the interior orifice of the vent, are verified by means of the chamber-gauge, the description of which will explain its use. An inspection of the chamber-reamer will be generally satisfactory in determining the size and shape of the chamber.

The vent is measured by the appropriate gauges, the smaller of which must enter freely, and the larger not at all. It is searched for roughness, or for cavities in the metal around it, by means of the searcher, the point of which should feel every part of it carefully.

Its inclination to the surface, and its position externally, are verified by means of the vent-guide furnished for the Dahlgren guns, and by the semicircular protractor and the vent-gauge.

In guns of the ordinary construction, the position of the vent is marked on the profile-board, and its inclination to the surface is determined by the protractor and vent-gauge.

The exterior lengths of the gun are measured by the profile-board, marked with the true dimensions, the differences being measured by the foot-rule, or, if minute, estimated by the eye.

The exterior diameters are measured with the calipers and square, or by the set-gauges used in turning, and a graduated wedge.

To verify the position and alignment of the trunnions of a gun, it is first necessary to ascertain, by means of the trunnion-gauge and of the calipers, their cylindrical form and their diameters, which should be the same, or allowance must be made for half the difference in measuring their axial distances from the base-line, by the trunnion-rule, which should next be done. These distances should be equal, or their axes do not coincide—an error not tolerated.

The trunnion-square is then placed upon the trunnions in the plane of their axis. The feet of its branches should coincide with the surfaces of both trunnions, throughout their length, above and in rear, and their inner edges with the faces of the rimbases. Then, with the beam-compass, scribe on the upper surface of the gun the distance of the axis of the trunnions from the base-line, and push the sliding-point of the square down, till, at that distance, it touches the surface of the gun, and screw it fast. Then turn the gun over, and again scribe on it the same distance from the base-line. The square, being again applied, will determine whether the trunnions are above or below the axis of the bore, which will coincide with that of the gun, if accurately bored, and turned on the same centres and bearings. If the branches rest upon the trunnions before the point of the slider touches the gun at the scribe, their axis is below; but if the point touch first, above the axis of the bore, by half the space between. The graduated wedge, being placed under the vertical sliding-point, will determine the amount. If both touch at once, both axes are in the same plane.

No gun can be received, the axis of the trunnions of which is above that of the bore.

The lengths of the trunnions are measured with the foot-rule, and the diameters of the rimbases by that of the exterior rim of the trunnion-gauge.

If the alignment of the trunnions be correct, it will serve as a means of determining the correctness of the line of sight, which, before the gun is removed from the lathe, should be distinctly traced on the sight-masses and the swell of the muzzle, and should be at right angles to the base-line, to the axes of the trunnions, and to the connecting piece of the trunnion-square, when its branches rest against their rear, with the plates across their upper surfaces.

The Inspector will further satisfy himself of the correct tracing of the line of sight on the gun, by examining the lathe and the manner of tracing it in the plane of the axis of the bore, at right angles to the axis of the trunnions, as by it are placed the sights and vent, and in their absence it serves as a line of metal sight.

The positions of the sight-masses are verified by the profile-board, and by reference to the line of sight, traced on them; their form and dimensions by the templates.

The positions of the lock-lugs and their forms are verified by means of the bronze pattern furnished to each foundry for each class of the Dahlgren guns, and their dimensions by the templates. For other guns the position of the lock-piece is marked on the profile-board, and their measures taken as above.

The opening of the cascabel and its curves, and those of the breech and the muzzle-swell, are verified by means of the "cylinder-block" and the templates.

30. The following variations from the proper dimensions may be tolerated by the Inspector, though every effort should be made to conform exactly to the drafts furnished by the Bureau of Ordnance.

			Inch.
In the diameter of the bore	more		0.03
	less		0.00
Exterior diameter	where turned or planed	more	.05
		less	.05
	where not turned or planed	more	.20
		less	.05
In the length	of the bore, more or less		.10
	from rear of base-ring or line to face of the muzzle, more or less		.25
	of the cascabel, from rear of base-ring to the end, more or less		.20
	of the reinforce, more or less		.15
From the axis of trunnions to base-line, more or less			.05
In the length of chamber, more or less			.10
In the position of the axis of the trunnions	above axis of the bore		.00
	below axis of the bore		.20
In the length of trunnions, more or less			.05
Diameter of trunnions, less			0.05
In the same gun, no variations to be tolerated in the position of the trunnions, or in their alignment.			
In the vent	diameter more		0.025
	do. less		.000
In lock-piece any dimensions	more		.10
	less		.00
Variation of position of exterior orifice of vent			.05
Idem of interior do. do.			.20
Depth of cavities	in the bore or vent		.00
	on exterior surface of reinforces, where turned or planed		.10
	elsewhere, where turned or planed		.25
	on trunnions, within one inch of rimbases		.10
	on trunnions, elsewhere		.25
Enlargement or indentation of bore by proof, not to exceed			.02

The measures are to be taken by scales corresponding with the standard measures of the United States.

If two or more cavities should be near each other on the exterior, the gun may be rejected, though the cavities should be of less depth than tolerated in the table.

If the trunnions are placed within the limits of toleration, the preponderance must not vary more than 5 per cent., more or less, from that fixed in the contract.

POWDER-PROOF.

31. The proof-charges shall be as follows:

	Calibre and Class of Gun.	Charge of Powder.	Projectile.	Wads.	No. of Fires.
		Pounds.			
Shell-guns.	XV-inch ....43,000 lbs.	35	Shell . . . 330 lbs.	....	3
		45	" "	....	3
		55	Cored sh. 400 lbs.	....	3
	XI-inch.............16,000 lbs.	25	Solid shot	Gromet .	1
		15	Shell..........	....	10
	X-inch..............12,500 lbs.	18	Solid shot	Gromet .	1
		12	Shell..........	....	10
	IX-inch............ 9,000 lbs.	15	Solid shot	Gromet .	1
		10	Shell..........	....	10
	8-inch of 63 cwt., or.... 7,000 lbs.	12	Shot..........	Gromet .	1
		10	Shell..........	....	10
	8-inch of............ 6,500 lbs.	10	Shot	Gromet .	10
	8-inch of 55 cwt., or... 6,000 lbs.	10	Shot	....	1
		8	Shell..........	....	10
	32-pdr. of........... 4,500 lbs.	8	Shot	....	10
Shot-guns.	130-pdr. of — cwt., or....16,000 lbs.	30	1 shot.........	Gromet .	10
	64-pdr. of 106 cwt., or...12,000 lbs.	20	do.	do. ..	10
	32-pdr. of 57 cwt., or... 6,400 lbs.	15	do.	do. ..	10
	32-pdr. of 51 cwt., or... 5,700 lbs.	13	do.	do. ..	10
	32-pdr. of 42 cwt., or... 4,700 lbs.	10	do.	do. ..	10
	32-pdr. of 33 cwt., or... 3,600 lbs.	10	do.	do. ..	10
	32-pdr. of 27 cwt., or... 3,000 lbs.	9	do.	do. ..	10

The cannon-powder for proof shall be of not less than 1,500 feet initial velocity, as determined by the gun-pendulum at the Ordnance Yard, Washington.

It shall be filled in service cylinders, and well settled.

For chambered pieces the increased charges should fill the chamber and necessary portion of the bore.

The projectiles shall be of full weight, and not below the mean gauge; the shells shall be filled with a mixture of sand and ashes, to bring them up to the proper weight of the filled shell.

Sabots for the shell and a gromet wad over the shot.

The gun should be fired on skids or a proving-carriage, to test the trunnions.

If five per cent. out of any lot offered for ordinary proof under a contract shall fail to sustain it, the whole may be rejected, as may be stipulated in the contract.

WATER-PROOF.

32. The pressure to be applied in the water-proof will be two atmospheres, or thirty pounds to the square inch.

The penetration of water in this proof through the metal of the piece, in any place, will cause the rejection of the gun; and if, on examination after the water-proof, there shall be any defects indicated by weeping or dampness in the bore, the gun shall be rejected.

The water-proof is alone to be depended on to detect minute clusters of cavities in the bore, which for this purpose should be perfectly dry, and examined by sunlight. All inspections, consequently, should take place in fair weather, and when the temperature is above the freezing-point.

MARKING GUNS.

33. Guns for the naval service, received by authority of the Bureau of Ordnance, are to be marked in the following manner, viz.:

On the cylinder, in the line of sight near the sight-mass, all accepted guns are to have stamped an anchor two inches long.

Drawings of these stamps will be furnished by the Bureau of Ordnance.

On the base ring or line, the initials of the foundry, the register number, and the weight of gun in pounds.

On the right trunnion, the calibre and year of fabrication.

On the left trunnion, the letter P. and the initials of the inspecting officer; all the above in one-inch letters.

On the upper jaw of the cascabel, the preponderance in pounds to be stamped lightly with half-inch figures.

On the end of the upper jaw, the cascabel block and head of the pin, the foundry number in quarter-inch figures.

The foundry number is also to be marked on the right rimbase.

Guns rejected for imperfections of any kind will have the letter C. stamped on the anchor, so as to partially obliterate it.

The founders are to be dissuaded from selling such guns to other parties, and required to break them up.

Guns rejected for such defects as render them dangerous to those who fire them, should be irreparably mutilated, with the consent of the founder.

EXTREME PROOF OF TRIAL-GUNS.

34. The extreme proof of guns intended for trial of metal, subject to such modifications by the Bureau as future experience may dictate, will be conducted as follows:

A suitable 'butt' shall be erected to arrest the flight of the projectiles used in proof, and to admit of their easy recovery, and a bomb-proof, readily accessible, for the protection of the firing party.

When practicable, the 'butt' should be made thick enough to allow the shot to just pass through, and be stopped by another beyond it, without penetrating the latter; this is, for XI-inch, about 12 feet.

With care, it is estimated that 130 shells may be fired 1,000 times, at the rate of one hundred rounds per day.

After undergoing the ordinary proof established for its calibre and class, the gun selected for extreme proof shall be subjected to at least 1,000 rounds with service charges.

It may be fired from the skids, or suspended, as the Bureau may direct.

During the trial the gun shall be frequently and critically examined, inside and out, for cracks or defects, especially about the interior orifice of the vent, of which impressions are to be taken in wax at regular intervals, in the manner prescribed on page 16, or in such other manner as the Bureau may direct. If they show that the vent is corroded in furrows, and enlarged considerably in diameter at its junction with the bore, a permanent impression is to be taken in lead, to show the conical enlargement. The following manner, practised at the Experimental Battery at Washington, is recommended:

IMPLEMENTS REQUIRED.

35. 1. A soft wire about 0.07 in. in diameter, and 3 or 4 fathoms long.

2. A lever about twice the length of the bore, and about 3 inches in diameter, and shod to suit the curve of the bore nearly.

3. A small button of soft lead, judged to be of sufficient size to fill the vent at least one inch from the bore. This is to be pierced lengthwise to receive the wire.

TO TAKE THE IMPRESSION.

36. Shove the wire through the vent; let it pass along the bore and out at the muzzle; put it through the leaden button and tie a knot at the end. Draw the wire back through the vent until the leaden button is introduced firmly into the inner orifice.

TYPES OF VENTS.

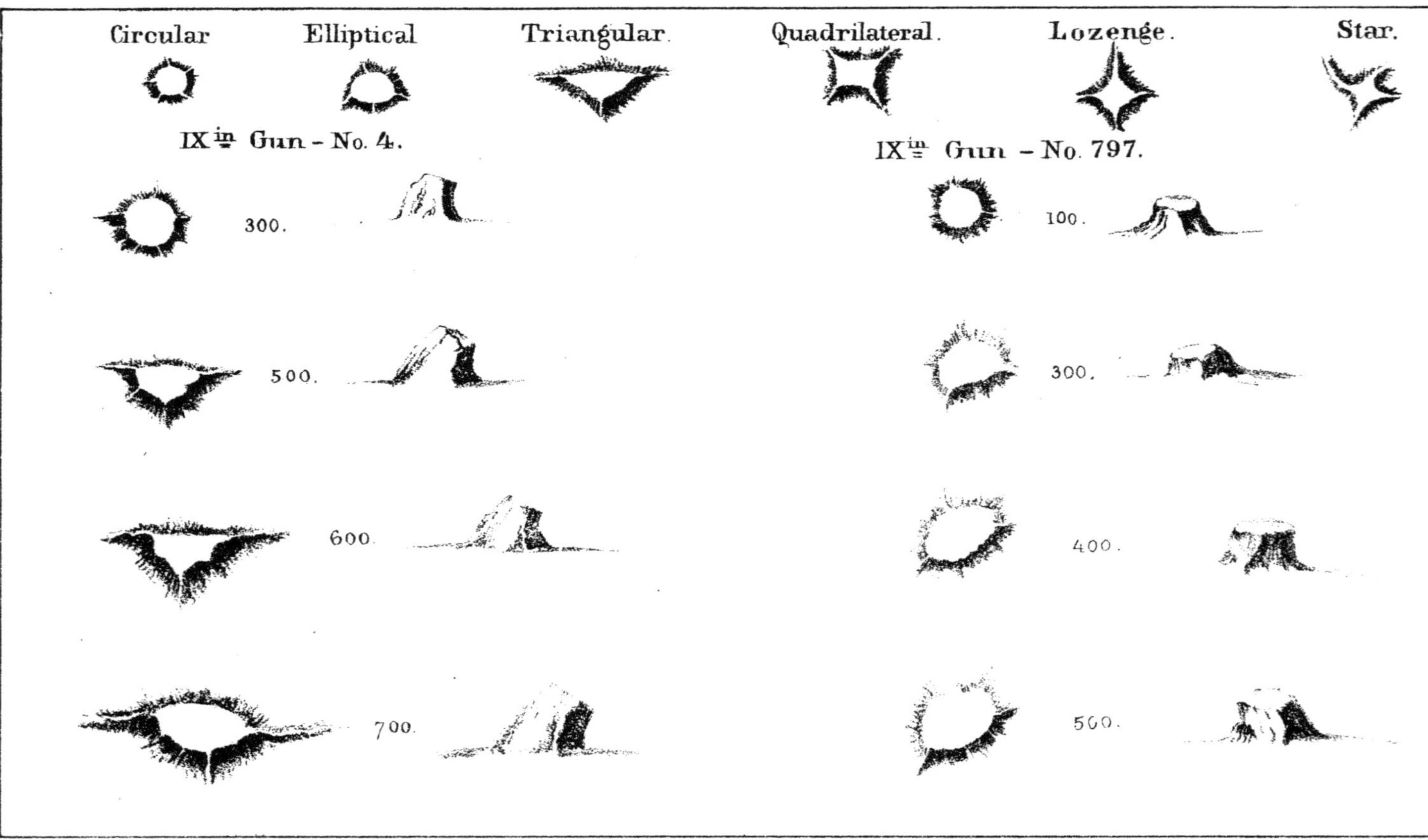

Lith. by J. F. Gedney, Washn.

Apply the lever, making its shoe bear on the button, and force it well in by repeated blows, the muzzle being the fulcrum. This done, disengage the button by pushing in the priming-wire.

In taking impressions of the vent and cracks, each button in turn is used as a pattern for moulding its successor, allowing for the progressive enlargement of the vent, or the cracks emanating from it. When the crack shows itself, the head of the button should be so enlarged as to include it.

These examinations should take place after every twenty fires, at least, and more frequently when any unusual enlargement of the vent or extension of cracks shall be developed, and indicate its speedy destruction.

Before each examination the bore of the gun is to be carefully washed and dried.

In recording the measurements of the bore in extreme proof and after service, distinguish between "indentation," which is the depression at the "seat of the shot," which is always below, and the "wear of the bore," which is generally above, and increase of bore, or "enlargement" from any other cause.

When from the appearance of the bore at the interior orifice of the vent, and especially when a crack or cracks appear to be extending rapidly, the vent so enlarged may be filled with melted tin, zinc, or Babbitt metal,—a tight-fitting sponge-head being pushed to the bottom of the chamber to close the interior orifice,—and the other vent be drilled through for the purpose of continuing the firing.

The precise time at which this is to be done will vary, according to circumstances; such as quality of metal, charge, and elevation.

The endurance of a smooth-bored gun with service charges may be surely predicted by observation of the progressive wear of the interior orifice of the vent.

There are certain general forms in which this enlargement takes place. They may be classed as triangular, lozenge, quadrilateral, star, circular, and elliptic. (See Plate.)

With the ordinary central vent, when subjected to a rapid, continuous fire, the enlargement usually takes the form of an isosceles triangle, the apex of one of the angles towards the muzzle, and the other two perpendicular to it.

With the lateral vent of the Dahlgren system it usually takes the lozenge form, the cracks extending from the opposite angles lengthwise of the bore.

With those rifled cannon in which the vent is bouched, the cracks appear around the bouching; and although the bouching preserves the vent, yet the formation of fissures around the enlarged orifice, when once commenced, causes a greater tendency to rupture. With the vent not bouched, the wear in rifled cannon is about double that of the smooth-bore.

So long as the wear of the vent is regular and without cracks, a mere enlargement is not indicative of danger; but when it reaches a diameter of four-tenths (.4) of an inch the vent should be closed and a new one opened.

A gun of large calibre should not in service be expected to endure more than 400 or 500 rounds before it will be necessary to open the new vent, which, however, will be of no advantage, unless the old one be closed at its interior orifice, on which the gases would otherwise continue to act as a wedge.

The first distinct appearance of the cracks, as shown by the button, is the proper limit.

After the gun bursts, make a sketch or draft showing lines of fracture, and reserve specimens to be sent to the Ordnance Yard at Washington for trial of density and tensile strength; and, if practicable, a photograph should be taken.

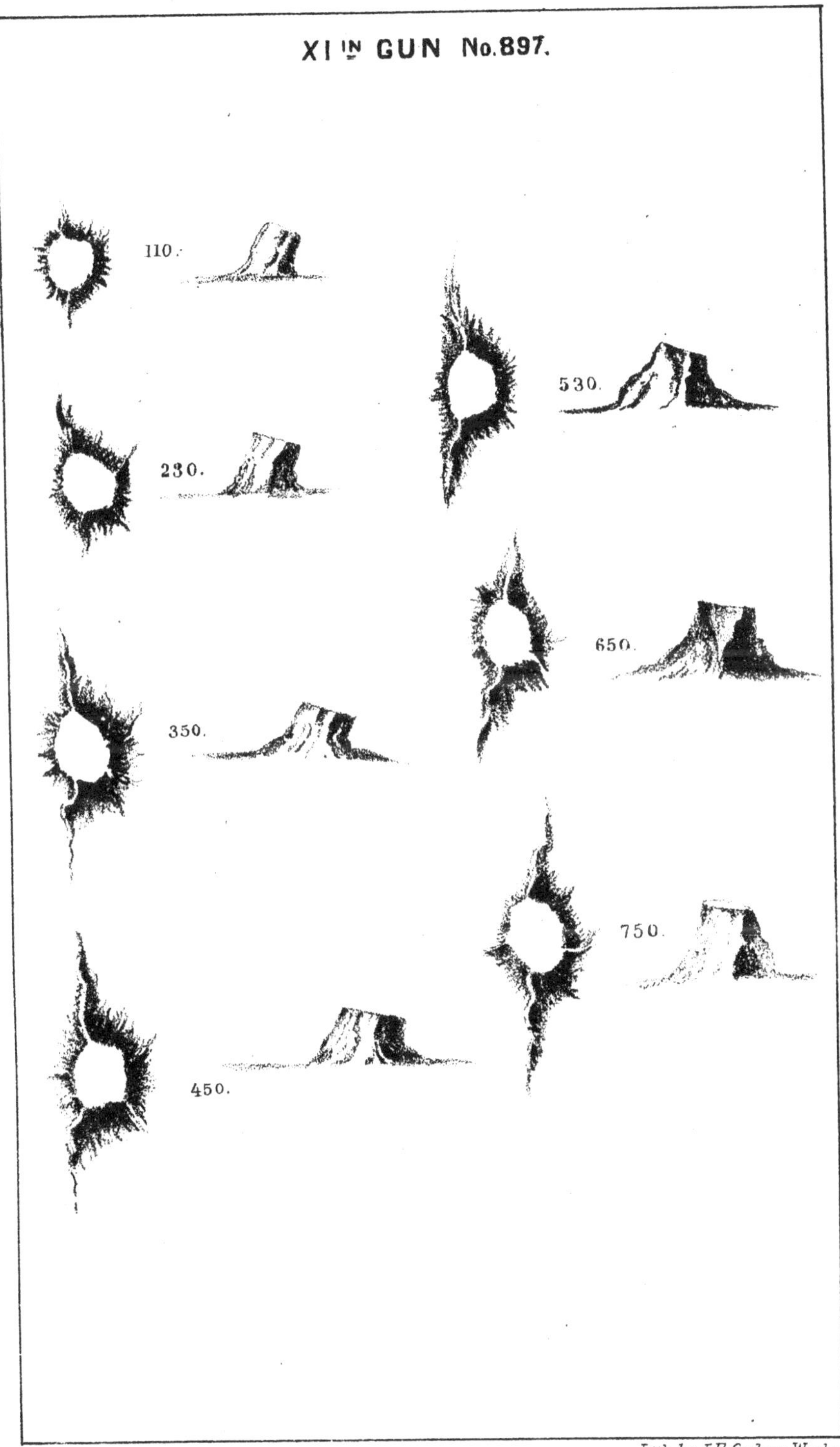

Lith. by J.F. Gedney, Washn.

PREPARATION OF GUNS FOR SERVICE.

37. After the guns have been received at the Navy Yards it is necessary to adjust the sights, and, in the guns of the Dahlgren pattern, cut the screw hole in the cascabel.

CUTTING THE SCREW-HOLE.

38. The boring and screw-cutting machine is a convenient portable hand drill-press, the use of which is readily understood by any machinist.

The gun being carefully levelled, and the trunnions placed horizontal, the position of the centre of the screw-hole, which in the guns of the Dahlgren pattern is tangent to the radius of the breech, is marked on the neck of the cascabel with a centre punch.

The machine is placed on the cascabel, the boring shaft inserted in the hollow leading bar, and its movable centre placed on the mark. The instrument is then set vertical, by a spirit-level on the cogged driving-wheel, and the four pairs of set screws on the clamp-head embracing the cascabel.

The centre is then removed, and a drill inserted in the lower extremity of the boring-shaft, which, being held firmly by a shoulder and turned by a four-armed wrench, while pressed up to the metal by slowly turning the cogged driving-wheel, cuts the hole. This is successively enlarged, by two or more counterbits, to the size of the body of the screw.

The cutter is then inserted in the leading bar, and the thread cut.

ADJUSTMENT OF THE SIGHTS.

39. The bore having been thoroughly cleaned, the axis is levelled by a spirit-level; this may be very conveniently done by the aid of the levelling-bar. The axis of the trunnions is to be laid horizontal, either by placing a small level on the trunnions, or, as more exact, by using the trunnion-square. If the trunnion-square is used it will be proper to verify the position of the line of sight, which is frequently incorrectly placed at the foundries.

The breech-sight is then to be adjusted.

A brass head or tompion, fitted with a vertical arm, on which there is a ledge for a spirit-level, is then introduced into the bore, and the arm placed vertical by the spirit-level and a tangent screw.

The arm is pierced on its centre line with two holes—one at the height of the prescribed diameter of the muzzle, the other at a height equal to the proper distance of the bottom of the sight-notch from the axis of the bore. A waxed thread or fine wire, being stretched from the upper hole to the centre of the sight-notch, will coincide with the line of sight traced on the swell of the muzzle, the top of the reinforce sight-mass, and the base-line, if they are correctly placed. It will also be parallel to the axis of the bore if the adjustment of the breech-sight is exact, and the top of the reinforce-sight is made to coincide with it.

This is, however, seldom the case, and after the adjustment of the reinforce-sight it is necessary to verify it.

This is done by the levelling-bar—a square steel bar with parallel faces, somewhat longer than the distance between the sights, the rear end of which is bevelled at 60° (the angle at which the sight is placed).

The outer end of this bar is placed on the reinforce-sight, which has been previously adjusted to the proper height, and the bevelled end in contact with the outer face of the sight-bar. The bar is then levelled by two screws placed near the inner end, and a spirit-level on its upper surface.

If then the bottom of the sight-notch coincides with the bottom of the bar, the line of sight is parallel to the axis; otherwise, the reinforce-sight or the sight-bar must be lowered until coincidence is obtained.

A centre line on the bar verifies the coincidence of the line of sight, and also the motion of the sight-bar in the vertical plane. The bevel verifies the angle of the bar; and the distance between the outer faces of the sight-notch and of the reinforce-sight, being also marked on the levelling-bar, verifies this adjustment.

Another method is sometimes and more advantageously used in adjusting the sights of guns which have not been turned.

Two iron or wooden disks are turned to the exact diameter of the bore, and placed on a rod two or three feet longer than the bore. One of the disks is placed near the bottom of the bore, the other just within the muzzle. On the part projecting beyond the muzzle there is a double square, each arm of which is divided into equal parts and traversed by a fine slit.

The square being set vertical by a spirit-level or plumb-line, and a waxed thread or wire stretched taut from the outer arm through the slit, cutting equal divisions on each, and passing through the centre of the slit, it is evident that a line of sight is obtained through the centre of metal and parallel to the axis of the bore.

This method has the advantage of adjusting the sights in any plane parallel to the axis, as in the case of the side-sights of rifled and other cannon.

ADJUSTMENT OF THE SIDE-SIGHTS.

40. The gun having been levelled, and the trunnions placed horizontal, a centre line is to be drawn on the top of the left (or right) rimbase.

The support for the sight is then to be fitted to the breech, at the distance from this line marked on the pattern-sight for its calibre, with the bottom of the sight-notch in the bar, exactly the height of the front sight (one inch) above the upper surface of the rimbase; the sight-bar perpendicular.

It is advisable to place a very thin sheet of rubber under the support, to prevent the heads of the screws from being jumped off by the vibration. The screws have the same thread as those for the present reinforce-sight.

After the breech-sight is adjusted, a parallel to the axis of the bore is to be drawn in the usual manner, and the front sight screwed in on the rimbase.

Some trifling adjustment may then be required, to bring the height of the top of the front sight and the bottom of the sight-notch parallel to the axis of the bore in both the horizontal and vertical planes.

PRESERVATION OF GUNS.

41. Guns received at Navy Yards are to be carefully placed on the ranges of masonry, capped with iron skids or bars. It is intended that these shall be so high that the guns may be rolled upon them without their trunnions touching the ground, and that the earth will not be beaten up against their muzzles by heavy rains.

42. The surface over which guns are to be stowed should be kept firm and clear of all vegetation, and for this purpose should be covered with cinders from the smiths' forges, or other substance unfavorable to or destructive of the growth of plants and grasses.

43. In stowing the guns they should be made to rest on one of the skids or bars, a little forward of the base-ring, the muzzle depressed, but not so much as to prevent the use of the sponge to clean out the gun; the axis of the trunnion of each to be inclined the same way, and just enough not to touch the adjoining gun; the vents to be upwards.

44. Before the stowage is finally made they should be carefully and thoroughly cleaned from rust and all improper coatings, and be lacquered internally and externally with such composition as may be directed by the Bureau. This should be applied, when practicable, when the guns are well warmed by the rays of the sun. The vents and all screw-holes are to be stopped with plugs made of soft wood or oakum dipped in tallow, after they have been protected by an application of beeswax dissolved in spirits of turpentine, or other composition that may be directed by the Bureau.

45. No tompions are to be put into the guns when they are stowed unless expressly directed by the Bureau; if so ordered, a score must be cut out from them on the lower side, half an inch wide and equally deep.

46. In lacquering guns care is to be taken to leave the distinguishing marks and numbers distinctly visible.

47. Shell-guns are always to be denominated by the diameter of the bore; shot-guns by the weight of their shot.

48. Guns of the same calibre and class, when it can be conveniently done, are to be stowed in the same tier or range, and those of each class belonging to or selected for any particular vessel kept together. Each tier or range of guns of a particular calibre or class is to be marked accordingly with paint on a sign-board, and the first gun of each class belonging to a vessel is to be marked with the name of the vessel.

49. The Officer on Ordnance duty will examine all the guns in the yard and on board vessels in ordinary, at least once in every two weeks, and take care that they are kept protected from rust or any other injury, and will report to the Bureau whenever any additional precautions or arrangements are required for their proper preservation, and which may not be furnished by the order of the Commandant of the Yard.

50. No cutting, boring, or chiselling of guns is to be done at any time without express authority from the Bureau.

51. No condemnation of guns or small arms belonging to the Navy is to be made, except upon surveys specially ordered, and confirmed by the Chief of the Bureau; nor of other articles which have been furnished under his authority, or by his direction, unless by surveys ordered or sanctioned by him.

52. When guns and their equipments are to be put on board vessels for their armament, the guns are to be carefully and thoroughly cleaned and examined, to see that they are in all respects in proper serviceable condition.

The vents should be examined with the vent-gauges and searchers, to see that they are clear from any substance which may obstruct the use of priming-wires and primers.

53. The carriages are also to be carefully examined, the trunnion-holes and arms of the axletrees cleaned, and saturated with boiled linseed oil, the cracks filled with putty, and rubbed smooth, and the trunnion-holes black-leaded. The iron work should be freed from rust, all screws be made to work easily, and be well cleaned and coated with proper composition.

54. The Ordnance Officers will see that the sights are properly fitted and marked for their proper guns. The greatest care should be taken that they are properly adjusted, as the efficiency of the ship depends on it, and it is difficult to detect or remedy any error after they are placed on board; that the beds and quoins are fitted and adjusted, and the quoins graduated to degrees or distances to correspond with those marked on the sight-bars. Porter's quoin is adopted for all carriages requiring quoins.

55. New guns are to have locks fitted to them before being put on board ship. Those having two lugs will have the one on the right fitted; the other is to be left solid.

56. When the guns are to be shipped for transportation merely, the same precautions are to be taken to guard them from injury as on shore, with the addition of a wad dipped into the composition which covers the bore, thrust into the muzzle, and connected with the tompion by a lanyard.

In the transportation of guns by rail—unboxed—the vents are to be plugged with soft wood, puttied over, and turned vent downwards on the trucks. All bronze howitzers transported by rail shall be boxed.

57. At the termination of a cruise the guns composing the battery of every vessel-of-war of the United States, shall be carefully examined by the Ordnance Officer of the Yard, and such others as may be directed, with the view to discover and report any injuries which they may have sustained in service, or any defects which may not have been developed in the original proof. In this examination the attention of the Inspecting Officers is to be directed to the following points, viz.:

Enlargement of the interior or exterior orifice of the vent.

Indentations or hollows produced by the shot balloting against the surface of the bore, or by the action of the gases.

Cuts or scratches in the bore, produced by fragments of broken or the roughness of imperfect shot.

Roughness or corrosion of the metal on the exterior, produced by neglect or exposure.

Similar injuries in the bore, or any enlargement of the bore, which is to be ascertained by measuring with the star-gauge, at every one-fourth ($\frac{1}{4}$) of an inch from the bottom of the cylindrical part to the seat of the shot, every inch from that point to the trunnion, thence every 5 inches to the muzzle, and the results recorded in the usual form, and reported to the Bureau, that they may be compared with those noted at the original inspection.

In rifled cannon, cracks or injuries produced by firing, or the rupture of shells, are to be sought for:—

Around and in rear of the vent bouching;

On the top of the bore, between the trunnions and reinforce band.

On the lower side of the bore, near the seat of the shot, at the junction of the lands and grooves.

Near the inside of the muzzle, caused by explosion of shells.

Care is to be taken that the distinguishing marks and numbers are always accurately noted, that the correct history of each gun may be preserved.

58. Before sailing, the Inspector of Ordnance will furnish the commander with a descriptive list of his battery, together with a statement of the number of times each gun on board has been fired, in the following form; a copy of which the commander shall transmit to the Bureau before sailing: this list shall be returned to the Inspector of the Yard to which she may return, with all additional firing noted opposite the number of each gun, certified "correct" by the commander.

In the list furnished by the Inspector, if the "number of fires" is *estimated*, it is to be entered in red ink (*See* Arts. 62–64), and so carried forward in the subsequent returns.

NAME OF VESSEL. STATION.

( ) ( )

Class of Gun.	Marks on Base-Ring.			Trunnions.		Pivot, or Broadside.	Where Received.	Number of Fires to Date.
	Reg. No.	Weight.	Foundry.	Right.	Left.			

Forwarded by ——————————— *Commanding.*

59. The Bureau directs that, whenever a gun is taken on board a vessel, the number of rounds which have been fired from it be ascertained by the Commander, a record made thereof, and forwarded with the descriptive list, in the above form, to the Bureau; and whenever a gun is landed or transferred to another vessel, a similar record is to be furnished the officer receiving it, which must be stated in the receipt for the gun, and a copy forwarded to the Bureau of Ordnance by the officer delivering the gun.

Tho Commander shall also transmit to the Bureau a quarterly return, according to tho prescribed form (*See* Appendix B, No. X.) of all firing whether with or without projectiles, in action or otherwise; noting particularly the kind of shell, species of fuze, kind, charge, and name of maker of the powder used in the gun and shell. He shall take care to note also the number of premature explosions of shells, and the point at which they take place, with the supposed causes thereof.

60. The Inspector will also furnish the commander with a set of leaden impressions of the interior orifice of the vents of the guns, secured in a suitable box, that he may be able to compare the wear and gradual enlargement. These will be transferred with the guns to other ships or when landed.

61. The protracted firing to which the Navy cannon have been subjected, and to which they will continue to be liable, renders it necessary not to exceed the number of fires designated for each vent.

These must never exceed five hundred (500) fires for each vent.

In the IX-in., XI-in., and guns of similar form, the right vent is always bored through, and the left initiated sufficiently to give it direction.

When five hundred (500) rounds have been fired from the right vent, it is to be closed by filling it with molten zinc or lead, and the left vent is to be bored, which will require a skilful mechanic.

When the left vent has been fired five hundred (500) rounds, the gun is to be disused, as it will then have been fired one thousand (1,000) times.

It may happen, from some peculiarity in the nature of the iron, that the vent may be worn to its full extent before five hundred (500) rounds have been fired, in which case the vent is then to be closed, and the other vent opened.

The gun should be frequently and critically examined inside and out for cracks or defects, especially about the interior orifice of the vent, of which impressions should be taken after every ten shotted rounds in practice, and at the close of an action.

The instrument described on p. 16 is convenient, but by no means indispensable—any small spar, such as a boat's mast, or even the rammer handle with a curved piece of wood seized to the end, will, in expert hands, take an impression of the vent or crack equally well.

62. As the best indication of the amount of firing to which any smooth-bored gun has been exposed, when it is not otherwise known, is given by the enlargement of the vent, particular attention will be paid, in the reinspection of the guns, to this point. The standard gauge will be used to ascertain the general enlargement, and the searcher to detect defects which may have been developed in firing. Impressions are to be taken of the lower orifice of the vent with softened wax, and if they show that the vent is corroded in furrows and enlarged considerably in diameter at its junction with the bore, a permanent impression is to be taken in lead to show the conical enlargement. (See mode of taking impressions, Arts. 35 and 36.)

63. When the number of rounds fired is not known, an estimate may be made from an examination of the vent by cylindrical gauges differing from each other by .01 of an inch passed through it. If the number is estimated, it is to be entered in red ink.

64. In all the guns of the Dahlgren pattern the vents are (.2) two-tenths of an inch in diameter. In all other guns .22 of an inch exterior, .2 of an inch on the interior.

Observation of the wear of the vent in proof firing of smooth-bored guns gives the following as the average diameter of the vent, after the undermentioned number of fires:

No. of rounds	100	200	300	400	500
Diameter of vent	.24	.26	.30	.35	.40

These, combined with examination of the interior orifice, will enable a very correct judgment to be formed of the probable number of fires sustained and duration of the gun.

The larger the calibre and the heavier the charge the more promptly the wear is manifested on the interior and exterior.

This enlargement does not extend very far from the lower orifice until the enlargement on the exterior has reached a diameter of .3 of an inch.

65. So long as the wear is regular, and the cracks, although numerous, do not exceed .5 of an inch in length, the indications are good. If the cracks are but few or diminish in number, running into each other and extending rapidly, it is a very unfavorable sign. In the rifle cannon (Parrott's) cracks athwart the bore either running into the bouching or in the rear of it are very unfavorable to the gun's endurance.

66. Whenever any premature explosions of shells take place within the gun or near the muzzle, a careful examination of the gun shall be made; and all the circumstances of the case, together with the opinions of the commander and officers in immediate charge as to the cause thereof, reported to the Bureau; taking care to state the kind of shell and species of fuze used; the mode of loading; whether the shell was lined or coated on the interior; kind, charge, and name of maker of the powder which was used in the gun and shell.

There is reason to believe that few failures of the Parrott rifles have occurred where the guns have not been previously, or at the time, injuriously strained by the explosion of shells within the bore.

67. Whenever a gun shall give away under fire, or an accident of any kind happen to one, the Bureau desires to be immediately informed of all the facts in relation thereto.

Particular attention should be paid to the following points:

1. The manner in which the gun was loaded, stating the charge and kind of powder used, and character and weight of projectiles.
2. The condition and appearance of the gun after it gave way, and what effect was produced on the carriage by the explosion.
3. What injuries, if any, occurred to the crew of the gun or vessel.

Sketches of the gun and fragments which remain should also be sent to the Ordnance Yard at Washington for trial of density and tensile strength, accompanied by the written statement in detail of the officers in immediate charge of the gun, and if practicable a photograph should be taken.

INSPECTION OF SHOT AND SHELLS.

RULES AND MEMORANDA FOR THE GOVERNMENT OF INSPECTORS.

68. All shot and shells for the naval service must be—

1st. Made from gray or mottled charcoal pig-iron.

2d. This iron must not be blasted with anthracite coal.

3d. It must be poured into sand moulds.

69. After being cast in this manner, the shot and shells must be—

1st. Spherical.

2d. Smooth on the surface.

3d. Free from the defects named in the following rules for the use of the inspecting instruments:

FOR SHOT.

70. Inspecting Instruments.—One large, small, and one medium ring gauge, and one cylinder-gauge for each calibre. The cylinder-gauge shall have the same diameter as the large gauge, made of cast iron, and three calibres in length. One hammer weighing two pounds, and having a flat face and a conical point; one searcher, of steel wire, with a handle; one pair of calipers and standard scale; one cold chisel; steel punches.

71. After having been well cleaned, each shot is placed upon a table, and examined to see that its surface is smooth, and that the metal is sound and free from seams, flaws, and blisters. If clusters of cavities or small holes appear on the surface, strike the point of the hammer into them, and ascertain their depth with the searcher. If the depth of the cavity exceeds 0.2 inch, the shot shall be rejected; it shall also be rejected if any attempt is made to conceal defects by plugging or filling holes in any mode whatever.

72. The shot must pass in every direction through the large gauge, and not at all through the small one; the calipers and scale will determine exactly the difference of diameters of the same projectile.

73. The ring and cylinder gauges shall be examined before each inspection, and when found to have enlarged 0.01 of an inch, must be laid aside and marked as unserviceable.

74. The shot are next to be passed through the cylinder-gauge, placed at an inclination of about two inches between the ends, and supported in such a manner as to be easily turned from time to time, to prevent its being worn in furrows. Shot which slide or stick in the cylinder shall be rejected; the latter must be pushed out from the lower end of the cylinder with a wooden rammer.

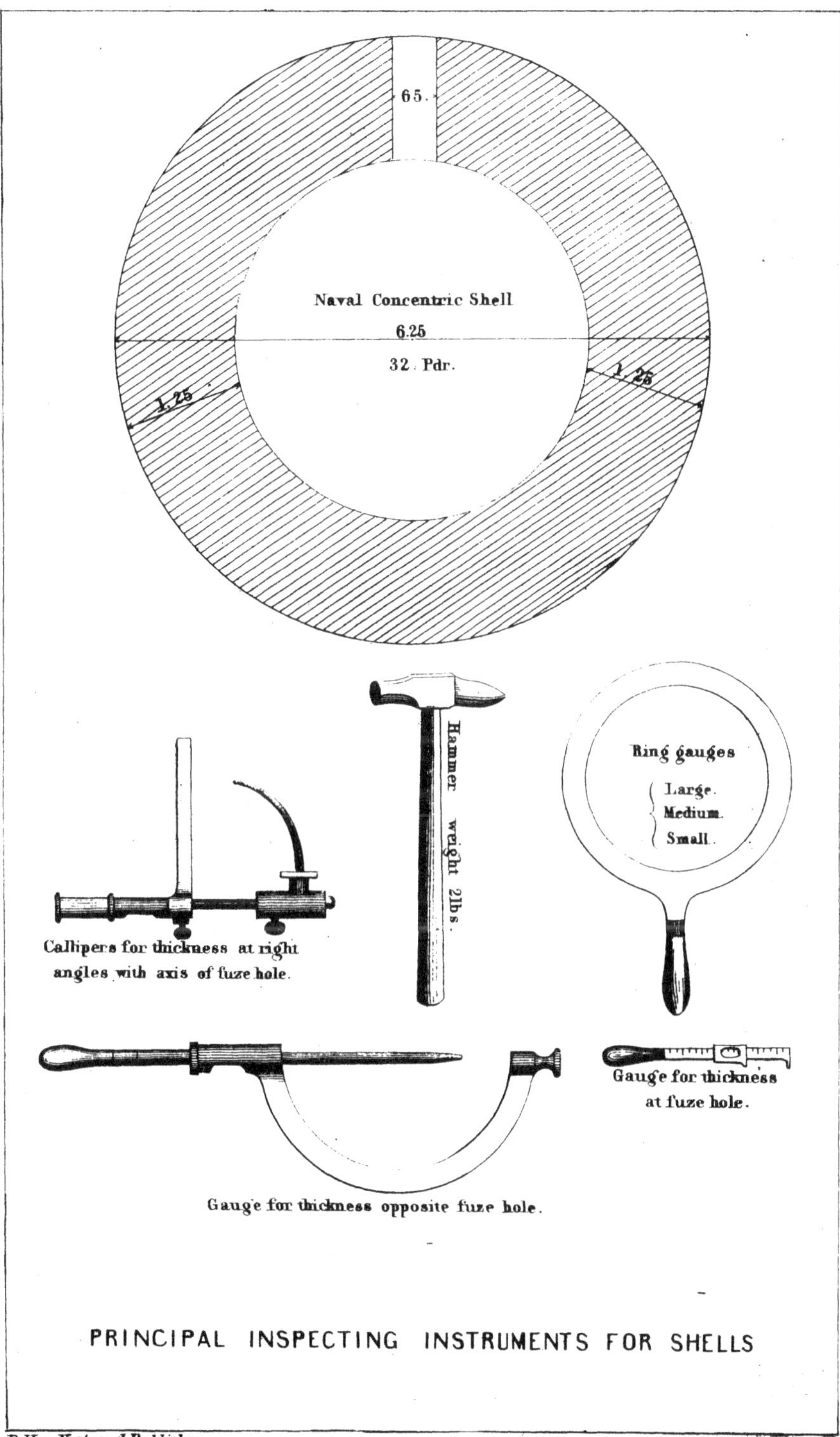

PRINCIPAL INSPECTING INSTRUMENTS FOR SHELLS

D. Van Nostrand, Publisher.

Julius Bien, pr.

75. The next proof of shot is to drop a few taken indiscriminately from the lot under inspection from a height of twenty feet on a solid platform of iron, or roll them down an inclined plane of the same height against a mass of iron; after which they are again examined for defects of metal.

76. The average weight of shot shall be determined by weighing at least three parcels, of from 20 to 50 each, taken indiscriminately from the lot. As many of the lightest shall be weighed separately as the inspecting officer may deem necessary, and all found to fall below the least weight allowed in the annexed table of the dimensions of shot and shells shall be rejected. Shot made of charcoal iron will be stamped with a * or "burr" near the gate.

SHELLS.

77. Shells should be cast on a half-inch hollow spindle, to allow the gas to pass freely from the core; the fuze-hole would then be sufficiently large to admit the gauge for thickness before the shells leave the foundry.

78. Inspecting Instruments.—In addition to the instruments for shot, there will be required calipers with steel points for measuring the thickness of the shell at points on the great circle at right angles with the axis of the fuze-hole; gauges for the thickness at and opposite the fuze-hole; a conical flat steel gauge for the fuze-hole, marked at the point to which it should enter; a pair of strong hand-bellows, with a wooden plug to fit the fuze-hole and the nozzle air-tight. (See Plate.)

INSPECTION.

79. The surface of the shell and its exterior dimensions, form, weight, and strength, are to be examined and tested as in the case of shot, and subject to all the conditions there specified.

80. The greatest care is to be taken to remove every particle of sand or fragment of iron from the interior when they are about to be loaded for service. And the Inspectors of Ordnance at foundries or Navy Yards will satisfy themselves that this has been done before accepting or preparing them for service.

81. The shell is next struck with a hammer, to judge by the ring or sound whether it is free from cracks; and the exterior and interior diameters of the fuze-hole (which should be accurately reamed) are to be verified, and the soundness of the metal about the inside of the fuze-hole ascertained. To determine the thickness of the metal, three points, at least, on the great circle at right angles to the axis of the fuze-hole are to be measured; also one at the fuze-hole and one at the bottom. No shell shall be received which deviates more than one-tenth of an inch from the proper thickness in any part.

82. The shell is next placed in a tub of water, which should be deep enough to completely cover the shell. Air is then forced by the bellows into the shell. If there are any holes in it, air-bubbles will rise on the surface of the water, and the shell shall be rejected.

83. This occasionally occurs from the escape of air from porous spots which do not extend to the interior of the shells. In this case the action of the bellows produces no increase of bubbles, which cease rising as soon as the spots or cavities are filled with water. Porous spots are also detected by their absorbing water and drying slowly when exposed to the air, and shall likewise cause the rejection of the shell.

84. The Inspecting Officers will stamp the shell at one inch from the fuze-hole with their initials, also those of the foundry at which they are cast.

The Inspector or one of his assistants must be present when shot or shell are inspected; and the stamps and marks are always to be retained in the possession of the Inspector.

85. Rejected shells are to be mutilated by chipping a piece out at the fuze-hole.

86. If, upon the inspection of shot or shells, any of them should be found not to conform strictly to these instructions or to the requirements of the contract under which they are offered for reception, the Inspecting Officer is not to receive them; but if, in his opinion, the defects, taken in connection with the general character of the articles, will not impair their efficacy or render them unsafe or hazardous, he may refer to the Chief of the Bureau of Ordnance for his decision, forwarding to him minute and full information on the subject.

87. Shot and shells shall be delivered for inspection at the places specified in the contract, at the expense of the contractor; and those which are rejected shall be immediately removed, also at his expense.

88. TABLE OF SHOT AND SHELL GAUGES.

SHOT.

DIMENSIONS, WEIGHT.	XV. (Cored.)	XIII.	XI.	X.	IX.	8.	32.
Diameter of large gauge for foundries.	14.83	12.83	10.83	9.83	8.83	7.88	6.28
Diameter of small gauge for foundries.	14.77	12.77	10.77	9.77	8.77	7.82	6.22
Mean of gauge for foundries.......in.	14.80	12.80	10.80	9.80	8.80	7.85	6.25
Mean w'ght required of foundries.lbs.	400.	276.	166.	124.	90.	65.	32.5
Least weight allowed foundries...lbs.	–	–	–	–	–	64.5	32.
Diameter of small gauges for service. 1st class.....in.	–	–	–	–	–	7.82	6.22
Diameter of small gauges for service. 2d class.....in.	–	–	–	–	–	7.80	6.20

89. SHELL.

DIMENSIONS, WEIGHT.	XV.	XIII.	XI.	X.	IX.	8.	32.
Diameter of large gauge for foundries.	14.83	12.83	10.87	9.87	8.87	7.88	6.28
Diameter of small gauge for foundries.	14.77	12.77	10.83	9.83	8.83	7.82	6.22
Mean of gauge for foundries.......in.	14.80	12.80	10.85	9.85	8.85	7.85	6.25
Thickness. Proper..............in.	2.85	2.37	2.	1.80	1.60	1.50	1.25
Thickness. Greatest............in.	2.95	2.47	2.10	1.90	1.70	1.60	1.35
Thickness. Least..............in.	2.75	2.27	1.90	1.70	1.50	1.40	1.15
Diameter of fuze-hole. Proper and least..	.65	.65	.65	.65	.65	.65	.65
Diameter of fuze-hole. Greatest.........	.75	.75	.75	.75	.75	.75	.75
Diameter of large gauge for strapped.	14.93	12.93	10.93	9.93	8.93	7.93	6.33
Mean w'ght required for foundries.lbs.	330.	208.	127.	95.	68.50	50.	25.
Least weight allowed foundries for any one ....lbs.	–	–	126.	94.	67.50	49.	24.5
Weight of filled and sabotted.....lbs.	352.	216.5	135.5	101.50	73.50	52.75	26.5

For gauges of boat-gun fixed ammunition, see Boat Armament of United States Navy, by Admiral Dahlgren, 2d edition, 1856.

90. SHRAPNEL.

DIMENSIONS, WEIGHT.	XV.	XI.	X.	IX.	8.	32.	24.	12.
Mean of empty case... Gauge.........in.	14.80	10.85	9.85	8.85	7.85	6.25	5.67	4.52
Mean of empty case... Thickness.....in.	1.25	1.	.87	.75	.69	.60	.55	.45
Mean of empty case... Weight.......lbs.	178.	76.	57.	38.	29.	15.	11.	6.5
Balls Number.............	1000.	625.	435.	350.	220.	235. lead	175. lead	80. lead
Balls Diameter......... in.	1.	.85	.85	.85	.85	.65	.65	.65
Balls Weight..........lbs.	140.	51.	33.5	27.	17.	14.	10.5	4.75
Sulphur ....lbs.	30.	10.	8.5	7.	5.	2.25	1.5	.75
Bursting charge..........oz.	10.	6.	4.	3.	2.5	1.25	450. grs.	350. grs.
Weight complete... " sabotted.... ..lbs.	358.	141.	101.	75.	52.	32.	24.	12.

91. DIMENSIONS OF SABOTS AND STRAPS FOR SHELL AND SHRAPNEL.

DIMENSIONS, WEIGHT.	XV.	XIII.	XI.	X.	IX.	8.	32.	24.	12.
Thickness.........................in.	5.	4.50	2.75	2.75	2·40	2.	1.50	1.90	1.50
Diameter.. greatest..............in.	14.25	12.25	10.50	9.50	8·60	6.90	6.	5.70	4.60
Diameter.. least.................in.	14.25	12.25	10.50	9.50	8·60	6.30	5.50	5.55	4.40
Depth of saucers...................in.	2.50	2.25	1.80	1.60	1·40	1.20	1.	1.50	1.30
Weights ....lbs.	8.90	5.50	2.70	2.40	1·85	.90	.50	.46	.22
Shell-straps.. Length ....in.	25.75	22.5	17.25	17.25	14·75	13.25	10.25	7.625	6.375
Shell-straps.. Width....... .....in.	1.25	1.	.75	.75	·75	.75	.625	.50	.375
Shell-straps.. Tin...............No.	XXD	XXD	XXD	XXD	IX	IX	IC	IC	IC
Tacks...........................No.	20	16	12	12	8	8	8	4	4

92. GRAPE.

DIMENSIONS, WEIGHT.	XV.	XI.	X.	IX.	8.	32.	24.	12.	RIFLE.	
									20.	12.
Weight of stand.............lbs.	-	34.75	26.10	20.4	15.7	8.75				
Weight of balls.............lbs.	-	89.10	71.70	52 20	37 12	24.80				
Number of balls..............	-	15.	15.	18.	18.	12.				
Diameter of balls..........in.	-	3.55	3.34	2.80	2.50	2.50				
Weight complete..........lbs.	-	125.08	98.62	74.10	53.25	33.50				

93. CANISTER.

DIMENSIONS, WEIGHT.	XV.	XI.	X.	IX.	8.	32.	24.	12.
Windage..................in.	.25	.25	.25	.25	.25	.25	.15	.15
Height. Empty case.....in.	15.50	13.50	11.75	10¼	9.75	8.65	5.	3.85
Height. Finished.........in.	14.	12.	10.5	9.5	8.75	7.75	6.	5.
Case notched, and turned over.......in.	.75	.75	.65	.50	.50	.45	4.65	3.52
Thickness of head Top.....in.	1	¾	¾	¾	.75	.50	.35	.3
Thickness of head Middle...in.	1.	¾						
Thickness of head Bottom...in.	2.	1.	1.	1.	.75	.50	1.90	1.90
Size of. Rod.............in.	$\frac{13}{16}$	½	½	½				
Size of. Nut diameter..in.	2.75	1.75	1.75	1.75				
Size of. Nut thickness.in.	1.50	1.	1.	1.				
Size of. Bale.............in.	½	¾	¾	¾				
Metal and thickness Iron........No.	20.	25.	25.	25.				
Metal and thickness Tin........No.	-	-	-	-	XXD	XXD	IC	IC
Balls. Number.............	600.	315.	290	230.	162.	100.	39.	39.
Balls. Diameter.........in.	1.30	1.30	1.30	1.30	1.30	1.30	1.30	1.
Balls. Weight..........lbs.	150.	85.	70.	65.	45.	28.	12.5	5.85
Weight finished.........lbs.	207.	120.	98.	70.	50.	30.	14.55	7.75

NOTE.—Bottom of XV-inch canister, of two thicknesses of oak, ash, or beech, crossing each other; put together with wrought-iron nails, clinched; spindle riveting on the bottom through a 3 inches square plate, ¼ thick; cast-iron hexagonal nut, with wrought-iron bale.

For XI, X, and IX-inch, bottom-head one thickness of one-inch oak, ash, or beech; spindle riveting on a plate 1¼ inches wide, by ¼ thick, running across the grain the whole width of bottom, with a rivet at each end of plate.

Top and centre heads of all made of white pine.

Iron cases to be well painted inside with red before filling.

94. Shot of the first class, or which do not exceed 0.18 of an inch windage, are to be entirely black, and those of the second class, having from 0.18 to 0.20 of an inch windage, to be marked partly white. Each class is to be piled and kept separate from every other. Both classes are to be considered and supplied as "serviceable shot;" but are to be stowed separately on board ship, and the returns to the Bureau are to show the number of each, respectively. The number of those having more than 0.20 of an inch windage are to be reported and retained until special orders may be given for their disposition. In case any should be taken as the foundation for piling serviceable shot, they are to be painted entirely white and their number returned as unserviceable.

PILING OF BALLS.

95. To find the number of balls in a pile—Multiply the sum of the three parallel edges by one-third of the number of balls in a triangular face.

In a square pile one of the parallel edges contains but one ball; in a triangular pile two of the edges have but one ball in each. The number of balls in a triangular face is $\frac{x(x+1)}{2}$; x being the number in the bottom row. The sum of the three parallel edges in a triangular pile is $x+2$; in a square pile, $2x+1$; in an oblong pile, $3X+2x-2$; X being the length of the top row, and x the width of the bottom tier; or $3m-x+1$; m being the length, x the width of the bottom tier.

If a pile consists of two piles joined at a right angle, calculate the contents of one as a common oblong pile, and of the other as a pile of which the three parallel edges are equal.

96. TABLE GIVING THE NUMBER OF BALLS IN A TRIANGULAR PILE, THE BASE OF WHICH IS X.

Value of X.	Value of S.	Value of X.	Value of S.	Value of X.	Value of S.	Value of X.	Value of S.	Value of X.	Value of S.
1	1	6	56	11	286	16	816	21	1771
2	4	7	84	12	364	17	969	22	2024
3	10	8	120	13	455	18	1140	23	2300
4	20	9	165	14	560	19	1330	24	2600
5	35	10	220	15	680	20	1540	25	2925

97. TABLE GIVING THE NUMBER OF BALLS CONTAINED IN A SQUARE PILE, THE BASE OF WHICH IS X, AND IN A RECTANGULAR PILE, THE SIDES OF WHICH ARE X AND X + N.

Value of X.	Differences. 2d.	Differences. 1st.	Value of N. 0.	1.	2.	3.	4.	5.	6.	7.	8.	9.	10.	Differences. 1st.	Differences. 2d.
2	7	9	5	8	11	14	17	20	23	26	29	32	35	3	3
3	9	16	14	20	26	32	38	44	50	56	62	68	74	6	4
4	11	25	30	40	50	60	70	80	90	100	110	120	130	10	5
5	13	36	53	80	85	100	115	130	145	160	175	190	205	15	6
6	15	49	91	112	133	154	175	196	217	238	259	280	301	21	7
7	17	64	140	168	196	224	552	280	308	336	364	392	420	28	8
8	19	81	204	240	276	312	348	384	420	456	492	528	564	36	9
9	21	100	285	330	375	420	465	510	555	100	645	690	735	45	10
10	23	121	385	440	495	550	605	660	715	770	825	880	935	55	11
11	25	144	506	572	638	704	770	838	902	968	1034	1100	1166	66	12
12	27	159	650	728	805	884	962	1040	1118	1196	1274	1352	1430	78	13
13	29	196	819	910	1001	1092	1183	1274	1365	1456	1547	1638	1729	91	14
14	31	225	1015	1120	1225	1330	1435	1540	1645	1750	1855	1960	2065	105	15
15	33	255	1240	1360	1480	1600	1720	1840	1960	2080	2200	2320	2440	120	16
16	35	286	1496	1632	1768	1904	2040	2126	2312	2448	2584	2720	2856	136	17
17	37	324	1785	1938	2091	2244	2397	2550	2703	2856	3009	3162	3315	154	18
18	39	361	2109	2280	2451	2622	2793	2964	3135	3306	3477	3648	3819	111	19
19	41	400	2470	2660	2850	3040	3239	3420	3610	3800	3990	4180	4370	190	20
20	43	441	2870	3080	3290	3500	3710	3920	4130	4340	4550	4760	4970	210	21
21	45	484	3311	3542	3773	4004	4235	4466	4697	4928	5159	5390	5621	231	22
22	47	529	3795	4048	4301	4554	4807	5060	5313	5566	5819	6072	6325	253	23
23	49	576	4325	4600	4876	5152	5428	5704	3980	6256	6532	6808	7084	276	24
24	51	625	4900	5200	5500	5800	6100	6400	6700	7000	7300	7600	7900	300	25
25	53	676	8525	5850	6175	6500	6825	7150	7475	7800	8125	8450	8775	325	26

The number contained in a square pile is found in the column 0 opposite the number X.

In a rectangular pile let the smaller side be 19 = X, the longer side be 26 = X + N. Then N = 7. Under 7 and opposite 19 we have 3,800. This table may be indefinitely extended by the aid of the columns of differences.

PRESERVATION OF SHOT AND EMPTY SHELL.

98. All round shot and shell are to be cleaned from rust and covered with a thin lacquer of such composition as may be directed by the Bureau when they are first received and when they are restowed.

99. For the present the following colors are established when put on board ship: All shot, black; shell, red; shrapnel, white; length of fuze stencilled on the shell. Special kinds of shell, as may be directed by Bureau. (Crane's shell, yellow; Pevey, blue.)

100. Empty shell, whether in store or in transportation, shall be most carefully protected from damp, and are to have the fuze-bouching coated with such composition as may be directed, and be stopped by a plug of very soft wood, well coated with a mixture of oil and tallow, screwed into them. The ends of the plugs should not be sawed off even with the shell, but left square and project sufficiently to allow them to be unscrewed by means of a wrench, and whenever these plugs are removed for the purpose of fitting the shells for service, they are not to be thrown away but preserved for future use.

They are to be piled with the fuze-holes down, and free from contact; under cover when practicable, but with free ventilation.

101. Platforms of masonry, or of condemned shot, are to be prepared to pile shot and shell upon, and are not to be wider, if space can be found than to stow fourteen 32-pdr. shot, or not exceeding eight feet in width. Square piles are to be preferred where there is room, but where this may be deficient, the piles may be extended in length.

102. Shot and shell, after having been piled, are to be so far examined in the first week of June in each year as to ascertain if they require to be cleaned, relacquered, and repiled to secure their proper preservation; and their condition reported to the Bureau, that if any work upon them is necessary it may be finished during the warm months of the year, when the lacquer can be best applied.

103. Whenever shot or shell are to receive lacquer care must be taken that the quantity applied does not increase the diameter more than is indispensably necessary, and in no case above the established high gauge. Old lacquer and rust should be removed by scraping, as far as can be conveniently done before a new coating is applied. For use at the Navy Yards, a milling machine performs this very expeditiously. Neither hammering nor heating is to be resorted to for this purpose.

NOTE.—After numerous experiments upon different lacquers employed for the preservation of shot and shell from rust, the French have abandoned all of them.

The shot and shell are simply piled, under sheds when practicable, or in the open air, and when put on board ship cleaned of rust and rubbed over with whale oil—the same means adopted every three months during the cruise.

PREPARATION OF SHELL FOR SERVICE.

104. The fuzes for shell will be prepared at the Laboratory in the Ordnance Yard at Washington, and distributed to other Navy Yards as they may be required. All fuzes taken from shell, or returned from ships which have been more than one year in service, are to be sent to the laboratory to be refitted. Fuzes of over two years date of manufacture, are not to be issued for service, but returned to the laboratory.

105. The charges of powder for spherical shell are to be as follows:

	XV-INCH.	XI-INCH.	X-INCH.	IX-INCH.	8-INCH.	32-PDR.	BOAT AND FIELD HOWITZERS.	
							24-pdr.	12-pdr.
	Lbs.	Lbs.	Lbs.	Lbs.	Lbs.	Lbs.	Lbs.	Lbs.
Bursting or Service Charge	13.	6.00	4.00	3.00	1.85	0.90	1.0	0.5
Blowing Charge................	1.0	0.25	0.25	0.25	0.25	0·25		

NOTE—The weight of charges for shells will vary slightly from those given in the table according to the size of the grain and density of the powder.

106. All empty shell, whether in store or in transpôrtation, shall be most carefully protected from dampness, and their fuze-holes invariably closed with wooden plugs. Whenever these plugs are removed for the purpose of fitting the shells for service, they are not to be thrown away, but preserved for future use. If by any accident the shell shôuld be damp in the interior, they are to be heated and dried, on the grillage prepared for that purpose.

107. The number of shell to be kept fitted at the Navy Yards will be determined by special directions from the Bureau.

In fitting shell to receive the bouching, great carelessness has been observed. The hole should be tapped with a full thread, and the proper shoulder left at the bottom to prevent the bouching from being driven in by the shock of firing and causing premature explosion.

108. All shell shall be filled with musket-powder of the highest initial velocity. The shell must be filled, and the powder well shaken down, leaving only room for the insertion of the fuze. A wooden plug the size of the lower part of the fuze will always determine this. The very common, but slovenly, practice of filling the shell, and then pouring out a quantity sufficient to allow the fuze to be inserted, is expressly prohibited. Shell have also been returned with the powder in the vicinity of the fuze compressed into a solid mass, owing to the fact that sufficient room had not been left for its insertion. No shell shall be fuzed unless it has been filled.

109. The date when shell are fuzed or filled, as well as that on which any of these arrangements are changed, or the shell are examined before issue to vessels, together with the initials of the officer superintending these operations, should be legibly written and pasted on the shell, or stencilled on the box.

110. The Ordnance Officer, or the Gunner of the Yard, is to see the shell supplied to all vessels properly conveyed on board, superintend the stowage, and furnish the Commanding Officer with a statement showing the number of each description of shell and fuze, and a plan of their stowage.

111. The condition of the shell, and especially of their fuzes, is to be frequently and carefully examined into, taking out a fuze occasionally so as to detect any injury which may arise from moisture, and to have such as may be found damaged replaced by the spare fuzes.

Boat shell and their spare fuzes are also to undergo a similar examination.

Shell have been sometimes returned with their fuzes entirely destroyed by moisture!!

112. It has been found recently, on drawing the charge of a 12-pounder howitzer in one of the small gunboats, that in cutting its fuze (Bormann) the incision had been made directly into the magazine.

Had the gun been fired, the explosion of the shrapnell must have occurred at the muzzle of the gun.

There is no doubt such errors will often account for the supposed defects of the fuze.

The attention of officers is therefore required to this subject; and, in making reports of defective ammunition, samples should be forwarded to Washington for examination.

It is of the gravest importance, not only because it involves the failure of the shell to act properly upon the object of fire, but may also endanger the lives of our own men.

113. Whenever it is expedient or necessary to examine the fuzes and loading of shell which have been already prepared, great care must be observed in removing the fuze. It should never be done in the shell-room.

114. The fuze-stock may generally be safely unscrewed with the fuze-wrench, taking care, in the first place, to strike the side of the shell gently with a wooden mallet, to detach the powder from the fuze, to work very slowly, and not to endeavor to overcome any unusual resistance.

115. Whenever it shall be necessary to load and fuze shell on board ship—a properly secured place being first prepared, as directed by the Captain, not in the shell-room and as far from the magazine as convenient—the shell, being strapped and sabotted, are to be examined to see that they are clean, both inside and out, and thoroughly dry. The greatest care is to be taken to remove every particle of sand or fragment of iron from the interior. The prescribed charge of powder is next to be poured into them through a proper funnel; care is to be taken that the end of the funnel passes below the screw-thread in the tap or bouching, to prevent any grains of powder entering it; any grains of it which may remain sticking to the thread of the bouching are to be brushed away carefully, and then, after putting a light coat of lacquer for small arms, or sperm oil, on this thread and on that of the fuze, the latter is to be screwed in carefully with the fuze-wrench. The lacquer should be of the consistency of cream, and when from evaporation, it becomes too stiff, should be thinned by adding more spirits of turpentine.

116. In emptying shell they are to be handled carefully and placed on a bench with a hole in it to receive and support the inverted shell. A wooden vessel placed below will receive the powder. *The powder which has been removed from shell shall only be used for filling shell, as it always contains a small quantity of grit, which renders it unfit for general service.* Should the powder have become caked, so as not to be easily removed from the shell, it is to be drowned and removed by washing out the shell. A handful of small iron shot put in the shell will facilitate this operation.

117. Loaded shell are to be painted red and placed in boxes or bags marked with a red cross, which boxes are to have the lengths of fuze painted on them in black. Shrapnel shell and the tops of their boxes shall be painted white, with the length of fuze stencilled on them in black. They are to be stowed in shell-houses prepared for that purpose. Loaded shell, whether in or out of their boxes, must be handled carefully. Shell-bags will be preserved, accounted for by the Gunner, and returned.

118. The greatest precaution must be taken in handling loaded shells fitted with percussion-fuzes. When returned from ships they must not be taken into the shell-houses until after the fuzes shall have been removed and the shell plugged.

119. Shell-houses, and the general condition of the shell they contain, are to be examined as often as once a fortnight by the Ordnance Officer, and every precaution taken to keep them as dry as possible.

120. The shell for boat guns are to be stowed in "the shell-houses" on shore, and "shell-rooms" on board of vessels, in their proper boxes.

121. One-fourth of the whole number of spare fuzes allowed for the great guns is to be for 5 seconds of time; one-fourth for 10 seconds; one-fourth for 15 seconds; one-fourth assorted of 3. 5, 7, and 20 seconds.

122. All the spherical shell, however, put on board ship, filled and fitted for immediate use, are to be provided with none other than the 5-second fuze. No fuze is, under any circumstances, to be put in shell which are not filled.

123. For rifled cannon the shell shall be fitted with one-half percussion, one-half time fuze. Parrott's shell will have bouching, or "adapting" rings for the naval time fuze. The new form of adapter, with a shoulder and washer beneath it, shall alone be used.

124. At ranges exceeding 1,400 yards the 10 or 15-second fuzes, according to such excess, are to be substituted for the 5-second fuze, by removing one and putting in the other; or, if preferred, those fuzes may be applied to shell which are not already fitted. The 5-second fuze is to be regarded as the general working fuze, and hence the reason the filled shell are to be fitted with it, as mentioned above. (See TABLE OF RANGES for proper lengths of fuze for all distances.)

125. The different kinds of fuzes shall be made up in separate packages, distinctly marked with the kind and length of fuze, and their use carefully explained to the Executive Officer and Gunner by the Inspector of Ordnance.

126. In consequence of numerous reports received from vessels in service of the inefficiency of certain fuzes, commanders of vessels are required to observe carefully the action and result of all fuzes, and report in detail to the Bureau of Ordnance whenever opportunities may occur, particularly specifying the number and kind fi·ed, elevation of gun, range, premature explosions, failures to explode, and satisfactory action. Also, whether the fire was direct or ricochet.

127. EXTERIOR DIMENSIONS, IN INCHES, FOR SHELL-BOXES.

For XV-inch shell, 18 × 18 by 20 high.
For XI-inch shell, 12·75 × 12.75 by 14.5 high.
For X-inch shell, 11.65 × 11.65 by 13.9 high.
For IX-inch shell, 10.63 × 10.63 by 12.9 high.
For 8-inch shell, 10.20 × 10.10 by 12.2 high.
For 32-pounder shell, 8.60 × 8.50 by 10.2 high.

128. AREAS OCCUPIED BY ONE TIER OF SHELL-BOXES.

XI-INCH.		X-INCH.		IX-INCH.		8-INCH.		32-POUNDER.	
No.	Ft. In.	No.	Ft. In.	No.	Ft. In.	No.	Ft. In.	No.	Ft. In.
72	15.5½ × 5.8½	75	15.2 × 5.3½	102	15.8¼ × 5.9¼	108	16 × 6	176	16 × 6
52	14.4 × 4.6½	56	14.2 × 4.1½	80	14.9¼ × 4.9½	85	15 × 5	140	15 × 5

GUNPOWDER.

STOWAGE, PRESERVATION, HANDLING, AND CHARGES.

129. The Bureau having adopted a new system of granulating Navy powder, the different classes will in future be known and designated as RIFLE, CANNON, and MUSKET.

Gunpowder intended for ordinary use in cannon is to have sufficient strength to give a 6-pounder shot the under-mentioned Initial Velocities, determinable by the gun-pendulum of the Ordnance Yard at Washington.

130. The size of the grains is determined by sieves, made by piercing round holes in thin plates of brass. These sieves are five in number, the holes being of the following diameters, viz.:

No. 1,	.3	of an inch	Initial Velocity	required,	1450 feet + 50 − 50,	for Rifle.
No. 2,	.15	do.				
No. 2,	.15	do.	do.	do.	1500 feet + 50 − 50,	for Cannon.
No. 3,	.10	do.				
No. 4,	.06	do.	do.	do.	1550 feet + 50 − 50,	for Musket.
No. 5,	.02	do.				

Rifle powder is used in the Parrott rifles of 8-inch, 100-pounder, and 60-pounder. Navy cannon powder in all other rifles and all smooth-bores.

131. Size of the grain is required to conform to the following:

Pass through No. 1....................	all	Rifle.
Remain on No. 2......................	all	
Pass through No. 2....................	all	Cannon.
Remain on No. 3......................	all	
Pass through No. 4....................	all	Musket.
Remain on No. 5......................	all	

Ten per cent. variation tolerated.

132. GRAVIMETRIC DENSITY, is the weight of a given measured quantity: it is usually expressed by the weight of a cubic foot in ounces.

This cannot be relied on for the true density, as the size and shape of the grain may make the denser powder seem the lighter.

Cannon powder should have a gravimetric density of about 875 oz., and not exceeding 900 oz., to the cubic foot. (It actually varies with different makers from 875 to 975.)

133. SPECIFIC GRAVITY.—The specific gravity of gunpowder is between 1.70 and 1.75.

All the powder of any lot being made of the same mill-cake, the specific gravities are equal although the gravimetric densities may vary.

134. Powder for small arms, or musket powder, should all pass through No. 4, none through No. 5, and average from 2,000 to 2,500 kernels in ten grains Troy.

All powder should be well glazed; for small arms more highly than for cannon.

135. The system of granulation adopted by the Army differs from that of the Navy, as follows:

	ALL THROUGH—	ALL ON—
Mammoth	0.9 in.	0.6 in.
Cannon	0.35	0.25
Mortar	0.10	0.06
Musket	0.06	0.03

It will be seen by this Table that under the Army nomenclature, Navy Rifle nearly corresponds to Army Cannon; that the Army Mortar is the nearest equivalent to Navy Cannon, but with much more fine grain, as it is what passes through the cannon-sieve, but remains on the musket-sieve; and that the Navy Musket has the same size for the larger grain, but contains more small grain than the Army.

In exchanging powder with the Army, it is necessary to attend to these distinctions.

136. Powder-houses or magazines on shore are to be inspected by the Ordnance Officers at least once in every week, and every precaution taken to guard them against danger of explosion, and to preserve the powder dry and in good condition.

137. Powder-barrels in magazines, where there are no racks, should be placed on their sides, with their marked ends towards the alleys, three tiers high, or four tiers, if necessary, with small skids on the floor and between the several tiers of barrels, using chocks at intervals on the lower skids to prevent the barrels from rolling. If it can be avoided, fixed ammunition should not be put in the same magazine with powder in barrels.

138. If it is necessary to pile the barrels more than four tiers high, the upper tiers should be supported by a frame resting on the floor; or the barrels may be placed on their heads, with boards between the tiers.

There should be an unencumbered space of 6 or 8 feet square at the doors of the magazine.

139. Whenever practicable, the barrels should be arranged in double rows, with a passage-way between the rows, so that the marks on each barrel may be seen at a glance, and any barrel easily reached.

140. Besides being recorded in the magazine-book, each lot of powder should be inscribed on a ticket attached to the lot showing the entries and the issues.

141. Magazines should be opened and aired in clear, dry weather, the ventilators kept free, and no shrubbery or trees allowed to grow so near as to shade the building from the sun.

142. The moisture of a magazine may be absorbed by chloride of lime, or charcoal, suspended in an open box under the arch, and renewed from time to time. The use of quicklime is dangerous, and forbidden.

143. When powder is handled in powder-houses on shore, either for the purpose of inspection or preparation for delivery to ships, the baize-cloth is to be spread, and the people, before entering the magazine, must divest themselves of every metal implement, empty their pockets, that nothing likely to produce fire may escape detection, and put on the magazine dresses and slippers. The barrels must be opened only on the floor-cloth, and no metallic setter used in driving either copper or wooden hoops.

Powder-barrels should never be opened except when required for use, as grains of powder falling between the staves would prevent their being tightened. Samples must be taken from the bung.

144. The attention of the Inspectors of Ordnance and Commanders of vessels is called to the Regulations regarding the stowage and service of powder and loaded shells in Magazines and Shell-rooms, ashore and afloat, and to the precautions which must be observed by every one who enters, or approaches for the purpose of entering, any Magazine or Shell-room.

The former Regulations are modified so far as to dispense entirely with the use of slippers made of either India-rubber or woollen; and in lieu thereof, slippers made wholly of buckskin or cotton canvas will be used in future. In hot climates, or in warm weather generally, the naked feet are preferred.

The terrible effect of the explosion of a Magazine or Shell-room, ashore or on board ship, can only be imagined. To avert it, by every human precaution, is an imperative duty with every one. The Bureau therefore directs that the Inspectors of Ordnance on shore and the Commanders of all vessels afloat will cause the existing Powder Regulations to be read, and copies placed within the reach of every officer and man connected in the remotest degree with the service of the Magazine and Shell-rooms; and no officer or other person is to be continued in such service who cannot within a reasonable time answer clearly and fully any questions relating to the requirements of existing Powder Regulations as contained in these "Ordnance Instructions."

145. The powder in barrels should be turned from time to time, at least as often as every three months, and, being arranged as mentioned above, the oldest powder will be at all times accessible for first delivery without disturbing that of more recent manufacture.

146. When powder is sent on board any vessel at the Yard, an Ordnance Officer or the Gunner is to see it properly stowed, and the Ordnance Officer is to hand to the Captain of the vessel a statement showing the quantity of powder, number and capacity of tanks, kind of charges contained in each, with the initial velocity, maker, and date of reception, with a list of small-arm and boat ammunition, fireworks, filled and other shells and projectiles, together with all the information directed by the three articles immediately following, with such remarks as he may deem proper to secure better precaution or more convenient arrangement, with a request that the memorandum, or a copy of it, may be delivered to the Ordnance Officer at the Yard where the vessel is refitted or laid up at the end of the cruise.

147. When cartridges are filled for issue to any vessel, the powder should be selected, as far as practicable, from deliveries made by the same person, and at the same time or date; and the tanks in which they are stowed must be marked with white paint on the upper sides, with the same marks as the barrels from which the powder was taken, giving the date of manufacture and the maker's name.

148. Great irregularities having been observed in the weights of cartridges supplied from different stations, it is ordered that at least ten measures shall be weighed at each filling, and allowance made for different densities. (See Art. 171.)

149. Whenever powder is returned into the powder-houses from vessels, and the powder emptied from the cartridges, care must be taken to have the barrels or other vessels in which the powder may be placed marked in the same manner and registered in the Magazine Ledger, so that the maker's name and date of manufacture of all powder may be correctly known and carefully preserved for reference.

150. The names of vessels from which powder is received, the length of time which the powder has been on board, and the station on which the vessel has been employed, should also be noted and reported by the Ordnance Officer, that reference may be had to the notes in case it should be desired in subsequent examinations of the powder.

151. In some instances where powder has been condemned by survey, it has been directed to be thrown overboard. This should never be done; the nitre contained, which forms three-fourths ($\frac{3}{4}$) of the powder, is still perfectly good, and can be made serviceable. In future, condemned powder is always to be returned to the United States.

152. The Ordnance Officers, when they supply vessels with powder, or remove any from them, must report to the Bureau by the earliest opportunity all the information which is required to be noted by Articles 147, 149, 150, immediately preceding; and when powder is received from vessels returning from cruises, or after it has been long embarked, they are to forward to the Ordnance Yard, Washington, a sample of two pounds and one-fourth, properly labelled, for every five hundred pounds landed, selected so as to show fair average samples of the whole, in order that its strength may be ascertained by the pendulum.

153. In case of necessity, powder for saluting may be purchased abroad in order to preserve a supply of our own proof powder for battle.

154. When a vessel is about to leave a foreign station and return directly to the United States, and other vessels belonging to the Navy are left on the station without a full supply of powder, the vessel which is about to leave may be directed to transfer to those remaining on the station any excess of powder that may be on board beyond fifty rounds.

155. Should it become necessary to use powder for service charges which has not been regularly inspected and proved in the manner required by regulations, such tests of it must be made as circumstances will admit.

The ranges given by it may be compared with those of service powder of known good quality under the same circumstances. If deficient in strength, the quantity of the charges should be increased until the ranges are equalized, in order that the sight-bars may still indicate the proper elevations for each charge and distance.

156. It is directed that vessels of war shall always receive their powder and loaded shells in the stream; unless, upon some great emergency, the nature of which shall be reported to the Bureau, it is deemed essential to put them on board at the Navy Yard.

157. When receiving or landing powder, the red flag is to be always hoisted at the fore, and all proper precautions taken to guard against accidents from fires and lights. The tanks should be passed through the ports most convenient to the magazines, and landed on mats, to prevent injury.

The red flag is always to be hoisted at the powder-houses when they are opened, and kept flying until they are closed.

158. When avoidable, gunpowder is not to be sent from vessels to powder-houses, nor from powder-houses to vessels, in wet weather, nor when there is a probability of wetting the barrels or cases; and the packages must be conveyed in covered boats or wagons showing a red flag.

159. The wharf or landing-place must be spread with old canvas, so that the barrels or cases may not come in contact with and convey sand or gravel to the powder-house. The barrels must not be rolled, but carried in slings to the trucks running on tramways of either wood or bronze, into the magazine.

160. The service charges for the different calibres and classes of naval smooth-bore guns now used in the Navy are as follows, and the cartridges are to be filled accordingly, viz.:

SERVICE CHARGES FOR NAVAL GUNS.

Ordnance.		Charges of Navy Cannon Powder.			Diameters of Cartridge-Gauge.	Saluting Charges, No. 50.
Calibre.	Weight.	For distant firing, 0.1	For ordinary firing, 0.6	For near firing, or two projectiles, 0.3		
		lbs.	lbs.	lbs.	Cylindrical.	lbs.
X-inch or 130-pounder..	16,000 lbs.	30.	18.	15.	9.00 inches.	
64-pounder............	106 cwt.	16.	12.	8.	7.00 "	6.
32-pounder............	61 "	10.	8.	6.	5.50 "	4.
32 do.	57 "	9.	8.	6.	5.50 "	4.
32 do.	51 "	8.	7.	5.	5.50 "	4.
32 do.	46 "	7.	7.	5.	5.50 "	4.
32 do.	42 "	6.	6.	4.	5.50 "	4.
32 do.	33 "	4.5	4.5	4.	5.50 "	4.
32 do.	27 "	4.	4.	3.	5.50 "	3.
Shell-Guns.				For near firing.	Conical.	
XV-inch...............	42,000 lbs.	50.	35.	35.		
XI-inch	15,700 "	20.	15.	15.	11 × 5.5 × 11	7.
X-inch	12,000 "	15.	12.5	12.5	10 × 5. × 10	6.
IX-inch	9,000 "	13.	10.	10.	9 × 4.5 × 9	5.
8-inch	6,500 "	7.	7.	7.	8 × 5. × 8	4.
32-pounder............	4,500 "	6.	6.	6.		4.
					Cylindrical.	
8-inch................	63 cwt.	9.	8.	6.	5.50	4.
8-inch................	55 "	7.	7.	6.	5.50	4.

N. B.—Two projectiles are not to be fired from any gun at the same time, except at objects within 200 yards' distance, and only when the advantages at the moment may be deemed by the Captain sufficient to justify the risk of injuring the guns and their equipments by the extra strain to which they will be exposed.

With the 15-inch guns at close quarters against iron-clads, 60 lbs. and a solid shot *may* be used for 20 rounds. So also with the 11-inch, 30 lbs. and a solid shot. With all the other guns, under like circumstances, and where penetration is desired, the *distant* firing charges should be substituted for the *near* firing.

Of the service charges, one-tenth shall be for distant firing, six-tenths for ordinary firing, three-tenths for near firing, or for two projectiles. Saluting charges to be of under-proof powder.

The calibre and class of guns for which the cartridges are intended must be distinctly marked near the top of the lid end of the tanks.

161. TABLE OF CHARGES FOR NAVY RIFLE GUNS.

GUN.	ORDNANCE.			CHARGE OF POWDER.		
	Calibre.	Diameter of Bore.	Weight.	Weight.	Kind.	Diameter of Cartridge-Gauge.
	Pounder.	Inches.	Lbs.	Lbs.		Inches.
Parrott	100	6.40	9,700	8.	Rifle.	5.50
Do.	60	5.30	5,400	6.	Rifle.	4.60
Do.	30	4.20	3,550	3.25	Cannon.	3.70
Do.	20	3.67	1,750	2.	Cannon.	3.25
Dahlgren	20	4.00	1,340	2.	Cannon.	
Do.	12	3.40	880	1.	Cannon.	

162. POWDER-TANKS.

CAPACITY OF TANK FOR POWDER IN GRAIN.	EXTERIOR DIMENSIONS.		WEIGHT, WHEN EMPTY.	APPROXIMATE WEIGHT, WHEN FILLED WITH CYLINDERS.
	Height in inches, including Lid and Handle.	Sides, in inches.		
200 pounds	$22\frac{1}{4}$	$16\frac{1}{2} \times 16\frac{1}{2}$	$67\frac{1}{2}$ pounds.	218 pounds.
150 "	$22\frac{1}{8}$	15×15	$59\frac{1}{2}$ "	170 to 180 lbs.
100 "	$20\frac{1}{2}$	13×13		
50 "	$16\frac{3}{4}$	$10\frac{1}{4} \times 10\frac{1}{4}$		

163. ACCOMMODATION AFFORDED BY POWDER-TANKS OF DIFFERENT SIZES FOR CARTRIDGES OF VARIOUS KINDS WHEN CLOSELY PACKED.

CAPACITY OF TANK FOR POWDER IN GRAIN.	WILL STOW CARTRIDGES AS FOLLOWS:																
DENOMINATION.	lbs. 20	lbs. 16	lbs. 15	lbs. 12.5	lbs. 10	lbs. 9	lbs. 8	lbs. 7	lbs. 6	lbs. 5	lbs. 4.5	lbs. 4	lbs. 3.25	lbs. 3	lbs. 2	lbs. 1.85	lb. 1
200 pounds	9	11	12	14	18	20	22	25	30	36	40	45	52	60	95	100	190
150 "	6	8	9	10	13	15	18	20	24	27	30	36	40	45	71	72	145
100 "	4	5	6	7	9	10	11	13	16	18	20	24	27	31	46	48	95
50 "	2	2	2	3	4	4	5	5	7	9	10	11	13	15	21	23	46
Powder-barrel	4	6	7	8	10	11	12	14	16	-	-	26	-	35	52	55	108

FIXED AMMUNITION FOR BOAT GUNS AND SMALL ARMS.

164. The charges for "boat and field howitzers" are—

	lbs.
For the 24-pounder of 1,310 lbs	2.00
For the medium 12-pounder of 760 lbs.	1.00
For the light 12-pounder of 430 lbs.	0.625

165. Dimensions of Boxes for Boat Ammunition.

PROJECTILES WITH CHARGE OF POWDER FOR HOWITZER ATTACHED, NOT TO BE STOWED IN THE MAGAZINE.

Calibre of Boat Howitzer.	Kind of Projectile.	Number of Projectiles Box contains.	Dimensions of Boxes, in Inches.	Weight, in Pounds.	
				Empty.	Filled.
24-pdr......	Shrapnel....	9	22 × 20.75 by 13.75 high.	35 1/3	270 1/3
24 "	Canister....	9	22 × 20.75 by 15.50 "	36 1/3	217 5/6
12 " heavy.	Shrapnel....	9	18.75 × 17.75 by 11.13 "	22 7/8	140 1/2
12 " "	Canister....	9	18.75 × 17.75 by 12.25 "	25 1/2	114 3/4

166. The cartridges for small arms are to contain the following quantities of powder:

For muskets.............................. 70 grains, Troy.
For muskets (marine)....................... 60 " "
For pistols .... 30 " "
For revolvers .... 18 " "

The ball-cartridges for rifles and rifled muskets are to be made with a single Minié ball.

167. Exterior Dimensions and Contents of Boxes

FOR SMALL-ARM AMMUNITION AND FIREWORKS.

Articles.	Exterior Dimensions.			Each Box contains	Remarks.
	Length.	Width.	Depth.		
	Inches.	Inches.	Inches.		
Musket-ball cartridges.............	12 1/2	8 1/4	8 1/4	500	
Do. blank do.	9 5/8	7 3/4	8 1/2	500	
Carbine rifle-ball do.	14 1/2	8 1/4	7 3/8	1000	
Pistol-ball do.	13 3/4	6 3/4	7 1/4	1000	
Blue-lights	20 1/2	13	6 7/8	30	
False fires.......................	20 1/2	13	6 7/8	30	
Port-fires........................	19 3/4	10 1/4	10 1/4	100	First size.
Do.	19 3/4	10 1/4	6 1/4	50	Second size.
Signal rockets....................	15 1/4	9 1/2	8 1/4	30	
Percussion-caps...................	11 3/4	9 1/4	7 3/8	6300	

N. B.—There is a variation in the dimensions of the above boxes, as made, of $\frac{1}{8}$ of an inch, on an average, in their exteriors.

168. Percussion-caps and bullets for small arms will be supplied from the Ordnance Yard at Washington.

169. The boxes in which cartridges for small arms, caps, primers, etc., are packed for distribution to vessels, are to be marked with the number they contain, and the kind of arm for which they are intended. At the expiration of the cruise they must be carefully returned into store, and the Gunner will be held pecuniarily responsible for their loss.

170. Standard powder-measures for filling cartridges for great guns will be made at the Ordnance Yard, Washington, and distributed as they may be required for the use of vessels and shore magazines. As the gravimetric density of powder varies from 860 to 940, the weight of the contents of ten measures should be ascertained for each lot, and allowance made accordingly before filling the cartridges.

171. In taking the weights, the powder is to be scooped up from the filling-chest with the measure until it is heaped, tapped twice moderately on the sides with the palms of the hands, and then struck with a wooden straight-edge. If the weight differs materially from that marked on the measure, a small compensating measure should be used to supply the deficiency or remove the excess.

CANNON-PRIMERS.

172. These are of two kinds, percussion and friction. Each percussion-primer is composed of a quill tube capped by an explosive wafer. The quills used for this purpose are first inspected by passing them through a gauge rather smaller than the vent.

The tube is filled with fine-grained powder.

The wafer is composed of a cap of cartridge-paper, enclosing a layer of fulminate of mercury combined with a small quantity of mealed powder. When pressed and perfectly dry, the wafer is coated with uncolored shellac, to preserve it from dampness.

173. Primers are to be kept in tin boxes containing fifty each, the lids of which are luted with shellac to exclude moisture until wanted for immediate use. These boxes are intended to fit in and form a lining to the primer-boxes which slip on the waist-belts worn by Captains of guns. For purposes of exercise no more of these boxes should be opened than are required; but for action a full box should be delivered to each Captain and 2d Captain of a gun.

174. A friction-primer consists of a tube charged with gunpowder, to the top of which is fastened a spur containing friction-powder, which is exploded by means of a slider pulled out by a lanyard. It is intended for use in case the lock should be out of order, or the other primers fail from any unforeseen cause. Friction-primers are packed in tin boxes in the same manner as percussion-primers. They are obtained from the Army as required.

175. Filled boxes of primers are kept in close laboratory cases, for which stowage must be provided in the general store-room of the ship, or other safe place.[1] They are on no account to be placed in the magazine, and the boxes must be so labelled before being put on board ship.

176. When primers have been returned from cruising ships, or have remained in store for one or more years, they must be tested by firing five per cent. of the number, and not issued again without special orders.

177. Damaged fuzes, primers, caps, and tubes, are always to be returned to the Ordnance Yard at Washington, in the condition in which they were received on the return of the ship.

178. The boxes containing metallic cartridges for breech-loading arms require the same care as percussion-caps, and are to be labelled, "On no account to be placed in the magazine."

179. PERCUSSION-CAPS for muskets, carbines, and pistols are made in the laboratory at the Washington Navy Yard. They are put up in small packages of water-proof paper, labelled with the number contained in the package and the date of fabrication, and stowed in tin cases containing 350 caps each.

180. Laboratory boxes, in which these are packed, are of the following dimensions: $11\frac{3}{4} \times 9\frac{1}{4} \times 7\frac{3}{8}$ inches, and will contain 6,300 percussion-caps each. These boxes are to be labelled, "On no account to be placed in the magazine." Stowage is provided for them in the general store-room.

CARTRIDGE-BAGS.

181. The material of which cartridge-bags are made is woven expressly for the purpose, and furnished by the Bureau of Ordnance as required. The color is white, and the calibre of the gun and the weight of the charge must be stencilled on the bag in figures two and a half ($2\frac{1}{2}$) inches long. When procured of necessity elsewhere, the stuff should be chosen of wool, entirely free from any mixture of thread or cotton, and of sufficiently close texture to prevent the finer particles of powder from sifting through. Wildbore, rattinet, merino, and bombazette are named as proper materials for cartridge-bags; of these the thinnest stuff, not twilled, but having the requisite strength and closeness of texture, is the best.

182. MAKING CARTRIDGE-BAGS.—Cartridge-bags for cylindrical chambers are made of a rectangle to form the cylinder, and a circular piece to form the bottom. The flat patterns, by which the cartridge-bags for the 8-inch and 32-pounder guns are cut, are, consequently, to be made rectangular for the cylindrical part of the bag, and circular for the bottom. The length

[1] Primers and percussion-caps should be divided into two or three lots, and stowed in different parts of the ship, so that an accidental explosion would not deprive the ship of the means of firing cannon and small arms.

of the rectangle is equal to the development of the cylinder, together with the allowance for seam; and its width, to the whole length of the bag before sewing, including the allowance for seam and tie.

Special patterns are furnished for those of XV-in., XI-in., X-in., IX-in., 8-inch of 6,500 lbs., and 32-pounder of 4,500 lbs. shell-guns, all of which have gomer chambers.

183. DIMENSIONS OF FLAT PATTERNS FOR CUTTING OUT CARTRIDGE-BAGS.

TO BE MADE OF PINE FOR THE 8-INCH AND 32-PDR. GUNS, AND OF METAL PLATES FOR THE "GOMER" CHAMBERS OF OTHER GUNS.[1]

DIMENSIONS.		10-INCH, OR 130-POUNDER.			64-PDR. GUN OF 106 CWT. 8-INCH RIFLE.			100-POUNDER RIFLE, 32-POUNDER GUN, AND 8-INCH SHELL-GUNS, HAVING CHAMBERS OF 32-POUNDER CALIBRE.								
Charges	lbs.	30	18	15	16	12	8	10	9	8	7	6	5	4.5	4	3
Width of rectangle (length of bag cut), including tie and four-tenths of an inch for seam.	in.	20.	15.2	14.	18.7	15.7	12.7	16.6	14.6	13.6	12.6	11.6	10.6	10.1	9.6	8.6
		Inches.			Inches.			Inches.								
Length of rectangle (cylinder developed), including eight-tenths of an inch for seam.		29.01			22.8			18.1								
Radius of circular pattern of bottom, including four-tenths of an inch for seam.		4.9			3.60			2.95								
Diameters of cylindrical formers for inspection of cartridge-bags.		9.00			7.00			5.50								
Additional length for one pound of powder.		0.40			0.80			1.22								

184. DETAILS OF CARTRIDGE-BAGS.

SHELL-GUNS WITH CONICAL CHAMBERS.

CALIBRE OF GUN.	XV-IN.			XI-IN.		X-IN.		IX-IN.		8-IN. OF 6500.	32-PR. OF 4500.
Charge of powder...lbs.	35.	50.	60.	20.	15.	15.	12.5	13.	10.	7.	6.
Diameter of cartridge. Large end.	13.5	13.5	13.5	9.85	9.85	9.	9.	8.13	8.13	7.25	6.
Diameter of cartridge. Small end.	–	–	–	5.50	5.50	5.	5.	4.50	4.50	4.	3.5
Width of stuff required to cut bag.......in.	24.	28.	30.	22.	20.	20.	20.	18.	18.	24.	22.
Whole length of bag cut, including tie and seam.	21.5	25.5	27.5	19.	17.5	18.5	17.75	16.5	15.5	12.6	11.6
Length of filled cartridge..........in.	12.	15.5	18.	12.	10.5	10.	9.	11.5	10.5	7.5	9.5
Additional length for one pound of powder.											
Quantity of stuff required to cut one hundred bags........yds.	122.	122.	122.	92.	92.	86.	86.	78.	78.	30.	30.

[1] The dimensions of those for the XV, IX, X, and XI inch guns, which have Gomer chambers, and cannot be conveniently tabulated, will be furnished to all vessels mounting such guns. The formers for inspection of bags will have the forms and dimensions of the Gomer chambers less 0.87 inch for the IX-inch, 1.0 inch for the X-inch, 1.15 inch for the XI-inch, and 1.50 inch for XV-inch guns, for windage at the large end, in accordance with the flat patterns furnished for cutting.

In cutting, the length of the rectangle should be taken in the direction of the length of the stuff, as it does not stretch in that direction, and the material should be chosen, as nearly as possible, of the width required for the length of the bags, to save waste in cutting.

The bags are to be sewed with worsted yarn, with not less than eight stitches to an inch; they must be stitched within four-tenths of an inch of each edge, and the two edges of the seam felled down upon the same side, to prevent the powder from sifting through. The edges of the bottom are felled down upon the sides.

The bags, when filled, must be tied with woollen thrums.

185. Cartridge-Bags for Saluting Charges.—Old cartridge-bags which have been condemned for service charges are to be repaired and used for saluting charges; and whenever it is necessary to make bags expressly for the purpose, or for immediate use, they may be formed by sewing together two rectangular pieces with semicircular ends.

186. Inspection.—The material especially procured for cartridge-bags is to be carefully inspected to detect any mixture of cotton with the wool, by burning a few bits taken at hazard from each piece; or, by dissolving it in a solution of ½ ounce of caustic potassa in a pint of water—the cloth to be put in when the water is boiling, which is to continue until dissolution takes place. The texture of the stuff is also to be examined and its strength tried, such standard for the latter being established as may be found sufficient to insure perfect efficiency.

After being made up, the empty bags are to be inspected, and those which are sewed with too long stitches, or in any other than the prescribed manner, must be rejected. The dimensions of each bag are to be verified, first by laying it flattened out, between two marks on a table showing the width of a pattern bag. A variation of 0.1 inch greater or less is allowed. The bags are also to be tried on mandrels, or formers, made according to the dimensions given on the preceding page.

187. Preservation from Moths.—Serge or any other woollen material employed for making cartridge-bags is never to be exposed on the shelves in store, either in the piece or when made up. It is to be protected by packing with the hydraulic press, by sewing it up in linen cloth, or by enveloping it in water-proof paper, hermetically sealed.

An infusion of coloquintida, in the proportion of 15½ grains Troy to a quart of water, is said to be a good preservative against moths. In case of using this preparation, the cartridge-bags should be steeped in the infusion, and, after being thoroughly dried, may be packed by the hydraulic press, and headed up in old whiskey barrels, if stored on shore, or packed in empty tanks, if on board ship.

Cartridge-bags, as well as the material for making them, must be frequently examined, to prevent their being damaged by moisture, as well as to guard against moths.

CHAPTER II.

MAGAZINES AND SHELL-ROOMS.

CONSTRUCTION, LIGHTING, STOWING, AND FLOODING.

188. No details of internal arrangement should be more carefully considered and executed than those relating to the stowage and delivery of powder, since a defect in these particulars, apparently insignificant, may lead to the instantaneous destruction of the ship; or, with the incendiary and explosive projectiles now used, to her becoming, comparatively, an easy prey to an antagonist. Every possible precaution, therefore, is to be taken to accommodate the full allowance of powder completely; to guard it to the utmost against injury and accidental explosion; and to deliver it at the magazine, as required, with facility and certainty. To these ends, and in view of the fact that all the powder for great guns is now put up in cubical copper tanks, made water-tight, THE FORM OF MAGAZINES should be as nearly rectangular as the shape of the vessel will admit, and they should be built strong enough to resist sufficiently the effect of her working in heavy weather, and also the pressure of water they will have to sustain in case of being flooded.

189. All magazines should have a light-box for each alley at one end, and a passage to deliver powder at the other; and the magazine and its passage, considered as one, must be made perfectly water-tight by caulking the bottom and sides, and then lining them internally, first with white pine boards, tongued and grooved, and again with sheets of lead of extra thickness, soldered together, over these boards. Both these linings are to extend entirely over the bottom or floor, and all the way up to the crown on all the sides.

190. When the magazine reaches the ceiling of the ship it must be battened off two inches; the lining of the floor must be battened up one, and also the magazine-deck, so that water leaking through the sides of the vessel may run by and under, and not into the magazine.

An external lining of sheet-iron must also be resorted to as a protection against fire, and to prevent the intrusion of rats.

191. A magazine aft in a ship is to have its passage for delivering powder adjoining its forward part; and one forward in a ship is to have this passage adjoining its after part, in order that it may not be necessary to pass the powder over the light-box scuttle.

192. As many doors are to be cut in the bulkhead separating this passage from the magazine-room as there are alleys to be left in the latter, between the racks or shelves on which the tanks are stowed, and these doors must correspond with those alleys. They are not only to afford a means of entrance to the magazine, but also for passing the tanks in and out. Through the upper part of each door a small scuttle is to be cut,—two, if necessary,—for the purpose of passing the cartridges out of the magazine-room with the door itself closed; and it is to have a lid so arranged as to open outwards only, and to close of itself when the scuttle is not actually in use.

193. Sailing ships-of-the-line and frigates should have two alleys for each magazine. In screw-vessels of large class, where the shaft will interfere with this arrangement, two alleys for the forward magazine. In smaller vessels one alley will suffice. In all cases the alley is to be not less than two feet and ten inches in breadth, and it ought to be more, if practicable, to prevent confusion and delay. Each alley is to be illuminated by a separate light.

If there is room in the magazine, there should be space left, at the end nearest the light, for a man to pass from one alley to the other without going into the passage.

194. Ships with two magazines—one forward and the other aft—are to have them as nearly equal, in point of capacity, as the shape of the vessel and other circumstances will admit.

Magazines should be constructed as low down as possible. Their floors may rest on the keelson, but should not come below it. Their height should be equal, only, to an exact number of times the height of a powder-tank when lying on its side, in addition to the thickness of the shelving. An additional inch for each shelf should be allowed for play or spring. The whole height in the clear should be limited by the condition that a man standing on the floor may reach the upper tier of tanks with ease. Four tiers of 200-lb. tanks, three of them resting on shelves two inches thick, and the other on inch battens on the magazine-floor, will, with an allowance of one and a half inch for play and spring, require a height, in the clear, of six feet two inches. Both safety and convenience would suggest this as the maximum limit in height, even for the largest magazine. Three tiers of these tanks will require a height, in the clear, of about four feet eight inches.

If, however, in ships of great draught of water, it should be found practicable to extend the height of a magazine so as to accommodate five tiers of tanks, then the lower or ground tier may be laid so as to occupy the whole of the magazine-floor; and on the top of this tier, in the alley-way, a light false bottom is to be placed for the men to stand upon to enable them to reach the upper tier, which is the one that should first be exhausted. This false bottom should be made of gratings, and in sections convenient for speedy removal.

195. When it is impossible to avoid extending the sides of the magazine so far out towards the skin of the ship as to leave only an air-passage on either side, the crown should be at least six feet below the deep load-line.

In all cases where this crown is less than six feet below that line, the sides should be made susceptible of protection by allowing a space to interpose materials, such as sand, coal, or water in tanks, between them and the inner planking of the ship.

An average space of six feet or more on both sides will be sufficient. Under no circumstances, however well the sides be guarded, should the crown of the magazine, if it can be avoided, be less than four feet below the deep load-line.

196. It is proper to add, in connection with this most important subject, that in order to increase security against the effects of lightning, a magazine should be placed, if practicable, so as not to include a part of a mast.

197. All the metallic fixtures about a magazine, delivering-passages, and light-rooms, must be of copper.

198. Each delivering-passage is to have, for the distribution of powder, at least as many passing-scuttles communicating with the orlop or berth deck as there are chains of scuttles above. The powder-man will thus always find at the scuttle the proper passing-box.

MAGAZINE-COCKS.

199. Each magazine, as a whole—that is, including the delivering-passage—being made, as stated above, water-tight, is to be provided with an independent cock for filling it rapidly with water; a waste-pipe leading from above the upper tier of tanks to carry off the superfluous water; and a cock just at the floor for letting the water off when the magazine is to be emptied after having been flooded. Both the cocks must be turned from the deck above, each having a lever to its spindle for the purpose, distinctly marked, with engraved letters, what it is and how it is to be used, and kept secured by a proper lock, the key of which is to be kept among those of the magazines. A short pipe to lead the water down into the hold is to be attached to the emptying cock, and with this the waste-pipe is to connect. All are to be well boxed over for protection against injury. A perforated disk, or strainer, is to be secured inside of the hole, at the upper part of the magazine, for the waste-pipe. All couplings of hose shall conform to the general naval standard.

LIGHTING THE MAGAZINE.

200. The magazine is to be lighted by means of one regulation-lamp, to correspond with each alley of the magazine-room, placed in a box arranged for the purpose. This box, of which a portion of the magazine bulkhead forms a part, is to be lined, internally, with soldered sheets of copper, and have a few inches of water in it whenever the lamp is lighted. The entrance to it is at the top, through a scuttle in the deck large enough to admit the lamp. For single-decked vessels this scuttle may be surrounded by a composition coaming pierced with holes one-fourth of an inch in diameter, on the forward and after sides near the top. The cover must be so arranged that, when placed in one position, all the holes will be closed —by turning it half round, they are all open; thus supplying air to the lamp and carrying off smoke. In the portion of the magazine bulkhead just alluded to, and so as to throw as much light as possible into the magazine-room, an opening with great bevelling is to be cut, which is to be covered by two plane glasses of suitable thickness, somewhat separated from each other, one of which, that next to the lamp, must be permanently fixed; and the other, or that next to the magazine, is to be let into a wooden frame so that it may be easily removed, and thus both glasses cleaned at any time with convenience and safety. The glasses are to be held in place by brass screws, after being closely fitted and having their edges made perfectly tight. A small dome or reversed funnel of copper, where it can be conveniently done, is to be placed above the lamp and fitted with a pipe of the same metal to convey the smoke off. This pipe may pass up through the covering of the light-box, which is to have a plug-hole, lined with brass, for the purpose, and then led farther, if necessary, taking care, however, to consult perfect safety throughout.

The admission of air to the light-box may be from the division of the hold in which it is placed, by small holes, near its top, through its side or back, protected with copper wire-gauze, inside and outside of the box.

The ceiling and bulkheads of all magazines and shell-rooms should be thoroughly whitewashed.

STOWING THE MAGAZINES.

201. In the stowage of magazines, reference must be had to the Gunner's duties (Art. 36, Part I.), and to Arrangements for Delivering and Distributing Powder (Art. 180, Part I.). Ledges on the shelves, or a bar of wood to ship and unship with facility, will be provided for each tier of tanks, on both sides of the alleys, to secure them from getting out of place when the ship rolls.

The Inspector of Ordnance will furnish the commander of the ship with an exact plan of the magazine and shell-rooms, which shall be returned to the Inspector of the Yard at which the ship refits or is placed in ordinary, with any suggestions the Commander may have to make relative to practicable changes which will render the service more safe or convenient.

SHELL-ROOMS.

202. Rooms for the stowage of loaded shells require the same care in construction and protection against an enemy's shot, and in provision for lighting and flooding, as magazines. Therefore, they should always be built with reference to these objects, as well as to affording room enough to accommodate conveniently the number of loaded shells allowed in their boxes, stowed in bulk. Each should have one light, arranged like those for magazines.

203. In vessels partially armed with shell-guns, the best place, perhaps, for these rooms is immediately forward of the spirit-room, but not communicating with it; and in those armed entirely with such guns, the additional shell-rooms necessary may be, perhaps, more conveniently placed abaft, and adjoining the delivering-passage of the forward magazine, than elsewhere.

204. With the introduction of rifled cannon, and various special projectiles, it is essential to devote more care to the stowage of shells, in order to avoid confusion in battle. Not only each kind and calibre, but each length of fuze, is to be stowed in separate tiers.

DAMPNESS OF MAGAZINES AND SHELL-ROOMS.

205. Sponge dipped in a solution of salt water, dried and weighed, is a means of ascertaining if dampness exists in these places. If it become heavier, the room is damp.

VENTILATION.

206. Provision must be made, by means of grating-hatches, for sufficient ventilation in action, to supply the magazine-men with fresh air, and allow the dampness caused by perspiration to pass off; and fan-blowers are to be fitted to increase the supply of fresh air, and assist the ventilation. The magazine should be opened and aired, at least once a fortnight, for a few hours, on bright, clear days.

SPACES REQUIRED
for working
DIFFERENT CLASSES OF GUNS
ON
TRUCK CARRIAGES.

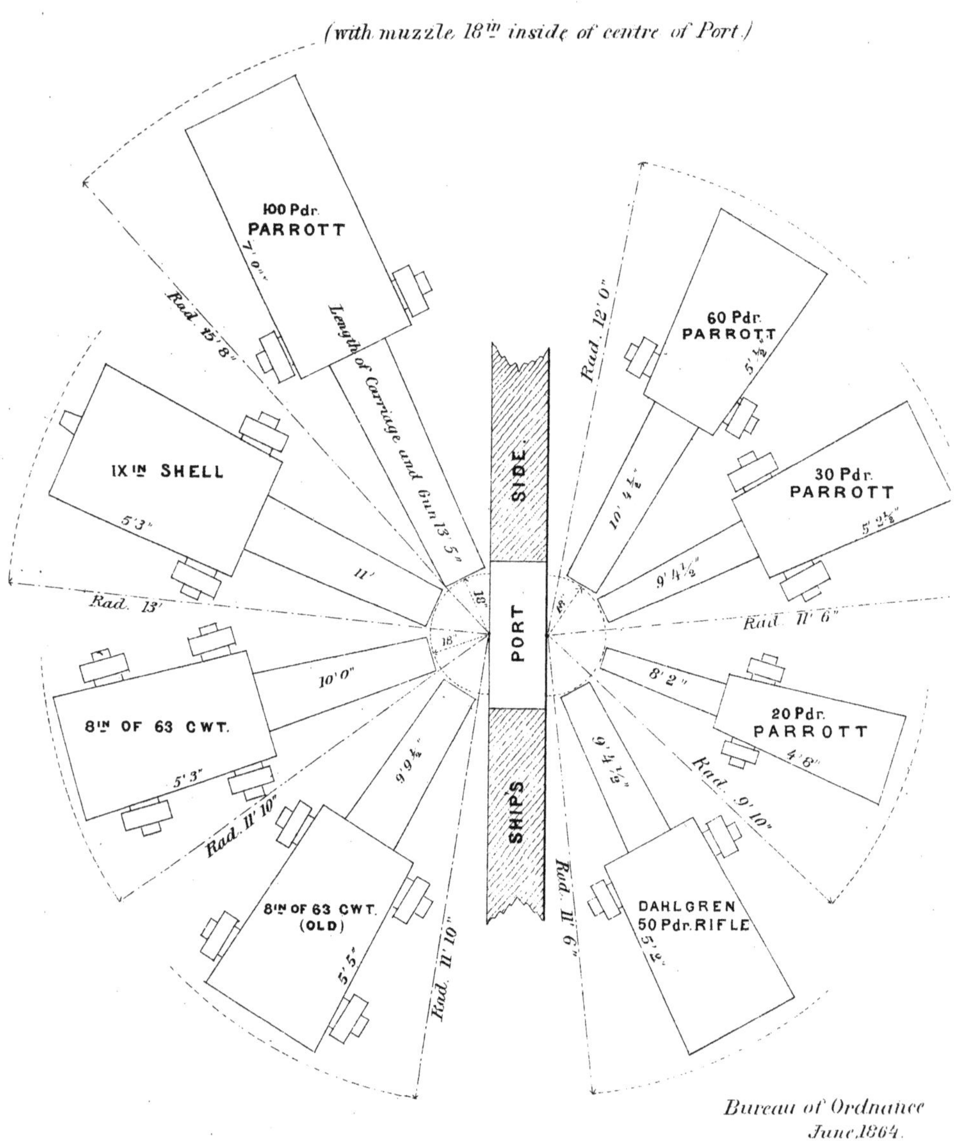

Bureau of Ordnance
June, 1864.

C.K. Stellwagen, del.

Lith. by J.F. Gedney, Wash.

SPACES REQUIRED

for working

DIFFERENT CLASSES OF GUNS

ON

TRUCK CARRIAGES.

(with muzzle 18 in. inside of centre of Port.)

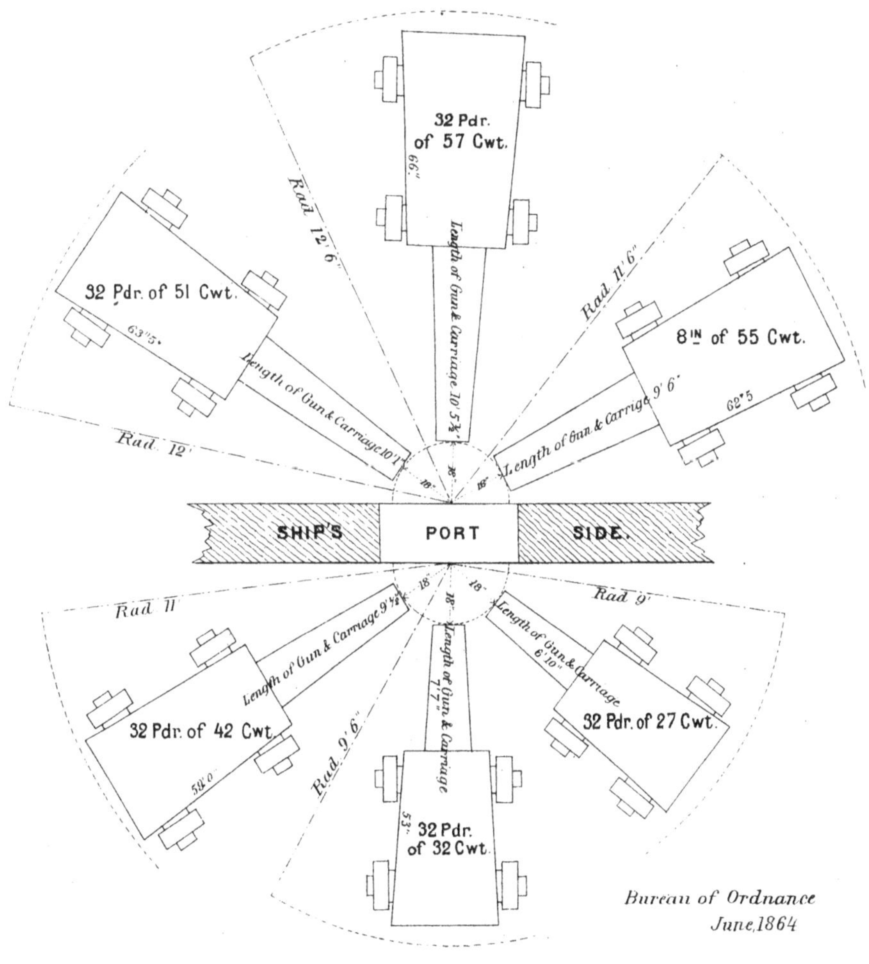

Bureau of Ordnance
June, 1864

C. K. Stellwagen, del.

Lith. by J. F. Gedney, Washn.

CHAPTER III.

GUN-CARRIAGES, GEAR, IMPLEMENTS AND EQUIPMENTS.

GUN-CARRIAGES.

207. All gun-carriages shall be constructed in exact conformity to the drawings furnished by the Bureau, and no alterations whatever will be permitted without its express sanction.

The Inspector of Ordnance will keep approved copies of all plans, and, in order to insure uniformity, will report to the Bureau any deviations from the standard drawings which he may observe in carriages received from other Yards.

The spaces required for efficient working of all guns are represented in diagrams X, Y, Z, and these, as well as the distances between pivot-centres, sizes and positions of bolts, are to be strictly adhered to.

The distance between pivot-centres of all XI-in., X-in., IX-in., and 100-pdr. carriages shall be either 142 or 117¾ inches, depending on the breadth of beam, position of hatches and other obstructions, and shall not be deviated from except by explicit directions of the Bureau, on a report of the particular circumstances in each case.

For the 60-pdr. Parrott, 130 inches between centres; and for the 30-pdr., 120 inches.

The sizes of sockets and pivot-bolts are established as follows:

	For XI-in., X-in., IX-in., and 100-Pdr.	For 60, 30, and 20-Pdr.
	Inches.	Inches.
Length of bolt under the head	18.	14.
Diameter of bolt	4.	3.
Do. hole in socket	4.1	3.1
Do. boss	10.5	8.
Height of boss	1.5	1.1

Slot in the pivot-plate, $\frac{1}{10}$ larger than the boss.

For XI-in., X-in., IX-in., and 100-pdr. carriages, the fighting and shifting sockets are bossed, the housing-socket plain.

For 60-pdr., 30-pdr., and 20-pdr. carriages, the shifting-socket alone is bossed.

For broadside-guns, the following positions for bolts are established:

	20 AND 24 IN. PORT-SILLS.	16 AND 18 IN. PORT-SILLS.
	Inches.	Inches.
Height of centre of lower bolt from deck..................	14.75	10.75
Distance between the bolts..............................	3.75	3.75
Do. of centre of 1st bolt from side of port............	14.	14.
Do. do. 2d bolt from side of port............	22.	22.
Do. do. training-bolt from side of port........	36.	36.
Height of training-bolt from deck........................	21.	14. & 16.
Height of securing-bolt (side-tackle bolt) above port-sill....	8.	8.

For IX-in. guns, the port-sill should not be less than 20 inches in height, and no port-sill less than 16 inches; otherwise, the carriages will not give sufficient elevation, and the position of the Gun Captain in aiming is exceedingly awkward and inconvenient.

Scraping and staining gun-carriages or keeping them bright is prohibited; they should be kept well painted, and the trucks, axletrees, and trunnion-holes oiled.

All new work shall be primed with red-lead.

Wrought-iron Broadside carriages, for IX-inch, new 8-in. of 6,500 lbs., and 32-pdr. of 4,500 lbs. shell-guns, have been designed by the Ordnance Bureau, submitted to trial with success, and are being issued for service at sea.

GUN-GEAR.

208. Breechings for all guns are to be made of the best hemp, of three-stranded rope, shroud-laid, and soft; and for smooth-bore guns not to measure less than seven and a half nor more than eight inches in the coil, excepting those for IX-inch guns, which are to measure nine and a half inches, and for XI-inch ten and a half inches.

209. The breeching-bolts must never be of less dimensions than those prescribed by regulation, and there must be double sets for the IX and XI inch guns.

210. In fitting breechings, a thimble is to be spliced into one end, the strands stuck through twice, and marled down. A thimble is to be turned into the other end, so that the length of the breeching may be conveniently altered. Thus fitted, when the gun is run in and levelled, breechings must be long enough to allow the muzzle of the gun to come a foot inside of the upper port-sill, if the breadth of the vessel will allow it. With guns of violent recoil this distance may be advantageously doubled, where there is room enough, as thereby the strain will be much lessened.

Breechings are neither to be covered, blackened, nor rendered less pliable in any way.

New 8 in. Gun of 6500 lbs, and Iron Carriage.

Side Elevation.

Plan.

Rear View.

Lith. by J. F. Gedney, Washn.

C. K. Stellwagen, del.

BREECHINGS.

CLASS OF GUN.	LENGTH OF BREECHING WHEN CUT.	LENGTH OF BREECHING WHEN FINISHED.	CIRCUMFERENCE OF BREECHING.	THIMBLE.				WEIGHT, INCLUDING THIMBLE.
				Diameter.	Depth	Radius of Score.	Diam. bolt-hole.	
Pivot.	Feet.	Feet.	Inch.	Inch.	Inch.	Inch.	Inch.	Lbs.
XI-inch	38.	32.	10.5	6.	4.	1.75	2.05	172.
X "	37.5	31.5	10.	6.	4.	1.75	2.05	170.
IX "	34.	28.5	9.5	6.	3 6	1.6	2.05	110.
100-pounder.........	37.5	31.5	9.5	6.	3.6	1.6	2.05	130.
60 "	33.	28.	8.	5.5	–	1.3	1.55	91.
30 "	27.5	23.5	7.	5.	–	1.2	1.55	43.
20 "	26.	21.	6.	4.	–	1.0	1.55	40.
Broadside.								
XI-inch	38.0	32.0	10.5	6.	4.	1.75	2.05	172.
X "	34.5	28 5	10.	6.	4.	1.75	2.05	160.
IX "	31.5	25.5	9.5	6.	3.6	1.6	2.05	100.
8-in. 63 cwt..	28.	23.3	8.	5.5	–	1.3	1.55	76.
8-in. { 55 cwt. 6,500 lbs. }	27.	22.3	8.	5.5	–	1.3	1.55	72.
32-pounder—57 cwt...	28.5	24.	8.	5.5	–	1.3	1.55	76.
32-pdr. { 42 cwt. 4.500 lbs. }	26.	21.5	8.	5.5	–	1.3	1.55	70.
32-pounder—33 cwt...	23 5	19	8.	5.5	–	1.3	1.55	65.
32 " 27 cwt...	22.	17.5	8.	5.5	–	1.3	1.55	61.
Broadside Rifle.								
100-pounder..	35.5	31.	9.5	6.	3.6	1.6	2.05	115.
60 "	28.	23.5	8.	5.5	–	1.3	1.55	80.
30 "	25.5	21.5	7.	5.	–	1.2	1.55	39.
20 "	23.	17.5	6.	4.	–	1.	1.55	34.

211. Gun-tackle falls will be made of Manilla or such other pliable rope as may be directed from time to time by the Bureau of Ordnance. It is prohibited to blacken them or to diminish their pliability. Three-inch rope will be found large enough for the heaviest, and from $2\frac{1}{2}$ to $2\frac{1}{4}$ inch for the lighter guns.

The rope being well stretched, the falls are to be cut of sufficient length to allow the full recoil, leaving end enough to hitch round the straps of their inner blocks, when hooked to the middle bolts.

212. Blocks for gun-tackles should have pins of hardened copper, turned smooth, and sheaves of lignum-vitæ without bouching. Those to reeve 3-inch falls to be 10 inches, those for $2\frac{1}{2}$-inch falls 9 inches, and those for $2\frac{1}{4}$ inch falls 8 inches long. The hooks of gun-tackle blocks are not to be less than one and a half inch diameter at the bend for heavy, and one and a quarter for light, broadside-guns.

Metallic blocks with nibs, which keep the blocks fair with the falls, and thus prevent the falls from fouling in the recoil, are to be supplied to all Marsilly and heavy pivot carriages.

GRIOLET.

213. The GRIOLET-PURCHASE for dismounting guns on covered decks is composed of—

A toggle-block, made of elm or oak, the outer end or head of which is made rather larger in diameter than the inner one, which exactly fits the bore of the gun. The head has two sheaves in it, so as to form the lower block of the muzzle-purchase, and is bound at the outer end with an iron band.

A double cascabel-block of iron is made either with a shackle or to fit between the jaws of the cascabel, where it is secured by the cascabel-pin. The iron pins on which the sheaves revolve are formed with eyes, for the convenience of hitching the standing part of the purchase.

Two iron treble-blocks, one for the muzzle and the other for the breech-purchase.

The muzzle-purchase block is so fitted as to be either shackled or toggled to the housing-bolt above the port, and the breech-purchase block has an iron strap terminating above, with an eye by which it is shackled to a bolt passing through the deck above the gun. This bolt has an eye in one end, and a screw or key-slit at the other, and, when in place, is secured above the deck with a nut or key, between which and the deck a washer of hard wood or iron of suitable breadth and thickness is placed.

The hole through which this bolt is put should be directly above the cascabel-block when the muzzle of the gun is under the housing-bolt, and may be bored at the time the gun is to be dismounted; it is to be stopped afterwards with a plug of wood coated with white-lead.

But as it is desirable that every division on the gun-deck should be exercised in mounting and dismounting its guns, a hole may be made in the deck above each division and bouched with a composition screw-tap.

The purchase-falls should not be less than three and a half inches in size, and should be made of Manilla rope, of sufficient length to reeve full, the gun being supposed to be on deck and the upper blocks in place, allowing also sufficient end for splicing in the thimbles and hitching the standing part of the purchase when rove.

An iron thimble, large enough to hook the double-block of a side or train tackle, is spliced into the end of each purchase-fall.

SELVAGEE WADS.

214. Selvagee wads are made by the wad-machine at the Navy Yards. This consists of pairs of disks adapted to each calibre of guns, which being placed face to face on a spindle and keyed, present an annular score, grooved in such a way as to make, when filled, a grommet of the requisite size.

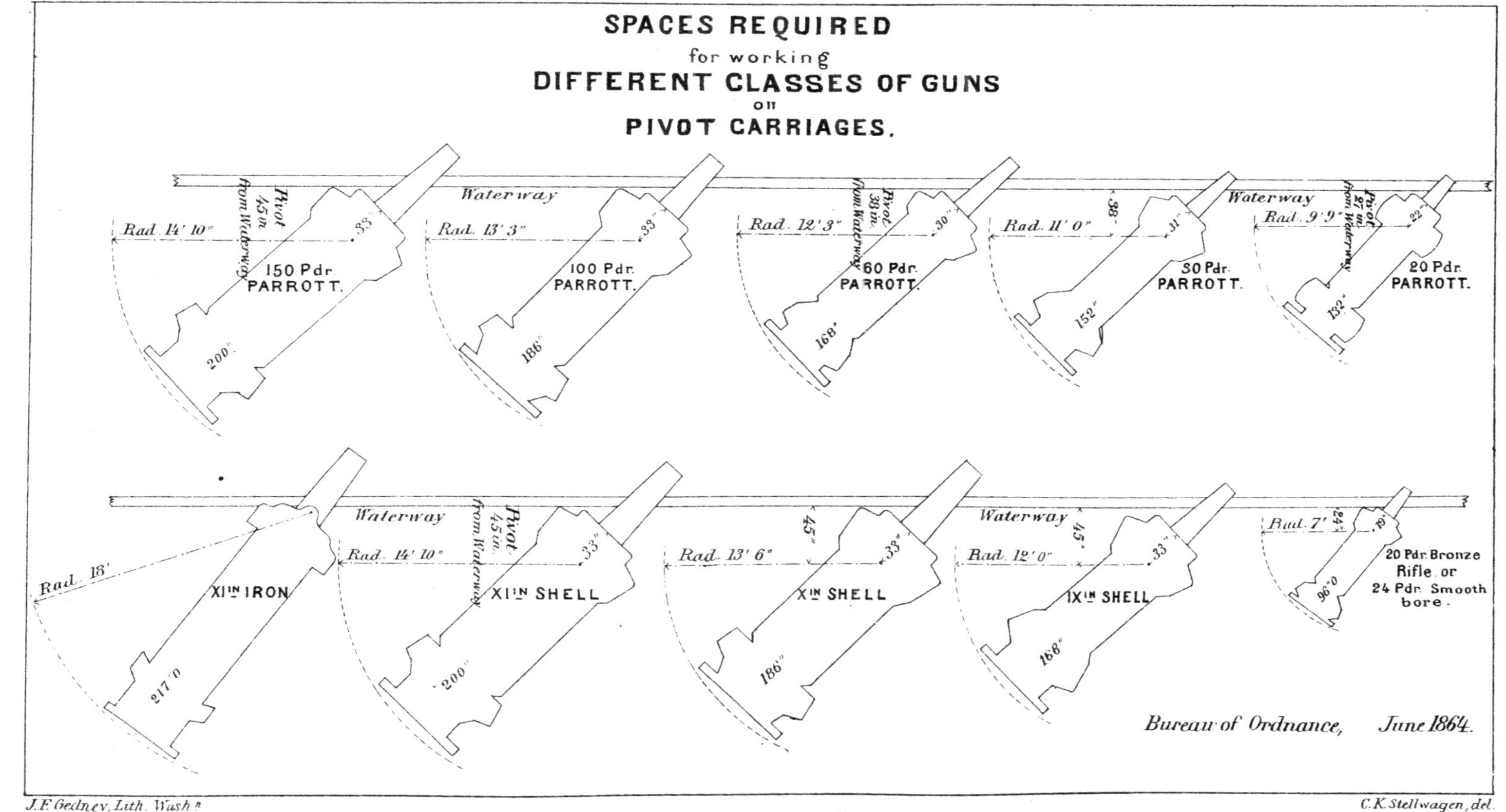

SPACES REQUIRED
for working
DIFFERENT CLASSES OF GUNS
on
PIVOT CARRIAGES.
Waterway
Rad. 14' 10"
Pivot 45 in. from Waterway
33"
150 Pdr. PARROTT.
200"
Rad. 13' 3"
33"
100 Pdr. PARROTT.
186"
Rad. 12' 3"
Pivot 38 in. from Waterway
30"
60 Pdr. PARROTT.
168"
Rad. 11' 0"
38"
31"
30 Pdr. PARROTT.
152"
Waterway
Rad. 9' 9"
Pivot 27 in. from Waterway
22"
20 Pdr. PARROTT.
132"
Rad. 18'
XI IN IRON
217"0
Waterway
Rad. 14' 10"
Pivot 45 in. from Waterway
33"
XI IN SHELL
200"
Rad. 13' 6"
45"
33"
X IN SHELL
186"
Waterway
Rad. 12' 0"
45"
33"
IX IN SHELL
168"
Rad. 7'
24"
19"
96"0
20 Pdr. Bronze Rifle, or 24 Pdr. Smooth bore.
Bureau of Ordnance, June 1864.
J.F. Gedney, Lith. Wash.n
C.K. Stellwagen, del.

Transverse notches are cut in the circumference of the disks to the bottom of the score, for the convenience of marling the wad before taking it off the mould.

In making the wad, the end of a rope-yarn is fixed in the score, and the mould is turned by a crank until the score is filled. The grommet thus formed is marled like a selvagee strap, and a section of about an inch is taken out of it, in order to make the wad, when swelled by dampness, enter the bore of the gun readily.

Selvagee wads should be made neither too hard nor too soft; and to avoid either of these extremes, a sufficient number of hitches only will be taken to give the wad the consistency required for service.

Sections of one-third or one-fourth of these wads will answer as well, in case of need.

MAGAZINE-SCREENS,

215. Are made of thick fearnaught, or of double baize, with holes through which to pass the powder; these holes to be covered by broad flaps of the same material. One screen is to be hung abaft, and another forward of the magazine passing-hatch and scuttles in sloops-of-war; in ships-of-the-line and frigates, one is usually to be hung abaft the fore, and one forward of the after, magazine-scuttle; but as ships are differently arranged, two to each magazine will be allowed, if required.

Canvas chutes for returning empty passing-boxes are to be supplied to each scuttle.

MAGAZINE-DRESSES,

216. Are to be of worsted, like a simple shirt, to reach to the knees—no metal buttons to be worn.

The shoes must be made wholly of cotton canvas or buckskin. In hot climates or warm weather generally, the naked feet are preferred. India-rubber and woollen slippers are prohibited.

RATTLES FOR CALLING BOARDERS,

217. To be made like those used by watchmen, of white oak, or some other similar wood. Rattle, 12 inches long; ratchet, 2 inches in diameter; spring, one inch in width, and of sufficient thickness and elasticity to produce the requisite sound. Weight enough should be given to the butt to cause it to revolve round the handle with ease.

Fixed rattles of greater power will be attached to suitable places on each deck.

SHELL-WHIPS.

218. To be made of two-inch rope, rove through two single blocks one above the other, in the shell-hatchway, and the ends knotted together. A hook is fixed on each part of the whip, near the block, so that the parts being bowsed on alternately, a full box is brought up on one hook and an empty one lowered by the other, at the same time.

FLASH-PANS.

219. Shallow copper bowls, large enough to hold an ounce of powder, with a handle two feet long, to be supplied to all vessels.

DARK LANTERNS.

220. To be made of copper, tinned inside, with two handles at the side, that the shade may be turned without taking hold of the top. The whole height, 12 inches; diameter, 4 inches.

BOAT GRAPNELS.

221. Are made of round iron, quite light, for throwing into the rigging or chains of the enemy, for the purpose of holding on when boarding; their prongs are barbed.

Six feet of small chain are to be attached to the ring, and connected with six fathoms of one and three quarter rope.

TARGETS.

222. In the construction of targets for practice at sea, the chief object will be to give buoyancy and stability to the screen, with sufficient development of its surface. To these ends, whiskey or beef barrels, supporting boards of sufficient length, will afford staging for the masts, yards, and screen; the heel of the mast passing through the stage, and having ballast attached to it. The stage should be so fitted as to be readily put together when wanted, and taken apart for stowage.

Harbor targets may be anchored, or supported on stakes; but it would conduce to good practice to stretch a screen of sufficient length to show, distinctly, four or six ports, with the proper intervals between. This will the better exhibit the lateral effect of the firing of each gun, and of the concentration of fire from several guns at known distances.

PACKING-BOXES.

223. Cartridges for small arms, primers, spur-tubes, percussion-caps, spare fuzes, false-fires, blue-lights, port-fires, and signal-rockets, will generally be supplied to vessels in boxes, in which they can be kept with little liability to injury, until wanted for use. (See Part I., Page 10, Art. 42.)

These boxes are to be safely kept and returned into store, or accounted for in the same manner as other articles of Ordnance stores, by those persons in whose charge they may be placed. They will be held pecuniarily responsible for their loss.

GUN-SLINGS

224. Must be made of chain of ¾-inch iron, and tested, to secure proper strength; the rings are to be of 1¼-inch iron. The length of the slings should exceed by one foot that of the longest gun on board. The two parts should be parcelled and marled together for a space of two feet before and one foot behind the trunnions of the longest gun, and a piece of three-inch rope spliced around both parts in the wake of the parcelling, long enough to take four or five turns round the chase of the largest gun.

TRUNNION-SIGHT FOR MORTARS AND PIVOT-GUNS.

225. The trunnion-sight is designed to be used only when the required elevation passes the limits of the other sights. It is formed of a bar of mahogany, or other hard wood not liable to warp, of about forty inches in length, two inches wide, and one inch thick, with a brass notch at the rear end and a point at the other, fixed in, and parallel to, the upper edge. It is attached, by a stout thumb-screw, to the axis of the left trunnion, around which it revolves when the screw is slack.

A semicircular plate, graduated to degrees, is attached to the bar, so that the sight may be used with the tables showing the corresponding ranges of the several classes of guns with their distant firing-charge. (*See* TABLES OF RANGES, Appendix D.)

The upper edge of the sight-bar corresponds with 0° when the line of sight is parallel to the axis of the bore. A small level let into the upper surface of the rear end of the bar shows when the bar is level.

In using this sight, the thumb-screw is first loosened, and the rear end of the sight raised until the mark on the trunnion coincides with the degree of elevation required for the range, as given in the Tables: clamp the thumb-screw, and elevate the gun until the bubble is at 0°, then give the lateral training.

226. Tangent-sights placed on the side of the breech, with a fixed front sight on the rimbase, as in rifled cannon, will hereafter be supplied to all pivot-guns; and these will give the sight with equal accuracy at all elevations.

RAMMERS AND SPONGES.

227. Rammer-heads are to be made of well-seasoned ash, birch, beech, or other tough wood, of the form and dimensions given in the drawings furnished by the Bureau to the different Navy Yards. The face of the rammer is hollowed, so as to embrace the front of the ball and press the selvagee wad home in its place. A hole is bored lengthwise through the head to admit the tenon, which is fastened by a pin of hard wood, three-tenths of an inch in diameter, passing transversely through the head and tenon. The diameter of the staff is 1.75, and that of the tenon 1.5 inch. The diameter of the rammer-head will be 0.25 inch less than that of the bore or chamber to which it is adapted.

For all chambered guns except those of the Dahlgren pattern, the rammers will be adapted to the chamber, but, as above described, will answer equally well for the shot and selvagee wad.

Staves are made of tough ash, and are one foot longer than the bores of the guns for which they are intended: they are to have grooves $\frac{1}{16}$ of an inch deep and $\frac{1}{4}$ of an inch broad cut in them to show when the "ordinary charges" are in place, and, by due allowances, the others also.

For rifled cannon, rammer-heads are made of composition, of the pattern prescribed by the Bureau.

228. Sponge-heads are to be made of poplar, or other suitable light wood. A hole 1.5 inch in diameter is bored through the axis to admit the tenon of the staff, into which the worm is previously secured by means of a brass pin which passes through an eye in its shank and the tenon. The worm is intended to project half an inch beyond the face of the sponge-head, when the tenon is in place, and to have free play back into its socket when pressed against the bottom of the bore. It must be two inches in length and one and a quarter inch in diameter, made of elastic brass or composition wire two-tenths of an inch in diameter, and tapering at the points, so as to preserve its elasticity and firmness. It is to be left-handed, in order to act when turned to the right, or with the sun.

The wood of which sponge-heads are made should be well seasoned, and gotten out of a size but little greater than the diameter of the heads for which it is intended, so that there may be as little shrinkage as possible in the finished heads.

The heads, when finished, should also be primed with several coats of boiled linseed oil or varnish, as the porous wood of which they are made is apt to become water-soaked, or to split on exposure to the air.

229. For chambered guns the sponges must fit the chambers and slopes, and a portion of the main bore, as shown in the drawings furnished by the Bureau. When made of wool, the whole surface is covered, and so sheared as to have no windage, and to be even with the points of the worm, that they make take effect. The heads for woollen sponges should be one inch less in diameter than the bores or chambers of the guns for which they are intended.

In future, sheepskins will not be allowed, but covers for sponge-heads made up ready to slip over the head and be tacked on.

230. The heads for the sponges of unchambered guns are to be eight inches long; and all sponge-heads intended to be covered with woollen material must be slightly tapered and secured by a thin copper hoop, fastened with copper tacks, on the inner end.

231. For Bristle Sponges the heads must be 1.5 inch less in diameter than the bores or chambers for which they are designed. The bristles are to be sheared so as to work easily and leave no windage. The worm must project one-fourth of an inch, in order to take the bottom of the bore, and special care is to be taken by the Inspector that it has both the necessary stiffness to act efficiently and elastically enough, when pressed home, to yield sufficiently to allow the bristles to act also. Spiral spaces extending the whole length of the sponge-head, including the portion adapted to the main bore in chambered guns, are to be left, in order to bring out the unconsumed portions of cartridges. These spaces must be left-handed like the worm.

Great care is necessary, in stowing them, to prevent the bristles from being crushed down by contact with hard substances. For this purpose fenders will be provided with copper tacks, on the inner end.

One will be allowed to each division, for each calibre, for cleaning guns.

232. Sponge-staves are to be made of tough ash, 1.75 inch in diameter, and must be 18 inches longer than the bores of the guns for which they are intended.

233. Sponge-caps are made of duck, and, except for spar-deck guns where they are exposed to the weather, should not be painted, but they, as well as the staves, should be kept clean by scrubbing. A becket should be attached to the end to haul them off by.

Sponges should be washed carefully and dried after use before putting the caps on, and frequently examined and dried to prevent their rotting.

ROBINSON'S WORM.

234. This worm consists of a screw, $1\frac{1}{4}$ inch in diameter, of two turns, at the end of a cylindrical iron shank, with a socket and straps riveted to the staff, which is 1.5 inch in diameter. The worm is supported in the axis of the bore by means of a guide-ring of composition, kept in place on the shank, six inches from the end, by a shoulder and forelock.

Thus adjusted, it is used to draw the junk-wad and cartridge; the latter being laid hold of by the tie, if the staff be held in the axis of the bore, is uninjured.

When the ring is removed the worm will be equally efficient in drawing the selvagee wad.

LADLES.

235. Ladles, when required, are to be made according to the patterns sent to each of the Navy Yards. Ladles which may be on hand are to be tried in drawing projectiles from the guns before they are issued for service. The Ladle will not draw rifle projectiles, and should not be used for that purpose.

SCRAPERS FOR BOTTOM OF BORE.

236. These consist of two steel blades, crossing each other in the middle, and having their edges conformed to the curve of the bottom of the bore. They are inserted in a sponge-head, and are designed to remove the cake usually caused by the adherence of the bottoms of the cylinders to the bottom of the bore.

The edges of the scrapers are so bevelled as to act only when turned to the right, or with the sun.

Scrapers are also to be supplied for rifled cannon, made to clean a groove and the adjacent lands.

ORDINARY HANDSPIKES.

237. Handspikes are to be made of well-seasoned white hickory, of the form and dimensions directed by the Bureau. They are always to be shod, stained black, and oiled. The Ordnance Officer of the Navy Yard will ascertain that they ship freely in the training-loops or sockets, and that the toe is sufficiently rounded not to cut the decks when held vertically.

Details of Handspikes.			No. 1.	No. 2.	No. 3.
Length	Total	in.	64.	60.	
	Square part	"	20.	20.	
	Octagon "	"	6.	6.	
	Round "	"	38.	34.	
	Shoe	"	18.	18.	
Diameter	of square	"	2.75	2·50	
	of small end	"	1.75	1·6	
Radius of quarter round		"	4.5	3·5	
Weight		lbs.	16.	12.	

ROLLER HANDSPIKES.

238. There are two sizes of roller handspikes: No. 1 for the IX-in. shell-gun and 100-pdr. Marsilly, or two-truck carriage; No. 2 for all other guns.

They are composed of—the head and socket of bronze, handle of hickory, and the roller of lignum-vitæ.

The boss on the head makes, with the handle, an angle of 70°, and, when vertical, lifts the carriage half an inch (0.5).

Commander Beaumont's roller handspike has been adopted.

It is a common error of seamen to stoop, with a view of raising the carriage higher. The lift is greatest when the end of the handle is at the hip.

Details of Roller Handspikes.			No. 1.	No. 2.
Length	Extreme	in.	70.5	66.
	of handle	"	63.0	62.5
	of socket	"	12.	7.5
	of boss	"	1.6	1.3
	of boss from centre of roller	"	4.5	3.6
	of axle-pin	"	9.5	7.5
Diameter	of roller	"	4.5	3.4
	of socket	"	2.9	2.5
	of hole in socket	"	2.6	2.25
	Small end of handle	"	1.5	1.50
	of hole for axle-pin	"	.75	.62
Width	of roller	"	3.60	3.00
	Exterior of head	"	9.00	7.00
Weight		lbs.	32	19.5

IMPRESSION-TAKERS.

239. All vessels carrying XI and IX inch guns, and all iron rifles, are to be furnished with an impression-taker and wax. Impressions of the vent and bore, as described in Art. 57, are to be taken after every ten shotted rounds in practice, and at the close of an action. The last one should be preserved for comparison with the succeeding one; and when, in the opinion of the Commanding Officer, the wear becomes excessive, or a decided crack shows itself, a duplicate must be forwarded to the Bureau for examination. In forwarding them, they should be tacked on a piece of thin board secured in the bottom of a box. If wrapped in cotton or oakum they are generally defaced. The date, number of fires, Register Nos. of guns, ship from which forwarded, and other remarks written and pasted on the under side of the box-cover.

In expert hands any small spar—such as a boat's mast—will take the impression equally well.

PASSING-BOXES.

240. Passing-boxes are to be made of strong and well-tanned harness or sole leather, strongly sewed, or of such other material as may be directed.

For 8-inch and 32-pounder guns they are to be of sufficient height to contain two near-firing charges.

Their diameters, in the clear, must be half an inch greater than those of the cartridges they are to contain.

Their tops must be distinctly lettered, in letters one inch and a half long, with the calibre and class of gun they are intended to serve, and made to slide on the beckets.

241. All passing-boxes are to be painted black, with the calibre and charge painted in white letters two and one-half ($2\frac{1}{2}$) inches long on the side, and one and one-half ($1\frac{1}{2}$) on the top.

242. If, however, there are any guns of the same calibre on spar-decks requiring lighter charges, the lower half of the box shall be painted white.

For gun-decks in similar cases the lower half shall be painted red.

FIRE-TUBS.

243. Fire-tubs should be made of oak, of the patterns furnished by the Bureau, the hoops being of iron. The top is to be provided with a stout hoop of wood, to ship and unship, with a grating across it of stout copper wire, the meshes of which must be small enough to prevent the passing-boxes from falling into the water when struck over the tub.

FIRE-BUCKETS.

244. Fire-buckets should be made of light well-tanned sole leather, according to pattern.

A few Rubber buckets have been issued for trial and report.

THE GROMMET MUZZLE-LASHING FOR HOUSING GUNS.

245. Consists of a grommet made of rope double the size of the gun-tackle falls, with two cringles worked into it for the frapping lashing, which will be of stuff half the size of the tackle-falls.

The grommet will be made large enough just to slip over the swell of the muzzle when the bight is over the housing hook-bolt, and the gun is in position for housing. It will be wormed throughout, and parcelled in the wake of the housing-bolt and frapping lashing, and where there is no swell, in the wake of the muzzle-ring.

Where the housing-bolt is an eye-bolt, the grommet is secured to it by means of a toggle which has a lanyard.

FUZE-WRENCHES.

246. For the Navy time-fuze these are made of steel, with a round shank, four inches long, four-tenths of an inch diameter. Prongs round, one and a half inch long, three-tenths of an inch diameter. Cross-handle of wood, with small forked screw-driver in one end for water-cap. The prongs of the wrench are flattened at the ends, and are nine-tenths of an inch apart.

A three-armed wrench is also required for the Parrott, Schenkl, and Hotchkiss fuzes, all of which differ.

Two to be allowed to each shell-room.

RIGGING STOPPERS.

247. Standing rigging, when stranded or shot away, is most readily and effectually secured for the moment by using stoppers composed of two small dead-eyes, fitted with double selvagee tails and lanyards, of sizes suitable to the rigging, whether lower or topmast. These are to be fitted on board ship, and set up by means of pendant-tackles or jiggers, as the case may require.

HARNESS-CASKS FOR BOATS.

248. For expeditions, the launches and first cutters of all vessels are each to be provided with a week's supply of pork, sufficient for all the boats' crews of the ship, kept in quarter barrels or kegs, adapted to the form of the boat and to convenient stowage.

ACCOUTREMENTS FOR CAPTAINS OF GUNS, BOARDERS, AND SMALL-ARMS MEN.

249. Waist-belts, to be made of buff leather—grained leather becomes stiff and horny when exposed to the sea-air—two inches wide, and from forty to forty-four inches long; a pattern buckle has been adopted.

The same belt is used by Captains of guns and boarders, as well as by small-arms men and the crews of field-howitzers; the frogs and boxes to hold the arms and ammunition being fitted with loops to slip on and off the belt as circumstances require, and in the following order:

1st and 2d Captains of guns, and of field and boat howitzers, wear the primer-box in front; if they are boarders, the sword on the left and the pistol-frog on the right hip. These equipments, consequently, will be slid on towards the loop end of the belt, in the order just named.

Other boarders, and guns' crews of howitzers when used as field-guns, wear their arms, as in the preceding case, without the primer-box.

Men armed with muskets, and acting on shore, will wear musket cartridge-boxes, fitted with frog and scabbard for bayonet on the waist-belt.

Men who may be armed with carbines on shore duty will wear cartridge-boxes with waist-belts. For boat duty, or when armed with pistols and swords, they will wear the waist-belt with the proper frog and boxes.

250. Instead of the sword-frog, the sword scabbards of Admiral D. D. Porter's pattern are fitted with a loop to slide on the waist-belt. This scabbard also dispenses with the brass mountings, which are replaced by leather ones. The whole is fastened by copper rivets, instead of being sewed.

251. Primer-Boxes, of black bridle leather, rectangular in form, and of the size to contain, loosely, the tin packing-box. Flap covering the top and front with a button-hole strap one inch in width, sewed near the bottom: brass button riveted to the bottom of the box. Loop, two inches wide, placed upright on the back of the box for the waist-belt to pass through.

252. Pistol-Frog—buff leather—wide enough at the mouth to cover the cock of the pistol, and at the lower part to accommodate the stock; upper part of the back of it turned down to form a loop large enough to admit the waist-belt. The stitches forming the side seams not to come nearer than 0.25 inch from the edges of the leather. To be worn on right hip.

Pocket—thin bridle leather—to contain three cartridges; flap, tongue, and loop.

Cap-pocket, like the cartridge-pocket; lining, a strip of sheepskin with the wool on, glued with fish-glue and sewed to the back at the mouth of the pocket.

These two pockets are of the same depth, and occupy the whole breadth of the pistol-frog.

253. Thumbstalls, of buckskin, with hair-stuffed pad, and thongs for the wrist.

254. Musket Cartridge-Box—black bridle leather—length, 7.2 inches; width, 1.6 inch; depth in front, 5.8 inches; inner cover—upper leather—4 inches wide, with end pieces sewed to it so as to cover the ends of the box; flap—harness leather—8.5 inches wide at the bottom, 8 inches at top, stamped U. S. N. in an oval on the outside; a button-hole strap, sewed near the bottom; brass button riveted to the bottom of the box; loop—bridle leather—with a hole in the middle to hook the shoulder-belt to, sewed to the back of the box for the waist-belt to pass through.

Cap-pocket—light upper leather—sewed to the front of the box; length, $4\frac{1}{2}$; depth, $2\frac{1}{2}$ inches; flap, tongue, and loop—bridle leather; lining, a strip of sheepskin with the wool on, 1.5 inch wide, glued with fish-glue and sewed at the mouth of the pocket; pocket for ball-screw and wiper sewed on the right, and for cone-key and cone-pick on the left of the cap-pocket.

Two tin linings, each with a lower division, 3 inches by 3.3 inches, open in front, to contain a bundle of ten cartridges, and two bundles of caps containing 25 each, packed in water-proof paper. Each tin has also two upper divisions, 2.7 inches deep—one of 2 inches by 1.35 inch for six cartridges; the other, 1.35 inch square, for four cartridges. The edges of the tins are turned over and soldered down, to prevent them from cutting the fingers.

All the tin linings should be made to slide freely in the boxes.

255. CARBINE CARTRIDGE-BOX.—The leather parts are like those of the musket cartridge-box; length, 6.4 inches; depth in front, 3.7 inches; width, 1.3 inch; inner cover, 3.5 inches wide; flap, 6.6 inches wide at top, 6.8 at bottom, 6 deep. Tin linings; two lower divisions, 2 inches deep, 2.9 inches long, 1.2 wide; five upper divisions, 1.2 inch wide by 1.15 inch long, and 1.5 inch deep, to contain forty cartridges, those below in bundles of water-proof paper.

256. CONE-PICK of steel wire, No. 18, 1.5 inch long, with a ring-handle 0.5 inch in diameter; it is carried, with the cone-key, in the pocket in front of the musket cartridge-box.

257. BAYONET SCABBARD—black bridle leather—length, 19.3 inches. Frog—buff leather—sewed to a socket of black leather, which is fastened to the top of the scabbard; the loop of the frog to be made wide enough to slide on the waist-belt.

MARKING SMALL ARMS.

258. It is directed that hereafter all small arms, when passed by the Inspector, be stamped in the following manner:

MUSKETS, CARBINES, AND PISTOLS.

On the top of the barrel, near the breech, with an anchor; and, on the lock-plate, the letter P over the initials of the Inspector, thus: $\frac{\text{P.}}{\text{A B.}}$

REVOLVERS.

On the top of the barrel, near the cylinder, with an anchor; and, on the face of the cylinder, the letter P over the initials of the Inspector, as above.

CUTLASSES.

On the blade, immediately below the guard, with an anchor; and the letter P over the initials of the Inspector, as above.

All arms in store or returned from ships will be stamped with the anchor before being issued.

The Bureau will furnish to each Inspector two sizes of stamps. MUSKETS, CARBINES, and CUTLASSES are to be marked with the larger, .15-in., and PISTOLS and REVOLVERS with the smaller, 0.1-in., size of stamps.

PRESERVATION OF SMALL ARMS.

259. The Captain will take care that the Small Arms are carefully cleaned and wiped dry after every exercise or use of them, before they are put away.

260. He will cause them to be frequently examined at other times, to prevent their being clogged with oil or lacquer, and to be sure that they are always ready for use.

He will strictly prohibit their being marked or otherwise defaced.

261. It is directed that the men who use them be taught to clean them properly, and to remedy any slight defects or obstructions to their use.

Chests not lined preserve them best, if there be no proper armory.

DIRECTIONS FOR CLEANING ARMS.

262. In taking apart and cleaning guns, there are required a screw-driver, wiper, wire-tumbler punch, and a spring vice. No other implements should be used in taking arms apart, or in setting them up.

263. DISMOUNTING AND CLEANING.—The rifle-musket should be dismounted in the following order, viz.:

1st. Unfix the bayonet. 2d. Insert the tompion. 3d. Draw the ramrod. 4th. Turn out the tang-screw. 5th. Take off the lock; to do this, put the hammer at half-cock, and partially unscrew the side screws; then, with a slight tap on the head of each screw with a wooden instrument, loosen the lock from its bed in the stock; turn out the side screws, and remove the lock with the left hand. 6th. Remove the side screws without disturbing the washers. 7th. Take off the bands in order, commencing with the uppermost. 8th. Take out the barrel; in doing this, turn the musket horizontally, with the barrel downward, holding it loosely, with the left hand below the rear sight and the right hand grasping the stock by the handle; tap the muzzle on the ground, if necessary, to loosen the breech. If an attempt were made to pull the barrel out by the muzzle, it would, in case it were wood-bound, be liable to split at the head of the stock.

The foregoing parts of the rifle-musket are all that should usually be taken off or dismounted

The breech-screw should be taken out only by an armorer, and never in ordinary cleaning. The mountings, cone and cone-seat screw, should not be taken off, nor should the lock be taken apart, except by permission of an officer.

264. To Clean the Barrel.—1st. Stop the vent with a peg of soft wood, or piece of rag or soft leather pressed down by the hammer; pour a gill of water, warm, if it can be had, into the muzzle; let it stand a short time to soften the deposit of powder; put a plug of soft wood into the muzzle and shake the water up and down the barrel; pour it out and repeat the washing until the water comes out clear; remove the peg from the cone and stand the barrel muzzle downward, to drain, for a few moments.

2d. Screw the wiper on the end of the ramrod, and put a piece of dry cloth or tow round it sufficient to prevent it from chafing the grooves of the barrel; wipe the barrel dry, changing the cloth two or three times.

3d. Do not put oil into the vent, as it will clog the passage and cause the first cap to miss fire; but, with a slightly oiled rag on the wiper, rub the bore of the barrel and the face of the breech-screw, and immediately insert the tompion into the muzzle.

4th. To clean the exterior of the barrel, lay it flat on a bench or board, to avoid bending it. The practice of supporting the barrel at each end, and rubbing it with a strap, buffstick, ramrod, or any other instrument to burnish it, is pernicious, and should be strictly forbidden.

5th. After firing, the barrel should always be washed as soon as practicable; when the water comes off clear, wipe the barrel dry and pass into it an oiled rag. Fine flour of emery cloth is the best article to clean the exterior of the barrel.

265. To Clean the Lock.—Wipe every part with a moist rag, and then a dry one; if any part of the interior shows rust, put a drop of oil on the point or end of a piece of soft wood dipped into flour of emery; rub out the rust and wipe the surface dry; then rub every part with a slightly oiled rag.

266. To Clean the Mountings.—For iron and steel parts, use fine emery moistened with oil, or emery cloth. For brass parts, use rotten-stone moistened with vinegar or water, applied with a rag, brush, or stick; oil or grease should be avoided. The dirt may be removed from the screw-holes by screwing a piece of soft wood into them. Wipe all parts with a linen rag, and leave the parts slightly oiled.

267. Dismounting by an Armorer.—The parts which are specially assigned to be dismounted by an experienced armorer will be stated in their regular order, following No. 8, viz.:

9th. Unscrew cone. 10th. Take out cone-seat screw. 11th. Take out band-springs, using a wire punch. 12th. Take out the guard-screws. Be careful that the screw-driver does not slip and mar the stock. 13th. Remove the guard without injuring the wood at either end of the plate. 14th. Remove the side screw-washers with a drift-punch. 15th. Remove the butt-plate. 16th. Remove the rear-sight. 17th. Turn out the breech-screw by means of a "breech screw-wrench" suited to the tenon of the screw. No other wrench should ever be used for this purpose, and the barrel should be held in clamps neatly fitting the breech.

268. Lock.—To take the lock apart: 1st. Cock the piece and apply the spring-piece to the mainspring; give the thumb-screw a turn sufficient to liberate the spring from the swivel and mainspring notch; remove the spring. 2d. The sear-spring screw. 3d. The sear-screw and sear. 4th. The bridle-screw and bridle. 5th. The tumbler-screw. 6th. The tumbler. This is driven out with a punch inserted in the screw-hole, which at the same time liberates the hammer. 7th. Detach the mainspring swivel from the tumbler with a drift-punch. 8th. Take out the feed-finger and spring. 9th. The catch-spring and screw.

269. As a general rule, all parts of the musket are assembled in the inverse order in which they are dismounted. Before replacing screws, oil them slightly with good sperm oil, as inferior oil is converted into a gum, which clogs the operation of the parts. Screws should not be turned in so hard as to make the parts bind. When a lock has, from any cause, become gummed with oil and dirt, it may be cleaned by boiling in soap-suds, or in pearlash or soda-water; heat should never be applied in any other way.

270. Precautions in Using.—In ordering arms on parade, let the butt be brought gently to the ground, especially if the ground be hard. This will save the mechanism of the lock from shocks, which are very injurious to it, and which tend to loosen and mar the screws and split the wood-work.

The ramrod should not be sprung with unnecessary force, for fear of injuring the corners of the grooves; and, in stacking arms, care should be taken not to injure the bayonets by forcibly straining the edges against each other.

No cutting, marking, or scraping the wood or iron should be allowed, and no part of the gun should be touched with a file. Take every possible care to prevent water from getting between the lock, or barrel and stock. If any should get there, dismount the gun as soon as possible, clean and oil the parts as directed, and see that they are perfectly dry before assembling them.

PAINTS AND LACQUERS.

COMPOSITION AND PREPARATION.

271. The proportions are given for 100 parts by weight of prepared colors, when not otherwise designated.

A gallon of linseed oil weighs	7.5 lbs.
" spirits of turpentine	7.25 "
" Japan varnish	7. "
" sperm oil	7.12 "
" neatsfoot oil	7.63 "

PAINTS AND LACQUERS.

Boiled oil.

Raw linseed	103. lbs.
Copperas	3.15 "
Litharge	6.3 "

Dryings.

Mixture of copperas and litharge taken from the boiled oil	60 lbs.
Spirits turpentine	56 "
Boiled oil	2 "

Putty (for filling cracks in wood).

Spanish whiting, pulverized	81.6 lbs.
Boiled oil	20.4 "

Another kind of putty, for the same purpose, is made by mixing fine sifted oak sawdust with linseed oil which has been boiled till glutinous.

White paint.

	Proportions.	
	For inside work.	For outside work.
White-lead, ground in oil	80. lbs.	80 lbs.
Boiled oil	14.5 "	9 "
Raw oil	0. "	9 "
Spirits turpentine	8. "	4 "

Grind the white-lead in the oil, and add the spirits of turpentine.
New wood-work requires about 1 lb. to the square yard for three coats.

Lead color.

White-lead, ground in oil	75. lbs.
Lampblack	1. lb.
Boiled linseed oil	23. lbs.
Litharge	0·5 lb.
Japan varnish	0·5 "
Spirits turpentine	2.5 lbs.

The lampblack and litharge are ground separately upon the stone, in oil, then stirred into the white-lead and oil; the turpentine and varnish are added as the paint is required for use, or when it is packed in kegs for transportation.

Black paint.

Lampblack	28 lbs.
Litharge	1 lb.
Japan varnish	1 "
Linseed oil, boiled	73 lbs.
Spirits turpentine	1 lb.

Grind the lampblack in oil; mix it with the oil, then grind the litharge in oil and add it, stirring it well into the mixture. The varnish and turpentine are added last.

This paint is used for the iron-work of carriages.

Paint for tarpaulins.

A square yard takes 2 lbs. for three coats.

1. *Olive.*—Liquid olive color	100 lbs.
Beeswax	6 "
Spirits turpentine	6 "

Dissolve the beeswax in the spirits of turpentine, with a gentle heat, and mix the paint warm.

2. Add 12 ounces of beeswax to a gallon of linseed oil, and boil it two hours; prime the cloth with this mixture, and use the same in place of *boiled oil* for mixing the paint. Give two coats of paint.

Lacquers for iron ordnance.

1. Black-lead, pulverized	12 lbs.
Red-lead	12 "
Litharge	5 "
Lampblack	5 "
Linseed oil	66 "

Boil it gently about twenty minutes, during which time it must be constantly stirred.

2. Umber, ground .... 3.75 lbs.
Gum-shellac, pulverized .... 3.75 "
Ivory-black .... 3.75 "
Litharge .... 3.75 "
Linseed oil .... 78. "
Spirits turpentine .... 7.25 "

The oil must be first boiled half an hour. The mixture is then boiled twenty-four hours, poured off from the sediment, put in jugs and corked.

3. Coal tar of good quality .... 2 galls.
Spirits turpentine .... 1 pint.

The turpentine to be added in small quantities during the application of the lacquer.

4. Anti-corrosion .... 40 lbs.
Grant's black, ground in oil .... 4 "
Red-lead, as a dryer .... 3 "
Linseed oil .... 4 galls.
Spirits turpentine .... 1 pint.

This mixture, when well stirred and incorporated, will be fit for use; but, as by long keeping in this state it becomes hard, no more should be mixed than may be required for immediate use.

Anti-Corrosion.—Slag from iron foundries, pounded .... 12 lbs.
Chalk .... 12 "
Soot, common .... 1 lb.

In applying lacquer, the surface of the iron must be first cleaned with a scraper and a wire brush, if necessary, and the lacquer applied hot, in two thin coats, with a paint-brush. It is best done in summer.

Old lacquer should be removed with a scraper, or by scouring, and not by heating the guns or balls, by which the metal is injured.

PLANTOU'S COMPOSITION FOR COATING IRON OR WOOD AS A PRESERVATIVE.

First composition.

Pulverized rosin .... 3 lbs.
Pulverized shellac .... 2 oz.
Pulverized charcoal, or cannel-coal .... 1 lb.
Spirits turpentine .... 1 oz.

Second composition.

Pulverized resin .... 3 lbs.
Beeswax .... 4 oz.
Pulverized charcoal, or cannel-coal .... 1 lb.
Spirits turpentine .... 1 oz.

The first two articles are to be dissolved in an iron vessel over the fire; the charcoal is then added, and briskly stirred until the whole is well intermixed; after which the turpentine is added, and stirred until it is well incorporated with the other ingredients. It is not safely made on board ship.

The composition is to be applied when hot, with a brush or spatula, and smoothed over with a hot iron. The wood, or iron should be perfectly dry, and freed from rust or other loose substances.

Lacquer for small arms, or for water-proof paper.

Beeswax	13 lbs.
Spirits turpentine	13 galls.
Boiled linseed oil	1 gall.

All the ingredients should be pure, and of the best quality. Heat them together in a copper or earthen vessel, over a gentle fire, in a water-bath, until they are well mixed.

Lacquer for bright iron-work.

Linseed oil, boiled	80.5	lbs.
Litharge	5.5	"
White-lead, ground in oil	11.25	"
Rosin, pulverized	2.75	"

Add the litharge to the oil, let it simmer over a slow fire for three hours; strain it, and add the rosin and white-lead; keep it gently warmed, and stir it until the rosin is dissolved. Apply it with a paint-brush.

Varnish for scabbards, or patent leather.

For 1st and 2d coats.—	Prussian blue, in lumps	4.	lbs.
	Sugar-of-lead	0.7	lb.
	Aquafortis	0.7	"
	Linseed oil, boiled	70.	lbs.
	Spirits turpentine	24.6	"

The ingredients, except the turpentine, are boiled together, in an iron kettle, eight hours, when the mixture will assume a brilliant black color. When the varnish is nearly cool, stir in the turpentine. The kettle in which the varnish is made should be of a capacity to hold double the quantity of varnish to be boiled. It cannot be safely made on board ship.

For the third or finishing coat.—COPAL VARNISH.

Gum-copal, in clear lumps	26.5	lbs.
Boiled linseed oil	42.5	"
Spirits turpentine	31.	"

This varnish is made in a copper vessel, smallest at the top, in the form of a still.

Put the copal in the vessel, set it on a charcoal fire for one hour, in which time it will melt, and all the watery particles will evaporate. Add the oil whilst the copal is warm, but not boiling hot. When nearly cool add the turpentine, which will give it a proper consistency for use.

For 5 lbs. copal, and the proper proportions of oil and turpentine, the vessel should hold six gallons. Not safely made on board ship.

Japan varnish.

Litharge	4 lbs.
Boiled oil	87 "
Spirits turpentine	2 "
Red-lead	6 "
Umber	1 lb.
Gum-shellac	8 lbs.
Sugar-of-lead	2 "
White vitriol	1 lb.

Japan varnish is generally purchased from the paint-sellers. It is made by boiling on a slow charcoal fire for five hours all the ingredients except the turpentine and a small portion of the oil. The latter is added as required to check the ebullition and to allay the froth which rises to the surface. It must be continually stirred with a wooden spatula. Great care is necessary to prevent it from taking fire, and therefore it cannot be safely made on board ship.

The turpentine is added after the varnish is nearly cool, and is stirred well in. The varnish must be kept in tin cans closely corked.

Olive paste.

Yellow ochre, pulverized	68. lbs.
Lampblack	1.1 "
Boiled oil	37. "
Spirits turpentine	0.4 lb.

Make a thick paste with the ochre and oil in a paint-pot, and with the lampblack and oil in another. Grind them together in small portions, and keep the mixture in a tin vessel.

Liquid olive color.

Olive paste	61.5 lbs.
Boiled oil	29.5 "
Spirits turpentine	5.5 "
Dryings	3.5 "
Japan varnish	2. "

Stirred together in a paint-pot.

Brainard's paint.

Dissolve 10 pounds of shellac in 10 gallons of boiling water, adding 30 ounces of saleratus. Mix this solution with an equal quantity of paint prepared in the usual manner. This paint is economical and durable.

Black stain (for wood-work).

Copperas	1 lb.
Nutgalls	1 "
Sal ammoniac	$\frac{1}{4}$ "
Vinegar	1 gal.

Stir it occasionally for a few hours, and it will be ready for use.

The wood must be clean and smooth, and the cracks filled with black putty, which must be allowed to dry. The stain to be applied two or three times, and left to dry for a day or two. Then it is to be rubbed with boiled oil until sufficiently polished. Until the oil is applied the color will be bluish. Scraping and staining gun-carriages, or keeping them bright, is prohibited. They should be kept well painted.

Impression wax for vents.

Beeswax	4 parts.
Tallow	2 "
Charcoal, finely powdered	1 part.

Melt the beeswax and tallow, and stir in the charcoal.

Paper parchment.

Immerse unsized paper for a few seconds in sulphuric acid, diluted with half its volume of water at about 60°; wash it well in cold water, then immerse it in a weak solution of caustic ammonia, and again wash.

It absorbs water, and becomes soft and pliable like animal parchment, but is water-proof. It is not affected by boiling water, is indestructible by most acids, and is not diminished in strength by wetting. It has about $\frac{2}{3}$ the strength of animal parchment when dry; the thinner kinds make capital tracing-paper, which takes ink readily.

Cement for the above.

Cheese-fresh, without salt, if possible	3 parts.
Quicklime	1 part.

Wash the cheese thoroughly three or four times in boiling water, and grind the materials on a stone and muller, adding cold water until it is of the consistency of honey.

Composition for lining the interior of rifle-shells.

Soap—common yellow, not salt-water soap	16 ounces.
Tallow	7 "
Rosin	7 "

The tallow should be melted first, then melt and add the rosin, and lastly the soap, bringing the mass to a heat that will make it *very* fluid.

The shells having been first thoroughly cleaned, fill them about one-third full of the composition, roll them slowly so as to spread the mixture over the whole interior surface, and then pour off the residue. This coating should be about one-tenth (0.1) of an inch in thickness, except at the bottom of the shell, where it should be about three-quarters of an inch thick. To obtain these thicknesses, the operation of coating should be performed twice; then pour into the shell enough of the composition to produce the desired thickness at the bottom, the shell standing on its base. After the composition is perfectly cool, immerse the shell in hot water at as high a temperature as the composition will stand without "running"—about 170 degrees. This second heating of the composition in the bath toughens it, and causes it to adhere more closely to the shell.

APPENDIX.

A. ALLOWANCE TABLE OF CREWS.

B. TABLES OF GUNNERY PRACTICE.

C. FORMS OF REPORTS OF INSPECTION AND OF TARGET PRACTICE.

D. TABLES OF ALLOWANCES OF ORDNANCE STORES.

APPENDIX A.

ALLOWANCE OF CREWS:

Embracing Officers and all others to be allowed each Vessel of the Navy, whatever may be her class, kind, or armament.

The number of men assigned in each case will be found adequate to man properly the battery, and also the Powder Division, together with the divisions of the Master and Surgeon.

DIRECTIONS.

1. Take from Table I., columns 3 or 4 (either or both, as the case may happen to require), the number of hands designated for each kind or class of gun the vessel may carry, and multiply these figures respectively by the number of guns of each kind to which they refer. In this way is to be obtained the aggregate number of hands necessary to man properly the battery itself. Call the result A.[1]

2. Then, in order to get at the additional number of hands necessary to man properly the powder division and the divisions of the Master and Surgeon, which additional number is to be called B, multiply A by the decimal—

	Decimal				Decks			Guns		
SAILING VESLELS.	.25	for a sailing vessel carrying on			3 decks	from		74 to 90	guns.	
	.29	"	"	"	2	"	"	36 to 60	"	
	.34	"	"	"	1 or 2	"	"	20 to 26	"	
	.36	"	"	"	1	"	"	16 to 20	"	medium of calibre.
	.60	"	"	"	1	"	"	14 to 18	"	light of calibre.
	.34	"	"	"	1	"	"	9 to 7	"	heaviest of calibre.
	.40	"	"	"	1	"	"	6 to 5	"	" "
	.50	"	"	"	1	"	"	4 to 3	"	" "
	.70	"	"	"	1	"	"	2 to 1	"	" "

STEAMERS.

- .25 for a steamer carrying on 2 decks from 36 to 60 guns, with broadside-guns on upper deck lighter than those on the other.
- .22 for a steamer carrying on 2 decks from 36 to 60 guns, with broadside-guns on upper deck as heavy as those on the other.
- .34 for all other steamers, including iron-clads.

NOTE 1.—Howitzers, when not really essentials of a battery, but intended rather as appendages to it for boat and field service, and for particular occasions, than to be used as commonly as the other guns of the vessel in general exercises, or in an engagement, are *not* to be included in applying these directions. The marines and available hands of the master's division are to be kept drilled to them, for the purpose of clearing the deck of an enemy.

In the case of a sailing vessel, *about* one-third of B will be the proportion of hands to be taken for the Master's division, and the rest, less those for the Surgeon's division (which is to be composed of the surgeon's steward and the nurses allowed), will be the number for the powder division.

And, too, in the case of a steamer of any kind, *about* one-third of B will also be the proportion of hands to be taken for the Master's division; but the rest, less those just mentioned for the Surgeon's division, is to be increased by one-third of the number of firemen and coal-heavers allowed, to constitute the powder division.

It is to be borne in mind that the powder division is always to command a preference over the master's, on the score of being sufficiently manned.

3. Add A and B together, and call their sum C.

4. To ascertain how many of the whole number of C are to be petty officers, &c., consult Table II.

5. One-sixth part of the whole number of C will give the number of seamen.

6. One-fourth part of the whole number of C will give the number of ordinary seamen.

7. One-fortieth part of the whole number of C will give the number of musicians (exclusive of the master of the band), when musicians are allowed, which is to be only to ships-of-the-line, frigates, and flag vessels having a totality of crew amounting to not less than 350 souls.[2]

8. The total number of petty officers, &c., seamen, ordinary seamen, and musicians, deducted from the whole number of C, will give the number of landsmen and boys.

9. The number of hands, in addition to the whole number of C, to serve as firemen and coal-heavers, when these are required, is to be ascertained by the annexed rule relating to the subject.

10. For the number and grades of officers, consult Table III.

11. For the number and grades of marines, consult Table IV.

12. An admiral of any grade, when appointed as the commander-in-chief of a fleet or squadron, is authorized to nominate to the Navy Department an officer not below the grade of a commander to serve as the head of his staff, or as the captain of the fleet, and to be borne on the books of the vessel carrying his flag in addition to her established complement.

13. Every officer appointed to the command of a fleet or squadron is authorized to nominate to the Navy Department an officer not higher in grade than a lieutenant, nor lower than an ensign, to serve as his flag lieutenant, or aid, and to be borne on the books of the vessel carrying his flag or broad pennant in addition to her established complement.

14. An admiral of any grade, appointed the commander-in-chief of a fleet or squadron, is to be allowed two seamen and two ordinary seamen, to be borne on the books of the vessel carrying his flag in addition to her established complement.

15. Every other officer appointed to the command of a fleet or squadron is to be allowed one seaman and two ordinary seamen, to be borne on the books of the vessel carrying his broad pennant in addition to her established complement.

16. The number of men in any rating, as above directed, is not to be exceeded, in any case, without the authority of the Secretary of the Navy, unless it be to make good deficiencies in superior ratings; and vessels, in time of peace, when otherwise ready for

NOTE 2.—If the number of musicians thus derived be even, one-half of them are to be of the first class, and one-half of the second class; otherwise, the bare majority are to be of the first class, and the rest of the second.

sea, are not to be detained on account of deficiencies in their complements, if the whole number of petty officers and persons of inferior rating be equal to nine-tenths of the number allowed as their crews.

17. The tctal number of a crew, as allowed above, is never to be exceeded without the express direction or sanction of the Secretary of the Navy.

18. Complements will be designated by the Navy Department for receiving vessels, practice vessels, apprentice vessels, store and supply vessels, and for any others intended for special or peculiar service.

TABLE I.

SHOWING THE NUMBER OF HANDS (*powder-man or boy included*) APPLICABLE TO VARIOUS KINDS OF GUNS IN USE, TO SERVE AS A BASIS TO DETERMINE THE NUMBER TO COMPOSE A VESSEL'S CREW, EXCLUSIVE OF OFFICERS, MARINES, FIREMEN, AND COAL-HEAVERS.

KIND OR CLASS OF GUN.	WEIGHT OF GUN, IN POUNDS, OR CWT., WHEN SO EXPRESSED.	NOTICES.	NUMBER OF HANDS FOR EACH—	
			Gun, when a pivot, or used singly.	Gun of both broad-sides.
Col. 1.	Col. 2.		Col. 3.	Col. 4.
XV-inch	42,000	In turrets of an iron-clad, and on carriage requiring but ten hands for a XV-inch and seven for an XI-inch, powder-men included.	20	These numbers, 20 and 14, give, intentionally, double crews.
XI-inch or 150-pounder	16,000 to 17,000		14	
XI-inch or 150-pounder	16,000 to 17,000	Elsewhere than in said turrets	25	12.5
X-inch or 64-pounder	12,000		21	10.5
IX-inch or 100-pounder	9,000 to 10,000		17	8.5
60-pounder	5,000		11	5.5
30-pounder rifle	3,000 to 4,000		9	4.5
20-pounder rifle	1,600 to 2,000		7	3.5
8-inch	63 cwt.	On lower deck of ship-of-the-line	17	8.5
8-inch	63 "	Elsewhere than on said deck	15	7.5
8-inch	56 " or 6,500 lbs.		13	6.5
32-pounder	57 "	On lower deck of ship-of-the-line	15	7.5
32-pounder	57 "	Elsewhere than on said deck	13	6.5
32-pounder	42 " or 4,500 lbs.		11	5.5
32-pounder	33 "		9	4.5
32-pounder	27 "		7	3.5
24-pounder howitzer	1,300 to 1,400		7	3.5
12-pounder howitzer	700 to 800		5	2.5

TABLE II.

Allowance of Petty Officers, and also of others NOT *Seamen, Ordinary Seamen, Landsmen, Boys, Firemen, Coal-heavers, nor Musicians, other than Master of the Band, for Sailing Vessels and Steamers of every description, including Iron-clads, when the amount of C is—*

RATINGS.	NOT LESS THAN 570 NOR MORE THAN 760.		NOT LESS THAN 375 NOR MORE THAN 570.		NOT LESS THAN 225 NOR MORE THAN 375.		NOT LESS THAN 175 NOR MORE THAN 225.		NOT LESS THAN 100 NOR MORE THAN 175.		NOT LESS THAN 80 NOR MORE THAN 100.		NOT LESS THAN 60 NOR MORE THAN 80.		NOT LESS THAN 40 NOR MORE THAN 60.		NOT LESS THAN 25 NOR MORE THAN 40.		NOT LESS THAN 12 NOR MORE THAN 25.	
S. V. means a Sailing Vessel. STMR. means a Steamer.	Col. 1.		Col. 2.		Col. 3.		Col. 4.		Col. 5.		Col. 6.		Col. 7.		Col. 8.		Col. 9.		Col. 10.	
	S. V.	Stmr.	S. V.	Stmr.	S. V.	Stmr.	S. V.	Stmr.	S. V.	Stmr.	S. V.	Stmr.	S. V.	Stmr.	S. V.	Stmr.	S. V.	Stmr.	S. V.	Stmr.
Chief Boatswain's Mate	1	......	1	1	1	1	1	1	1	......	......	......	......	......	......	......	......	......	......	......
Boatswain's Mate in charge	......	......	......	......	......	......	......	......	......	......	......	......	1	1	1	1	1	1	......	......
Boatswain's Mates	5	......	3	3	2	2	2	2	2	2	2	2	1	1	......	......	......	......	......	......
Chief Gunner's Mates	1	......	1	1	......	......	......	......	......	......	......	......	......	......	......	......	......	......	......	......
Gunner's Mates in charge	......	......	......	......	......	......	......	......	......	......	......	......	1	1	1	1	1	1	......	......
Gunner's Mates	3	......	1	1	1	1	1	1	1	1	1	1	1	1	......	......	......	......	......	......
Chief Quartermasters	1	......	1	1	1	1	1	1	1	1	1	1	1	1	......	......	......	......	......	......
Quartermasters	9	......	7	7	5	5	3	3	3	3	3	3	3	3	3	3	2	2	1	1
Coxswains	10	......	8	8	7	7	6	6	4	4	4	4	2	2	1	1	1	1	......	......
Captains of Forecastle	4	......	4	4	2	2	2	2	2	2	2	2	2	2	1	......	1	......	......	......
Captains of Tops	8	......	6	6	6	4	4	2	2	......	2	......	2	......	1	......	......	......	......	......
Captains of After-Guard	2	......	2	2	2	2	2	2	2	2	2	2	1	1	1	1	......	......	......	......
Quarter Gunners	18	......	12	12	6	6	4	4	4	3	3	2	2	2	2	2	1	1	1	1
Carpenter's Mates	2	......	2	2	1	1	1	1	1	1	1	1	1	1	1	1	......	......	......	......
Sailmaker's Mates	2	......	1	1	1	1	1	1	1	1	1	1	1	1	1	1	......	......	......	......
Painters—1st class	1	......	1	1	1	1	1	1	1	1	......	......	......	......	......	......	......	......	......	......
Painters—2d class	1	......	1	1	......	......	......	......	......	......	1	1	1	1	1	1	......	......	......	......
Coopers	1	......	1	1	1	1	1	1	1	1	1	1	1	1	......	......	......	......	......	......
Armorers	1	......	1	1	1	1	1	1	1	1	......	1	......	......	......	......	......	......	......	......
Armorer's Mates	1	......	1	1	......	1	......	......	......	......	1	......	......	......	......	......	......	......	......	......
Captains of Hold	2	......	2	2	2	2	2	2	1	1	1	1	1	1	1	1	......	......	......	......
Ship's Cooks	1	......	1	1	1	1	1	1	1	1	1	1	1	1	1	1	1	1	1	1
Bakers	2	......	2	2	1	1	1	1	1	1	......	......	......	......	......	......	......	......	......	......
Yeomen	1	......	1	1	1	1	1	1	1	1	1	1	1	1	1	1	1	1	......	......
Master-at-Arms	1	......	1	1	1	1	1	1	1	1	1	1	1	1	......	......	......	......	......	......
Surgeon's Steward in charge	When there is no Medical Officer provided, the Surgeon's Steward allowed is to become the Surgeon's Steward in charge.																			

TABLE II.—Continued.

RATINGS.	NOT LESS THAN 570 NOR MORE THAN 760.		NOT LESS THAN 375 NOR MORE THAN 570.		NOT LESS THAN 225 NOR MORE THAN 375.		NOT LESS THAN 175 NOR MORE THAN 225.		NOT LESS THAN 100 NOR MORE THAN 175.		NOT LESS THAN 80 NOR MORE THAN 100.		NOT LESS THAN 60 NOR MORE THAN 80.		NOT LESS THAN 40 NOR MORE THAN 60.		NOT LESS THAN 25 NOR MORE THAN 40.		NOT LESS THAN 12 NOR MORE THAN 25.	
S. V. means a Sailing Vessel. STMR. means a Steamer.	Col. 1.		Col. 2.		Col. 3.		Col. 4.		Col. 5.		Col. 6.		Col. 7.		Col. 8.		Col. 9.		Col. 10.	
	S. V.	Stmr.	S. V.	Stmr.	S. V.	Stmr.	S. V.	Stmr.	S. V.	Stmr.	S. V.	Stmr.	S. V.	Stmr.	S. V.	Stmr.	S. V.	Stmr.	S. V.	Stmr.
Surgeon's Stewards	1	......	1	1	1	1	1	1	1	1	1	1	1	1	1	1	1	1	......	......
Paymaster's Stewards	1	......	1	1	1	1	1	1	1	1	1	1	1	1	1	1	1	1	......	......
Schoolmasters	1	......	1	1	1	1	1	1	1	1	1	1	1	1	1	1	......	......	......	......
Ship's Writers	1	......	1	1	1	1	1	1	1	1	1	1	1	1	1	1	......	......	......	......
Ship's Corporals	2	......	2	2	2	2	1	1	1	1	......	......	......	......	1	1	1	1	......	......
Masters of the Band	1	......	1	1	and	one to	every	other	vessel	allow	ed a	band.								
Coxswains to Commander-in-Chief. Stewards to Commander-in-Chief. Cooks to Commander-in-Chief	One	of eac	h, to	be bor	ne on	the bo	oks of	the v	essel c	arryin	g his	flag in	additi	on to	her c	omple	ment.			
Cabin Stewards	1	......	1	1	1	1	1	1	1	1	1	1	1	1	1	1	......	......	......	......
Cabin Cooks	1	......	1	1	1	1	1	1	1	1	1	1	1	1	1	1	......	......	......	......
Ward-room Stewards	1	......	1	1	1	1	1	1	1	1	1	1	1	1	1	1	1	1	......	......
Ward-room Cooks	1	......	1	1	1	1	1	1	1	1	1	1	1	1	1	1	1	1	......	......
*Steerage Stewards	1	......	1	1	1	1	1	1	1	1	1	1	1	1	1	1	......	......	1	1
*Steerage Cooks	1	......	1	1	1	1	1	1	1	1	1	1	1	1	1	1	......	......	1	1
*Forward Officer's Stewards	1	......	1	1	1	1	1	1	1	1	1	1	......	......	......	......	......	......	......	......
*Forward Officer's Cooks	1	......	1	1	1	1	1	1	1	1	1	1	......	......	......	......	......	......	......	......
*Carpenters, including Caulkers	12	......	10	10	8	8	6	6	4	4	2	2	2	2	1	1	1	1	......	......
*Nurses	2	......	2	2	2	2	2	2	2	2	1	1	1	1	1	1	......	......	......	......
TOTAL	107	......	88	88	68	67	58	56	51	47	44	41	38	36	30	28	15	14	5	5

NOTE.—Those ratings marked * are *not* Petty Officers. Iron-clads without spars not to be allowed any Captains of Tops.

TABLE III.

Allowance of Officers when the amount of C is—

GRADES.	NOT LESS THAN 570 NOR MORE THAN 760.		NOT LESS THAN 375 NOR MORE THAN 570.		NOT LESS THAN 225 NOR MORE THAN 375.		NOT LESS THAN 175 NOR MORE THAN 225.		NOT LESS THAN 100 NOR MORE THAN 175.		NOT LESS THAN 80 NOR MORE THAN 100.		NOT LESS THAN 60 NOR MORE THAN 80.		NOT LESS THAN 40 NOR MORE THAN 60.		NOT LESS THAN 25 NOR MORE THAN 40.		NOT LESS THAN 12 NOR MORE THAN 25.	
S. V. means a Sailing Vessel. STMR. means a Steamer.	Col. 1.		Col. 2.		Col. 3.		Col. 4.		Col. 5.		Col. 6.		Col. 7.		Col. 8.		Col. 9.		Col. 10.	
	S. V.	Stmr.	S. V.	Stmr.	S. V.	Stmr.	S. V.	Stmr.	S. V.	Stmr.	S. V.	Stmr.	S. V.	Stmr.	S. V.	Stmr.	S. V.	Stmr.	S. V.	Tugs.
Commodore	1	......	1	1	......	......	......	......	......	......	......	......	......	......	......	......	......	......	......	......
Captain	......	......	......	......	1	1	......	1	......	1	......	......	......	......	......	......	......	......	......	......
Commander	......	......	......	......	......	......	1	......	1	......	......	1	......	1	......	......	......	......	......	......
Lieut.-Commander	1	......	1	1	1	1	1	1	1	1	1	......	1	......	1	1	1	1	......	......
Lieutenant	2	......	1	1	1	1	1	1	1	1	......	1	......	1	......	......	......	......	......	......
Master	3	......	2	2	1	1	1	1	1	1	3	2	2	1	1	1	1	1	......	1
Ensign	3	......	2	2	2	2	2	2	2	2	2	2	3	3	4	4	3	3	1	......
Midshipman	12	......	8	8	6	6	4	4	4	4	4	4	......	......	......	......	......	......	......	......
Surgeon	1	......	1	1	1	1	1	1	1	1	......	......	......	......	......	......	......	......	......	......
Assistant Surgeons	3	......	2	2	2	2	1	1	1	1	2	2	1	1	1	1	1	1	......	......
Paymaster	1	......	1	1	1	1	1	1	1	1	......	......	......	......	......	......	......	......	......	......
Assistant Paymaster	......	......	......	......	......	......	......	......	......	......	1	1	1	1	1	1	1	1	......	......
Chaplain	One to each Flag-ship.																			
Boatswain	1	......	1	1	1	1	1	1	1	1	1	1	......	......	......	......	......	......	......	......
Gunner	1	......	1	1	1	1	1	1	1	1	1	1	......	......	......	......	......	......	......	......
Carpenter	1	......	1	1	1	1	1	1	1	1	1	1	......	......	......	......	......	......	......	......
Sailmaker	1	......	1	1	1	1	1	1	1	1	......	......	......	......	......	......	......	......	......	......
Chief Engineer	......	......	......	1	......	1	......	1	......	1	......	......	......	......	......	......	......	......	......	......
1st Assistant Engineer	......	......	......	2	......	2	......	2	......	1	......	2	......	1	......	1	......	1	......	......
2d Assistant Engineer	......	......	......	2	......	2	......	2	......	2	......	2	......	2	......	2	......	1	......	1
3d Assistant Engineer	......	......	......	3	......	2	......	2	......	2	......	2	......	2	......	2	......	2	......	2
Secretary	One for each Commander of a Squadron.																			
Clerk to Commanding Officer	1	......	1	1	1	1	1	1	1	1	1	1	1	1	1	1	1	1	......	......
Clerk to Paymaster	1	......	1	1	1	1	1	1	......	......	......	......	......	......	......	......	......	......	......	......
Master's Mates	......	......	......	......	......	......	......	......	......	......	......	......	3	3	2	2	2	2	1	1
TOTAL	33 to 35	......	25 to 27	33 to 35	22 to 24	29 to 31 •	19	26	18	24	17	23	12	17	11	16	10	14	2	5

NOTE.—Iron-clads without Spars are not to be allowed either Boatswains or Sailmakers.

No Paymaster or Assistant Paymaster shall be allowed a clerk in a vessel having the complement of one hundred and seventy-five persons or less, excepting in supply steamers and store vessels.

TABLE IV.

Allowance of Marines when the amount of C is—

GRADES.	Not less than 570 nor more than 760.		Not less than 375 nor more than 570.		Not less than 225 nor more than 375.		Not less than 175 nor more than 225.		Not less than 100 nor more than 175.		Not less than 80 nor more than 100.		Not less than 60 nor more than 80.		Not less than 40 nor more than 60.	
S. V. means a Sailing Vessel. Stmr. means a Steamer.	Col. 1.		Col. 2.		Col. 3.		Col. 4.		Col. 5.		Col. 6.		Col. 7.		Col. 8.	
	S. V.	Stmr.	S. V.	Stmr.	S. V.	Stmr.	S. V.	Stmr.	S. V.	Stmr.	S. V.	Stmr.	S. V.	Stmr.	S. V.	Stmr.
Captain	1	1	1	1	......	......	......	......	......	......	......	......	......	......	......	......
Lieutenants	2	2	1	1	1	1	1	1	1	1	......	......	......	......	......	......
Sergeants	3	3	3	3	2	2	2	2	2	2	2	2	2	2	1	1
Corporals	4	4	4	4	4	4	3	3	2	2	2	2	2	2	2	2
Drummers	2	2	1	1	1	1	1	1	1	1	1	1	1	1	......	......
Fifers	2	2	1	1	1	1	1	1	1	1	1	1	1	1	......	......
Privates	50	50	40	40	30	30	20	20	16	16	12	12	10	10	8	8
Total	64	64	51	51	39	39	28	28	23	23	18	18	16	16	11	11

APPENDIX B.—No. I.

GRADUATION OF SIGHTS AND MEAN RANGES

OF

UNITED STATES NAVAL SMOOTH-BORE GUNS.

(*From Results of Practice, by Admiral* DAHLGREN, *United States Navy.*)

The graduation commences from the bottom of the head of the bar resting on the sight-box.

The aim is supposed to be taken at the water-line of a ship.

		32-POUNDER OF 27 CWT.		32-POUNDER OF 33 CWT.	
Charge		4 lbs.		4½ lbs.	
Axis of bore above load-line		7 feet.		7½ feet.	
Distance between sights		Old Model. 29¼ inches.	New Model. 26¾ inches.	31 inches.	
ELEVATION.	RANGE.	GRADUATION.	GRADUATION.	RANGE.	GRADUATION.
Degrees.	Yards.	Inches.	Inches.	Yards.	Inches.
Level.	250	0.353	0.324	287	0.350
1°	545	0.746	0.684	581	0.792
2°	800	1.266	1.161	857	1.343
3°	1,047	1.801	1.652	1,140	1.909
4°	1,278	2.337	2.144	1,398	2.478
5°	1,469	2.870	2.633	1,598	3.044
6°	1,637	3.398	3.116	....	....

APPENDIX B.—No. II.

		32-Pounder of 42 Cwt.		32-Pounder of 57 Cwt.	
Charge		6 lbs.		9 lbs.	
Axis of bore above load-line		7½ feet.		8 feet.	
Distance between sights		Old Model. 40.5 inches.	New Model. 37.1 inches.	42.5 inches.	
Elevation.	Range.	Graduation.	Graduation.	Range.	Graduation.
Degrees.	Yards.	Inches.	Inches.	Yards.	Inches.
Level.	313	0.446	0.408	360	0.412
1°	672	1.016	0.931	760	1.042
2°	988	1.742	1.596	1,150	1.808
3°	1,274	2.488	2.280	1,440	2.597
4°	1,505	3.235	2.964	1,710	3.384
5°	1,756	3.974	3.641	1,930	4.162
6°	....	....	....	2,140	4.930

APPENDIX B.—No. III.

8-Inch of 55 Cwt.			8-Inch of 63 Cwt.		
Charge....................		7 lbs.	9 lbs.		
Shell.....................		51½ lbs.	51½ lbs.		
Axis of bore above load-line..		7½ feet.	8 feet.		
Distance between sights.....		37 inches.		Old Model. 43.50 inches.	New Model. 38.20 inches.
Elevation.	Range.	Graduation.	Range.	Graduation.	Graduation.
Degrees.	Yards.	Inches.	Yards.	Inches.	Inches.
Level.	283	0.429	330	0.460	0.402
1°	579	0.949	660	1.100	0.964
2°	869	1.603	970	1.878	1.647
3°	1,148	2.280	1,260	2.678	2.350
4°	1,413	2.958	1,540	3.478	3.051
5°	1,657	3.632	1,770	4.273	3.749
6°	1,866	4.300	....	....	....

APPENDIX B.–No. IV.

	IX-Inch Shell-Gun.		XI-Inch Shell-Gun.		XI-Inch Shell-Gun.	
Charge	10 lbs.		15 lbs.		15 lbs.	
Shell.........	72 lbs.		135 lbs.		135 lbs.	
Axis of bore above load-line	10 feet.		10 feet. [Screw-sloops.]		20 feet. [2d deck above water.]	
Distance between sights	39 inches.		48 inches.		48 inches.	
Elevation.	Range.	Graduation.	Range.	Graduation.	Range.	Graduation.
Degrees.	Yards.	Inches.	Yards.	Inches.	Yards.	Inches.
Level.	340	0.461	306	0.600	420	0.87
....	700	0.983	500	0.945	700	1.48
....	900	1.514	700	1.442	900	2.01
....	1,100	2.073	900	2.040	1,100	2.62
....	1,300	2.646	1,100	2.651	1,300	3.25
....	1,500	3.222	1,300	3.295	1,500	4.92
....	1,700	3.813	1,500	3.953	....	....
....	....	....	1,700	4.681	....	....

APPENDIX B.—No. V.—*Approximate Ranges of Shell-Guns.*

Class of Gun.	Kind of Projectile.	Weight of Projectile.	Charge, lbs.	Height above Plane.	Elevation in Degrees.—Ranges in Yards.—Time of Flight in Seconds.															
					P. B. or 0°	1°	2°	3°	4°	5°	6°	7°	8°	9°	10°	11°	12°	13°	14°	15°
XV-inch	Cored shot	400	....	....	....	....	....	....	....	....	....	....	....	....	....	....	....	....	....	....
	Shell	350	35	....	300	620	920 1.9	1,200 3.7	1,470 4.3	1,700 5.7	1,900 6.5	2,100 7.7	....	....	....	....	....	....	....	....
XI-inch	Shell	136	15	10	306 .84	631 1.72	918 2.8	1,208 3.88	1,472 4.9	1,712 5.81	1,914 6.74	2,105	2,300	2,500	2,687 10.2	'2,870 11.70	3,022 12.15	3,160	3,300	3,400
	Shell	136	15	20	421 1.16	679 1.96	992 3.	1,257 3.94	1,524 4.99	1,757 6.04	1,950	2,140	....	....	....	....	....	....	....	....
	Shell	136	20	10	410	665 1.9	1,000	1,340 4.1	1,660	1,975	2,255	2,490 8.6	2,690	2,870 10.2	3,025	3,170 11.8	3,305	3,435 14.	3,550	3,650 16.5
	Shrapnel	141	15	10	295 .8	620 1.7	910 2.7	1,200 3.7	1,465 4.7	1,710 5.6	....	....	....	....	....	....	....	....	....	....
X-inch	Shell	103	12½	11	340 .1	705 2.	970 2.9	1,230 3.9	1,490 4.9	1,740 5.8	1,960 6.7	2,210	2,430 8.5	2,640	2,840 10.1	3,000	....	....	....	....
	Shrapnel	101	12½	....	....	....	....	....	....	....	....	....	....	....	....	....	....	....	....	....
IX-inch	Shell	72½	10	10¾	332 .9	718 1.96	962 3.	1,218 4.	1,471 5.1	1,710 5.96	1,933	2,133 8.	2,314	2,484 8.6	2,644 11.5	2,788 12.9	2,927	3,045 13.5	3,190	3,357 14.7
	Shell	72½	13	....	350 .1	740 2.08	980 2.84	1,275 4.04	1,520 5.20	1,750 6.24	1,980 7.16	2,200 8.36	2,395	2,580	2,750	2,910	3,055	3,190	3,320	3,450
	Shrapnel	75	10	....	332 .8	718 1.9	960 2.9	1,215 4.	1,470 5.	1,690 5.9	....	....	....	....	....	....	....	....	....	....
8-inch, 63-cwt	Shell	51½	9	8	330 .8	660 1.89	970 3.07	1,260 4.34	1,540 5.32	1,770 6.32	....	....	....	....	....	....	....	....	....	....
	Shrapnel	52	9	....	340 .9	670 1.8	980 3.	1,270 4.2	1,550 5.2	1,775 6.2	....	....	....	....	....	....	....	....	....	....
8-inch, 55-cwt. and of 6,500 lbs.	Shell	51½	7	7½	283 .8	579 1.7	869 2.9	1,148 3.75	1,413 4.78	1,657 5.82	1,866 6.90	....	2,315	....	2,600 9.70	....	....	....	....	....
	Shrapnel	52	7	....	290 .8	590 1.6	880 2.8	1,160 3.9	1,420 4.9	1,660 5.8	....	....	....	....	....	....	....	....	....	....

APPENDIX B.—No. VI.—*Approximate Ranges of Shot-Guns and Howitzers.*

Class of Gun.	Kind of Projectile.	Weight of Projectile.	Charge.	Height above Plane.	Elevation in Degrees.—Ranges in Yards.—Time of Flight in Seconds.															
					P. B. or 0°	1°	2°	3°	4°	5°	6°	7°	8°	9°	10°	11°	12°	13°	14°	15°
32-pdr. of 57 cwt.	Shot	32	9	8	360 1.0	760 2.2	1,150 3.4	1,440 4.3	1,710 5.3	1,930 6.6	2,140 7.7	2,310	2,460	2,610	2,731 10.7	....	....	....	....	....
	Shell	26	6	....	370 1.04	780 2.00	1,090 3.14	1,360 4.20	1,620 5.30	1,850 6.40	....	....	....	....	....	....	....	....	....	....
	Shrapnel	32	9	....	360 1.0	760 2.2	1,150 3.4	1,440 4.3	1,710 5.3	1,930 6.6	....	....	....	....	2,619 10.8	....	....	....	....	....
32-pdr. of 42 cwt. and of 4,500 lbs.	Shot	32	6	7½	313 .90	672 2.0	988 3.0	1,274 4.0	1,505 5.0	1,756 6.0	....	....	....	....	....	....	....	....	....	....
	Shell	26	6	....	330 .90	710 1.90	1,012 3.05	1,270 4.15	1,495 5.32	1,710 6.50	....	....	....	....	....	....	....	....	....	....
	Shrapnel	32	6	....	313 .8	672 1.8	988 2.8	1,274 3.8	1,505 4.8	1,756 5.8	....	....	....	....	....	....	....	....	....	....
32-pdr. of 33 cwt.	Shot	32	4½	7½	287	581	857	1,140	1,398	1,598	....	....	....	....	....	....	....	....	....	....
	Shot	32	4½	15¼	366 1.1	655 2.	929 2.9	1,152 3.9	1,385 4.9	....	....	....	....	....	....	....	....	....	....	....
	Shell	26	4½	7½	295 .90	660 1.85	952 2.85	1,205 3.85	1,435 4.90	1,648 6.00	....	....	....	....	....	....	....	....	....	....
	Shrapnel	32	4½	7½	297 1.	581 1.8	857 2.7	1,140 3.8	1,398 4.9	1,598 6.	....	....	....	....	....	....	....	....	....	....
32-pdr. of 27 cwt.	Shot	32	4	7	250 .7	545 1.4	800 2.6	1,047 3.7	1,278 4.5	1,469 5.4	1,637 6.3	....	....	....	....	....	....	....	....	....
	Shell	26	4	....	320 1.	660 1.95	920 2.90	1,120 3.85	1,300 4.80	1,460 5.75	1,610 6.7	....	....	....	....	....	....	....	....	....
	Shrapnel	32	4	....	250 .7	545 1.4	800 2.6	1,047 3.7	1,278 4.5	1,469 5.4	1,637 6.3	....	....	....	....	....	....	....	....	....
24-pdr. howitzer.	Shell	20	2	7	280 .90	590 1.80	810 2.75	980 3.65	1,125 4.63	1,270 5.68	....	....	....	....	....	....	....	....	....	....
	Shrapnel	26	2	....	255 .96	555 1.92	790 2.87	960 3.80	1,140 4.75	1,308 5.70	....	....	....	....	....	....	....	....	....	....
12-pdr. heavy howitzer.	Shell	10	1	7	270 1.0	516 1.65	730 2.35	875 3.1	990 3.9	1,085 4.8	....	....	....	....	....	....	....	....	....	....
	Shrapnel	13	1	....	250 1.	500 1.9	700 2.8	870 3.7	1,015 4.6	1,150 5.4	....	....	....	....	....	....	....	....	....	....

APPENDIX B.—No. VII.—*Approximate Ranges of Rifle-Guns.*

Class of Gun.	Kind of Projectile.	Weight of Projectile.	Charge, lbs.	Height above Plane.	P. B. or 0°	1°	2°	3°	4°	5°	10°	15°	20°	25°	30°	35°
					Elevation in Degrees.—Ranges in Yards.—Time of Flight in Seconds.											
Parrott—100-pounder	Solid shot	100	No. 7 10	......	......	......	......	......	......	2,200 6½	3,810 13	5,030 18¼	6,125 22½	6,910 29	......	......
	Hollow shot	80	10	......	......	......	......	......	......	......	......	5.190 19	6,338 23	7,180 29½	7,988 32¾	8,453 36¾
	Long shell	100	10	......	......	500	920	1,400 4¼	1,700 5½	2,150 6½	3,700 13	4,790 18	5,853 21¾	6,820 28	......	......
	Short shell	80	10	......	......	......	......	......	......	......	......	......	......	......	7,810 32½	......
	Shrapnel	......	......	......	......	......	......	......	......	......	......	......	......	......	......	......
Parrott—60-pounder	Shot	60	6	......	......	......	......	......	......	......	......	......	......	......	......	......
	Shell	50	......	......	......	......	......	......	......	......	......	......	......	......	......	......
	Shrapnel	......	......	......	......	......	......	......	......	......	......	......	......	......	......	......
Parrott—30-pounder	Shot	......	......	......	......	......	......	......	......	......	......	......	......	......	......	......
	Shell	29	Can. 3¼	......	......	660	1,100	1,500	1,860	2,200 6⅞	3,500 12¼	4,800 17⅝	5,700 21¼	6,700 27	......	......
	Shrapnel	......	......	......	......	......	......	......	......	......	......	......	......	......	......	......
Parrott—20-pounder	Shot	......	......	......	......	......	......	......	......	......	......	......	......	......	......	......
	Shell	19	Can. 2	......	......	600	1,020	1,365	1,700	2,100 6½	3,350 11¼	4,400 17¼	......	......	......	......
	Shrapnel	20	Can. 2	......	......	620 1⅞	950 3⅛	......	......	......	......	......	......	......	......	......
Dahlgren—20-pounder	Shot	......	Can. 2	......	......	......	......	......	......	......	......	......	......	......	......	......
	Shell	20	2	8	370 1.4	815 2.4	1.155 3.4	1.440 4.5	1.715 5.5	1.960 6.5	......	......	......	......	......	......
Dahlgren—12-pounder	Shot	......	Can. 1	......	......	......	......	......	......	......	......	......	......	......	......	......
	Shell	12	1	8	360 1.0	750 2.0	1,050 3.0	1,305 4 0	1.550 5.0	1,770 6.0	......	......	......	......	......	......

APPENDIX B.—No. VIII.

[1] *Table for Finding the Distance of an Object at Sea.*

To use the Table, let an observer from the cross-trees measure the angle between the distant horizon and the enemy's water-line, and look into the Table with that angle; opposite to it, in the column marked distances, will be found the distance of the object in yards.

Yards.	Height of the Eye above the Level of the Sea, in Feet.								
Distance.	20	30	40	50	60	70	80	90	100
	° ′	° ′	° ′	° ′	° ′	° ′	° ′	° ′	° ′
100	3.44	5.37	7.29	9.21	11.11	13.00	14.47	16.34	18.16
200	1.50	2.46	3.43	4.39	5.35	6.31	7.27	8.23	9.18
300	1.12	1.49	2.26	3.04	3.41	4.19	4.56	5.33	6.11
400	.52	1.21	1.48	2.16	2.44	3.12	3.40	4.03	4.36
500	.41	1.03	1.25	1.48	2.10	2.32	2.54	3.17	3.39
600	.34	.52	1.10	1.29	1.47	2.05	2.24	2.42	3.01
700	.28	.44	1.01	1.15	1.31	1.46	2.01	2.18	2.34
800	.24	.38	.51	1.05	1.18	1.32	1.46	2.00	2.13
900	.21	.33	.45	.57	1.09	1.22	1.33	1.45	1.57
1000	.18	.29	.40	.50	1.01	1.12	1.23	1.34	1.45
1100	.16	.26	.35	.45	.55	1.05	1.15	1.24	1.34
1200	.15	.23	.32	.41	.50	.59	1.08	1.17	1.26
1300	.13	.21	.29	.37	.45	.53	1.02	1.10	1.18
1400	.12	.19	.27	.34	.41	.49	.57	1.04	1.12
1500	.11	.18	.24	.31	.38	.45	.52	.59	1.07
1600	.10	.16	.22	.29	.35	.42	.48	.55	1.02
1700	.09	.15	.21	.27	.33	.39	.45	.51	.58
1800	.08	.14	.19	.25	.31	.36	.42	.48	.54
1900	.08	.13	.18	.23	.29	.34	.39	.45	.50
2000	.07	.12	.17	.22	.27	.32	.37	.42	.47
2100	.06	.11	.16	.20	.25	.30	.35	.40	.45
2200	.06	.10	.15	.19	.24	.28	.33	.38	.42
2300	.05	.10	.14	.18	.22	.27	.31	.36	.40
2400	.05	.09	.13	.17	.21	.25	.29	.34	.38
2500	.05	.08	.12	.16	.20	.24	.28	.32	.36

No correct use of this Table can be made when the proximity of land may interfere with the distance of the horizon.

[1] By Lieutenant W. P. Buckner, U. S. N. See a pamphlet "On the Determination of Distances at Sea," by Captain A. P. Ryder, R. N., for more extended tables of this and other methods.

APPENDIX B.—No. IX.

REPORT OF TARGET PRACTICE WITH GREAT GUNS ON BOARD

MADE THIS ——— DAY OF ———, 18 , AT ————.

Kind of Projectile.	Distance of Target, in Yards.	Calibre of Gun.	Class of Gun.	Charge of Powder.	Number of Fires.	Length of Fuze, in Seconds of Time.	Elevation of Gun, for Yards.	Fall of Projectile.					Bursting of Shells.			
								No. of Hits.	Short of Target.	Beyond Target.	Right of Target.	Left of Target.	At or near Proper Time.	Too soon.	How much too soon.	Not at all.

U. S. S. ——————————, —————————— COMMANDING,

ARMAMENT { ——————————————— }

Shells not Burst.			No. Fires Direct.	No. Fires Ricochet.	N. B.—Each kind of projectile, distance of target (measured or estimated), class of gun, and charge of powder, require a separate line across the page. REMARKS.
No. Patches of Fuzes returned.	Range sufficient to burn Fuzes.	Range not sufficient to burn Fuzes.			

REPORT OF TARGET PRACTICE WITH SMALL-ARMS ON BOARD THE U. S. S. ————, ———— COMMANDING, MADE THIS ———— DAY OF ————, 18 , AT ————.

KIND OF ARM USED. (Each kind requires a separate line.)	Distance of Target, in Yards.	Size of Target, in Feet (say 6 by 1½ Feet).	Single Shots with Deliberate Aim.			Volleys at Order "Fire."				Whole Number of Shots Fired.	Kind of Ball Used.	Charges of Powder.
			Number Fired.	No. of Hits.	No. within 6 Inches of Centre of Bull's-Eye.	Number Fired.	Number Shot in each Volley.	Number of Hits.	No. within 6 Inches of Centre of Bull's-Eye.			

Remarks on each kind of arm used, and the general results of practice; names of those who made the best *average* of shots; Officers whose *divisions* fired best.

APPENDIX B.—No. X.

It being of great importance to know the endurance of guns in service, Commanding Officers are directed to fill up the blanks of the annexed Circular issued by the Bureau of Ordnance, November 5, 1863, as far as in their power, and forward it to the Bureau at the expiration of every quarter.

When the "total number of fires to date" cannot be ascertained, the number since the vessel has been in commission is to be stated.

NAME OF VESSEL. STATION.
( ) ( )

CLASS OF GUN.	Register No.	FOUNDRY.	Date of Fabrication.	Charge of Powder.	Shot.	Shell.	Shrapnel.	Grape.	Canister.	No. of Fires during Quarter.	Total No. of Fires to Date.

.............................., *Commander.*

...................., 186 .

The object of this circular is to enable the Bureau to know, *at all times*, how many rounds have been fired *from every gun in the service;* and the following directions are to be observed in making the quarterly return of firing:

"CLASS OF GUN."—Under this head give the kind of gun; if rifled, state it; and if a 32-pounder or 8-inch, give the *weight.* It is not necessary to give the position of the gun in the vessel.

"REGISTER NO."—Be careful to give the register number correctly, as this is most important.

"FOUNDRY."—Under this head give the initials on the base-ring.

"Date of fabrication" will be found on the right trunnion.

"Charge of powder" in pounds.

"Projectiles" to be entered under their appropriate heads in the blank.

"Kind of fuze" to be stated.

"Number of fires during quarter," must be given *for each gun separately.*

"Total number of fires to date," must include *all rounds fired from each gun separately;* and each succeeding quarterly report must have the "total number of fires to date" from the report next preceding (a copy of which is always to be kept on board the vessel) brought forward, added to the total for the quarter, and the aggregate placed in the last column.

The Bureau often receives reports *with the last column left blank*, or with "not known" written therein. Reports sent in this way are of no value whatever to the Bureau.

If a record of the total number of fires of any gun has not been kept, or if it cannot be ascertained from the Log, then vent-impressions of such gun are to be taken; and the Commanding Officer must determine, as nearly as possible, judging from these impressions, the total number of fires, and enter the same on his return. (*See* ORDNANCE INSTRUCTIONS, Part III.)

The Bureau expects that all Commanding Officers will, in future, have this return *carefully made out;* and that they will not sign or forward one of them without first being satisfied of its correctness.

APPENDIX C.—No. 1.

REPORT OF AN INSPECTION

Of the U. S. ________________, ________________ *Commanding,*

made by ________________, *this* ________ *day of* ________, 186 ,

at ______________________________

ARMAMENT.

{ ____ }
{ ____ }

[These inspections are required to be made of each vessel—when first commissioned and before proceeding to sea, chiefly with reference to the completeness of her equipment and the proper stationing of her crew; semi-annually during the cruise; and at the end of it, before being paid off. As a general rule, the first and last inspections are *not* to take place alongside of the Navy Yard, but in the stream.]

1. What time has the vessel been in commission, and what opportunities has she had for exercise and target practice?

2. Date of last inspection?
3. Date of last target practice?

			Hours.	Minutes.
4.	Times in which each division reported ready for action.	*Gun Divisions.*		
		1st, commanded by		
		2d, " "		
		3d, " "		
		4th. " "		
		5th, etc. " "		
		Master's " "		
		Powder " "		
		Engineer " "		
		Marine " "		

5. Were *all* the divisions properly prepared? If not, state what divisions were found defective, in what particulars, and from what causes. Include in the answer to this question the condition of *division-boxes, spare implements, and equipments*, and their readiness for use.

6. Are the men well skilled in the exercise of the great guns, including working both sides at once, and in pointing and firing?

7. Time required to dismount, shift carriage, remount, load, and run out any broadside-gun selected by the Inspecting Officer. State its position and weight.

8. Time required to transport a gun from one side to the other, and back, giving numbers of ports and weight of gun.

9. Time required to shift breechings, trucks, and tackles.

10. Have the prescribed arrangements been correctly made for supplying the batteries with powder and projectiles; are the men properly stationed for these purposes, and are they expert in the performance of these duties? Is the supply ample, and without confusion of charges?

11. Condition of magazines, shell-rooms, shot-lockers, and lighting apparatus.

12. Are the men well trained in securing masts and spars, stoppering rigging, and repairing injuries to the steering apparatus, and in getting springs on the cables? State the time required to perform *efficiently* the most important of these operations; for instance:

Bowsprit shot away, to secure foremast;
Port main rigging and main stays disabled, to secure mainmast;
To fish a lower mast and yard;
Steering apparatus disabled, what means of repairs or substitutes prepared.

13. Are the prescribed arrangements for stopping shot-holes complete, and the men well trained to that duty?

14. Are the arrangements for boarding and repelling boarders efficient? Note the time required to assemble each division properly armed. Are the boarders and others well trained in the use of the single-stick or broadsword?

15. Is the *whole crew* well trained in the use of small-arms, and in company and battalion drill? If not, state the reasons assigned. State also the condition of the armory, small-arms, and their ammunition.

16. What is the state of the equipment and preparation of boats for armed service? If defective, in what particulars and for what assigned reasons?

17. Times from the call "ARM AND AWAY" to the shoving off of each boat. Time to form a line abreast. Time required for other evolutions. Time required to land small-arm men, from the signal or order given when near the shore. Time to land howitzers, specifying their weights. Time to embark them; to shift from bow to stern. Time to load properly and fire safely three rounds. Are the crews expert in these points?

18. Are the arrangements and apparatus for extinguishing fire efficient? If not, state deficiencies and their causes. Times required to get the several streams of water to the designated point; time required for complete readiness.

19. Have the "ORDNANCE INSTRUCTIONS" been fully complied with in this ship? State exceptions and reasons assigned, if any.

20. General condition of the vessel in point of armament, carriages, and other ordnance equipments, and of the crew as to efficiency for action, stating particular exceptions, if any, and what remedies have been suggested or applied.

GENERAL ORDER.

NAVY DEPARTMENT, *April* 5, 1861.

Flag Officers are required to hold the semi-annual inspection of each vessel under their command, according to the foregoing form given in Appendix C, No. 1, ORDNANCE INSTRUCTIONS.

Commanding Officers of vessels acting singly will hold the same general inspection, and in either case, the reports will be forwarded to the Bureau of Ordnance by the first favorable opportunity after the inspection has taken place.

GIDEON WELLES,

Secretary of the Navy.

APPENDIX C.—No. II.

FORM OF REPORTS OF TARGET PRACTICE.

QUESTIONS TO BE ANSWERED AT LENGTH IN THE "REMARKS" ON TARGET PRACTICE, IN ADDITION TO FILLING THE TABLES. APPENDIX B.—No. IX.

Was the ship at anchor or under way?

Under what sail?

Water rough or smooth?

Force and direction of wind in reference to line of fire?

Roll of the ship, in degrees by pendulum, during firing?

When "carrying sail" by the wind, does heel of ship cause the weather or lee guns to "wood" before they are level?

Was target to windward or to leeward?

How was its distance measured?

Append sketch of target, showing its dimensions, mode of construction, and materials, with the "hits," and fall of projectiles around it.

The degree of strain on breechings of weather batteries?

Were the chocking-quoins necessary?

Probable causes of the failure of the shells to burst?

Such other remarks as appear important or suggestive of improvement; such as the best mode of constructing a floating target of 20 by 10 feet (the size used at the Experimental Battery of the Ordnance Yard, Washington).

APPENDIX D.

TABLES OF ALLOWANCES OF ORDNANCE EQUIPMENTS AND STORES.

Note.—Allowances not proportioned to guns or to ships are proportioned to the complements of Petty Officers, Seamen, Ordinary Seamen, Landsmen, and Boys, and must vary with them. The Armaments are designated by special order of the Bureau of Ordnance.

NAMES OF ARTICLES.	Proportion to each Gun.	Ships-of-the-Line.	Frigates.	Sloops-of-War. Classes. Razees.					Brigs.	Steamers. Screw. Classes.				Steamers. Side-wheel. Classes.			
				1st.	2d.	1st.	2d.	3d.		1st.	2d.	3d.	4th.	1st.	2d.	3d.	4th.
Complements........................	....	721	402	265	235	156	135	97	67	521	333	110	61	224	187	75	50
Howitzers, Equipments, and Implements.																	
Ammunition-Chests..................	11																
Containing Canister.........No.	27																
" Shell.........No.	18																
" Shrapnel.........No.	54																
Boat, Pivot-Clamps.........No.		One set for each boat carrying a gun.															
" Traverses for Boat-Carriages.........sets.																	
" Skids for landing.........sets.																	
" Tracks for Field-Carriages.........sets.																	
" Wrenches for Pivot-Clamps.........No.																	
Boring-Bits.........No.	2																
Boxes, Passing, 24-pounder and 20-pounder, No.	3																
" " 12-pounder, field.........No.	12	Two only, if used only as guns of battery.															
" for spare articles.........No.	1																
" Caisson, or Transporting.........No.	....	Two to each field-carriage.															
" Primer.........No.	2																

Tables of Allowances of Ordnance Equipments and Stores—Continued.

NAMES OF ARTICLES.	PROPORTION TO EACH GUN.	SHIPS-OF-THE-LINE.	FRIGATES.	SLOOPS-OF-WAR. Razees. 1st.	SLOOPS-OF-WAR. Razees. 2d.	SLOOPS-OF-WAR. Classes. 1st.	SLOOPS-OF-WAR. Classes. 2d.	SLOOPS-OF-WAR. Classes. 3d.	BRIGS.	STEAMERS. Screw. Classes. 1st.	STEAMERS. Screw. Classes. 2d.	STEAMERS. Screw. Classes. 3d.	STEAMERS. Screw. Classes. 4th.	STEAMERS. Side-wheel. Classes. 1st.	STEAMERS. Side-wheel. Classes. 2d.	STEAMERS. Side-wheel. Classes. 3d.	STEAMERS. Side-wheel. Classes. 4th.
COMPLEMENTS	....	721	402	265	235	156	135	97	67	521	333	110	61	224	187	75	50
Howitzers, Equipments, and Implements—Continued.																	
BREECHINGS, for Broadside 24 and 20 pounders....No.	1	If required.															
CHARGERS, for Rifle-Shells, copper....No.	1																
CHOCKS, Shifting....No.	1																
COMPRESSERS, spare, for Boat-Guns....No.	1																
DISMOUNTING BARS....No.	1																
" STRAPS....No.	1																
DRAG-ROPES for Field-Guns....No.	1																
ELEVATING SCREWS, 24 and 20 pounders....No.	2	Three to two guns, if used only as guns of the battery.															
" " 12-pounder....No.	2																
FORMERS, for Cartridge-Bags....No.	....	One for each class of howitzers.															
FUNNELS, Copper....No.	1																
FUZE-CUTTERS....No.	....	One in each box of shell and shrapnel. To be accounted for.															
" EXTRACTORS, wrench....No.	1																
" GAUGES.... for Rifle-Howitzers....No.	1	If required by kind of fuze furnished.															
" MALLETS.... for Rifle-Howitzers....No.	1																
" PLUG EXTRACTORS.... for Rifle-Howitzers....No.	1																
" REAMERS.... for Rifle-Howitzers....No.	1																
FUZES, BORMANN'S, spare....No.	5	For exercising crews in cutting fuzes.															
HAVERSACKS....No.	1																

Tables of Allowances of Ordnance Equipments and Stores—Continued.

NAMES OF ARTICLES.	PROPORTION TO EACH GUN.	SHIPS-OF-THE-LINE.	FRIGATES.	SLOOPS-OF-WAR.					BRIGS.	STEAMERS.							
				Classes.						Screw.				Side-wheel.			
				Razees.						Classes.				Classes.			
				1st.	2d.	1st.	2d.	3d.		1st.	2d.	3d.	4th.	1st.	2d.	3d.	4th.
COMPLEMENTS	....	721	402	265	235	156	135	97	67	521	333	110	61	224	187	75	50
Howitzers, Equipments, and Implements—Continued.																	
HOWITZER ... No.	....	As may be ordered.															
" Boat-Carriage ... No.	1																
" Field-Carriage ... No.	1																
LADLES ... No.	1																
LOCKS for Howitzers ... No.	2																
LOCK-LANYARDS ... No.	3																
LOCK-TOGGLES ... No.	2																
LOOP-PINS ... No.	2																
PIVOT-BOLTS ... No.	2																
PRIMING-WIRES ... No.	2																
PRIMERS for Howitzers ... No.	250																
RAMMERS and SPONGES, connected ... No.	2																
SHIFTING-SPAR ... No.	....	One to each class of howitzers.															
SIGHTS for Howitzers (long and short) ... No.	2																
SIGHT, Thumb-screws ... No.	2																
SCREW-DRIVERS for Fuzes for Rifle-Howitzers ... No.	1	Three-armed to unscrew the different kinds.															
TACKLES for Broadside 24-pounders and 20-pdrs ... set.	1																
TOMPIONS, with wads and lanyards ... No.	$1\frac{1}{10}$ 1																

Tables of Allowances of Ordnance Equipments and Stores—Continued.

NAMES OF ARTICLES.	PROPORTION TO EACH GUN.	SHIPS-OF-THE-LINE.	FRIGATES.	SLOOPS-OF-WAR. Classes. Razees. 1st.	SLOOPS-OF-WAR. Classes. Razees. 2d.	SLOOPS-OF-WAR. Classes. 1st.	SLOOPS-OF-WAR. Classes. 2d.	SLOOPS-OF-WAR. Classes. 3d.	BRIGS.	STEAMERS. Screw. Classes. 1st.	STEAMERS. Screw. Classes. 2d.	STEAMERS. Screw. Classes. 3d.	STEAMERS. Screw. Classes. 4th.	STEAMERS. Side-wheel. Classes. 1st.	STEAMERS. Side-wheel. Classes. 2d.	STEAMERS. Side-wheel. Classes. 3d.	STEAMERS. Side-wheel. Classes. 4th.
COMPLEMENTS	....	721	402	265	235	156	135	97	67	521	333	110	61	224	187	75	50
Howitzers, Equipments, and Implements—Continued.																	
TRAIL-BARS for Field-Howitzers ... No.	1																
TRAIN-ROPES for Broadside 24-pdrs. and 20-pdrs. No.	3																
VENT-GUARDS ... No.	1																
WHEELS, spare, for Field-Carriages ... No.	1																
SHELLS for Rifle-Howitzers ... No.	90																
SHRAPNELL for Rifle-Howitzers ... No.	10																
CANISTER for Rifle-Howitzers ... No.	10																
CHARGES for Rifle-Howitzers ... No.	100																
JUNK-WADS for Rifle-Canister ... No.	10																
Articles under proportion to Guns of Battery.																	
APRONS, Brass, for Locks ... set.	$1\frac{1}{10}$																
" " Breech-sights ... set.	$1\frac{1}{10}$																
" " Reinforce-sights ... set.	$1\frac{1}{10}$																

NOTE.—Each rifle or smooth-bore howitzer used in the ship's battery, and also as a boat and field gun, shall be furnished with fifty per cent. addition to the above ammunition.

Tables of Allowances of Ordnance Equipments and Stores—Continued.

NAMES OF ARTICLES.	PROPORTION TO EACH GUN.	SHIPS-OF-THE-LINE.	FRIGATES.	SLOOPS-OF-WAR. Classes. Razees. 1st.	Razees. 2d.	1st.	2d.	3d.	BRIGS.	STEAMERS. Screw. Classes. 1st.	2d.	3d.	4th.	Side-wheel. Classes. 1st.	2d.	3d.	4th.
COMPLEMENTS	....	721	402	265	235	156	135	97	67	521	333	110	61	224	187	75	50
Articles under proportion to each Gun—Continued.																	
BEDS. No.	$1\frac{1}{10}$																
BLOCKS, double, spare. No.	$\frac{2}{10}$																
" single, spare. No.	$\frac{2}{10}$																
BOLTS, Pivot, for Pivot-Guns, spare, bronze. No.	1																
" Breeching, spare. No.	$\frac{2}{10}$																
BORING-BITS, Cannon. No.	$1\frac{4}{10}$																
BOXES, Passing, for Guns. No.	$1\frac{1}{10}$																
" Primer, for Gun Captains. No.	$1\frac{1}{10}$																
BREECHINGS, fitted, for Friction-Carriage. No.	1	and 2 for pivot-guns.															
" " for Truck-Carriage. No.	2																
BUCKETS, Fire. No.	1	and four for each top.															
" " lanyards. No.	1	and four for each top.															
CANISTER, for smooth-bore Pivot-Gun. No.	10																
" " Broadside-Gun. No.	5																
" for XV-in. Guns. No.	5																
CARRIAGES, Gun. No.	1																
" " spare, in parts. No.	....	One for each class of guns on trucks over 32 cwt.															
CHOCKS, Shifting, for Pivot-Guns. No.	4																
" Rail " " No.	2																
" Housing, lower deck. No.	2																
COVERS, canvas, for Pivot-Guns. No.	1																

Tables of Allowances of Ordnance Equipments and Stores—Continued.

NAMES OF ARTICLES.	Proportion to each Gun.	Ships-of-the-Line.	Frigates.	Sloops-of-War. Classes. Razees. 1st.	2d.	1st.	2d.	3d.	Brigs.	Steamers. Screw. Classes. 1st.	2d.	3d	4th.	Side-wheel. Classes. 1st.	2d.	3d.	4th.
Complements	....	721	402	265	235	156	135	97	67	521	33[illegible]	110	61	224	187	75	50
Articles under proportion to each Gun—Continued.																	
Dismounting Apparatus (Griolet) ... No.	....	One to each gun-deck.															
Division-Bags ... No.	....	One to each division, of No. 8 canvas.															
Flasks, Powder ... No.	$\frac{1}{4}$																
Fuze-Pickers ... No.	2																
Gauges, Shell ... No.	....	One for strapped shell for each calibre on board, and one for each calibre of rifled projectiles.															
Grenades, Hand, 3 pounds ... No.																	
" " 5 " ... No.																	
Guns of Battery ... No.	....	As may be ordered.															
Gun-Scrapers ... No.	$\frac{1}{10}$																
" " to fit on Rammer-head ... No.	....	One to each calibre of chamber.															
Handspikes, Ordinary ... No.	$2\frac{1}{2}$																
" Roller ... No.	$1\frac{3}{10}$																
Heavers for Selvagees ... set.	1																
Impression-Taker for Vents ... No.	1	For each class of gun of 32-pdr. calibre and upwards, and all iron rifles.															
Ladles, Shot ... No.	....	One to each calibre.															
Lanyards, Port ... No.	5	And one tricing-line for ports requiring them.															
Lanterns, Battle, gun-decks ... No.	1																
Lashings, Breast ... No.	1																
" Housing-straps ... No.	1																
Linch-Pins, Spare ... No.	$\frac{1}{10}$																

Tables of Allowances of Ordnance Equipments and Stores—Continued.

NAMES OF ARTICLES.	PROPORTION TO EACH GUN.	SHIPS-OF-THE-LINE.	FRIGATES.	SLOOPS-OF-WAR. Classes. Razees.					BRIGS.	STEAMERS. Screw. Classes.				Side-wheel. Classes.			
				1st.	2d.	1st.	2d.	3d.		1st.	2d.	3d.	4th.	1st.	2d.	3d.	4th.
COMPLEMENTS	....	721	402	265	235	156	135	97	67	521	333	110	61	224	187	75	50
Articles under proportion to each Gun—Continued.																	
LOCKS, Cannon. No.	$1\frac{1}{4}$																
" Strings. No.	3																
" Toggles. No.	2																
" Screws and Nuts. set.	$1\frac{1}{4}$																
" Blanks, Composition. No.	$1\frac{1}{4}$																
MATCH-STAVES. No.	$\frac{1}{10}$																
MUZZLE-BAGS. No.	1																
PINS, for Breeching Shackles, spare. No.	2																
" " Shackles in brackets of Carriages, spare. No.	2																
PORT-FIRE STAVES. No.	$\frac{1}{10}$																
PRIMERS for CANNON, quill. No.	...	One hundred and twenty for each 100 rounds.															
" " " friction (copper). No.	50																
" " " " lanyards, complete. No.	2																
" Packing-boxes, wood. No.	..	As many as needed, to be accounted for by Gunner.															
" " " tin. No.	..	As many as needed, to be accounted for by Gunner.															
" " " Keys for. No.	..	As many as needed, to be accounted for by Gunner.															
PRIMING-WIRES, Cannon. No.	2																
PUNCHES for SHACKLE-PINS. No.	$\frac{2}{10}$																
QUOINS, Ordinary, for Carriages requiring them. No.	$1\frac{1}{10}$																

Tables of Allowances of Ordnance Equipments and Stores—Continued.

NAMES OF ARTICLES.	PROPORTION TO EACH GUN.	SHIPS-OF-THE-LINE.	FRIGATES.	SLOOPS-OF-WAR. Classes. Razees. 1st.	2d.	1st.	2d.	3d.	BRIGS.	STEAMERS. Screw. Classes. 1st.	2d.	3d.	4th.	Side-wheel. Classes. 1st.	2d.	3d.	4th.
COMPLEMENTS	....	721	402	265	235	156	135	97	67	521	333	110	61	224	187	75	50
Articles under proportion to each Gun—Continued.																		
QUOINS, Chocking ....No.	2																	
" Transom, for Pivot-Guns ....No.	2																	
RAMMERS ....No.	$1\frac{2}{10}$																	
SABOTS, for Bouched Shells ....No.	....	One for each empty shell: with tacks and lashing.																
SCREWS, Compressing, for Friction-Carriages, spare. No.	1																	
" Elevating, for guns needing them ....No.	$1\frac{1}{10}$																	
SELVAGEES for BREECHINGS ....sets.	1																	
SHELLS in boxes, loaded and fuzed, for Broadside Smooth-bore Guns .... No.	40																	
SHELLS in boxes, loaded and fuzed, for Pivot Smooth-bore Guns .... No.	60																	
SHELLS in boxes, loaded and fuzed, for Broadside Rifled Guns .... No.	40*																	
SHELLS in boxes, loaded and fuzed, for Pivot Rifled Guns .... No.	60*																	
SHELLS in boxes, not loaded nor fuzed, for Broadside Smooth-bore Guns .... No.	20																	
SHELLS in boxes, not loaded nor fuzed, for Pivot Smooth-bore Guns .... No.	30																	
SHELLS in boxes, not loaded nor fuzed, for Broadside Rifled-Guns .... No.	25*																	

* Fuzes, one-half percussion, one-half time.

Tables of Allowances of Ordnance Equipments and Stores—Continued.

NAMES OF ARTICLES.		Proportion to each Gun.	Ships-of-the-Line.	Frigates.	Sloops-of-War. Classes. Razees. 1st.	2d.	1st.	2d.	3d.	Brigs.	Steamers. Screw. Classes. 1st.	2d.	3d.	4th.	Steamers. Side-wheel. Classes. 1st.	2d.	3d.	4th.
Complements		....	721	402	265	235	156	135	97	67	521	333	110	61	224	187	75	50
Articles under proportion to each Gun—Continued.																		
Shells in boxes, not loaded nor fuzed, for Pivot Rifled-Guns	No.	35*																
Shells in boxes or bags, loaded and fuzed, for XV-inch Guns	No.	50																
Shot, Grape, stands for each Smooth-bore Pivot-Gun	No.	5																
Shot, Grape, stands for each Smooth-bore Broadside-Gun	No.	5																
Shot, Cored, for XV-inch Guns	No.	5																
† " Solid, " " "	No.	10																
" " " Broadside Smooth-bore Guns	No.	10																
" " " Pivot " " "	No.	10																
" " Rifle, for Broadside Rifled Guns	No.	10																
" " " " Pivot "	No.	15																
" " (round) for Broadside "	No.	10																
" " " " Pivot "	No.	15																
Shrapnel, for Broadside, Smooth-bore Guns	No.	15																
" " Pivot " "	No.	35																
" " Broadside Rifled "	No.	15																
" " Pivot " "	No.	25																
" " XV-inch guns	No.	15																

* Fuzes, one-half percussion, one-half time.
† When *steel* shot are to be furnished, the number will be designated by the Bureau.

Tables of Allowances of Ordnance Equipments and Stores—Continued.

NAMES OF ARTICLES.	PROPORTION TO EACH GUN.	SHIPS-OF-THE-LINE.	FRIGATES.	SLOOPS-OF-WAR.					BRIGS.	STEAMERS.							
				Classes.						Screw.				Side-wheel.			
				Razees.						Classes.				Classes.			
				1st.	2d.	1st.	2d.	3d.		1st.	2d.	3d.	4th.	1st.	2d.	3d.	4th.
COMPLEMENTS	....	721	402	265	235	156	135	97	67	521	333	110	61	224	187	75	50
Articles under proportion to each Gun—Continued.																	
SHELL-BEARERS for all Pivot-guns of heavy calibre. No.	2																
SIGHTS .... sets.	$1\frac{1}{10}$																
" Reinforce .... No.	$1\frac{1}{10}$																
" " Bands, Screws .... No.	$1\frac{1}{10}$																
" Bolts and Nuts .... No.	$1\frac{1}{10}$																
" Screws for Reinforce .... No.	$1\frac{1}{10}$																
" Thumb-screws, spare .... No.	1																
" Breech-side or Trunnion, for Pivot-Guns .. No.	1																
SPONGES, Sheepskin .... No.	$1\frac{3}{10}$																
" Bristle .... No.	....	One to each division for each calibre, for cleaning guns.															
SPONGE-CAPS, Canvas .... No.	$1\frac{3}{10}$																
STRAPS for Bouched Shells .... No.	....	One for each empty shell															
TACKLES, Gun .... set.	1																
" " Spare .... No.	1																
" " Pivot, if required .... set	1																
" " Port, lower deck .... No.	2																
THUMB-STALLS .... No.	2	Eight to each reserve box.															
TOMPIONS, with wads and lanyards .... No.	$1\frac{1}{10}$																
TRUCKS, spare, lignum-vitæ .... No.	$\frac{2}{10}$																
TRANSPORTING TRUCKS .... sets.	....	One for each class of guns on friction carriages.															
" AXLES .... No.	....	One for each class of guns on friction carriages.															

Tables of Allowances of Ordnance Equipments and Stores—Continued.

NAMES OF ARTICLES.	PROPORTION TO EACH GUN.	SHIPS-OF-THE-LINE.	FRIGATES.	SLOOPS-OF-WAR.					BRIGS.	STEAMERS.							
				Classes.						Screw.				Side-wheel.			
				Razees.						Classes.				Classes.			
				1st.	2d.	1st.	2d.	3d.		1st.	2d.	3d.	4th.	1st.	2d.	3d.	4th.
COMPLEMENTS	....	721	402	265	235	156	135	97	67	521	333	110	61	224	187	75	50
Articles under proportion to each Gun—Continued.																	
TUBS, Division ... No.	....	One for each division.															
VENT-DRILLS, with Braces ... sets.	....	One for each division.															
VENT-GUARDS ... No.	1																
VENT-PUNCHES ... No.	$\frac{2}{10}$																
WADS, Junk ... No.	10																
" Selvagee ... No.	....	One to each shot and shell. Not to be put in box.															
WORMS, Robinson's ... No.	$\frac{2}{10}$																
WRENCHES, Fuze, with water-cap drivers ... No.	$\frac{2}{10}$																
" Screw, Patent ... No.	....	Two to each vessel for tightening bolts.															
Small Arms.																	
ARM-CHESTS (not lined) ... No.		As required.															
AXES, Battle, with frogs ... No.	....	Number required by Article 101, Part I., to arm crew.															
BELTS, Waist ... No.	....	Sufficient to supply arms furnished.															
CAPS, Percussion, Navy ... No.	....	200 per piece.															
" " Revolver ... No.	....	200 per piece.															
" " Packing-boxes, wood ... No.	} ..	As many as needed. To be accounted for by Gunner.															
" " " tin ... No.																	
" " " Keys for ... No.																	

Tables of Allowances of Ordnance Equipments and Stores—Continued.

NAMES OF ARTICLES.	PROPORTION TO EACH GUN.	SHIPS-OF-THE-LINE.	FRIGATES.	Sloops-of-War. Classes. Razees. 1st.	Razees. 2d.	Sloops-of-War. 1st.	2d.	3d.	BRIGS.	Steamers. Screw. Classes. 1st.	2d.	3d.	4th.	Side-wheel. Classes. 1st.	2d.	3d.	4th.
COMPLEMENTS	....	721	402	265	235	156	135	97	67	521	333	110	61	224	187	75	50
Small Arms—Continued.																	
CARTRIDGE-BOXES, Musket, leather. No.	..	Sufficient to supply arms furnished.															
" " Carbine or Rifle, leather. No.																	
" " Pistol or Revolver, leather. No.																	
" " Revolver, leather. No.																	
" PAPER, reams. No.	....	3	2	1	1	1	1	1	½	2	1	1	½	2	1	½	½
CARBINES or RIFLES. No.	....	Number required to arm the crew as allowed by Art. 101, Part I.															
" Ball-moulds. No.	....	If needed.															
" Bayonets, if needed, with scabbards & frogs. No.	....	Number required to arm the crew as allowed by Art. 101, Part I.															
" Cones. No.	....	120	100	80	80	70	60	50	20	100	80	50	20	80	70	30	20
" Cone-picks. No.	....	12	10	8	8	7	6	5	2	10	8	5	2	8	7	3	2
" Screw-drivers and Cone-keys. No.	....	12	10	8	8	7	6	5	2	10	8	5	2	8	7	3	2
" Wiper-rods. No.	....	12	10	8	8	7	6	5	2	10	8	5	2	8	7	3	2
" Wipers. No.																	
CUTLASSES and SCABBARDS. No.	....	Number required to arm the crew as allowed by Art. 101, Part I.															
" Frogs. No.	....	Number required to arm the crew as allowed by Art. 101, Part I.															
LACQUER, for Small Arms. galls.	....	8	6	5	5	5	5	5	2	6	5	5	3	5	5	3	2
" Tin Cans for. No.		As required.															
MUSKETS, Rifled. No.	....	Number required to arm the crew as allowed by Art. 101, Part I.															
" Ball-moulds. No.	....	1	1	1	1	1	1	1	1	1	1	1	1	1	1	1	1

Tables of Allowances of Ordnance Equipments and Stores—Continued.

NAMES OF ARTICLES.	Proportion to each Gun.	Ships-of-the-Line.	Frigates.	Sloops-of-War. Classes. Razees. 1st.	Razees. 2d.	1st.	2d.	3d.	Brigs.	Steamers. Screw. Classes. 1st.	2d.	3d.	4th.	Side-wheel. Classes. 1st.	2d.	3d.	4th.
COMPLEMENTS.	....	721	402	265	235	156	135	97	67	521	333	110	61	224	187	75	50
Small Arms—Continued.																	
MUSKETS, Ball screws and wipers.....No.	....	27	12	8	8	7	6	5	2	12	8	5	2	8	7	3	2
" Bands, sets.....No.	....	14	6	4	4	3	3	2	1	6	4	3	1	4	3	2	1
" Bayonets, Scabbards, and Frogs.....No.	....	Sufficient for arms furnished.															
" Breech-screws.....No.	....	7	3	2	2	2	2	2	1	3	2	2	1	2	2	1	1
" Cartridge-formers.....sets.	....	2	2	2	2	2	2	2	1	2	2	2	1	2	2	2	1
" Cones.....No.	....	270	120	80	80	70	60	50	20	120	80	50	20	80	70	30	20
" " picks.....No.	....	27	12	8	8	7	6	5	2	12	8	5	2	8	7	3	2
" Guard-screws.....No.	....	14	6	4	4	4	3	3	1	6	4	3	1	4	4	2	1
" Hammers.....No.	....	14	6	4	4	4	3	3	1	6	4	3	1	4	4	2	1
" Hand-vices, spring.....No.	....	14	6	4	4	4	3	3	1	6	4	3	1	4	4	2	1
" Locks, complete.....No.	....	7	3	2	2	2	2	2	1	3	2	2	1	2	2	1	1
" Lock-screws, spare, small.....No.	....	75	30	20	20	18	15	13	5	30	20	13	5	20	18	8	5
" Screw-drivers and Cone-keys.....No.	....	27	12	8	8	7	6	5	2	12	8	5	2	8	7	3	2
" Side-screws, spare.....No.	....	27	12	8	8	7	6	5	2	12	8	5	2	8	7	3	2
" Springs.....sets.	....	14	6	4	4	3	3	2	1	6	4	3	1	4	3	2	1
" Tang-screws.....No.	....	14	6	4	4	3	3	2	1	6	4	3	1	4	3	2	1
" Triggers.....No.	....	7	3	2	2	2	2	2	1	3	2	2	1	2	2	1	1
" Wire and Tumbler Punches.....No.	....	14	6	4	4	4	3	3	2	6	4	3	2	4	4	2	2

Tables of Allowances of Ordnance Equipments and Stores—Continued.

NAMES OF ARTICLES.	PROPORTION TO EACH GUN.	SHIPS-OF-THE-LINE.	FRIGATES.	SLOOPS-OF-WAR.					BRIGS.	STEAMERS.							
				Classes.						Screw.				Side-wheel.			
				Razees.						Classes.				Classes.			
				1st.	2d.	1st.	2d.	3d.		1st.	2d.	3d.	4th.	1st.	2d.	3d.	4th.
COMPLEMENTS	....	721	402	265	235	156	135	97	67	521	333	110	61	224	187	75	50
Small Arms—Continued.																	
MUSKETS, Wipers, bristle ... No.	....	27	12	8	8	7	6	5	2	12	8	5	2	8	7	3	2
" Worms and Scrapers ... No.	....	14	6	4	4	4	3	3	2	6	4	3	1	4	4	2	2
" Scraper, Crane's ... No.	....	Half the above.															
PISTOLS, Navy ... No.	....	Number required to arm the crew as allowed by Art. 101, Part I.												2	2	2	2
" Ball-moulds ... No.	....	2	2	2	2	2	2	2	2.	2	2	2	2	2	2	2	2
" Cartridge-formers ... No.	....	2	2	2	2	2	2	2	2	2	2	2	2	2	2	2	2
" Cones, spare ... No.	....	18	11	8	8	6	5	4	2	12	8	4	2	8	6	3	2
" Frogs ... No.	....	Sufficient for arms furnished.															
" Screw-drivers and Cone-keys ... No.	....	18	11	8	8	6	5	4	2	12	8	4	2	8	6	3	2
" Worms and Scrapers ... No.	....	18	11	8	8	6	5	4	2	12	8	4	2	8	6	3	2
" Revolvers ... No.	....	Number required to arm the crew as allowed by Art. 101, Part I.															
" " Bullet-moulds ... No.	....	2	2	2	2	2	2	2	1	2	2	2	1	2	2	2	1
" " Cone-wrenches ... No.	....	18	11	8	8	6	5	4	2	12	8	4	2	8	6	3	2
" " Extra bolts ... No.	....	18	11	7	7	6	5	4	2	12	8	4	2	7	6	2	2
" " Cones ... No.	....	185	110	76	76	60	50	40	20	120	80	40	20	76	60	25	20
" " Hammers ... No.	....	30	20	15	15	10	10	8	5	20	15	10	5	15	10	5	5
" " Hands ... No.	....	18	11	7	7	6	5	4	2	12	8	4	2	7	6	2	2
" " Lock-screws ... No.	....	18	11	7	7	6	5	4	2	12	8	4	2	7	6	2	2
" " Triggers ... No.	....	18	11	7	7	6	5	4	2	12	8	4	2	7	6	2	2

Tables of Allowances of Ordnance Equipments and Stores—Continued.

NAMES OF ARTICLES.	PROPORTION TO EACH GUN.	SHIPS-OF-THE-LINE.	FRIGATES.	SLOOPS-OF-WAR.					BRIGS.	STEAMERS.							
				Classes.						Screw.				Side-wheel.			
				Razees.						Classes.				Classes.			
				1st.	2d.	1st.	2d.	3d.		1st.	2d.	3d.	4th.	1st.	2d.	3d.	4th.
COMPLEMENTS	....	721	402	265	235	156	135	97	67	521	333	110	61	224	187	75	50
Small Arms—Continued.																	
PISTOLS, Revolvers, Main and Sear Springs ...... No.	....	30	20	15	15	10	10	8	5	20	15	10	5	15	10	5	5
" Flasks ...... No.																	
" Frogs ...... No.	....	Sufficient for arms furnished.															
" Spring-vices ...... No.																	
PIKES, Boarding ...... No.	....	Number required to arm the crew as per Art. 101, Part I.															
" " Guards for ...... No.	....	Number required to arm the crew as per Art. 101, Part I.															
SINGLE STICKS ...... No.	....	70	60	50	50	40	40	30	20	60	50	40	20	50	40	30	20

Tables of Allowances of Ordnance Equipments and Stores—Continued.

NAMES OF ARTICLES.	PROPORTION TO EACH GUN.	SHIPS-OF-THE-LINE.	FRIGATES.	SLOOPS-OF-WAR.					BRIGS.	STEAMERS.							
				Classes.						Screw.				Side-wheel.			
				Razees.						Classes.				Classes.			
				1st.	2d.	1st.	2d.	3d.		1st.	2d.	3d.	4th.	1st.	2d.	3d.	4th.
COMPLEMENTS	....	721	402	265	235	156	135	97	67	521	333	110	61	224	187	75	50
Magazine Stores, &c.																	
ADZES, Copper ... No.		One to each magazine.															
BUCKETS, Water, Copper-bound ... No.	....	One for each magazine and shell-room.															
BRUSHES, Dusting ... No.	....	Two to each magazine.															
" Paint ... No.	....	Two to each gun, assorted sizes.															
CANS, Water, Copper-bound ... No.		Two to each magazine and one to each shell-room.															
CARTRIDGES, Carbine, ball ... No.	....	100 per piece, 200 if breech-loader.															
" Musket, ball ... No.	....	100 per piece.															
" " blank ... No.	....	20 per piece.															
" Buckshot ... No.	....	20 per piece.															
" Pistol, ball ... No.	....	100 per piece.															
" Revolver, ball ... No.	....	100 per piece.															
" Packing-boxes for Carbine ... No.																	
" " " Musket ... No.																	
" " " Rifle ... No.																	
" " " Pistol ... No.	..	As required. To be accounted for by Gunner.															
" " " Revolver ... No.																	
" " " Keys for ... No.																	
CARTRIDGE-BAGS, spare ... No.	10																
DUST-PANS, Copper ... No.	....	One to each magazine.															

Tables of Allowances of Ordnance Equipments and Stores—Continued.

NAMES OF ARTICLES.	PROPORTION TO EACH GUN.	SHIPS-OF-THE-LINE.	FRIGATES.	SLOOPS-OF-WAR. Classes. Razees. 1st.	Razees. 2d.	Classes. 1st.	2d.	3d.	BRIGS.	STEAMERS. Screw. Classes. 1st.	2d.	3d.	4th.	Side-wheel. Classes. 1st.	2d.	3d.	4th.
COMPLEMENTS	....	721	402	265	235	156	135	97	67	521	333	110	61	224	187	75	50
Magazine Stores, &c.—Continued.																	
FIREWORKS, Blue-lights, new pattern ... No.	....	50	45	40	40	25	20	15	10	50	40	25	10	40	25	15	20
" Red " " ... No.	....	50	45	40	40	25	20	15	10	50	40	25	10	46	25	15	20
" White " " ... No.	....	50	45	40	40	25	20	15	10	50	40	25	10	40	25	15	20
" Port-fires ... No.	....	25	20	15	15	10	5	5	5	25	12	10	5	12	10	5	5
" Rockets and Staves ... No.	....	100	60	50	50	40	20	20	20	100	50	40	20	50	40	20	20
" Packing-boxes for blue, white, and red lights ... No.	..	As needed. To be accounted for by Gunner.															
" Packing-boxes for Port-fires ... No.																	
" " " Rockets ... No.																	
" " " Keys for ... No.																	
FORMERS, for cutting Cartridge-Bags ... sets.	....	One set to each class of cartridges.															
FUNNELS, for filling Cartridges ... No.	....	One to each magazine.															
" " Shells ... No.	....	Two to each shell-room.															
FUZES in metal stocks, 5″ ... No.	....	One in each loaded shell.															
" " " 5″ ... No.	...	One for every four empty shells. (Spherical.)															
" " " 10″ ... No.	....	One for every four empty shells. (Spherical.)															
" " " 15″ ... No.	....	One for every four empty shells. (Spherical.)															
" " " 20″ ... No.	....	One for every four empty shells. (Spherical.)															

Tables of Allowances of Ordnance Equipments and Stores—Continued.

NAMES OF ARTICLES.	PROPORTION TO EACH GUN.	SHIPS-OF-THE-LINE.	FRIGATES.	SLOOPS-OF-WAR. Classes. Razees. 1st.	Razees. 2d.	Classes. 1st.	2d.	3d.	BRIGS.	STEAMERS. Screw. Classes. 1st.	2d.	3d.	4th.	Side-wheel. Classes. 1st.	2d.	3d.	4th.
COMPLEMENTS	....	721	402	265	235	156	135	97	67	521	333	110	61	224	187	75	50
Magazine Stores, &c.—Continued.																	
FUZES, Percussion for Rifle-Shell ... No.	....	One-half the number of shell.															
FUZES, in metal stocks, spare, assorted, 3½, 7, 20 sec. No.	....	One to four shells.															
FUZES, TIME, for Rifle-Shell ... No.	....	One-half the number of shell.															
" Packing-boxes for ... No.	} ..	As needed. To be accounted for by Gunner.															
" " " Keys for ... No.																	
" Plug-extractor ... No.	....	One to each shell-room.															
HOSE, with Pipes ... No.	....	One to each magazine and shell-room.															
KNIVES, Copper ... No.	....	One to each magazine.															
LAMP-FEEDERS, Tin ... No.	....	One to each magazine.															
LANTERNS, Copper, with Lamps ... No.	....	One to each light-box.															
" Glass Chimneys for ... No.	....	Six to each lamp requiring them.															
MAGAZINE-DRESSES ... suits.	....	10	8	8	8	6	3	4	2	8	6	4	2	8	6	4	2
" SHOES ... pair.	....	10	8	8	8	6	3	4	2	8	6	4	2	8	6	4	2
POWDER, Rounds ...	110,	and 65 extra for each Pivot-gun.															
" Musket ... lbs.	....	150	100	60	60	50	50	50	50	110	65	50	50	60	50	50	50
" Saluting ...	50	and 730 extra for each flag ship. Not to be given to vessels less than six guns.															
" Shell-Charges in Bags ...	....	One for each empty shell.															
" Measures, Copper ... sets.	....	One to each magazine and shell-room.															
" Whips ... No.	....	As required.															

Tables of Allowances of Ordnance Equipments and Stores—Continued.

NAMES OF ARTICLES.	PROPORTION TO EACH GUN.	SHIPS-OF-THE-LINE.	FRIGATES.	SLOOPS-OF-WAR. Classes. Razees. 1st.	SLOOPS-OF-WAR. Razees. 2d.	SLOOPS-OF-WAR. Classes. 1st.	SLOOPS-OF-WAR. Classes. 2d.	SLOOPS-OF-WAR. Classes. 3d.	BRIGS.	STEAMERS. Screw. Classes. 1st.	Screw. 2d.	Screw. 3d.	Screw. 4th.	STEAMERS. Side-wheel. Classes. 1st.	Side-wheel. 2d.	Side-wheel. 3d.	Side-wheel. 4th.
COMPLEMENTS	....	721	402	265	235	156	135	97	67	521	333	110	61	224	187	75	50
Magazine Stores, &c.—Continued.																	
SCISSORS, Lamp ... No.	....	One pair to each light-box.															
SCOOPS, Copper ... No.	....	Two to each magazine.															
SCREENS, Baize ... No.	....	Two to each magazine and shell-room, if required.															
SWAPS ... No.	....	Two to each magazine, if required.															
TANKS, Powder, Copper ... No.	....	Enough to hold *all* the powder.															
TANK-SCREWS, Spare ... No.	....	One to ten tanks.															
" Wrenches ... No.	....	One to each magazine when necessary.															
" Heavers, Copper ... No.	....	One to each magazine.															
VICES, Copper ... No.	....	One to each vessel.															

Tables of Allowances of Ordnance Equipments and Stores—Continued.

NAMES OF ARTICLES.	PROPORTION TO EACH GUN.	SHIPS-OF-THE-LINE.	FRIGATES.	SLOOPS-OF-WAR. Classes. Razees. 1st.	Razees. 2d.	1st.	2d.	3d.	BRIGS.	STEAMERS. Screw. Classes. 1st.	2d.	3d.	4th.	Side-wheel. Classes. 1st.	2d.	3d.	4th.
COMPLEMENTS	....	721	402	265	235	156	135	97	67	521	333	110	61	224	187	75	50
Miscellaneous Articles.																		
AWLS, Saddler's . . . No.	....	36	24	18	18	12	12	12	6	24	18	12	6	24	18	12	6
AXES, Wood . . . No.	....	6	5	5	5	4	4	3	2	5	5	4	3	5	4	3	2
BEESWAX . . . lbs.	....	One pound to each gun, two to each shell and pivot gun.															
BOLTS, Clevis . . . No.	....	As required.															
BOXES, Division, Supply, and Reserve . . . No.	....	One of each to each division of guns.															
CALLIPERS . . . No.	....																
CAMPHOR . . . lbs.	....	6	5	4	4	3	3	2	1	5	4	2	1	4	3	2	1
CHESTS, Arm, for Boats . . . No.	....	One to each launch and first cutter.															
CHUTE, Powder . . . No.	....	One to each scuttle.															
EMERY (for Armorer's use) . . . lbs.	....	5	4	3	3	2	2	2	1	4	3	2	1	4	3	2	1
FILES, Rat-tail, for Spikes for Howitzers . . . No.	. 2																
FLASH-PANS, Copper . . . No.	....	2	2	2	2	2	1	1	1	2	2	1	1	2	2	1	1
GLASS, thick plates . . . No.	....	Half set to each battle-lantern, cut to fit.															
GONGS . . . No.	....	One to each gun-deck.															

Tables of Allowances of Ordnance Equipments and Stores—Continued.

NAMES OF ARTICLES.	PROPORTION TO EACH GUN.	SHIPS-OF-THE-LINE.	FRIGATES.	SLOOPS-OF-WAR. Classes. Razees. 1st.	2d.	Classes. 1st.	2d.	3d.	BRIGS.	STEAMERS. Screw. Classes. 1st.	2d.	3d.	4th.	Side-wheel. Classes. 1st.	2d.	3d.	4th.
COMPLEMENTS.	....	721	402	265	235	156	135	97	67	521	333	110	61	224	187	75	50
Miscellaneous Articles—Continued.																	
GRUBBING-HOE and PICKAXE, combined ... No.	....	One to each field-carriage.															
HAMMERS, Claw ... No.	....	2	2	2	2	2	2	2	1	2	2	2	1	2	2	1	1
" Saddler's ... No.	....	2	2	2	2	2	2	2	1	2	2	2	1	2	2	1	1
KNIVES, Shoe ... No.	....	3	2	2	2	2	2	2	2	2	2	2	1	2	2	2	1
LADLES, Shot, great guns ... No.	....	One to each calibre.															
LANTERNS, Dark (small, with Reflectors) ... No.	$\frac{1}{10}$																
LEAD, Black, pulverized ... lbs.	....	24	12	6	6	6	5	4	3	12	6	5	3	6	5	4	3
LOCK-STRINGS, spare ... faths.	3																
LOCKS, PAD, Brass, and Keys ... No.	....	Two to each magazine and light-box scuttle and arm-chest.															
MATCH-ROPE ... lbs.	....	50	40	30	30	25	25	20	10	40	30	20	10	40	30	20	10
MUSLIN for TARGETS ... yds.	....	50	50	50	50	40	40	40	20	50	50	40	20	50	50	40	20
OIL, Sperm, for Small Arms ... galls.	....	10	8	6	6	5	5	5	3	8	6	5	3	6	5	3	3
" " Tin Cans for ... No.	....	As needed.															
NAILS, 3d, for strapping Shell ... lbs.	....	10	5	3	3	2	1	2	1	5	3	2	1	5	3	2	1
PENDULUM ... No.																	
PUTTY, in Bladders ... lbs.	....	100	75	50	50	45	20	40	20	75	50	40	20	50	40	20	20
QUADRANT, GUNNER'S ... No.																	

Tables of Allowances of Ordnance Equipments and Stores—Continued.

NAMES OF ARTICLES.	PROPORTION TO EACH GUN.	SHIPS-OF-THE-LINE.	FRIGATES.	SLOOPS-OF-WAR. Classes. Razees. 1st.	Razees. 2d.	1st.	2d.	3d.	BRIGS.	STEAMERS. Screw. Classes. 1st.	2d.	3d.	4th.	Side-wheel. Classes. 1st.	2d.	3d.	4th.
COMPLEMENTS	....	721	402	265	235	156	135	97	67	521	333	110	61	224	187	75	50
Miscellaneous Articles—Continued.																	
RATTLES for calling Boarders, Hand ... No.	$\frac{2}{10}$																
" " " Fixed ... No.	....	One at wheel and one on each gun-deck.															
SCREW-DRIVERS ... No.	....																
SCREW-PLATE and TAP, fuze, Navy ... No.	....	One set for each vessel armed with shell-guns.															
" " " " Parrott ... No.	....	One set for each vessel armed with these guns.															
SHEARS, Sheep ... No.	....	One pair to each vessel.															
SHELL-WHIPS ... No.	....	As required.															
SHOVELS, Intrenching ... No.	....	Two for each field-carriage.															
SIGNAL-LIGHT DISCHARGERS ... No.	....	One for each vessel.															
SHEEPSKIN, covers for Sponge-heads (made up) .. No.	1½																
SLINGS, Gun, chain ... No.	....	2	2	1	1	1	1	1	1	2	1	1	1	1	1	1	1
TACKS, Copper, for Sponge-heads ... No.	....	1000	500	300	300	200	200	200	100	500	300	200	100	500	300	200	100
" Iron, for strapping Shell ... No.	....	4000	2000	1200	1200	1000	1000	1000	600	2000	1200	1000	600	2000	1200	1000	600
TARGET FRAME ... No.	....	One to each vessel; to be fitted on board.															
THREAD, Shoe ... lbs.	....	3	2	1	1	1	1	1	½	2	1	1	½	2	1	1	1½
TONGS, Shot ... No.	....	As required.															
TUBS, Fire ... No.	....	One to each chain of scuttles.															

Tables of Allowances of Ordnance Equipments and Stores—Continued.

NAMES OF ARTICLES.	PROPORTION TO EACH GUN.	SHIPS-OF-THE-LINE.	FRIGATES.	SLOOPS-OF-WAR. Classes. Razees.					BRIGS.	STEAMERS. Screw. Classes.				Side-wheel. Classes.			
				1st.	2d.	1st.	2d.	3d.		1st.	2d.	3d.	4th.	1st.	2d.	3d.	4th.
COMPLEMENTS	....	721	402	265	235	156	135	97	67	521	333	110	61	224	187	75	50
Miscellaneous Articles—Continued.																	
WAX, for taking Vent Impressions...lbs.	½																
WICKS, Woven...gross.	....	One-half to each lamp requiring them.															
" Cotton...lbs.																	
YARN, Worsted...lbs.	....	2	1	1	1	½	½	½	½	1	1	½	½	1	1	½	½
" Coarse Woollen ("Thrums")...lbs.	....	2	1	1	1	½	½	½	½	1	1	½	½	1	1	½	½
21-thd. HEMP, Boat's service...lbs.																	
18-thd. " " "...lbs.																	

Tables of Allowances of Ordnance Equipments and Stores —Continued.

BOOKS.

Book	Allowance
1. Ordnance Instructions	One to Commander, one to Executive Officer, one to each divisional officer, and one to the Gunner of every ship.*
2. Boat Armament—Dahlgren's	One to each vessel of 1st, 2d, and 3d rates.
3. Shells and Shell-Guns, do.	" " " " " "
4. The Naval Howitzer Ashore and Afloat—Parker	Two to each vessel above 4th rate; one to 4th rate.
5. Naval Gunnery—Sir H. Douglas	One to each vessel above 4th rate.
6. " " Simpson	One to each vessel.
7. Ordnance and Armor—Holley	One to 1st and 2d rates.
8. Experiments on Gunpowder—Mordecai	One to 1st, 2d, and 3d rates.
9. Gunnery Catechism—Brandt	Same allowance as the "Ordnance Instructions," with the addition of one to each Captain of a gun.*
10. Ordnance Circulars	Same allowance as the "Ordnance Instructions."*
11. Blank-Books and Returns	One set to each vessel.
12. Table of Ranges—Buckner	Two to each vessel above 4th rate; one to 4th rate.

* All of these books to be receipted for by the persons receiving them, accounted for, and turned over to successor or Inspector of Ordnance.

INDEX.

I N D E X.

C.

E.

F.

N.

O.

Q.

R.

T.

V.

www.ingramcontent.com/pod-product-compliance
Lightning Source LLC
LaVergne TN
LVHW011159110826
845150LV00006B/1261

* 9 7 8 1 4 2 5 5 4 5 6 6 6 *